PETER HOWARD
LIFE AND LETTERS

Peter Howard in London, 1964

PETER HOWARD
LIFE AND LETTERS

by

Anne Wolrige Gordon

HODDER AND STOUGHTON

92

H 8341w

174251

For
JULIETTE, JOHN, KATE, PATRICK
EMMA, TOM and CAROLINE

Author's Note

I have dedicated this book to Peter Howard's grandchildren. As they grow up they will hear a great deal about their grandfather, both favourable and critical, and I want them to know him from his words and letters.

This book is not a biography. For one thing, I do not believe that close family members should write biographies. For another, it is too soon to publish much of the available material. Many of my father's friends are still alive and his work was, by its nature, concerned with the deepest and most personal aspects of their lives. People told him things which they told no one else. He did not talk about these things and he would not have wished his letters about them to be read by others, particularly in their lifetimes. These friendships were his daily experience, and without them his story is incomplete.

That there are omissions in this book I admit at once. Most are made for the sake of the living not the dead, and I make no apology for them. Others are due to the fact that his parents kept none of his letters and papers.

I have tried to write a book about a man not a movement – to catch a glimpse of what Peter Howard made of life at a time when life itself is treated so callously the world over. I have assumed that those who wish to know more of the results of his and his friends' work can read the numerous books which have been written on the subject.

The effects of my father's work are not for me to judge. I know that, in spite of extensive research, I have found only a small percentage of the people who were influenced by him. Every year I hear of more of them, and of many I shall never know. To me, he was a father whom I loved and respected. He should have written this book himself for he would have done it far better than I can. I hope, nevertheless, that it will be of interest to those who knew him and will introduce him to those who did not.

I would like to thank the following for their recollections and help during the writing of this book:

Mrs. Edie Alley, Mr. Harry Almond, Wing Commander Charles L. de Beaumont, O.B.E., Mr. Tom Beeton, Miss Hilary Belden, Mr. K. D. Belden, Dr. Paul Campbell, Mrs. Russell Carpenter, Mr. A. R. N. Carter, Mrs. J. Coulter, Mr. Geoffrey Coxon, His Eminence Cardinal Cushing of Boston, Dr. James Dyce, Mr. Vincent Evans, Mr. Michael Foot, M.P., Professor

John Forbes of Virginia, Shri Rajmohan Gandhi, Miss K. Green, Mrs. Alton H. Gross, Mrs. F. T. L. Guilbride, Helen, Lady Hardinge of Penshurst, Mr. Michael Henderson, Mr. William Hood, Mr. Anthony Howard, Mr. Philip Howard, Mr. Conrad Hunte, Mrs. Omar Ibargoyen, Mrs. M. L. Jacks, Mr. William Jaeger, Mr. William Lang, Miss Mary Lean, Dame Flora MacLeod of MacLeod, Mr. A. E. Oliver, Mr. Colin Oliver, Mr. Frank Owen, the Hon. John F. Powers, Miss Mary Rutherfurd, M. Michel Sentis, Mr. Peter D. Strachan, Mr. Arthur Strong, Mrs. Carroll Wax, Mr. Peter H. Webb, Mr. J. E. Whitehead, Miss Joy Wimbush, Mr. Keith Winter, Mr. A. Lawson Wood.

I would also like to thank the following for permission to use extracts from speeches, messages or letters received at the time of my father's death:

Mr. F. J. A. Cruso, Mr. Charles Graham, the Rt. Hon. Quintin Hogg, Q.C., M.P., the Rt. Hon. Keith Holyoake, Speaker John W. McCormack, His Eminence Cardinal Tisserant.

I would especially like to thank the following:

Sir Max Aitken, for the use of the *Daily Express* Library; the Trustees of the Beaverbrook Foundations for permission to use two letters from the late Lord Beaverbrook; Beaverbrook Newspapers for permission to quote from articles in the *Daily Express*, *Sunday Express* and *Evening Standard*; Mr. Garth Lean, for invaluable sub-editing; the Council of Management, the Oxford Group; Miss Muriel Upton, my father's secretary, for many months of untiring work in preparing the manuscript; my husband, Patrick Wolrige Gordon, for constant support and advice; my mother, Mrs. Peter Howard, for the complete use of all her personal letters and papers, and without whom this book would never have been written.

A. W. G.

Illustrations

Peter Howard (Frontispiece)   facing page

Peter Howard, aged 5, at Crescent House School   38

Peter Howard — Wadham College, Oxford, 1928–31   38

England rugger trial at Twickenham in 1931   39

The British bobsleigh team, 1939   39

Peter Howard in the Daily Express office, 1939   46

Peter and Doë Howard at their country cottage, 1940   46

On his farm in Suffolk, 1964   47

The Howard family, 1945   62

Peter Howard with his family, 1951   62

Sri Rajagopalachari receives Dr. Frank Buchman and Peter Howard   63

Peter Howard and Dr. Paul Campbell with Congress leaders,
Hyderabad, 1953   63

Dr. Frank Buchman and Peter Howard in America, 1960   126

The Hon. John F. Powers, His Eminence Cardinal Cushing and
Peter Howard in Boston, 1964   126

Peter and Doë Howard in Tokyo, 1963   127

Howard and Rajmohan Gandhi, 1964   127

Howard and his eldest son Philip in Kenya, 1955   142

Howard meets American Indian chief in New Mexico, 1964   142

Howard addresses dock workers, Rio de Janeiro, 1965   143

Howard greets Chancellor Konrad Adenauer, 1963   190

Howard arrives in Rio de Janeiro, 1965   190

Howard during his tour of the American universities, 1964   191

Howard escorts Dame Flora MacLeod to his daughter's wedding,
1962   206

Howard talking to students following speech to the Royal
Commonwealth Society, 1964   206

Doë and Peter Howard, Dame Flora MacLeod, Patrick and Anne
Wolrige Gordon in California, 1964   207

9

Chapter 1

PETER HOWARD came from a family which had farmed the land at Meldreth in Cambridgeshire for nearly three hundred years. They were solid, prosperous folk. James Howard was a Church Warden in 1680 and his son, John, in 1710, was one of the six parliamentary electors in the village. John's grandson, James Howard, owned a house and eleven acres. He started to buy much of the game shot in that part of Cambridgeshire, which he sent up in wicker baskets to be sold at Leadenhall Market. He was a Deacon of the independent chapel at Melbourn and, on his return journeys from London, would bring students back on his wagon to "preach with a view".

James's sons did not turn out quite as he had hoped. His second son, John, in particular, became the outstanding black sheep of the family. He was sent to prison for debt more than once and, having deserted his wife for another woman, died in 1850, and was buried in a pauper's grave. Through his sons, Henry and Ebenezer, he was the grandfather of both Peter Howard's own grandparents.

Henry had emigrated to Canada in 1841, and his wife, after his death, started a ship-chandler business in Halifax, Nova Scotia. It prospered, and she returned to England leaving the business in the hands of her sons, Ebenezer and John. On arrival in England, she naturally got in touch with her brother-in-law, Ebenezer, who had married a wealthy Yorkshire mill-owner's daughter, and himself become a prosperous property owner in the City of London. He and his wife had one daughter, Gracie, with whom her cousin, Ebenezer Howard of Halifax, promptly fell in love when he came to visit his mother in the "old country". These two became the grandparents of Peter Howard.

Young Ebenezer made his first visit when Gracie was fifteen years old. His schooling in Halifax had been rather primitive, but he was a well-read man, deeply versed in the Bible and a strong puritan. He wrote clear and excellent English and was an outstanding public speaker. But he was also a dreamer — and bone lazy. He could not even be bothered to finish what he was writing, and often broke off in the middle of a sentence. Gracie wrote, "My mother said that Eben Howard was over from Canada on a short visit, and added that he was the best-looking young man she had ever seen. Soon after Christmas I saw him for the first time. He came into our drawing room at 28, Old Steine, and my mother said, 'Kiss your cousin,' which I thought unnecessary as we were strangers to each other. The two of us went riding on the Downs together, and I thought him rather a bad rider."

Gracie has left a vivid account of their courtship and life together:

"On one occasion, I was paying a visit to an old lawyer friend of my father's in Camden Square, and Eben was invited to dinner. He came in evening dress, and after the meal was over, about eight o'clock, he whispered, 'What about going out?' I said, 'Impossible. These people will think us very rude.' 'Never mind that,' said he, 'let us go.' And off we went, after I had offered a few words of explanation to my host and hostess.

"When we came back, after going to the entertainment – not a theatre – Mrs. Webber gave Eben a letter to post addressed to my mother. The result was that the next day I had a wire saying 'Return at once.' "

The Howards discouraged meetings between Eben and Gracie, although it was impossible to avoid them altogether. On one occasion, Gracie and her mother went to tea with a cousin, not knowing that Eben was in the house. "Eben appeared and when we bid goodbye said he would see us off. My mother declared this to be unnecessary, and when his back was turned she slipped the sitting room key out and locked Eben therein. When we arrived on the platform, there stood Eben. He had lifted the sitting room window, jumped into the area and away to the station before us."

Just after Gracie's 21st birthday the family moved to a house near Hastings, because it was thought that the air would be good for her father whose health was rapidly failing. One Saturday evening Eben and another cousin appeared unexpectedly and announced that they were staying at an hotel for the weekend. They were invited to Sunday lunch and stayed for tea and supper.

"It was a perfect October night, October 13, 1878," Gracie recalled. "After supper Eben whispered to me, 'What about a walk?' Together we climbed, saying little, till we passed St. John's Church, and reached an open space. I suppose it may have been eight-thirty or nine o'clock for all the stars were out. He looked at me quietly and said, 'I wonder, dear, could you some day ever love me?' And I said, 'Yes, I think I love you now.' "

So Eben and Mary Grace became engaged, but her parents continued to oppose the marriage. Gracie was warned by her mother: "She told me fearsome tales of what resulted from the marriages of first cousins. And in my heart I offered a prayer that I might never bring such misfortunes as she described into the lives of innocent beings."

On April 17, 1880, Gracie and Eben were married. "Father was accustomed all his life to putting on every day a fresh clean boiled shirt with attached stiff collar. And he dressed with great care on this occasion.

"A fine carriage and pair came to our door and he and I got in saying nothing. My mother and cousins came later and stood behind me during the ceremony. When it started some old memories came back to my poor old father, and as Eben said the words so he repeated after him, 'I, Ebenezer, take thee, Mary Grace, to be my wedded wife.'

"I could feel my cousins shaking with laughter behind me, but I felt turned to ice, both in soul and body, and was not very far from tears.

"That evening, when my father heard I had gone away to Windsor, he put a £5 note into Matlock's (the butler) hand saying, 'Bring her back, bring her back.' "

On this sad note Eben and Gracie began their married life. Their first child, Ebenezer, Peter Howard's father, was born a year later on February 10, and four more children – Kitty, Arthur, Catherine, who died in infancy, and Geoffrey followed. None of them inherited the deformities forecast by their grandmother. They were all extremely handsome, over six foot, with strong foreheads and deep-set eyes. They had remarkable memories, and were gifted both in sport and intellect.

The three boys were sent to Haileybury and Oxford; the girl to Roedean. Ebenezer held the record for the mile at school and both he and Arthur were excellent rugger players. Arthur played cricket for Oxford and Sussex. Geoffrey was an able writer and entertainer, and later became a Q.C. and High Court Judge. They were outspoken, sometimes to the point of cruelty – but endowed with enough charm to allow people to overlook it. Their friends were many, for they had wit and courage, and their parents were hospitable.

Gracie and Eben were not as happy as they had hoped. The children felt closer to Gracie, who had a lightness of touch and gaiety to which children naturally responded. Their father was a remote figure, with what they came to regard as strict and Victorian points of view. He was also head-strong. He founded a paper called *Wit and Wisdom*. Its editor, Alfred Harmsworth, later Lord Northcliffe, suggested they go into partnership, but he refused saying that he preferred to run his own paper. He ran it to death and the *Daily Mail* rose gloriously to life. He collected many famous manuscripts by such men as Barrie, but as he refused to publish them, they were found unused upon his death. However, his shares in the London Glove Company, which he had bought before his marriage, brought in a lot of money.

He entered local politics and ran against Lord de la Warr (of whose divorce he disapproved) as Mayor of Bexhill. He won the election and became the first Mayor of the Borough.

Eben Howard took his faith seriously, preaching strong sermons almost every Sunday morning in church. His sons did not respond. They found his brand of Christianity too restricting. The eldest, Ebenezer, came down from Oxford and read for the Bar. Just before the final examination he fell in love with Evangeline Bohm, and decided he could not wait to be married. His parents, who had already paid the £100 fee, were furious, but in the family tradition Ebenezer took no notice. He married Evangeline and went to teach at the Cornwallis preparatory school near Oxford. His home was at 5, Garden Road, Maidenhead. It was a poor little house, as they had almost no money and he was estranged from his parents because of the marriage.

In the early morning of December 20, 1908, a son was born to them. They named him Peter Dunsmore Howard.

Chapter 2

PETER'S ARRIVAL drew the family together, but the announcement that he was to be called Peter, and not Ebenezer, created renewed ill-feeling. Even so, Gracie and her daughter, Kitty, travelled to Maidenhead soon after Christmas to see the new baby. During the visit Kitty expressed an interest in her nephew's legs and feet and, drawing back the covers to take a closer look, discovered to her horror that his left leg was extremely thin, and the back of his foot was attached to the knee joint — the whole calf being bent in a semi-circle.

Gracie insisted that Peter be brought to London immediately to see the best medical men of the day. Cost was to be no obstacle. Evangeline protested that there was no need for this, that she was sure everything would be all right in time. It would be hard to understand her attitude, except that she blamed herself utterly for Peter's deformity. She had never been accepted by the family and was afraid that this tragedy would make matters worse. She was also suffering from shock. In the end good sense prevailed and Peter was taken to London. His leg was cut and straightened but the doctors held out little hope of permanent cure. It was the beginning of almost weekly visits to the doctor, which continued throughout his childhood.

Evangeline Howard was a strikingly lovely woman of Austrian descent, with ice-blue eyes, reddish hair and a hasty temper. She was affectionate and gay, loved children and lavished affection on Peter. Her husband Eben, on the other hand, was a strict disciplinarian and an eccentric. He took cold baths in the morning, exercised by running or skipping before breakfast — a habit he continued until his dying day — and ate sparingly and in his own way. He enjoyed huge chunks of brown bread with cheese and a packet of dates. He disliked "fuss and bother", and was absolutely determined that Peter should be brought up in the same way as other boys he had anything to do with, and if possible more strictly.

In 1909, when Peter was just over a year old, his father bought for £100 a half share in Crescent House School, Cliftonville, Brighton. The family moved from Maidenhead and Ebenezer Howard became headmaster. The school, which consisted of a handful of boys, had until then belonged to the widow of a Mr. Thomas, who had been headmaster for many years. Thomas had been something of a scholar, and a Latin Primer which he wrote was a standard work in many schools at that time. Crescent House had been in existence since 1860. Ebenezer Cecil Howard became known to his boys as E.C.H.

When E.C.H. moved to Brighton, Miss Irene George was employed to look after Peter as well as to act as school matron. Nanny George, as she became known, was only twenty years old. She had come from tragic family circumstances in London, and had been trained as a children's nurse in Yorkshire. She was a strict nanny in the Victorian tradition, but she took to Peter at once.

E.C.H. was an exceptional teacher. He had a gift for imparting knowledge to boys in ways in which they would never forget. Most of his boys were not well off, and their only chance of a public school education was a scholarship. He worked tirelessly to this end. He believed in cutting out half-holidays and weekends in order to get a boy through an exam, and often used beatings as an extra spur. His humour was of a strange variety. One of his favourite jokes was to ask new boys at breakfast on their first day whether they would like porridge or to "wait for the bacon and eggs". Most of the newcomers decided to wait for the main course. It never came for there was no bacon and eggs. New boys soon learnt to accept porridge at once.

It was on the question of food that Nanny George had her first disagreement with the Howards. She told them that Peter was not getting enough to eat and that more food must be sent to the nursery. Often there was only a pennyworth of herring to share between the two of them for a meal. Her request was refused. From that day Nanny George would spend most of her wages on buying food for Peter. She would tuck it under the blankets of the pram and smuggle it home for the cook, Clara, to prepare. She also spent her money on clothes in the cold weather, for Peter had the barest minimum to wear. The Howards, it was true, were very short of money. But these deprivations were more a matter of principle than finance, or meanness. They were part of Ebenezer's way of bringing up Peter.

From the age of one till seven Nanny George would massage Peter's lame leg daily with coconut butter. Each week she would take him to the doctor. Peter would be given an anaesthetic so that the leg could be manipulated. It was on these occasions only that he showed fear. He would refuse to lie down on the couch unless Nanny was beside him. He would then insist that she put cotton-wool over her mouth and nose before he would take the mask himself. Nanny George would always oblige.

In her affection Nanny George was generous. She was a perfectionist in the home, keeping rooms and belongings tidy and spotless. She liked expeditions and outings of all kinds and would take Peter to the beach at Brighton, to the Downs and for picnics in the fine weather. Every Sunday afternoon Nanny George took him to church for the children's service. It was a regular and enforced visitation, which Peter remembered:

"From the pulpit the preacher asked questions which the children had to answer. 'Who killed the giant Goliath?' he would ask. Half the children were scared to answer that white-surpliced figure which towered above them. Half the children did not know the answer. I belonged to both halves.

"But the stern and be-boned elbow of Nanny would give me a dig. 'David,' the voice would whisper in my ear. Then another dig, 'Go on, say David.' And obediently I would gulp and mutter 'David' from our pew. 'Very good, very good,' the preacher would remark from the heights above and a smile like a sunrise would dawn above the surplice, while Nanny would proudly look around, taking to herself the admiration of her charge. I quickly lost my sense of fright at answering the preacher. As soon as the preacher asked his questions, I would eagerly listen for the prompting answer swiftly lest anyone should beat me. I was in such a hurry to reply that one day I shouted 'Abraham', when the answer should have been 'Ahab'."

Nanny George was a sport. She was also scrupulously fair. Outspoken in her criticisms to the Howard parents themselves when she felt their treatment of Peter unfair, she would never allow one word of comment to pass in Peter's hearing. Nor would she allow Peter any liberty of criticism.

"In that nursery in Brighton they brought in a little dish with butter made into balls," wrote Peter. "I saw a maid come in and pop one in her mouth. I thought what an extraordinary thing to do. After the maid had gone out, Nanny came in. I said, 'Do you know what the maid did?' I told Nanny. She said, 'Tell tale tit, your tongue shall be split, and all the dogs in Brighton shall have a little bit.' "

A young boy, William Hood,[1] came to Crescent House as a boarder in 1911. "When the front door was opened by the cook, Clara, on my arrival, I had a large chunk taken out of my calf by a fox terrier called 'Trimmer', and the wound had to be dealt with at once by the painful application of a caustic stick. Ebenezer Howard remarked rather unsympathetically that the dog only bit tradespeople.

"Peter Howard was only about two years old, a good-looking child, very like his mother to look at, with an inward turning foot and wasted leg which he was inclined to trip over as he rushed madly about the place. He also had his mother's hasty temper.

"I owe my scholarship to Haileybury entirely to Ebenezer Howard, though it meant no half-holidays for at least two years."

[1] From 1946 Master of the Supreme Court (Tax Office).

When war broke out in 1914, Peter Howard's much-loved Uncle Arthur joined up: "Uncle Arthur was of lean and tempered steel. He was blue-eyed and blond, unlike the other black-browed, tough-hided Howards. He was a hero, so gay and so gallant. He was a magnificent footballer and the crowds roared as he swept forward with the ball.

"Once he set me on his back and ran with me down the street so I felt the air rush by and a sense of peril and yet of escape from the world, as if I were borne forward in the crow's nest of a tall-masted and lithe ship through tumbling seas. It was a relief and a regret when Uncle Arthur set me down. I said, 'Again, uncle, again,' and then gulped with apprehension as he gripped and hoisted me aloft."

Uncle Arthur went off to France to fight the Germans. The family gave him a patent body shield. This was a steel waistcoat, proof against bullets and shell splinters. It covered a man from the neck down to the small of the back. Arthur Howard made jokes about it before he said goodbye. To young Peter he was an indestructible conqueror:

"I remember the trains full of troops pulling out and the trains full of wounded pulling in as dusk fell. The feverish cheers and hectic laughter. The songs, 'It's a long way to Tipperary', 'Pack Up your Troubles', 'Keep the Home Fires Burning' — the potency of such music to tear the heart. These were the last words so many mothers, wives, daughters heard their menfolk sing as the trains, slowly but with gathering speed, disappeared south into the darkness.

"The sudden silence after the troop trains had departed — all conversation ceased, no need now to pretend to be cheerful so as to send the boys off with the memory of a smile — the huddles and clusters of women, standing silent for a moment or two, straining their eyes after the red tail-lights of the trains, then turning and quietly, quickly, heads down, slipping off through the barriers towards their empty homes."

So Peter as a child of six was to remember saying goodbye to his Uncle Arthur. But the war was to make an even more direct mark upon him: "Uncle Arthur and a sergeant were out one night on patrol in No Man's Land. Someone from the German lines fired a Very light. Uncle Arthur and the sergeant lay still on the ground. A shell exploded nearby. Presently the sergeant said, 'It's all right, sir, we can get up now.'

"Uncle Arthur answered, 'I'm trying to get up, sergeant, but I can't seem to manage it.' They wheeled him to an emergency hospital in a barrow. A piece of shrapnel had severed his spine. The shrapnel was the size of half a lump of sugar. It had penetrated his spine about half way down, just at the point where the covering of the body-shield would have been most adequate.

"But Uncle Arthur was generous as well as gay. That night on patrol it had been the sergeant's turn to wear the body-shield."

Never again of his volition did Arthur Howard move the lower half of his body. The child Peter watched a living man disintegrate year by year, week by week, day by day for seven long years:

"Uncle Arthur's lower half shrivelled to the proportion of a mummy. Those valiant legs which had kicked and run and leapt to the clamour of applauding multitudes. He died. Most families in the world have the savagery and sadness of war focused for them by some personal tragedy. It made me dislike war. I perceived its futility. I believed that Uncle Arthur had fought in the war to end wars and that therefore war could not be for me."

                    .   .   .

When in 1916 Peter was seven years old, his father decided that he should join the lowest class at Crescent House. To prove that there was no favouritism, E.C.H. decided that whenever any boy was punished Peter would be punished too. It meant that Peter was punished regularly both for things he did not do, and for plenty that he did:

"We had a thing called the strike list, and if you got strikes you sat at table without talking and if there was any special food going you did not get it. I was on those strike lists. Nanny was amazing. She never said a word to me about my mother or father they would not have been glad to hear. But she used to fight furious battles on what she felt was justice for 'rat' Howard."

Peter was a bright and energetic schoolboy. He learnt fast. Nanny would read to Peter for hours — adventure stories, fairy stories and tales of animals and wild life. Unlike other adults, who were all too apt to treat Peter differently from other children because of his leg, Nanny insisted that he learn how to do things for himself. She taught him how to make his bed, clean his room, wash clothes and tidy them away. He learnt how to dress himself with an iron on his leg and never to be a "cry-baby" when it hurt. For all this Peter was an invariably scruffy schoolboy, exceptionally untidy and always on the run. Red-faced, hot and tousle-haired he would charge into a room with ink all over his face and hands, usually on his way to perform some practical joke. His leg was something noticed by others but never by himself. This was perhaps because neither his father nor Nanny George allowed it to interfere with his life, except that he had to go to bed ten minutes earlier than the other boys to have his leg massaged.

One of the new boys to join Peter at Crescent House was Geoffrey Coxon:[1]

"I was delivered two days prior to the official commencement of the term. I spent those two days in the company of the Headmaster's son, Peter Howard, and Miss George, who acted as school matron. Peter was dressed in a short covert coat and cap to match and my first impressions were of his large brown expressive eyes, his vitality and the sadly thin leg with which he had been born. The stocking on this leg would always come down, and although he dragged it when tired, he never let it interfere with his intense activity. On those two days we went for walks, once on the Brighton front in a gale and with a rough sea. Peter's idea of fun was rushing out on the groyne near the Palace Pier and then retreating at speed as the sea dashed over us.

"The Headmaster, Ebenezer Cecil Howard, was a character. Huge and dark, he seemed to tower over us. Always dressed in a sports coat and flannel bags of some antiquity. He must have worked tremendously hard to teach us, and the record of scholarships and entry into the Navy was a tribute to this. I think he was harder on Peter than any of us, just because he wished there to be no favouritism. I, fortunately, got on well with him and have affectionate memories of this rather eccentric but brilliant schoolmaster. His wife, Peter's mother, Evangeline Howard, called 'Madam' by us boys, was very handsome. Although E.C.H. was tough with Peter, he was always his mother's son.

"Peter must have been very bright for he was doing work with those of two years older before I left at the end of 1920. He was a rumbustious lad, always charging about and getting hot and dirty. He was nicknamed unkindly either 'Beetroot' or more unkindly 'Dunsmuck'. The latter a pun on his second Christian name of Dunsmore.

"I recall in him an inherent kindness and generosity. Sometimes when his mother had lashed me with her tongue, he would come and say, 'She doesn't really mean it.' He liked to make gifts and I recall his giving me a postcard album.

"Finally, the outstanding characteristic was his courage. That thin leg would have held back a more timid character but never Peter. He was always in the thick of a fight or a football match. We used to do some boxing and to my own intense surprise, for I hated fighting, I proved to be fairly good at it. I was wont to await an attack and then counter with a pretty hard right which earned some respect. Peter must have studied this and made a plan to undo me. He waited until I had delivered my hard right, ducked it, and then before I could recover my guard, planted his own right smack on my chin! It was a grand blow and in later years I should have been out for the count. Happily for Peter, his father came in

[1] Later became a bank manager.

just in time to see it and for once praise flowed for his son in his words, 'That was a good one.' "

E.C.H. had a system called "N.T.N.T." It meant, "No translation no tea". Boys had to do their translation, do it perfectly and neatly or they did not go down to tea. Hungry boys would watch others going down to tea and know that unless that translation was finished it was "N.T.N.T." The last person down to tea, after the final translation was perfectly done, was E.C.H.

In Peter's first year at Crescent House he fell on the rugger field and sprained his thin leg. The doctor who examined the sprain said to Peter, "Well, cricket is a better game for you. Don't play football. You stick to cricket, there's a good boy."

"It was at that moment that the desire to be a footballer sprang to life inside me," wrote Peter later. "As my father and Uncle Arthur had both been rugby footballers, rugby was the game for me." So Peter took no notice of the doctor's advice. His father did not appear to object.

But life was not all sport or work. Among Peter's enjoyments at Crescent House was collecting birds' eggs. Many of the boys did this, and one of them possessed a small egg with spots on it which Peter much coveted. Peter stole it and put it in his desk. The owner reported the loss to E.C.H. and the Headmaster ordered that all desks should be searched. The egg was found in Peter's desk. E.C.H. ordered Peter to return the egg in front of the class. But that was not all. Peter owned a penknife. It was his most treasured possession, "It had a thing for taking out corks, a thing for taking out stones from horses' hooves, and three different blades for cutting." "You stole that egg. Now you give him your knife," said E.C.H. "To give that boy my knife — it was as if something had been ripped out of my guts," said Peter. But he handed it over. He learnt the penalty of theft.

E.C.H. hated the ties of human dependence. He wanted his boys to leave Crescent House able to stand on their own feet. Though not without a tender heart underneath, he never allowed it to rule him. One hot summer day Peter was playing in the long grass at the edge of the cricket field. He put his hand down in the grass and was about to sit down. "I sprang up and there was a great gash right over my hand. My father was there, and with my hand bleeding I ran over to him and showed it to him. My father looked at it and bound it up with his handkerchief. Then he looked at me and said, 'Now, you know where the doctor lives?'

" 'Yes,' I said.

" 'You have got to go there. He may have to put some stitches in it, and if he does it will hurt, but it will be over in a minute. I want you to be brave. Now off you go.'

"I went off with my cut hand thinking, 'My God, he has let me go alone.' "

One of the blessings of Crescent House was the long summer holidays. The Howards usually spent them near Harlech in North Wales, fishing, walking and golfing. E.C.H. would set off early with his rod, and walk for miles into the hills. Sometimes he took Peter with him and taught him to fish for brown trout in the deep pools. They were days when very little was said, and Peter learnt to love the sound of rushing water and the squelch of peat bog under his feet. At teatime they would meet Evangeline and Nanny George at a pre-arranged place. They would brew tea and have hot food ready. Oh the hunger and the enjoyment of that meal! The excitement of discussing the day's adventures, the number of fish caught, the number that got away. It was on one of these holidays that Nanny George learnt to ride a bicycle. She mounted and wobbled precariously out of sight down the hill, pursued hotly by Peter shouting, "Come back, come back Nanny, or you will be gone for ever." But Nanny returned. She would take Peter to Harlech beach and they would bathe on those glorious yellow sands, build endless castles and moats, boil shrimps for tea and run for miles in the sea air.

From an early age E.C.H. took Peter golfing. Peter was a child of eight and E.C.H. was a good golfer. But he did not allow that to mar their games together. They would set off in the morning by train along the coast and they would play two rounds (thirty-six holes) at the Royal St. David's Golf Club. E.C.H. could not afford a caddy, so they carried their own clubs. Afterwards they would walk the two and a half miles home. Between the first two telegraph poles they would walk, and between the next two they would trot, all the way home. For Peter it was the best holiday on earth. "I loved it. It built something into me of comradeship. sweat and go. I took it all so much for granted. My father was pushing fifty. I don't think that after two rounds of golf he particularly liked running two and a half miles home with a boy."

In 1918, when Peter was ten years old, his only brother, John, was born. They were so far apart in age that it was almost as if they belonged to different generations. John's arrival was followed by the departure of Nanny George. Perhaps Evangeline Howard felt Nanny had become too close to Peter. Whatever the reasons, her departure remained a mystery, and one which caused great sorrow to young Peter, just as the new baby was becoming the focus of all attention. John was a fair-haired boy, with blue eyes, unlike Peter in almost every way. For Evangeline it was a great happiness to have a son with no physical deformity whatever – something she had feared could never happen.

In the summer of 1921 Peter won an open scholarship to Mill Hill School. He was thirteen years old. At the end of July he left Crescent House School and put his childhood behind him.

Chapter 3

THE PIGEONS OF ST. PAUL'S

There are no nightingales in London now,
No larks or finches, crested wrens I trow,
No garden warblers flutter by the walls;
Still, still remain the pigeons of St. Paul's.

Like Hermes flash they swiftly through the air,
Their smooth grey necks stretched low, as if in prayer.
Kind folk with crumbled bread fetch with their calls
The clear, the friendly pigeons of St. Paul's.

Best loved of all the London beasts and birds.
Their very loveliness beyond all words
Until the majesty of London falls
Still will be loved the pigeons of St. Paul's.

P. D. Howard
Mill Hill, Summer 1924

Mill Hill School is set, as its name implies, on top of a hill. It is surrounded by green playing fields and trees, under which you can sit on a clear summer evening and see the great smoke-bound city of London stretching away as far as the eye can see. It has a non-conformist tradition. The buildings are Victorian, set apart from each other, but bound together by that strange unity which surrounds an English public school. The corridors and hallways seem to echo to the sound of everlasting boys' voices and running feet. In the centre of it all lie the playing fields — so green and rich in summer time, and so muddy and rough after the winters of rugger and hockey.

It was on September 22, 1922, that Peter Howard arrived at Mill Hill School for the first time. Unlike other boys, he was not accompanied by his parents. E.C.H. had felt it would be better for him to go off on his own. Peter said goodbye to his parents at Gracie and Eben's home in Inverness Terrace. Like all boys arriving for the first time at public school, he was apprehensive and nervous. At Golders Green Station he passed the war memorial, "Courage: Justice: Loyalty: Honour". For many a year he was to pass that memorial on his way to school.

Peter's House was Priestley. His form the Upper Fifth. A scholar of thirteen he found himself working with boys of fifteen years of age. His Housemaster said, "He was placed so high because of his classics. He had first-rate Latin and Greek. It was done deliberately because we wanted to encourage Peter's main subjects, knowing he would catch up on the rest."

For Peter it was a difficult burden to bear. The boys of his own age thought him a prig. The boys in his form considered him an intruder. They noticed his leg-iron and made fun of it: "We used to bathe in the school swimming bath. The other boys asked me questions about my thin leg, and I soon came to suppose there was a shame and uncleanliness in possessing it."

At the worst moments, Peter would visit "Buster Brown", one of the Mill Hill masters, for tea and crumpets: "Those teas saved my life," he used to say afterwards. He had few friends and he felt lonely and unhappy. He turned his attention to the rugger field. E.C.H. had been doubtful about the wisdom of allowing Peter to play games in the tougher surroundings of a public school. As soon as possible Peter sought out the school doctor, Dr. Edwin Morley, and being a born persuader got him to agree that if his parents said "Yes" he could shed his leg-iron and play games. Whether or not E.C.H. agreed we do not know, but anyway Peter cast off the leg-iron and played. He developed a rollicking gallop on the field, which made up in speed for what he lost in lameness.

The Headmaster, Mr. M. L. Jacks, was to remember Peter in his first year at school: "He was the inkiest, untidiest scrap of small boyhood that I have ever known, and one of the most active and irrepressible. This activity and irrepressibility continued as he grew. There was always about his doings a flavour of the old saying, 'Go and see what Billy is doing and tell him not to.'"

In 1923, at the age of fourteen, Peter passed his School Certificate and was moved up to the Classical Sixth. Here he was to stay until he left Mill Hill. Among his few friends was a boy his own age called Tony Carter: "Peter was rather unpopular at the beginning of his school life, but he didn't appear to give a damn about other people's opinions. And it was this that first attracted me about him."

Tony Carter[1] and Peter were in the same House. But in 1924 a new House, Winterstoke, was built and volunteers from established Houses were asked to start it. Most boys were getting on comfortably where they were and had no intention of moving. Not Peter. He joined Winterstoke. His new Housemaster was Mr. J. E. Whitehead. It was to Mr. Whitehead that Peter would take the occasional letters he received from home:

[1] Later joined the family leather business, John Carter & Sons, Bishopsgate.

"Peter's father treated him very much like another pupil. Whenever he wrote him at school he never began the letter 'Dear Peter', but started straight in with some criticism of his last Latin essay or translation, and ended the letter with his initials, 'E.C.H.' Peter did not at any time have a chip on his shoulder about this. He would bring the letter to me and ask for the necessary help with his work. It was Peter's acceptance of correction without anger that made him unusual."

But Peter could be maddening as his classics master, Mr. Whitehorn, discovered: "I would be lecturing on Greek history. I could see Peter looking out of the window, his mind miles away. He would then, at the end of some point I had made, suddenly say, 'I don't agree at all,' and proceed to argue the opposite of what I had said."

Suddenly Peter began to make his way at school. He started to make friends and enjoy himself. His imagination ran riot. He would devise methods of "catching" unsuspecting masters on the prowl, spending precious pocket money scattering sugar in the corridors outside their studies. The crunching footsteps could be heard a long way off. He plotted long hours on how to help Winterstoke win some sporting event.

In the tug-of-war, at which Winterstoke was not strong, they were drawn against the top team. Peter gave orders that on the first pull the Winterstoke side should let the rope go slack altogether. When the whistle blew the opposing side, taken by surprise, landed flat on their backs and were pulled helplessly across the line. On the second pull, the opposition was wise. They were prepared for the same thing to happen again and did not pull too hard. Peter gave orders for Winterstoke to pull like mad the moment the whistle blew. The opposition flew across the line, this time flat on their stomachs.

Peter's parents seldom came to visit him at Mill Hill. When they did E.C.H. took no trouble with his appearance. If Peter was "scruffy", E.C.H. was deplorable. He would arrive in old clothes and show far more interest in the classics papers and the library than in his son. Peter would often lose track of him altogether. One Foundation Day, Peter finally accosted Mrs. Whitehorn and said, "Have you seen my father wandering around in a mackintosh too ghastly to be seen? We must find him and get it off him."

In 1926, E.C.H. left Crescent House and went to teach for a year at Worksop College. In April 1926 Peter set out to join him there for the holidays on his new motor-cycle. On the way he skidded and collided with a truck. He found himself bruised and bleeding in a ditch, but assured the driver of the truck that there was nothing wrong. He managed to borrow a pedal cycle and pedalled twelve miles to the Worksop Hospital, only to discover on arrival that his thin leg was broken in two places. He went straight to the operating theatre. Coming round after the anaesthetic he heard the doctor saying, "I shall have to take this leg off." For Peter it was a moment of cold horror. He begged the doctor to do nothing until his parents had been seen. Finally the doctors agreed that if Peter would remain in hospital for four months, they could save the leg: "I sat out those four months with my leg propped up on the window-sill, but I did not mind because my leg was still there."

Peter missed that whole summer term at Mill Hill. It was the term he should have taken an exam held annually at Mill Hill, using old scholarship papers, giving boys a chance to practise for the Oxford scholarship exam a year later. E.C.H. finding hospital no excuse for laziness, looked up the syllabus and sent Peter the books which he had to read for the exam in July. Two weeks before examination day, Peter had a letter from a friend at school, from which he inferred that he might be reading the wrong books. He wrote to Mill Hill and discovered that this was indeed so. The correct books arrived and he had just over a week left to read them: "I think I must have read day and night for that whole week," he said afterwards. He passed the exam.

In September 1926, Peter returned to school and went straight into the Second XV rugger team. On December 20 he had his seventeenth birthday, and 1927 was just ahead. It was a year which held great prospects for him. In September 1927, Peter returned to school to find himself a House Monitor. Before the school year was out he was in the First XV rugger side, opening bat for the First XI cricket side, a member of the Boxing Eight, a member of the Athletics side, Vice-President of the Debating Society, and the winner of an Open Exhibition to Wadham College, Oxford.

Peter spent many holidays with Tony Carter: 'We used to go to Hertford every Whit Sunday to play cricket, and we always brought a signpost home with us. At least Peter did. He was the only one strong enough to pull the things out of the ground. We had quite a collection of them in Alton House (the Carter family home) all pointing the incorrect way to remote villages in Hertfordshire."

At Winterstoke Peter was in charge of the big dormitory of twenty-one beds. His Housemaster says, "He was quite outstanding in the way he kept all the boys quiet." One night, however, there was trouble brewing against Tony Carter in a neighbouring House, and Peter leapt out of the window to protect his friend. He was fortunate that twenty-one small boys did not follow him. At the end of the year he was made Head of Winterstoke House.

In rugger Peter played in the front row of the scrum. He had grown to six feet three inches, and was broad shouldered and strong. He excelled in the line-outs, where he seemed to tower above the others. He was fortunate to play rugger for Mill Hill when the sport was at its height – Mill Hill at that time producing several of the England international players, including Sobey and Spong. Peter's success on the rugger field did not satisfy his own sense of ambition: "I only managed to get into the school football XV in my last year there. I was not pleased with that at all. I wanted to be the best player in the school. But there were at least nine others who played better than I did."

The summer term came almost too soon. It brought with it long days of cricket. In the final House match between Winterstoke and Priestley, Peter and Tony Carter were lined up against each other. In the first innings Carter bowled Howard, and in the second innings Howard bowled Carter, so they were all square: "Winterstoke opened disastrously, Beven being run out through a misunderstanding after scoring one. Howard and Aish[1] were obviously not at ease to the bowling of A. R. N. Carter on a wicket affected by rain. Aish was l.b.w. to Carter for the second time in the match with ten to his credit. Howard and Das[2] then knocked off the necessary runs. If Howard had not been missed early in his innings owing to an unfortunate misunderstanding, the result of the game might easily have been changed. As it was, he was undefeated for thirty-eight, and Winterstoke won by eight wickets."

Peter and Tony Carter were both in the First XI cricket side and so they shared the enjoyments of their final term. Carter was an excellent spin bowler, Howard a batsman.

Cricket Report 1928, P. D. Howard:

"A very hard-hitting batsman, who scored runs quickly and who knew how to sit on the splice when it was required. A very good runner between the wickets. A very good fielder in most positions, preferably at mid-off. A capable and efficient secretary."

Mr. Whitehorn remembers him as "an exceptionally good cricketer, who ran so fast between wickets that it was embarrassing if you were in with him because he was over in three strides before you had taken off."

The summer term rushed gloriously to its close, bringing with it the numerous rewards and prizes which every end of year will bring. For Peter the list was long. He was Senior Champion in Athletics. He also took a lively interest in the school magazine which he edited, in the Music Circle and the Scriptorium Committee. On leaving he won "In Memoriam", the top prize of the school.

Success came easily to Peter Howard, or so it seemed. His friends saw little of the struggle which had brought a thirteen-year-old schoolboy with little to his credit to a young man of eighteen with the world at his feet.

[1] Killed in action in World War II.
[2] Later War Controller of Supplies in Bombay.

"To back up this success," said his Headmaster, "he had a tremendous capacity for enjoying life, a fertile and lively mind, and a nice wit. He was indeed a figure that challenged attention and enjoyed and courted the challenge. It was not to be expected that a person with so strong a drive to triumph over a physical handicap that might well have kept a lesser individualist permanently in the shadow of the touch-line, should not at times come into rough contact with other boys, and with authority in general. Or should not, indeed, have been to some degree self-centred; he was. It was perhaps his most solid achievement that he learned to subdue these strong qualities to the service of the spiritual welfare of mankind."

Chapter 4

PETER HOWARD went up to Oxford in October 1928. He had his Exhibition to Wadham College. Mr. Jacks, his former Headmaster, had helped him to acquire a small Government grant on the understanding that he would become a teacher after he had obtained his degree. Howard had no serious intention of becoming a teacher, but he needed the money. His parents could not afford an Oxford education, nor could they supply him with the adequate pocket money. For Howard the grant made Oxford possible and, above all, pleasant.

Like many other public schoolboys, Howard found the freedom of university exhilarating. He loved Oxford – its colleges and walks; the Isis on lazy summer days; the parties that went on till breakfast; the college scouts with their observant eyes and dry humour; and the winter evenings spent arguing in smoke-filled rooms for hours on end about little or nothing. In 1928, between the two Great Wars, Oxford seemed the ideal place to be. It was full of undergraduates who either wanted to forget 1918 or dreamed that 1939 would never come.

Perhaps the best picture of Howard at Oxford is given by his friend Keith Winter, the novelist and playwright:

"What do I remember about Peter?

"Quickly, without reflection, that he was an experience, a vividly arresting, quite unforgettable happening. I was a year his senior at Oxford (though no one felt 'senior' to Peter for long!) but we met first in his last term at Mill Hill when I accompanied a college friend on an afternoon visit to his old school.

"In a study which seemed too small for his large, athletic frame I was introduced to a darkly handsome youth whose rabelaisian humour and extraordinary conversation were far removed from anything I'd encountered in an English public school – or anywhere else, for that matter.

"'What did you think of him?' asked my friend as we drove back to Oxford.

"'Mad,' I replied promptly. But I added after a moment's reflection, 'In the right way though.'

"The following October he came to Oxford and we became immediately, and rather improbably – on a superficial level we had about as much in common as Othello and Iago – great friends.

"The relationship was neither cosy nor placid. Standing up to his steam-roller personality was almost a whole-time job, but worth it, I rather grudgingly decided.

"Frequently maddening, intermittently unreliable (he had no sense of time, and to him an appointment was less a fact than a whimsical possibility), on occasions socially outrageous, to people who bored him frequently very rude, he was never, under any circumstances, dull.

"Finance, or rather the lack of it, was one of our more constant pre-occupations. Once, after we had treated ourselves to a handsome meal on the terrace of the Trout Inn at Godstow, I produced a shilling from my pocket and stared at it sombrely. 'My last,' I announced, 'literally my last.'

"Peter took it from my hand and threw it into the river. My stunned expression clearly delighted him. 'Now,' he said, roaring with laughter, 'you'll have nothing to worry about.' I might state here that whatever the conditions of his finances he was always fantastically generous. In cash, kind or spirit, he gave without thought.

"Without thought, too, he sometimes hurt and offended people. Stopping to think was not a habit of our generation. Even so, there was no malice in Peter, nor any kind of meanness.

"The range of his acquaintances at Oxford was wide but he belonged to no particular set or clique. He was a natural athlete and a brilliant rugby football player, but one could spend days in his company without gathering he knew one end of a ball from another.

"He was a classical scholar, but one never heard about it; a poet, but it required heavy detective work to unearth the fact. This was less false modesty than a sense of proportion developed to an unusual degree.

'A time will come when the flowers are faded,
A time will come when the year is dead.
But now the shoots are newly springing,
No petal yet to the day is spread.
What shall we have to remember?
That is the test.
Only bright flowers, please God, to remember,
Only the best.'

"Again, this was not shown to me by the proud author but discovered quite by chance in a back number of a magazine. It wasn't the sound one would have expected to emerge from the seething heart of a rugby scrum. At the time I was deeply impressed by its simple beauty. I still am.

"There were occasions when he appeared no more than a noisy, over-ebullient extrovert primarily interested in the devising of wildly extravagant and usually extremely funny pranks, but his real achievements were made swiftly, silently and without fuss.

"In my last year at Oxford I published a novel. For better or worse, come hell or high water, I was going to be a writer!

"But where was the turbulent, meteoric mass of energy that made up Peter going to land?

"I knew, as did all his more intimate friends, that he was a born leader. But that, when one is a very young tiger 'burning brightly' only within the mellow confines of an ancient university, can spell, as often as not, less glory than a disillusioning smack in the eye.

"After all, what was he going to lead? And who? And whither?

"One shouldn't, as it turns out, have worried."

.   .   .

Peter Howard's great ambition upon going to Oxford was to play rugger for the University. He was a good public school player, but that was a long way from becoming an Oxford Blue. In November 1928, one month after he had arrived at Wadham, he had a piece of good fortune:

"One cold Thursday, a winter afternoon, when the Oxford University Greyhounds (the University Second XV) were playing Cheltenham, a member of the team fell ill. By a series of chances I was the person available to take his place. I was pulled in at the last moment.

"Everything went right for me in that game. Next Saturday I was picked to play for the University.

"I cannot describe the exhilaration which filled me when I heard this news. I telegraphed to my parents.

"I played for the University all through that season until a fortnight before the University match. I felt sure of my Blue. All my friends – and it is odd how many friends a man has who is playing football for a University – told me it was certain.

"Then I was dropped from the side. I heard that the captain of the team took the view that my thin leg might snap in the Varsity match. He would not risk it.

"The decision seemed silly, as I had played in first-class rugger matches all the way through the season, two days a week and sometimes more, without my leg snapping. In any case, it was a terrible blow to me, and my pride bled and suffered."

For Howard the disappointment was unbearable. He was bitter and angry when he went home in December – and even more determined to win his Blue:

"My father and mother bore with me in these tiresome circumstances. I behaved very badly, becoming ill-tempered, venomous and surly."

Howard's anger did not last long:

"My only hope rested in the following rugger season. During the spring I thought of rugger. During the summer I thought of rugger. And when the autumn came I started training for rugger.

"As I left my home to go up to Oxford and try to win my Blue, my father and mother stood on the doorstep. We had always been close together as a family, in spite of the fact that all three of us possess determined and potentially violent dispositions, hurting each other and sorry for it afterwards. My father said with emphasis: 'Well, I hope to God you don't get your Blue. That's all. You're too damned conceited already.'

"I turned and went away.

"I know now that my father wanted above everything else in the world that I should get a Blue. But he knew how disappointed I had been at my earlier failure. He dreaded that I might fail again. He was resolved that, if I did fail, I should not feel that he and my mother were also disappointed in me.

"This is now plain to me. Not so at the time. I was wounded and resented the wound. I felt dislike for my father."

In the autumn of 1929, Howard was picked to play for Oxford: "I got my Blue. The days passed in a daze of delight."

Oxford won the Varsity match at Twickenham.

.   .   .

That November he started writing regularly for the University magazine, Isis. His first contribution was on November 20 under the heading, *Death by Misadventure*:

Oh, there are many ways, grotesque, bizarre — let us be even more frank and say funny — by which we may come to our deaths, and I expect even in this present whirl of mechanism and immaturity, of laughter and caprice, above all of eating and drinking, there are not a few who give an occasional thought to the end of the story, and discuss with themselves in their leisure moments their inevitable and ultimate duty of dying. I am such a one, and if I had the choice I would prefer to emulate with my ending those happy few who have confounded the pessimists by dying from laughter. If only God had been sufficiently kind to a man that he could die with laughter at the sight of his own face in a mirror; that would be a king of jokes indeed. But I, alas, am not unhandsome.

Isis followed in December with a feature on their new recruit. It was entitled, "Peter the Great", and was reprinted in the *Daily Sketch*:

Peter Howard is a giant from Wadham, with extremely black hair and a disarming manner. Born in 1908, he seems to have conducted his life on the principle that what is worth doing is worth doing violently.

Strong as a bull, and shaped across the shoulders very much like one, he is no man to meet when he is in a whimsical humour, for his sense of a joke is liable to lead him to drop his friends over Magdalen Bridge, if he felt so inclined.

He does a lot of work on the Isis, which office seems entirely full when he is in it, and in his capacity as a member of the Isis staff he is perhaps more irresponsible and irrepressible than anywhere else.

The Oxford Mail followed suit:

Peter Howard is the big blue boy. He is quite young and may grow bigger. He may yet be known and famous on many fields.

He is neither a proud nor conceited man. He thinks nothing of himself as either a footballer or a cricketer, but he fancies his chances at ping pong. Do you know he believes himself to be the finest ping pong player in the world? He is nothing of the kind.

I have heard it said in dark and obscure corners that he has written poetry; that's not the sort of thing one likes to hear about big men; but then we all have our enemies.

If Howard had enemies they were few. The fame of the rugger field made him more boisterous than ever. His friends enjoyed it and egged him on. He and some friends organised massive practical jokes. It was customary for undergraduates who misbehaved to receive a summons in writing from the Proctors (University disciplinary authorities) to appear before them at a specified hour. One morning every male undergraduate at Oxford came down to breakfast to find they had received a Proctor's summons for a certain day the following week at 10.30 a.m. By some error of judgment, some women undergraduates at Lady Margaret Hall had also received cards. Unlike the men, they were outraged and frightened. They went straight to the Dean. The Dean got in touch with the Proctors and, being forewarned, the iron gates to the Proctor's lodgings were firmly shut and locked. None-the-less, at 10.30 on the morning concerned a crowd of some two thousand had gathered outside the Proctor's gates, waving their cards in the air and demanding to be let in. At this point somebody took the precaution of telephoning the Oxford Fire Brigade to inform them that the Proctor's house was in flames. As the fire engines arrived and tried to make their way through the wild excitement of the crowd, the Pathé News cameras were in operation on the roof of the building opposite and shot an excellent film of the whole proceedings.

The Oxford authorities tried without success to discover where the cards which had started the whole affair had been printed. Nobody could be found who knew anything about it. The Oxford Fire Brigade could not trace the call which had brought them out to deal with a non-existent fire. Pathé News did not know who had given them the information. The whole matter had to be overlooked, with a statement from the Proctors that such behaviour would be severely dealt with in future.

Though Howard was in training for rugger, he attended many parties and gave some himself. They did not always end cheerfully. On one occasion a piano was forced through an upper window at Wadham, and landed in the quad below with its insides a tangled mess of wires and hammers. The noise was deafening and the owner, returning to find his piano in bits in the quad, was naturally distressed.

On other occasions, Howard would join his rugger friends at OICCU (Oxford Inter-Collegiate Christian Union) meetings and heckle from the back:

"Are you saved?"

"Yes, we are," the chorus would reply.

During the readings from the New Testament one of Howard's friends would ask, "Who said that?"

"Peter, Peter," the others would shout.

God, who at Mill Hill had been a formal and unmentioned subject, became at Oxford a term of abuse. What little faith Howard had, he soon lost. He was later to say, "I rationalised what I knew was wrong, and before long I saw nothing wrong in it at all." At the time, he would not have said that. He felt it was realist and adult to discard faith in the face of his doubts as to its truth. He was often cruel in his condemnation of those who possessed faith: "I found it repulsive to see anybody reading a Bible in a railway carriage." More often he found it ridiculous and made fun of it.

At the beginning of 1930, Oxford had become the centre of Howard's life. He immersed himself in its politics and its people, but all too little in its work. At the beginning of January, however, something happened which was to take him out of Oxford a good deal:

"Tuning in the radio one evening, I heard the announcer give the names of the players picked to represent England against Wales. My name was there. The news threw me altogether off balance. I walked as a man like a god.

"My first International match was to be played at Cardiff. The England team went to Penarth two days beforehand. 'Are you coming to see the game?' I asked my father. 'No, I shan't bother,' he replied. 'It's a long way to go, you know, and I think I'll stay at home.'

"I was angry that my father should not be willing to travel to the end of the earth, let alone to Wales, to witness the glorification of his son. So I packed.

"At Cardiff the match was played. We were expected to lose. Instead we came away with victory perched on our banners. It was tremendous, exhilarating, triumphant. In addition to the success of the team, I had the satisfaction of knowing that I myself had played well.

"As I changed back into my ordinary clothes with the rest of the team, I was told someone was waiting at the dressing room door to see me. There stood my father.

"I hurried on my overcoat and we walked out together on to the Cardiff Arms Park. It was almost dark and round us we could see the tiered stands, which before had trembled with cheers, but now were deserted except for newspapers and other bits of débris left by the crowd and flapping in the gale.

"My father and I walked across the muddy, trampled turf, where half-an-hour before I had been rolling about, fighting, kicking, running and tumbling.

"He told me he had taken a day excursion from London, that he had to go back very soon. Then he caught hold of my arm. He is not a man who shows his emotions easily. For the only time in my life I saw him burst into tears.

"It was a terrifying and rending experience. I put my arms round him and tried to comfort him. 'Whatever is the matter, my dear?' I asked.

" 'Oh, I can't tell you what this all means to your mother and me,' he said. 'Sorry — so sorry to make such a fool of myself. So sorry. But you know, you with your lame leg. It's always been sad for us. We've blamed ourselves for it. And now to see you playing for England, and the crowd and the cheering, I can't explain to you how much it means to us both.'

"This strange incident on the Cardiff Arms Park had two effects upon me. From that day to this I have never been troubled again about my thin leg. It has meant no more to me, good or bad. It does not matter to me in the slightest, one way or another.

"And from that day I never felt the same fever for football."

The fever for football may have left Howard, the ability to play it had not. On February 8, he was capped for England to play against Ireland:

"I remember landing in Ireland for that game, after a night crossing the Irish Sea, with the cameramen and the reporters to meet and greet us.

"The wonder of achievement was still fresh upon me.

"In the Shelbourne Hotel, Dublin, I was conscious of the looks which followed each member of the team — and walked through the lounge several times in order to enjoy them.

35

"We drove out to the ground for the match next day. I had lunched off hot steak and cold milk. I had the theory that I played better after this diet of contrasts.

"When I opened my bag at the ground, with the hum and moan and gabble of the multitudes bursting through the window, a frightening but intoxicating sound, I discovered that I had failed to bring my puttees from England. I was determined that the England selectors should never notice on the field how thin my left leg really was in case they took fright and dropped me from the side. So I used to roll two puttees around it, mould them into the shape of a sound leg and pull my stocking over them.

"Now the puttees were gone. The game was due to begin in five minutes. I ran into the wash place. I grabbed a towel from the rail, rammed it somehow around my leg and tied my stocking over it.

"Off we ran on to the field. The air was blurred with the uproar of the Dublin crowd, co-mingled with the shouts of the boatloads of English supporters who had made the night crossing to watch the game. The whistle blew.

"I can see that ball now, silhouetted like a yellow lemon against the grey Dublin skies, dropping and twisting towards us. I caught it and kicked to touch as three Irishmen sprang on top of me and knocked the breath out of my bones against the grass.

"It was a wearing, tearing, worrying, scurrying game. Once, breaking from the scrum, I caught the ball inside our own twenty-five line and ran up the field. Three times Irishmen tried to tackle me – three times I ran on after a stumble and stagger. Finally the full-back crashed me down only a few yards from the Irish line.

"It was during the last twenty yards of the run, which sticks in my mind because it was far the longest distance I ever was allowed to carry the ball in a first-class game, that I sensed rather than saw something white snapping or worrying at my heels as I moved. I thought it might be a terrier dog escaped from the crowd.

"As the full-back knocked me over, I perceived a shriller sound of merriment mixed with the deep baying of the multitude's applause. Then I noticed that the towel with which so urgently I had padded my leg was trickling behind me. I snatched it off, pretending to laugh. But I felt bitterness within me – forty thousand people all laughing at me."

Not everyone laughed. Oxford was pleased. *Isis* wrote:

It would be almost invidious to wish Peter further success, because he possesses in a rich measure all those qualities that will bring it to him in the natural course of things. We can only wish him 'fun tomorrow' – for undoubtedly he knows his C. E. Montague well enough to recognise the phrase – and assure him of the sincere warmth of our regard.

In February, Howard was invited to join the England rugger tour of New Zealand. He was tempted to accept. But before doing so he wrote for advice to Lord Birkenhead, an Honorary Fellow of Wadham College, and High Steward of the University. Lord Birkenhead replied:

> 14, Waterloo Place,
> London, S.W.1.
> February 28, 1930

Dear Howard,

I am very glad to give you my advice for what it is worth.

No one can possibly guarantee you employment on your return to England from the New Zealand tour. The prospects depend entirely upon your own capacity, the influence of your friends and the state of the Labour Market in any field in which you desire to compete.

I do not suppose for an instant that you want to spend your life in writing criticisms about Rugby Football. It would certainly be a poor career.

My old friend Baxter naturally wants to take the strongest team that he can to New Zealand and if you were a young man of means who could afford a six months' holiday I could not imagine a more agreeable way of spending it. But I gather that you are not. After all you have gathered enough football laurels. You have got your Blue and are admitted to be one of the best forwards in England. It might help other people if you went to New Zealand; but how is it going to help you? Your business in life is to equip yourself with such capacity as you possess for the very acute competition of modern life. You were a scholar of your school and an Exhibitioner of Wadham. In my judgment fresh football laurels can mean nothing to you while the obtaining of a degree which after all, the College which gave you an Exhibition is entitled to expect from you, would give you some further equipment in that struggle for existence which today is so acute.

I do not know whether in a letter I could add any more, though my opinions are fairly clear. My son Furneaux is coming over on Sunday to lunch at my house near Banbury. If you got into touch with him either at Micklem Hall where his lodgings are, or the Vincent's Club he would I am sure arrange to drive you over on Sunday and I should be very glad to discuss the matter with you verbally.

> Yours very sincerely,
> B.

The advice was good and Howard took it. When the rugger season came to an end, he firmly resolved to do some work. But it was easier said than done. The rising unemployment in Britain, and the lack of any party to remedy it made Howard bitter and scornful. Being by nature on the side of the underdog, his politics were to the Left and radical. Sir Oswald Mosley had resigned from the Socialist Party and formed the New Party. In 1930, Howard joined it. He saw in it a hope of some political alternative which would enlist the younger generation in Britain and alleviate the hardships of the working man. Later, he was to see how naïve it was.

Howard joined friends in the New Party, among them Harold Nicolson and Randolph Churchill. It was unfortunate that Howard's entry into politics should come at a time when he needed to work.

"Howard is a scrim-shanker," wrote Isis early in 1931. "Think of old Howard sneaking out of Oxford into the Big World in search of adventure. He's gone to romp, taking a knuckle-duster, the Pro-Milone and a nice new pair of trousers. All this to protect Sir Oswald and Lady Cynthia Mosley. Howard belongs to the New Party, and believes in youth and getting on with it."

Howard certainly did get on with it, as the Daily Express of May 28 reported:

Mr. Hugh Speaight, the leading spirit in the recent flight of the Oxford Balloon Union, was the host at a freak party held at Oxford tonight when a party of undergraduates toured the city sewers in canoes.

The invitations sent out by Mr. Speaight stipulated that his guests should wear nautical dress.

The party included Mr. Peter Howard, the Oxford Rugby Blue, Mr. A. Hopkinson of the editorial staff of the undergraduate newspaper Isis, and Mr. Wall, Chairman of the Charles Fox Association.

They entered the city sewers at a point in East Oxford and by the aid of electric torches found their way under the centre of the city, and emerged at a point south of Carfax where the sewer joins the River Thames.

Six canoes were used to convey the party and one was wrecked in an attempt to negotiate an iron gate into the Thames, and the occupants were thrown into the stream, but rescued.

In what spare time he had left, Howard worked for Isis. He wrote short stories, feature articles on Oxford events, and each week covered the Union Debates:

Isis, May 14, 1930.
The subject for debate last Thursday at the Union was "That one can be happier in America than in England".

The three visiting Americans were good, but there was rather too much "Halitosis" (with explanations of its inner significance) in some of their joking for it to be anything but deplorable.

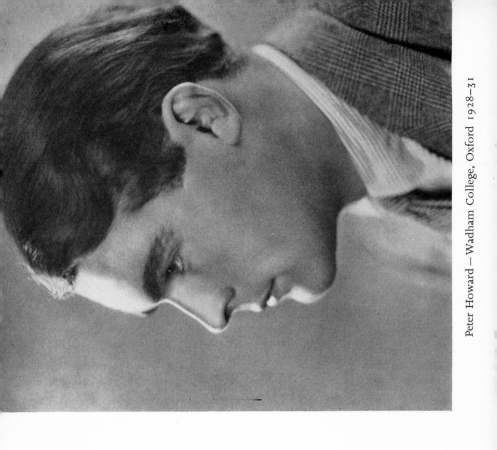

Peter Howard – Wadham College, Oxford 1928–31

Peter Howard, aged 5, at Crescent House
School

England rugger trial at Twickenham in 1931

The British bobsleigh team at Cortina d'Ampezzo, 1939, after breaking the world record

Mr. R. M. McClintock[1] (Stamford College) had a pleasing voice, an unusual virtue in an American. He thought that happiness in America was more ubiquitous in scope than elsewhere. The Englishman took too much for granted and therefore failed to appreciate his happiness: he was inclined to accept it in the same way as he accepted his breakfast. Education in England tended to keep a man in his own class; in America to raise him above it. Each country had a different standard of happiness, and to each the standard of the other seemed unreal and strange.

And now how can I adequately express my perfervid admiration of Mr. S. A. Boyd-Carpenter[2] (Balliol). He positively leaped to his diminutive feet to defend the honour of old England. Happiness, he said with a sprightly jump to the left, is a matter of opinion. Business is the mainspring of America, he declared, giving a practical and coquettish demonstration. No persecution of individual thought or individual life for us, he thundered, nimbly turning a somersault to the right. He finished his speech in as nearly an upright position as ever he attained, but I was left wondering whether I was sitting on my head or my heels.

Mr. H. E. S. Bryant-Irvine (Magdalen) seemed not only a dull dog but an insolent one to boot. He was an unfortunate choice for this particular subject, as he is entirely without a sense of humour. He made some remarks about the Standing Committee which were, I think, in very bad taste, and afterwards became merely smug and dreary. Later on he was again impertinent — on the subject of the Prince of Wales this time. I was fascinated by only one part of him, his trousers, which were hitched up on Thursday night a good three inches too high.

Mr. P. H. Gore-Booth[3] (Balliol) was the first speaker who treated the subject seriously. His chief argument seemed to be that America was unsafe and therefore unhappy. He also discussed American liberty and pleasure, which seemed non-existent. I liked him very much.

Mr. T. N. Fox (Hertford), Teller for the Ayes, said that Americans were well satisfied with themselves and failed to perceive that an Englishman's chief delight was to throw mud at everything English.

Mr. A. J. Ayer[4] (Christ Church) must speak more slowly. But he was the second speaker of the evening to treat the subject seriously and successfully. America pursues happiness as an end in itself and fails to realise that it only comes during the pursuit of other ends. A good speech. At 11.28 p.m. England emerged victorious.

Isis, May 22, 1930
The motion: "That India should receive her Independence".

[1] Later American diplomatist and Ambassador to Argentina from 1962.
[2] Later the Rt. Hon. J. A. Boyd-Carpenter, Conservative M.P.
[3] Later Sir Paul Gore-Booth, Head of the British Foreign Office.
[4] Later Wykeham Professor of Logic, the University of Oxford.

The Hon. Quintin McGarel Hogg[1] (Christ Church), ex-President, must take full blame, I think, for the irritating and tedious hour we spent last Thursday before the debate opened. He proposed it in no very skilful manner, arguing that the Union should not rush in where the daily press feared to tread — this seemed a little illogical — and declaring with a sob in his voice that he had never forfeited the confidence of the Society, but was moved by a sincere desire for its good.

It was a pity that Hogg thought fit to spring so often to his feet on points of order. It was a pity that McGarel objected so bitterly to personal allusion to himself by other hon. members. It was a pity that Quintin never hesitated himself to allude to others in person. The President must be warmly congratulated on his behaviour in what was a very trying situation. We shall long remember the firm and inimitable manner in which he so often was forced to order the Hon. Quintin McGarel back to his seat.

Mr. Randolph Churchill[2] (Christ Church) was very, very British. This is not a compliment. Nor, strangely enough, is it an insult. He argued that the English had done an inestimable amount of good to India, but little harm, and that he would be the last person to thwart the country of self-government when it was ripe for it. He made the damaging admission that he had studied the question of how to make the Society laugh. I wish he would write and tell me. Despite the fact that several later speakers, some of them on his own side of the house, saw fit to abuse the proposer, I thought this was a good speech.

Mr. F. R. Moraes[3] (St. Catherine's) made one of the best speeches I have heard in the Union. He declared that, before the British came, Moslems and Hindus lived peaceably together and that in states at present under Indian rule relations between them were still cordial.

Mr. Pinto (Wadham), whose Christian name, gloriously and happily enough, is Ignatius, made a good speech to oppose the motion. No country, he said, could be declared unfit for self-government which had never been given the opportunity of trying it. If she was not given freedom, India would fight for it. Ignatius should speak again.

Mr. H. Z. A. Kabir[4] (Exeter) is a gymnast second only to one. He bounced from his seat and leaped about positively incoherent with excitement. It was lovely to watch him, but alas, nobody except possibly the President could understand anything he said.

A good debate, marred only by the behaviour of one or two hon. members, who, while adding nothing to the debate themselves, con-

[1] Later the Rt. Hon. Quintin Hogg, Q.C., M.P., member of successive Conservative Governments.
[2] Son and biographer of Sir Winston Churchill.
[3] Later Editor of the Indian Express Newspapers.
[4] Humayun Kabir, M.A., M.P., Indian politician and writer.

stantly interrupted speakers whose views did not coincide with their own.

.   .   .

The long summer holidays were some of the happiest times Howard ever had with his parents. Together with his brother, John, they went to North Wales, Cornwall or the Highlands of Scotland:

"Dear young and only brother John. I remember him as a fat, wriggling baby, searching the carpet for imaginary animals called 'Beadles' which he pretended to stuff down your neck.

"I remember him winning the race at his prep. school, so proud and so eager he was, with father and me cantering along beside him cheering him to victory as he entered the straight towards the tape.

"He was lucky at fairs – I can see him carelessly bowling pennies down to the board of squares and going off presently with his pockets full of cash, the showman scowling and the girls who had gathered to look on, all giggling and nudging each other.

"He was a slashing cricketer and scored more direct hits on the body with his own fast bowling and more direct hits on other people's fast bowling with his own bat than almost anybody else I know.

"I can picture him hot and happy running in the sunshine or with a cool, serious gaze studying some book, then bursting into roars of laughter, hurling it from him and springing half-way across the room with a single galvanic bound."

These brothers were so alike, and yet so different. John was fair and blue-eyed; Peter dark and brown-eyed. They admired each other greatly but envied one another often. Peter envied John's closeness to his parents. It was natural, for John was still a child when Peter was already a man. John envied Peter's fame on the rugger field; his easy success. These feelings were deep and unexpressed. The Howards did not easily show each other affection or its opposite. Instead, they walked for days in the hills, by rushing torrents and peaceful lochs. They fished and swam – and enjoyed being together.

Although Howard had made new friends at Oxford, he did not lose sight of the old ones: "I used to spend many weekends in Oxford with Peter meeting rather nervously all the king pins of the day, with whom he was friends, and enjoying the wonderful company and constant fun he provided," writes Tony Carter. "He was on holiday with us at Filey in Yorkshire in 1930. As we were walking along the beach one day, father pointed out the wreck of a submarine in the distance and remarked what a deceptively long way away it really was. He knew as he had been there before. Peter did not think it was very far. 'You'll never reach it in twenty minutes,' said my father, and meaning it. Without a word, off went Peter, clambering, hobbling and dancing over the rocks, and within a quarter-of-an-hour he was there. He was always ready to meet a challenge, especially if it seemed impossible."

In October 1930, Howard returned to Oxford. He was in training for rugger. He was also made sub-Editor of Isis, and stopped doing the weekly reports of the Union.

Isis, October 15, 1930.
This is principally for the benefit of Freshmen: at the same time I should advise all of you to read it. I feel sure that you will understand the Society better when you have done so. Besides, you may get a mention. If you don't, I will guarantee that (for the relatively small sum of five shillings, to be sent in a plain envelope to the Isis office) you will get one next week.

The new Isis reporter is, of course, with the exception of the President, the most important person at the debates. Even in this office, that seat of wit and discrimination, he is conspicuous for the brilliant sharpness of his tongue. No more need be said. Except, of course, that I shall myself be sorry to attend the debates in an unofficial capacity. I shall, of course, attend all the debates. All the best chaps do.

If by any chance you want a mention next week, don't forget the five shillings. Puffs come more expensive – half-a-guinea a time. We are, of course, willing to come to some arrangement about puffing you all through the term. Good-bye until Thursday evening.

At the beginning of February the OUDS (Oxford University Dramatic Society) presented Flecker's Hassan at the New Theatre, Oxford. The cast included Peggy Ashcroft and George Devine. Howard played the part of Masrur, the Executioner. His principal memory of the performance was the hours taken to make up his face, and the longer hours taken in cleaning it off again. He also enjoyed helping to lower Peggy Ashcroft from the heights in a basket.

"Mr. P. D. Howard," wrote Isis (February 19, 1931) "made a most impressive figure, who in his scene with Yassim gave a real impression of sinister power, which was assisted by a wonderful lighting effect."

On February 26, England was to play Ireland at Twickenham. Sam Tucker, the English captain, had gone down with 'flu. In his place, Howard was picked to captain the side. He was twenty-two years old.

The Daily Telegraph, February 1931.
I am glad the selectors have made this choice, for Howard is young enough, and good enough, to play for England for some years to come. Moreover, he has the sort of personality which makes for satisfying leadership, and his knowledge of the game is considerable.

42

On Howard's visits to London he would go to his grandparents' at Inverness Terrace. Ebenezer Howard was by that time an old man, but he and Gracie showed much kindness to their grandson. It was on one of these visits that Howard intended to raise with his grandfather the question of his Oxford finances. By this time, the bills were pouring in steadily, and there was no money to pay them. The opportunity arose when Howard took his grandfather to the station:

"When my grandfather was over eighty, I sought his advice on a certain course of action. Already I had decided to take that course, whatever advice my grandfather offered. But I hoped the old gentleman would be pleased and flattered at my inquiry. The following conversation took place between us:

"Myself: 'Grandfather, there's something I want your advice about.'

"Grandfather: (fiercely) 'Well, Peter, you shall have my advice, but you won't pay attention to it.'

"Myself: (stung by the truth of this observation) 'You see, I am wondering whether I should. . . .'

"Grandfather: 'Don't bother to tell me about it. I don't want to hear it. My advice to you and all young men is, don't do it. Then they usually do do it, and afterwards they are sorry.'

"No more would my grandfather, Ebenezer, say. He climbed puffing into the train. The train climbed puffing out of the station. I was left, punctured, on the platform."

Disappointed in his hopes that his grandfather might pay his debts, Howard decided to leave Oxford in April 1931. He did so without a degree. He considered that with unpaid bills amounting to over one thousand pounds, a job was more important to him than an Oxford degree. Financially he was right. Scholastically he was wrong.

His departure had unpleasant repercussions for many people. His old Headmaster, Mr. Jacks, had great difficulty in explaining his action to the Grants Committee. Those to whom Howard owed money felt that he was running away from responsibility. For many young men such a bad start would have signified a poor future. For Howard it was the beginning of financial wisdom, which lasted him all his life. Though he received many offers of loans he accepted none of them. He was determined to earn enough to pay all his debts. He was to do so within two years.

Chapter 5

I never knew a heart could break
So easily — with only pain
To make it never live again.
No sounds or cries,
When a heart dies.
Only dumb and misunderstanding pain.

I never knew a heart could still,
When it was broken and had died,
Love with its happiness, its pride —
   And broken, still
   Beat down my will —
Still love you, when the blood of it had dried.

In the months after he left Oxford, Peter Howard took on not one job, but three.

The first was offered him by Sir Oswald Mosley, and he was persuaded to accept it by Harold Nicolson.[1] He was to be National Secretary of the New Party Youth Movement: "At that time public duty made no strong appeal to me, though I was flattered to imagine that men of the standing of Nicolson and Mosley should select me as a member of the patriot band to save Britain.

"I was offered a total of £650 a year for my services. I accepted the job and the money.

"Those were the days when Mosley was declaiming his bitter opposition to Fascism and all its ideology. 'We don't want any ice cream from Italy,' he exclaimed. Also he described British Fascists of that day as 'black-shirted buffoons, making a cheap imitation of Italian ice cream sellers'."

[1] The Hon. Sir Harold Nicolson, politician and author.

Howard was to be responsible for the political organisation of the youth clubs and was to write regularly for the New Party paper, *Pioneer*.

The Howard family, desiring him to have a more stable job, insisted that he should read for the Bar. He started to work on the necessary books.

Meanwhile, Howard needed something to bring in money quickly. Through Lord David Cecil, then a Wadham Don, he heard of a boy, Sir John Dyer, who needed special coaching to get into Oxford the following year:

"His parents offered me five pounds a week and all expenses to take him to Switzerland for six months and coach him.

"This suited me well. It gave me the prospect of setting aside five pounds a week for the next six months and also would put me outside the reach of my creditors for the same period."

.   .   .

Howard arrived at the Kulm Hotel, St. Moritz, in the early summer of 1931. The young baronet whom he was to tutor was a pleasant boy but in poor health, as a result of which he wore a metal frame on his back. He was accompanied by his grandmother and sister. Also at the Kulm Hotel was a young American, John Forbes:[1]

"Peter was very good for John Dyer – checked him in the midst of introducing himself as 'Sir John' with a 'Mister Dyer'!

"My mother and I, Peter and John Dyer used to walk the mile or two from St. Moritz 'Dorf' to St. Moritz 'Bad' to hear the band play in the park at the Kurhaus daily at about eleven.

"Peter was an interesting mixture of very old and very young. The latter was reflected in the harmless vanities – University tags like 'subfusc, gentlemen, subfusc', patronising references to people smaller than himself as 'little people'; mysterious references to the story he was one day going to write under the title 'Death of a Rose'; the announcement that he was wearing 'my grandfather's dinner jacket', when from other allusions it was a reasonable guess that his grandfather did not own one. (In fact, Howard did own his grandfather's dinner jacket, and wore it for many years.)

"He had a pleasantly witty way of expressing himself. A not very attractive English girl at the hotel wore a ribbon in her hair. Peter named her 'the filleted female'. He was very diverting company, had the usual British reserve about speaking of his athletic career, and was certainly the handsomest young man I ever saw."

St. Moritz in 1931 attracted European society. Film stars, millionaires, sporting personalities, as well as mountaineers and ordinary men and

[1] Later Professor of Business History at the University of Virginia.

women in varying degrees of health, found their way to St. Moritz. The summer tennis tournament brought some of the French champions, at a time when French tennis was at its height. Howard, though only a moderate player himself, decided to enter for the Men's Handicap Doubles with a Cambridge undergraduate, Mr. William Farquhar,[1] who edited the University magazine *Varsity*. The Kulm Hotel had some excellent hard courts beside it, where players could practise. Howard could watch them as he did his work:

＇s sitting in the sunshine of our hotel balcony, teaching my pupil how ｉscover if the hands of a clock were together at five-and-a-half minutes past one at what exact moment they would next be together again.

"I looked over the hotel balcony and saw a girl. She was playing tennis on the hard court below. I fell in love with her. Three days after I met her, I had proposed to her. Three seconds later she had refused me."

The girl was Mlle. Doris Metaxa. She was just twenty years old, and a Junior Tennis Champion of France. Known later to her friends as "Doë", she was a slender, dark girl with lightning speed on the tennis court. Doë was French by birth and by upbringing, but her parents were Greek. John Metaxa, her father, was over six feet tall, a native of the Island of Ithaca:

"John Metaxa's mother once hid him in the bread oven saying pirates might come to the Island of Ithaca where he was born. For pirates used to shanghai small boys from Ithaca, carry them off as cabin hands and cook boys on expeditions of smuggling and violence.

"So one of John Metaxa's first recollections is of his mother's pale hands fluttering like moths toward him through the darkness of the oven, thrusting forward a cup of sweet wine and a hunk of bread stuffed with black olives, and swiftly withdrawing.

"Metaxa ran barefoot on Ithaca. His body grew strong and hard. He plunged it in the Bay of Ithaca where, on calm days fathoms deep, they say you still can see pinnacles and fluted pillars of age-old palaces drowned in the ageless ocean.

"John Metaxa was bred to responsibility and vision. For his family is one of the oldest in Greece."

Metaxa had left Greece, never to return, after Venizelos[2] had broken a promise made to him at the time of Venizelos's rise to power. He had spent many years in Bombay with Ralli Brothers, and was a neighbour

[1] Later Director of the Chase-Manhattan Bank in Paris.
[2] Prime Minister of Greece for 14 years between 1910 and 1933.

Peter Howard in the *Daily Express* office, 1939

Peter and Doë Howard at their country cottage, Old Thatches, in 1940

On his farm in Suffolk, 1964

and friend of Jinnah, with whom he would often ride and talk. He married Irene Theologo, also Greek, and they had three children – two girls, Myrto and Doris, and a son, Marc. They were a family of considerable wealth, though not of luxury. John Metaxa was outstandingly generous with his money, and when he died it was found that, unknown to his family, he had been giving financial help to over two hundred people. He had a warm heart and a hot temper. Of his three children, Doë was perhaps the one he loved most, though he would never have said so. Both he and his wife were sad that Doë had chosen to play tennis for France, rather than Greece. But Doë had learnt her tennis in France, with French tuition and French people. It seemed inconceivable for her to play for Greece, a country she hardly knew.

At the age of twelve, Doë had first taken a racquet and ball and played for hours against a stable wall near their home in Marseilles. From there she went regularly to the club, and entered the Riviera Tennis Tournaments, of which there were many. At the age of eighteen she had become the Ladies' Junior Tennis Champion of France. At the age of twenty, she was one of the great lawn tennis players of the day.

Howard was amazed by her:

"It was a surprise and shock to me when I first saw the force and fury generated by so slight a person. I felt something of the wonder which would fill the mind of the onlooker if he saw a gazelle kicking buffaloes to extinction."

It was William Farquhar who first introduced Doë to Peter Howard. It was apparent to all their friends that they were very fond of each other. Howard tried hard to deny it. He protested, although no one had taxed him with it, that he was not all that interested. As he sat with Farquhar beside the tennis courts watching Doë smash another opponent into oblivion, Farquhar began to whistle "Three Little Words". Howard was furious, and asked him what he meant by it. "Nothing at all. I just mean game, set and match to Miss Metaxa."

Howard found meeting Doë none too easy.

"I soon discovered that to walk and talk with John Metaxa's daughter was not so ready an affair as to become familiar with some of my English friends. No appointment with the daughter could be made without sanction of the sire.

"I used to telephone the hotel where the Metaxas were staying. 'Would it be possible for Mr. Howard to see Mlle. Metaxa this afternoon?' Presently the concierge would bring a message, 'Mademoiselle would be happy to walk at two-thirty.'

"At two-thirty I would go to the hotel. There would be Doë. And there would be John Metaxa too, with walking stick, neat clothes, and the kindly but penetrating gaze of an eagle.

"Doë and I would walk in front. Behind, like the detective who protects royalty, never within earshot, ever within eyeshot, ever detached, never removed, strode John Metaxa.

"He was at that time over seventy. It was hot weather, the dry, parching heat of an Alpine summer. I tried to walk faster than he did to leave him far behind. But I never succeeded. He always looked cool and faintly amused as we said goodbye, while I always was sweating and faintly uncomfortable.

"The man who had spent his youth on the precipitous goat-tracks of Ithaca found the tourist tracks of St. Moritz very small beer by comparison.

"It would be hypocrisy to pretend that I enjoyed his manoeuvres. But I conceived an admiration and affection for his character."

The Metaxas were not pleased with Peter Howard's attentions. They had no idea who he was, or whether he had any prospects. Doë had been brought up on strict and sheltered lines. Howard seemed oblivious of anything except that he was in love with their daughter. He entered the golf tournament with her. The first prize was a Cartier handbag and a gold wrist watch. Howard was very keen to win the handbag for Doë. He played a brilliant game. At the first tee Doë hit the ball with some force backwards over a precipice. They were disqualified. The hazards of a golf match could not now come between them. They were deeply in love.

At the end of August the Metaxas left St. Moritz and took Doë back to Paris. Hardly a day passed when Peter Howard did not write to her. Unfortunately, he seldom dated his letters.

P.D.H. to Doë   Kulm Hotel,
                                                     St. Moritz
                                                     August 1931

This afternoon a wonder arrow of silver-coloured birds flew across the lake from the river. And I turned very quickly as I was walking on the hillside and said, "Look, Doë darling," before I realised you weren't there. But you see how close you still are to me. You remember the last time I wrote you a letter when I knew that at any moment you might come in through the door and find me, which you did. You are just as near to me now as you were then. I believe you will always be as close to me as this when I am writing to you, even also at most times when I am not writing to you.

With you in life I feel I could and can do anything. You touch all the best of my very great ambitions and all the best of my capabilities. Without you in life, now I have known you, I should disappear. To

48

accomplish things for myself, even for my mother, now seems a very trivial thing to me.

Up here some few times you saw the truth and felt and knew it to be the truth. I believe the memory of those months will help you to sift things in your heart and feel sure of yourself. I shan't say any more of this until you speak to me of it again.

The mountains are nearer tonight than they have ever been. I once thought I hated them, but the mountains and the sea and big rivers have always been my friends and they will be kind to us now. I have spoken out loud to you so often today and I swear you are with me in body and spirit as I write this. I could never feel so happy if you were not here.

P.D.H. to Doë   St. Moritz
                                                                          August 1931

Things that happen to me when you are not here are just stupid waste of time. This evening the sun crossed the lake and the valley and climbed up the mountains where valkyries hide. And there were those streaks of gold on the peaks which we looked at together. And there was just a moment when the sun went away when everything was quiet and the earth so lovely that it was difficult to breathe. And it meant very little to me. Beauty without you to enjoy it only makes me angry.

The photos were enlarged by an assistant who has spoiled them, as you see. They are being done again. I had the golf shot one enlarged to illustrate what is wrong with the finish of your shot. You must not have the weight of your body anywhere but on your left leg at the end of your shot, the right knee bent and the left knee braced. In the photo your arms are absolutely right, but you seem to have taken your eye off the ball.

Doë, a French Bachelor of Arts, and brought up in an intellectual atmosphere, found his letters young and immature.

P.D.H. to Doë   St. Moritz
                                                                          August 1931

It makes me unhappy to think that my letters to you are not the right sort of letters. It is young, I suppose, to enjoy the stars and the mountains and call them your friends, and to invent curious phrases for them, like, the stars hanging in the rich fields of darkness, or the clouds wandering over the pure lakes of the sky. And it is young, too, to love someone so that nothing else on earth matters. It is younger still to say so. And youngest of all to write it in a letter. And it is young to say that you will go through hell to help someone you love. So young as to be almost old-fashioned. And it is young to be thrown out of one's old life suddenly into a new and strange and frightening one, to allow oneself to be thrown out of everything that has mattered like that.

But now I will try so hard to be old and obvious and unhysterical. Perhaps you will say it is young to want to change yourself, or even your letters, to please someone. Well, may be, but with your help it shall be the last act of my youth. I will not have any more emotions and I will talk about God as if He were a close personal friend, with rather boring ideas Who comes to lunch every Sunday, and His digestion, poor fellow, is always upset by your roast beef and Yorkshire pudding. And I will remember that the clouds are only atoms of dirt and water, when all is said and done, and the stars only melted stones remote and unconcerned, stuck into space like plums in a pudding.

And as for going out of my way to help you, why, you know that in future my good sense will prevail and I shall stay where I am and speak and make money, and dictate to my secretary sixteen pages of good advice to you, culled from my own experience. And as for loving you, probably it is only the mountain air which has a galvanic effect on the stomach, the seat of most human emotions. And all this is the most utter nonsense. When I write to you I feel young. My love for you is a young love. I should hate to degrade you by loving you like an experienced person of forty.

But my letters to you must be old. I think perhaps that I can make them older if I try. To be middle-aged or at least conventionally middle-aged, you only have to criticise everything and everyone, and to imply that you could do far better in their place, to scoff at youth because you are so bitterly jealous of it, and to praise the cynical pleasures of life which you know, or knew, were wrong.

Do let me know how you would like me to write to you. It is heart-breaking to know that when you are with me I satisfy you, but when you read my letters you can only smile.

P.D.H. to Doë   St. Moritz
                                                        August 1931

Your sweet letter came just before lunch today. It will be a little while still before I see the stars again as stars not stones, and clouds as clouds not dirty water, and God as a Spirit not an old bore poking His nose into our business because His own is too insignificant to occupy His attention.

It does seem strange that I should seem most like myself in my letters to you when I am being bitter, or cynical, or cross. Was I so utterly horrible up here? Because as a matter of fact, although I have been trying for years to turn myself into an amiable vegetable, or better still into a really wicked person with no feelings at all, I have succeeded very poorly. I still believe that it is a more beautiful thing not to allow your body and your desires to overrule your conscience, or what loose-livers call your early Victorian prudery. I still believe it is bad to get drunk. I still see nothing unmanly in grasping at shadows, in loving beautiful things, in writing poetry and in talking to the moon and stars. And I shall always know that love is the most important thing in life now.

I have just had a long letter from Mosley. He thinks that the recent crisis in England will help the party enormously as being the only one which has got constructive plans for placing the industrial position on a firm basis. Myself, I don't think so. This crisis has not hit the vast and phlegmatic lump which is the great British public hard enough yet for them to take any new steps. You know, in England to get anything done, people always have to be ridiculed, starved and martyred. And even then what is done is usually done twenty years too late. But still, they are good sports, bless their fat hearts and stomachs. And they hate damn dagos, and anyhow something has always turned up in the past. I shall one day write a very amusing essay about my countrymen. It will be amusing because it will be true.

Mosley in his letter also says, "As regards clothes, I think the note for you to strike is simple cleanliness. I think you may continue to appear hatless. On the other hand, to dress too untidily will give the impression you are trying to look like a Labour agitator, and that is the sort of impression we do not wish to convey.'

Will you please come to my tailors with me on the 18th and order the right things for me?

P.D.H. to Doë   St. Moritz
                                                    August 1931
I have got something rather disagreeable to say to you. I wouldn't say it, but we did promise that if there is anything in the other which we thought needed putting right, we would say. So you will forgive me.

Here are the two things I have to tell you about yourself, which you must try very hard to put right. First, you spell Wednesday "Wednesday" — not Wensday. Second, you spell address "address" — not adress.

You are by no means alone in disliking Mosley's face, even in disliking Mosley himself. He is probably the most unpopular person in England today. But you have to be rather a big person to be as hated as that, especially in England. He is rather Mussolini-like, you know, when you talk to him. I must introduce you to him in London. He has rather shifty eyes. He is the most vindictive hater of anyone I know, even more horrible in real rage than I am myself. He is very courageous, and by a long way the best orator in England today. But what endears him to me (by this I do not mean I am devoted to him as a person. I am not, but I would never desert him while he still needed me in politics) is that he is alight with his own cause. He really does believe he can save the British working classes and no one else can. And I think you would like this part of him as much as I do.

When the Metaxas had left St. Moritz, they had planned to come to England in September. But now they decided to cancel the journey in the hopes that Doë would forget Howard.

P.D.H. to Doë   St. Moritz
                                                                September 1931

I and Richey were going to climb today. There were too many clouds for it to be safe. So he has gone off in his car to Zürich and I have sat in the hotel after taking John for a long walk, waiting for your letter from Paris telling me why your plans have gone awry.

I rejoice that I have found a relationship with someone sufficiently strong and enduring and large to be able to absorb small tragedies like this and make me see them as the little things they are.

Try to see it like this and remember, however much fate may seem to be against us, yet "God fulfils Himself in many ways, lest one good custom should corrupt the world".

I myself have been brought up to believe that I should not love lightly, that the love I should one day have for a woman would be the greatest thing which would ever happen to me, and the only thing to which I must expect to sacrifice my heart and myself; my body and my brain to winning money or fame as she might desire, yes, but myself for her alone and my heart to be plucked out for her and for no one else, should she actually want it.

And now this thing has come to me. In two short months I am changed, as my mother told me I would be, from the person I was before, rather selfish and so damnably successful at everything I touched, just because it never occurred to me that I should not succeed, and because I wanted to do so for the sake of my pride. Yes, to think that I was so very proud a person that believed, "From quiet homes and first beginning out to the undiscovered ends, there's nothing worth the wear of winning, but laughter and the love of friends."

And even then friends seem to fall into my lap without my having to wear myself to win them. And now I am no longer the same person. I no longer know I shall be successful. It doesn't matter at all. And sometimes now I, who used to be so brave and stand on rocks and perilous places and not be afraid to go down before the fiercest forward rush at Twickenham, and who would swim in the fiercest sea, and never hesitated to tell anyone the truth as I saw it, looking into their eyes, am often so terribly and ashamedly afraid for myself that I know myself to be a coward.

Personally, I have always pictured truth as a young and vigorous person. It has to be strong. It has the hardest tasks to perform – not an old, old man with a goatee beard, rather like Uncle Sam with the same self-satisfied and inane look on his face.

My thoughts and my prayers cannot but help you, keep you safe and give you strength to laugh at the discouragements around you. More things are wrought by prayer than this world dreams of. I know my prayers for you will be heard.

Howard had now been invited to stand as a New Party candidate in Bristol for the forthcoming election. He accepted the offer.

P.D.H. to Doë   St. Moritz
                                                         September 17, 1931
Whatever you do, don't ever get to a state of bitterness in which you believe that all family life is the sort you seem to lead. I am certain that family love is one of the greatest joys life can offer, and one of the best ways in which we can know we are doing good as we are meant to. I don't mean that any family goes on without members of it thinking differently about different things. You will always find one lot of people enjoying things which grate on the nerves of the others and so on. But in a family, as a family should be, you will find a spirit of unselfishness based on an absolute trust and reliance and love between the members of it, which we will not find in another group of human relationships, and which makes everyone see the storms of life as the small things they are, and to give way instead of crashing into the feelings and souls of the others. So don't think that all families shout and quarrel and hurt, because they don't.

In December I have a Bar exam and next summer a diploma in political economy which I haven't yet begun to read for. So you can see that with all these things and my Oxford House activities, I have plenty to occupy myself. Also, I have to turn out a weekly article for the *Pioneer*, whose first number appears on October 1. I have got an important rugger match on September 23 (England and Wales versus Scotland and Ireland, which Sam Tucker gets up every year). And also I expect on October 3, I shall play versus the South Africans. Unfortunately, I am not at the moment at all interested, but I expect when I receive my first buffet on the head I shall become a little more enthusiastic.

I wonder if I will ever get back that old flame which used to drive me to do things better than other people so that my own pride could be satisfied. For my pride has gone.

You ask about my work in England. My first wireless talk is on September 27. With Mosley I go to Bristol almost as soon as I get back to England to be introduced to my constituents, poor fools. I hope they will not suspect that the young ass with nodding ears, which is me, is lurking behind the voice which will tell them how, if they send me back to Parliament, they will inevitably find their bread costing them less. I speak in the Temple some time before the end of the month, and I start the three Pioneer Clubs — two in London and one in Birmingham. That should take about three weeks. I am speaking at Stratford on Sunday, October 25 on world peace. Also, before the end of the year, I have to find time to go to every town in England, Scotland, Northern Ireland and Wales where I think it likely I can get a New Party Club started and address a meeting there.

Howard left St. Moritz and returned to England, but whenever he had a weekend to spare he would catch the boat train on Saturday night for Paris. Doë would know he was coming. Her father would not:

"I used to telephone to their hotel from the Restaurant Griffon where the proprietor loved romance even to the extent of once cashing a cheque for me.

" 'Mr. Howard finds himself in Paris for the day. Could he call and see Mademoiselle Metaxa?' The answer would be, 'Will Mr. Howard take luncheon with the family Metaxa at one o'clock?'

"So I wandered around Paris on the Sunday mornings, unknown and knowing nobody. I used to drink a glass of Dubonnet, watch the anglers in the Seine, stroll and follow the pigeons and children in the Louvre Gardens – and at one o'clock I would go to the Hotel Napolèon.

"There would be a family lunch. I would grab a few sentences with Doë. Then goodbye again.

"In the afternoon, a solitary cinema, often incomprehensible, for I did not speak French in those days. Then back to the dear, drear Gare du Nord with its odour of fresh coffee and stale garlic, trains and drains and the prickling, tangy smell which is France. Away again on the night journey to Dunkirk and Tilbury, and to my office at Westminster by nine on Monday morning."

P.D.H. to Doë   The Griffon, Paris
                                                               September 27, 1931
I am writing this between the courses of my dinner. At the thought that you are within a mile of me and yet I am to go away without seeing you, sadness returns to me. But yet I cannot altogether be sad after today. Just after you went into the hotel I nearly made a fool of myself and came as far as the door for a last chance of seeing you, and I wandered down the Avenue with a breaking heart.

Forgive me if I was dirty or dull today. I am terribly, terribly tired, but happier than I ever hope to be able to be. I never thought I would spend twenty-six hours out of thirty-six free hours travelling to see anyone, except my mother, and I so rejoice that I was sensible enough to come.

The journeys home were long and tiring. Doë was tormented with doubts and fears, which were encouraged by her parents, and the partings were difficult.

54

P.D.H. to Doë   New Party Headquarters
                                                 London
                                                 September 28, 1931

It was rather hellish that journey back last night. I sat in the train at the Gare du Nord and as we began to move I blew a kiss to you up to the lovely full moon. Paris looked so lovely, and I so hated leaving it and you.

I think that the mistake you have made in the past is that you have known the truth now for some time deep in yourself, but whenever you have had bad moments – and we all of us have them you know – you have not argued with the truth that you know is your strength and with me beside you. You have not said, "I have known and I know that Peter loves me and will always love me. And I have known and I know that I will always love him." Don't hazard our future and great happiness by refusing to fight thoughts which you know deeply in yourself are untrue, and which, if you don't at once kill with the truth as we have known it, could grow stronger in time.

P.D.H. to Doë   London
                                                 September 1931

I am hiding in a little café near the Houses of Parliament called the Pewter Jug. Everyone in the office is hunting for me and very cross because I have gone off. But I can't go on any longer without writing to you.

I arrived at Stoke-on-Trent at four-thirty and had to arrange for the stewarding of the hall where Mosley was to speak. Also interview several people for him and make a short speech of thanks and encouragement to the local New Party committee. At seven-thirty his meeting started. I had to stand on a statue outside the Town Hall and speak for an hour-and-a-half to all the people who couldn't get inside to hear him, a crowd of about 7,000. Well, you try speaking even in an ordinary tone without stopping for an hour-and-a-half and see how tired you feel, but to pitch your voice in the open to carry to 7,000 is a terrific task, and I was really almost fainting at the end.

P.D.H. to Doë   London
                                                 October 1931

I am sorry that you do not like me being devoted. It doesn't mean quite the same thing to me as it does to you. By devoted, I don't mean that I shall always be crawling at your feet and saying you can do no wrong, and doing always what you say. Such a life is impossible to me. I have got my own ideas of the way to go about things and I shall put them to you for your approval, just as I hope you will put your ideas to me. But any grovelling subservience is bound to kill affection.

About my clothes, that is a thing about which I shall definitely be at your feet. I am no good at choosing them myself. It is far better that you should choose them for me. I think myself that a cream bow would be nicer in your hat than a yellow one, unless you have got exactly the right shade of yellow. This won't be very helpful, I am afraid, but you see I do remember little things about you, even in the middle of this babel. The noise in election time is the worst part of it — telephone bells, typewriters, people dictating letters. It never stops.

P.D.H. to Doë   October 1931
Yesterday I had to go and see Mosley. After he had finished talking to me I had no time even to finish off my letter and post it. But I have carried it in my bag down to Cardiff. After my speeches there last night I came to Merthyr, where I am now.

Merthyr has been a Labour seat for the last forty years and everyone says it is madness to fight it. We are the only Party which has put up a candidate against the Socialist wall-head and we are doing very well here.

We have a crowd of about 8,000, and if it wasn't for you I would be feeling very afraid. Most of them will be hostile at the beginning, as our policy is not a popular one, and it doesn't promise the voters much for another year.

You see, I am only a little boy sometimes — very nervous and afraid of big things I have to do. This is not an easy speech I have to make in an hour's time. It will be the hardest I have to make in the whole election, except the one at Glasgow on Monday.
Later
I have just come in from making a speech to the miners at Treharris as they came up out of the ground from their work in the pit. It was rather wonderful, a thing I won't forget. I was standing on a heap of slag making my speech and the sun was going down very red and splendid (you know what a British winter sun is like) behind the pithead and the other black slag heaps. All the miners came pouring out of the shaft with coal-black faces, tired from their work, and looked up at me and listened. It was strange and wonderful. My body was the only white thing and everything else black, except the red sun.

It was in South Wales during the election campaign that Howard was to see the torment of unemployment for the first time:

"I went in a car along the valleys of the Rhondda. Presently I saw a crowd of people, three or four hundred of them, squatting on a hillside, gazing at a pond. There they were on the grass, crouching down on their heels as miners do, like a flock of black crows against the green and grey of the Welsh landscape.

"For two days before I arrived they had sat stolidly from dawn to dark gazing at that pond (the water was not more than fifty yards across).

A miner bathing in the pond had been drowned. They were dragging the water for his body.

"And all the miners from the village turned out and watched these operations. For they had nothing else to do. Nothing at all. They were all unemployed. For years the older men had done no work. Many of the younger men had never done a day's work in their lives. So now they spent their time watching the pond. It was their only occupation in life.

"I learned that they sat there for another whole day after I left the Rhondda, until the steel drag caught firm in the dead arm of the drowned miner, lying thirty feet below the surface, and hauled him into the daylight. When the ambulance had taken the body off, the unemployed miners went home. They had no excuse to watch the pond tomorrow.

"It was in the Valleys that I first saw how women take on men's countenances when they are in grief – then the taut, still, chiselled lines of the women's faces have a masculine appearance. The shape of one such face is etched for ever in my memory, the lips slightly parted, bitterness fighting faith in the deep lights of the eyes, the cheeks and chin soaking wet, though no rain had fallen.

"Class means nothing and hatreds mean nothing, and the old political cries and slogans mean nothing at the pithead on days like these. Manager's wife and miner's wife brew tea together, stamping to keep warm on the blackened mud around the shaft. It is a sisterhood of sorrow.

"Men from pit-face and office who for years have not spoken about each other except in terms of abuse, go down together to face the trouble – they work until clothes, hands and nails are torn. Sometimes they die in company, taking risks to cut their way swiftly to the entombed men. It is a brotherhood of travail.

"In one street I saw twenty or thirty children playing. I stopped to watch them. And in a moment, anger, pity, humiliation, a compound of every deep feeling of the human heart rose within me. For I saw that almost every one of those children had mis-shapen legs or ankles.

"They had felt the weakening drag of malnutrition, because there was so little money coming into the mining areas at that time.

"When I asked a Member of Parliament about this tragedy, he said, 'Well, it's very sad. But if they spent the dole on milk for the children instead of beer for themselves, they'd be better off.'

"Perhaps there was some truth in the remark. I cannot say. But it sounded so cynical and it was so inadequate. It filled me with fury. I cursed God and man, especially that man."

P.D.H. to Doë   October 1931
    This is the first time since I left you that I have been able to sit down with you and be alone with you and speak with you for more than a few minutes. They will come for me in a quarter-of-an-hour and take me

away and give me food before I speak. They look after me like a child these people all over the country, for I am so utterly exhausted after I have made a long speech as I put all of myself into it. I am so utterly tired nowadays that I really have passed the stage where I can think of things like food and sleep for myself. But I eat when they tell me, and sleep when they tell me.

Tomorrow (Sunday) I am in Birmingham; Monday and Tuesday in Glasgow — the Great Central Hotel. After that until October 28 at the Stafford Hotel, Stoke-on-Trent. Mosley is having a grim fight there to keep his seat and wants me to be with him until the poll.

Howard's election visit to Glasgow was as difficult as the one to Wales. The memory of it never left him:

"I was sent to canvass a street in one of the Glasgow constituencies which a supporter of Mosley was fighting. In the basement of a house there, I found a man living in a single room with five children. The eldest was about fifteen, the youngest near two. There was no window at all in this dug-out. The place stank. On the faces of the children, except of the smallest, there were sore scabby places, looking like scrum pox.

"The man stood talking to me quite politely. He told me that he was not interested in politics and did not mean to vote in the election at all. 'You see none of these fellows do anything for me,' he said. I explained that the New Party was really a new party, it attempted to give expression to all the hopes and ambitions of men of goodwill, it planned to right the wrongs of the submerged millions of our population and to make a new Britain with equality of opportunity and justice and work.

"The fellow was just not interested. 'They all say the same,' he said. Then, in a more forthcoming voice, because I was doing all I could to make him like me — and succeeding — he added, 'You know, they none of them do anything for me, because they none of them can. It's all a hopeless muddle.'

" 'Well,' I said, 'if you do change your mind and vote, vote for the New Party.' 'Maybe,' he answered, grinning at my persistence. 'If the New Party was in power,' I told him, 'you'd get a better place than this to live in — more room.' He replied in ordinary conversational tones, 'Oh, we were more crowded a week ago. There was another kid here then. She died down here last Friday.' He gave me this information exactly as if he had told me that he liked kippers for supper. Life had so beaten this fellow that he just no longer cared about anything at all.

"I heard from his neighbours that the daughter, aged nine, had died down there among them all one night, and next morning the father had carried the corpse in a sack over his back to a place where arrangements had been made to bury the child."

·   ·   ·

By this time both the Metaxas and Howards were keen to end the romance between Peter and Doë. The Howards felt Doë was a foreigner and there were plenty of good English girls around. The Metaxas wanted references from England to assure them of Howard's good character.

P.D.H. to Doë   October 1931

This is going to be a very serious letter. It is the first time I have had a chance to write for the last three days. I have never known such a rush as this. I have made over twenty speeches in three days, some of them more than an hour long. I spoke before Mosley at the meeting in Birmingham. You may have read about when the Communists tried to kill us with chains and bottles and I got cut on the head (I am sending a photo of it) just before the real fighting began. You see how dishevelled and angry I am looking. I and Mosley had just been fighting with batons and clearing the space round the platform. All our speeches in Glasgow were made in places where there was rioting less than a month ago. We are going to have another meeting in Birmingham once the election is over.

I have just answered your mother's letter and said that if she will wait, as she herself has suggested, until after the election, it would be better as I can give her a far fuller and more detailed answer then.

As to the question of nationality, I am afraid I do not think as your mother does about this. If you come to me with the determination of making yourself into an English woman with a love of England which would exceed your love for any other country, even if you succeeded, the love you formed would be a love which you had forced upon yourself, not a natural love at all, and you never would wholly succeed.

Of course, you love France best. It would be unnatural if you did not. If you come to me resolved to turn your ideas and ideals into English ideals for my sake, it implies that you belong to me far more than I belong to you, and I don't think this should be so.

I shall think of the people I will get your mother to write to. Harold, yes, and "Buster" Brown, who has known me and my family for years. And Lord David Cecil, who has known me all through my Oxford days. And as soon as I get home at the end of the month, I will get my mother to write both to yours and to you, but it is better for you not to write to her, I think, until I have seen her. She will be a little sad although she has known that it was going to happen.

I am glad to say that I think the national government is safe for a majority now. As for our own candidates, they are doing far better than at one time we dared to hope, but we have a long, long way to go yet. My own people have been sorely hit by this new emergency budget. Unless we reorganise our trade, none of us will have any money left. If this is a bad winter there will be fighting and looting in the streets I am afraid.

The General Election took place on October 27, 1931. For the New Party it was a fiasco. Every one of the twenty-four candidates, including Mosley and Howard, was defeated. After the election, Howard spent a few days with his parents in Bexhill, before returning to London. In London he spent many nights on a houseboat in Chelsea, going to his grandparents' home for occasional hot baths. It was not surprising that he caught 'flu.

P.D.H. to Doë   The Studio, London
                                                           November 1931

I am better but very, very tired. So odd, I got a great rugger press on Saturday. Evidently some reporter mistook me. It was fun to read about how well you had played when you had been lying in bed. I hope I will be able to stay up in a few days. I shouldn't really have got up yesterday.

P.D.H. to Doë   The Studio, London
                                                           November 1931

A little better, but temperature still up. Each day the office boy, Charlie, comes at about six o'clock from head office and brings your letters. It is funny when you are ill how it seems quite impossible that one could ever get really well.

Worn out from the election campaign, 'flu and his increasing work, Howard was less and less able to resist the pressure from his family. They urged him to break off his attachment to Doë. He could not say he no longer loved her. He did. He took the only course which in his weakened state seemed open to him. It involved telling Doë an elaborate lie.

P.D.H. to Doë   December 1931

Here baldly is the truth. No man could love a woman more than I love you. I hurt my leg at rugger a fortnight ago and was ill also afterwards, but was only in bed three days. On examining my leg the doctor says it is diseased. When I asked if it would pass to my children, if any, he said yes. I hadn't the courage until you found me out to tell you the truth. Here it is. You may have been unhappy yourself, but what of me now?

P.D.H. to Doë   London
                                                           December 24, 1931

In the course of the next few weeks I am going to see all the best London surgeons. It was pure chance that I had to go to a doctor to have this rugger injury put right or I wouldn't have found out about this. This seems almost more than I can bear. You must forget me as soon as ever you can. If you want difficult things done I shall be here to try and do them. I have not lost my courage, but just my faith and hope.

P.D.H. to Doë   Christmas Day, 1931

This is only going to be a short letter. I have written so very many long ones lately and all they have done is to make me more sad. As things are now, you are the last person I would marry because you are the person I am most fond of. Your letters made me so very sad that although it is almost unbearable, I have not opened the last six. I am sorry. I will when I am better able to do so. You must if you love me be sensible and know that in time you will get over this and find someone you will love.

My father is the only one of my family who knows of my misfortune. I will have to tell my mother soon, I suppose.

P.D.H. to Doë   Boxing Day, 1931

I don't think I will write again for a few weeks if I can bear not to. We shall both be in hell for a long time, I am afraid. We may always have memories of a hillside in Switzerland and a cinema in Paris. Bless you always. I am thinking of taking a job in the Sudan I have been offered. It would be a change.

.   .   .

For three months the letters ceased. Doë knew that the leg injury was not the real reason for the silence. She feared that the true reason might be another girl. She was wrong.

During the months which followed Howard became disillusioned with the New Party. Mosley became increasingly Fascist in his outlook, and Howard felt the days of the New Party were finished.

Harold Nicolson records the beginning of the end in his *Letters and Diaries 1930–39*:

March 15, 1932

"We suggest . . . that the New Party can now acknowledge its own death. Peter Howard is summoned and speaks out in this sense with an openness which neither Bob Forgan nor I have as yet dared to assume. An important meeting, in that the death of the New Party has now been frankly discussed and the ice broken."

April 5, 1932

"We decide to dissolve the New Party as a political or electoral organisation . . . This means sacking Peter Howard."

The sacking came as no surprise to Howard. It was more with relief than regret that he left the New Party. Howard wrote:

"Funds were declining. Mosley's thoughts began to turn to Fascism, which Harold Nicolson — and I — detested. There was plenty of talk about it and about. But Mosley's shirt darkened as day followed day. Presently,

61

Nicolson picked his hat off the peg. I was handed mine. And we both walked out of the New Party together."

The break with Mosley seemed to clear the air for Howard. Other aspects of his life began to fall into place. In April 1932, he wrote his first letter to Doë for three months.

P.D.H. to Doë   4, Chepstow Villas,
                                                 Bayswater, W.
                                                 April 1932

Will you just send me one letter to show me you are still there? I wonder if you care for me as much as you did? Only one thing is sure that, such as I may be, I love you.

P.D.H. to Doë   New Party Headquarters
                                                 April 1932

I think for the last few months my whole mind has been ill. When are you coming to England? Let me see you when you do. It will be better to speak to each other I think. It is today for the first time I have had a hope that things may come right, though I am so dreading that you have been too unhappy ever to want to see me again, or to forgive.

P.D.H. to Doë   North Stafford Hotel
                                                 Stoke-on-Trent
                                                 April 1932

I have been so very happy since your letter came to me this morning. I can scarcely breathe. You say why wait if there is hope. There is more than hope. My leg is perfectly all right so far as marriage goes.

Will you send me directly you get this your address in Rome? I will send to there the whole sad story of my stupidity.

P.D.H. to Doë   April 1932

Our news made my parents so happy. Mother came into my bedroom and kissed me goodnight and said, "I do so hope she likes us, Peter." That was her only worry. So I assured her that you would, and things there could not be better.

I had not mentioned you at all to my father and mother for three months. I felt rather awkward about it, but you will see now that things with them could not be better than they are. They are both coming to London to see me tomorrow, and we are going together to a theatre in the evening.

On the insistence of the Metaxas that he must get a steady job, Howard gave up reading for the Bar, and joined Brown's, Solicitors of Bishopsgate, as an Articled Clerk. Then he wrote once more to the Metaxas asking their

The Howard family, 1945

Peter Howard discussing
a speech with his wife
and children, 1951

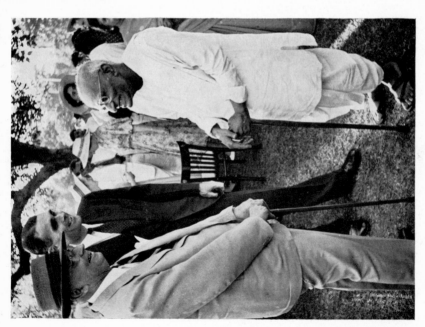

Sri Rajagopalachari receives Dr. Frank N. D. Buchman and Peter Howard in Madras, January 1953

Peter Howard and Dr. Paul Campbell confer with Gener...

permission to marry Doë. She was not yet twenty-one. The Metaxas were still resolved to stop the marriage. They were to spend Easter in Montreux and Howard had hoped he would be invited.

P.D.H. to Doë   1, Great George Street
                                                 London
                                                 April 1932

This is an important letter because I have just had your mother's answer to mine. I am going to tell you the bones of what she says with quotations in inverted commas.

She thanks me for my very kind and straightforward letter. She is glad that I and my family are very devoted and says, "With us it is the same, and I hope that we will live all our lives in loving union with our children."

She says that my position and prospects are secure, which means a great deal. "What you earn and what we intend to give Doris should allow a young couple to live comfortably if carefully. But I am wondering if Doris is capable of being careful. She probably thinks she is, but the nomadic life we have lately been obliged to lead has accustomed her to luxuries which she does not get at home and have made her restless and exacting. It is almost impossible for her to remain quietly at home or without company. It has given her false ideas of values and made her recklessly extravagant. She spends her pocket money almost as soon as she receives it, and then either borrows or owes, but does not attempt to deny herself the things she wants or thinks she needs.

"For justice to yourself, I think you ought to make sure that she will be content with the simple home and pleasures you can afford her, and that she will not crave for the constant limelight and expensive amusement of that position of society to which the *Daily Mail* devotes most of its columns. She has social ambitions as well, visions of herself married in London, the centre of an admiring circle of your literary and political friends, and where her tennis acquaintances are always welcome to her small but perfectly appointed flat, where she gives smart little dinner or supper parties that are the talk of the town, and over which she presides in beautiful clothes from the best Paris dressmakers, (where we cannot afford to have her frocks made) driving her own Rolls-Royce or Packard to fetch her husband from his office and take him on to Queens Club or Roehampton. She means to go off in her own aeroplane for weekends.

"I should be distressed to know that any child of mine was wasting its precious use in such a way and I feel that with her many qualities, Doris is made for a better and more useful life. I think she can be brought to see it, but it may take some time to show her that she is dazzled by false glamour. And I do not think she should marry before she realises that married life is made of constant sacrifice and that we enjoy what we give far more than what we receive or take.

"I hope this does not sound like cant. I am very much in earnest and am striving for my little girl's happiness, and yours too."

I seem to have copied out most of her letter for you and very boring and trying it has been. You see for yourself two snags about the answer she has sent me. She doesn't say anything about asking me to Montreux. And it is difficult to say to her that I think she has a wrong impression of Doris altogether. She naturally likes aeroplanes and Rolls-Royces and Roehampton. Who doesn't? But they are not indispensable to her happiness. And as for the salon of young authors and politicians, I know most of them and she could see as much of them as she wanted. But she knows or should know that the days of famous London hostesses have gone, and that people who get their names in the papers are mostly climbers who send in the account of their own dinner parties.

But what on earth am I to say to your mother? If I say that she is wrong about you and that your good sense is capable of separating the truth from the false, and although we both like expensive treats we also like inexpensive treats. Then her complete answer will be, "Well, I suppose I know my own daughter better than you do," to which I would answer, "No you don't." And there we reach a deadlock.

I do resent her taking the line that you are going to be the wrong sort of wife for me. After all, you and I must be the best judge of that. And according to her, the only husband who could be happy with you and make you happy must be a fat and incredibly rich vegetable with no love for you yourself as a person, just as a hostess, and no love of simple things like flowers and poems and the country and golf and so on, and no more feeling than putrefying codfish.

P.D.H. to Doë   April 1932

I have just written to your mother thanking her for her letter and saying that although the news of all your wicked tendencies and ambitions is disturbing, I think you are far too sensible a girl to have them long, even if you do have them now, and will she write as soon as she comes to any conclusions with you and your father. I thought it best policy not to argue by letter.

Doë wrote anxious letters about Peter's health. In truth, she was worried that he would not be fit enough to come to Switzerland. The Metaxas had invited him but were keen that he should not be known as Doë's fiancé.

P.D.H. to Doë   London
                                                                     April 1932

Hello grannie! I see that when we are married I shall have to wear my winter woollens from September onwards until June, and never go out within three hours of a hot bath, and never run about the house in the early morning in bare feet, which I may say is a thing I always do. I am to be so coddled and comforted that I shall grow fat and red and sluggish and have an enormous chocolate-coloured beard to keep my chest warm, and wear one of those appalling red flannel things that I think the Victorians called "comforters" around my middle. You are a silly ass. Of course I take care of myself. I am far too fond of myself not to do so.

When I come to Montreux, I seem to have to be, (a) your brother, and, (b) a friend of a relation of your mother's who is there on business. A very difficult dual role to perform. Who am I to be in front of which people? What business exactly have I come to carry out? It is annoying of your mother to refuse to acknowledge that we are engaged. But if she insists upon blinding her eyes to the truth, there it must be.

Howard left for Montreux. It was only a weekend visit.

P.D.H. to Doë   En route to England
                                                  April 1932
I had breakfast on the train and one of the wildest rides in a taxi from station to station that I have ever had. I was sure I was about to be killed. Then I sent a telegram to you — a great argument with a man in my best French as to whether 'sweetheart' was one word or two.

The engagement was still not announced and impatience was setting in.

P.D.H. to Doë   London
                                                  May 1932
I will have a determined attack at your father in Paris and see what that brings forth. I propose with your consent to say this to him: all I want is to marry Doris without the unpleasantness of doing it against your wishes. Both of us would hate that. If you will give us your blessing, you need not bother to give us your money. If on the other hand, you feel this may be hard for Doris, as indeed it may, give us your blessing and give her the money. I will not touch it. I will support her and myself in the best way I am able with the money I earn, and she can have her own money for her own absolutely to spend on her clothes and her entertainment.

P.D.H. to Doë   Knole, Sevenoaks
                                                  May 1932
We went to Sissinghurst yesterday and Harold and Vita[1] were too sweet to us. Harold has a tiny scrap of a terrier bitch called Rebecca, and his golden spaniel, Sally, is very, very jealous.

[1] Harold Nicolson, and his wife, Vita Sackville-West, author and poet.

I have two contracts with the BBC but can be dismissed in two months. I am not likely to be, but I can be. Everyone else in the BBC is in just the same boat. And if your mother supposes that anything else is the rule in England, except in business, which I will not go into, she is mistaken. Of course, I shall never make as much money as your father. He is plainly particularly competent in that line of country, which I am not.

After dinner, Eddy[1] played for us and he plays at least as beautifully as anyone I have ever listened to. Then I went early to bed. This morning Lord Sackville and I played golf. Eddy doesn't play but walked round with us. I played rather well which was fortunate.

This place is with no exception at all the most inspiring and beautiful I have ever been in. Everything left untouched for the last five hundred years, and most of it for longer.

Doë was due to come to England at the end of June for Wimbledon. It seemed possible that both families would agree to an engagement being announced then.

London
May 1932

Just as I was writing this the post came with your mother's letter. It is very nice and charming, and a very long way the most definite thing I have got out of her. She says, after a long explanation of why she isn't coming to England and so on and so forth, "If I can possibly go over to England for a few hours even, we might arrange to meet your parents after the tournament, and if we can settle things to our mutual satisfaction, the engagement might be announced then. The marriage might be fixed up for the end of the year or the beginning of next, according to how you would be able to fix it in a few days' leave."

She keeps on telling me that she has my happiness as well as yours at heart, and ends by saying, "Do not leave your work to meet the boat as it will enrage my husband. And I should also advise you, if you wish to preserve his good opinion of you, to refrain from familiarity of attitude and language, which are not usual with us who are naturally more reserved outwardly than northern people." Now, what have I been up to?

Howard left for a weekend in Paris.

P.D.H. to Doë Harlech
June 1932

Money always seems to be cropping up as a bugbear between us. I am entirely sincere when I say that money is of no importance to me, because I know by experience that it can contribute little or nothing to my happi-

[1] Edward Sackville-West, later Lord Sackville.

ness. As for your statement about charity and your enquiry as to what is the use of a kind smile without money to back it up, I think that you are a little wrong. Remember that Christ, who presumably invented charity as a virtue, had seldom if ever any money to distribute. And you may remember the story of the widow's mite?

In June, Doë came to London with her father for the Wimbledon fortnight. John Metaxa planned to return to France with Doë the day she was knocked out of the tournament. He was anxious to attend to some business. Doë was eager to stay in England as long as possible.

During the first round of the championship, when Doë had match point against her, John Metaxa produced a telegram form and, in full view of Doë who knew what he was doing, began to draft a message to his wife in France saying that he and Doë would cross the Channel that night.

Doë won that match. She went on to win the finals of the Women's Doubles at Wimbledon.

Howard watched that match:

"Doë led five games to four, and forty love. Her opponent was serving. The first service Doë hit with terrific force, a foot beyond the base line. Fifteen-forty.

"The second she hit even harder and it landed about three inches beyond the base line. Thirty-forty.

"The third. She hit it as hard as ever I have seen a tennis ball hit. The ball looked elliptical as it travelled. The chalk flew up in a cloud from the corner where it landed, a perfect winner. But the linesman called it 'out'. The umpire questioned him. Doë's opponent told the umpire it was in. But the linesman remained obdurate. So deuce was called. Doë lost that game.

"But she won the set and the match. Some people sail more strongly and steadily the harder the harsh winds blow. Doë is a warrior. She has the steel quality of the undaunted. She has vividness coupled with warmth, and that is an exceedingly rare combination."

On July 9, 1932, Peter Howard and Doë Metaxa announced their engagement.

Chapter 6

Out of the hills ran a wind, heavy with dust for the plains
Where the vines and olives stand thirsty for springtime rains.

Drenched in the sun it ran, laden with smells of flowers
Over the brick red plough where oxen plodded the hours.

Twitched with its hand as it came from my shoulders the
    load of the years,
The hopes that were never fulfilled, the foolishness of my fears.

Twitched them away to the sky with never a syllable said,
As a frolicsome wind in England steals the hat from an old
    man's head.

I stood there laughing and crying under the southern sky
And again in Provence this winter there is only you and I

With a life to live before us, and the past all left behind,
Twitched from my foolish shoulders by the breath of
    Provençal wind.

                                                        P.D.H.

Howard's engagement brought him security and happiness. He had
already managed to pay off his Oxford debts. Now he learned the solici-
tor's job in the office by day and worked for his exams by night. He found
the law fascinating:

P.D.H. to Doë   London
                                                December 5, 1932
    Two attendances before the Master tomorrow, for which I shall have to
prepare. We have managed to get the timber case adjourned again. But

the anti-fire and anti-Cunard appeals are coming before the Divisional Court, and we can't adjourn that. I am afraid I will not be able to attend it, though I ought to as Geoffrey[1] is pleading it for us. Four people this afternoon with appointments and two of them waiting outside now — some of them to take proofs of evidence which take at least forty minutes.

I took three-quarters-of-an-hour today to have lunch with Tony's[2] father because I hoped to get some work out of him, and sure enough I did. Only a small claim for damages from a North Wales hotel proprietor. If we get them which, on the evidence, I believe that we will, he will give us more work I hope. That would be a help as his leather business is enormous. Sorry to talk about work, but it is spinning in my head today.

But, as December 17 approached, his excitement grew:

P.D.H. to Doë   December 11, 1932
Today week we shall be a married couple. Isn't it lovely to remember that? I think of it all the time. Today the weather is filthy. I have got a bit of a cold so I stayed in bed rather late this morning and then got up, wrapped myself up in about half-a-dozen overcoats and went into the garden to pick roses. Isn't it wonderful that in spite of frost and cold winds, summer is still blooming here?

Howard travelled to Marseilles with Tony Carter who was to act as his best man. None of the Howard family went to the wedding, though Geoffrey lent his nephew his tail coat and Gracie paid the fares — a return for Tony Carter and a single for Peter! They arrived two days before the wedding and stayed at a small hotel. The wedding itself, as Howard was later to write, was something of a marathon:

"I have been five times wed. It is only fair to add, for the delusion of the wise and the confusion of the ignorant, that each time it was the same girl who plodded with me through the ceremonies. So we can stake out a claim, which is unique within my experience, to be a quintuple couple, five times a husband and five times a wife.

"Doë and I finished this steeplechase of a marriage at Marseilles — once at the English church there, twice and at great length at the Greek Church, once at the English Consulate, and again at the French Mairie.

"I was so gay on the morning of the first day that I bowled sous down the gutter of the Rue St. Jacques and the little French children screamed and fought for them.

"The French Mairie had a tricolour scarf so tightly reefed about his middle that his flesh swelled out top and bottom of it like twin waves of the ocean

[1] Howard's uncle, Geoffrey Howard. Later Q.C. and High Court Judge.
[2] Tony Carter.

with a trough between. His stomach bulged with each breath. It was a poignant spectacle, and the onlookers gasped and sweated in sympathy. He took eight-and-a-half minutes to marry us. Then he got up steam and steered towards me to kiss my cheeks. He would have done so had I not, with English pride, out-sailed him.

"At the Greek Church an unseen choir chanted from a gallery overhead Young girls moved before us scattering rosebuds and living orange blossoms at our feet, as thrice in a holy ritual we followed the bearded priests around the sanctuary. Over each head, Doë's and mine, a crown of wrought and delicate gold was held by friends – held at arm's length for ninety minutes without pause or respite.

"At the English Church, where on the afternoon of the third day the ceremonies came to an end, I had lost all nervousness. By then getting married was to me a commonplace and, indeed, an everyday affair. I sang 'The Campbells Are Coming, tra la, tra la' in an undertone to my best man as Doë and her father came up the aisle.

"We spent two days getting to England. That was our honeymoon. I remember the pigeons, living and rotund, on the street by the Concorde Gardens in Paris, and the thrushes, dead and roast, on the spit in the café at Avignon. We ate them with thick black gravy and thick red wine.

"Arrival in England was an ordeal for Doë. Her life had been in France and her friends in England few.

"My mother wept when I left England before marriage. Doë's mother wept when she left France after marriage. It was with this salty background that Doë and I strode across the gangway onto the shore at Dover to savour the tang of life.

"The stars were tender to us and the earth was warm. Doë and I were deeply in love."

The Howards took a flat in Disraeli's old house at 22, Theobald's Road off Gray's Inn. It was a home full of secret cupboards and doors. The bathroom was hidden behind sliding bookshelves in the drawing room and gave plenty of scope for Peter's practical jokes. For Doë it was a lonely life, but she learnt to find her way to French shops in Soho and brought home croissants, mussels, olives and hors d'oeuvres which gave her a taste of her much-loved Provence.

On Sundays they would walk together through the silent City streets. They came to know London so well that soon it was hard to believe they had not lived there always. Doë began to speak perfect English. Peter was working long hours and often late into the night. His eyesight began to be affected, and Doë was afraid that the intense work might do him permanent damage.

On November 2, 1933, their first child, a son, was born. He had dark hair and brown eyes, and they called him Philip. "I was astonished,"

Peter Howard records. "There is a feeling of wonder when the things you have often heard about happen to you. But coupled with the feeling of astonishment was one of irritation and a tiny fear." The irritation was because something had occurred which was beyond his control and the fear was financial. "The child would multiply our financial commitments, while in a measure subtracting from our pleasures, liberties and comforts." There was still no steady income coming into the house.

Two months later, in January 1934, a new source of income presented itself. The *Sunday Express* asked Howard to report rugger matches on Saturday afternoons. It would not interfere with his legal work and would bring in £1 10s. a week. He accepted.

One evening, the following June, a friend took Howard along to Lord Beaverbrook's political club, the Empire Crusade Club. There he heard a number of speeches advocating Empire Free Trade. Howard thought it all a lot of rubbish. He got to his feet and said so with his usual vigour. He relates:

"Afterwards a funny little fellow looking rather like an ape in a suit of clothes came up to me and said, 'Mr. Howard, I listened with close attention to every word you said and it will all be in the *Evening Standard* tomorrow.' Next day there was a paragraph in the *Evening Standard* 'Londoner's Diary' praising my abilities. Two weeks later, Beaverbrook phoned my office and asked me to go and see him. As I entered his room, he said, 'Howard, I hear you are going to write a political column for me.' It was the first I had heard of it."

Beaverbrook made it clear that if Howard accepted, he would have to give up the law and devote his entire time to the *Express Newspapers*. It was a hard decision. Everything in Howard wanted to accept Beaverbrook's offer, but it seemed mad to leave yet another unfinished career behind him. In the end Howard took a calculated gamble. He was not to know that from his first political article in June 1934, which earned him only £9 12s. 3d., he was within five years to become one of the highest paid political journalists on Fleet Street, earning nearly £60 a week:

"For seven long years I gave Fleet Street my life. In return Fleet Street gave me three F's — Fun, Fame and Fortune. It was a more ample return than is received from most things to which men devote their lives.

"At nine o'clock each night those massive steel and concrete structures in Fleet Street begin to quake and tremble like corn before the evening breeze. The very pinnacle of the roof shakes and oscillates at the moment when, embedded fifty feet below the surface of the earth, the sprawled machines begin to revolve and pour forth million upon million of newspapers to every corner of Britain until the daylight comes again.

"Life in Fleet Street is a bug. It burrows beneath your skin and into your blood-stream.

"There is a loyalty and a gaiety of comradeship and a zest and a stir among the Black Brotherhood of Ink. Life tastes strong and distinctive in the Street. Its flavours there are full and grip the throat.

"You are of the world and in the world and yet above the world. You scan life from a crow's-nest, the waves and tides of humanity surge and struggle and break around you. You perceive the toil and triumph, the suffering and success, the tears and tumult, the complaints and the applause. You groan and rejoice in sympathy – for every good reporter must feel in his own heart, and so understand, the emotions and the motives he describes. Yet all the time you remain a spectator and an observer. And some can still be found in Fleet Street, not enough, but a valiant section, who hold their pens unimpassioned and without bias, servants only of the truth and masters of humanity.

"With it all, life in the Street can be a jungle business – the survival of the foremost and death to the hindmost. The dives and joints which surround Fleet Street are awash with those who for one reason or another have not stood their feet and have been carried off by the tide."

Beaverbrook immediately took Howard in hand and the training was both rigorous and detailed:

"At all hours of the day and night my telephone bell would ring. Sometimes at two o'clock in the morning I would hear that tough Canadian voice saying, 'Peter? You're a young man and it's just the time to be up and working. Now get out of bed, there's a good boy. Put on your clothes. Get to it. We need an article for today's *Evening Standard*.'

"Every word of almost every article I wrote was chewed, swallowed or spewed forth in disgust by that hungry and discriminating jaw. He would read through some effort, scanning it slowly and carefully. Then a dialogue something like this would take place.

"Lord B: 'Did you do this all by yourself?'

"P.H. (puffing with pride): 'Yes.'

"Lord B: 'Did you write every word of it yourself without getting help from anyone at all?'

"P.H.: 'Yes.'

"Lord B. (scrumpling up the papers and throwing them on the floor): 'I can't believe it of you, Peter. It's so bad. Now there's a typewriter in the other room. Go outside and do it all over again.'

"From his criticisms I learned to create. The training I had was beyond price. The truth is that if I paid back all I earned that sum never could buy what Beaverbrook gave me.

"When I worked with him his praise was lavish. His blame no less so. Sometimes I thought of him as Santa Claus, sometimes as Satan. Sometimes it was Christmas, sometimes the Day of Judgment. Though you were often conscious of being a goose, he had the encouraging and endearing habit of always expecting you to lay a golden egg."

Howard was found to have two natural assets for his new job. He had a phenomenal memory. He never took a notebook or pencil with him on his journalistic jobs. He did not need them. A conversation, even of four or five hours, was so imprinted on his mind that he could reproduce it word perfect the following morning. He seldom asked for an interview, and politicians did not know when they were giving one. Many of his best stories came from the House of Commons where, over a social drink, Howard would listen to the chatter of unsuspecting M.P.s. It was a new kind of journalism, ruthlessly employed.

His second asset was an exceptional speed of writing. He would rise early and finish four articles by mid-morning. Later in life, he would do fifty letters, then proceed on to speeches and articles, all before breakfast; and complete the first draft of a play or book in three days.

His journalism was terse, tough and often cruel. He sometimes recalled that a previous political journalist, Harold Begbie, had called himself, "The Gentleman with a Duster". "If I had to choose a pen-name for my own excursions as a political journalist," added Howard, "I should call myself 'A Man with a Knuckleduster'."

His entry into Fleet Street provided him with a platform for the unspoken hatred which he felt for men in positions of power, a hatred which he first conceived in Oxford and which had grown through the days of the 1931 election. One of his colleagues in Fleet Street remembers him like this:

"Malice to be sure glowed through his veins and came out of his pen — mostly gall and often pure vitriol. In short, Peter was all for Peter Howard. He was out for glory and gold, not minding how he got it. Beaverbrook and his newspapers were made to measure for him. Whatever tune was called by the Beaver, Peter would play it. He was a ruthless and buccaneer political journalist. He seemed to love malice for malice's sake. He used his pen (never once did I see him at the typewriter) like a dagger.

"He would say of some politician he was attacking, and he was a master of invective, 'I pin him wriggling on the point of my pen.'

"He relished office intrigue and office gossip, lolling over a glass of beer or sprawling in his chair, a cynical grin on his good-looking face, as he relayed the latest bit of poison."

Howard himself said much the same in other words:

"After a time in Fleet Street I developed a philosophy of writing. My philosophy was that each man should make up his mind where he was going—and go there—ruthlessly. If an opponent strikes at you, strike him back twofold. Stand on your own legs. Be your own friend. Rely on nobody but yourself. Always be pleasant to those who can be of use to you—jolly them along. Be as pleasant as you like to other people. But let 'em down with a bump if that suits your convenience. (Of course, in the case of a friend you loved, it did not suit your convenience to betray him. For you felt wretched afterwards.)

"I was, in short, a materialist, handicapped by an annoying streak of affection in my nature, which in tough moments I derided to myself as sentimentality."

There was little sentimentality about Howard's writing. In his column entitled "Politicians and Politics", later known as "Cross-Bencher", he specialised in printing information about M.P.s which they wished to hide. He did it regularly:

"Politicians and Politics" by P.D.H.
Sunday Express, August 5, 1934

In this age of Youth Ballyhoo, hundreds of young men have been given their chance in politics. Not one of them has taken it. I do not see one young man in politics today who is worth a fig, or a snap of the fingers.

Someone will write to me to say that Mr. Hore-Belisha[1] is an exception.

Perhaps he is. But is he old or young? He is a man of all the ages. A birthday chameleon. He changes his age as readily as some politicians change their party. Perhaps he'll change that soon too. I think he'd do better for himself if he did.

Will he tell us if he intends to do so? Not he. He gives away nothing. He doesn't even give away his own age in the 1934 Who's Who, nor Dod's Parliamentary Companion, nor Kelly's Handbook.

But look at this:

In 1932 Who's Who gave his birthday as September 1898. Dod agreed with the month and gave the day of it—September 8.

But the year was 1895.

The Liberal Year Book of 1933 made no guess at the day or the month, but plumped for 1895, also. The 1932 Debrett's House of Commons said his birthday was September 7, 1893. Kelly's Handbook said 1893, and left it at that.

[1] Secretary of State for War and President Army Council 1937–40. Member of War Cabinet. Minister of National Insurance 1945.

Miss Thelma Cazalet,[1] M.P. for East Islington, is another political athlete. She plays tennis. She serves underhand, and moves slowly about the court. She does not play as well as she used to, but she is not at all bad for a woman of her age.

How do I know her age? Not from any reference book. She doesn't give it. She may think it a secret. But I'll tell you.

She's thirty-five. She was born on May 28, 1899.

I asked one of my aunts who knows her.

Following this article Beaverbrook made one of his normal comments:

"I was bidden by Lord Beaverbrook's secretary to come and hear the Master's Voice on the tape. It ran something as follows:

" 'Now Peter, the article you sent me. Baldwin — too long, too long, too long. Lloyd George — too long, too long, too long. Churchill — too long, too long, too long.' Then the voice rose in tone nearly an octave. It bubbled with glee and malice. It said, 'And the lady you mention, Peter — too young, too young, too young.' "

"Politicians and Politics" by P.D.H.
Sunday Express, November 25, 1934

Now for Dr. Summerskill.[2]

She is the Socialist candidate for Putney. I know that she is, for I saw her name up outside her committee rooms.

But inside it is a different story, for Dr. Summerskill's husband, the other Mr. Samuel, with blue eyes and a yellow tie, does all the talking.

"Why do you want to go into politics?" I asked Dr. Summerskill. 'I will tell you,' said Mr. Samuel. He did.

"How is the fight going?" I asked Dr. Summerskill. "I will tell you," said Mr. Samuel. He did.

I should be astonished if Dr. Summerskill were elected. But in one way I should be pleased. For I should like to hear her do her own political talking. She might get a chance at Westminster.

Mr. Samuel, her husband, would not be there.

[1] Later Mrs. Thelma Cazalet-Keir, National Conservative M.P. for East Islington, 1925–45.

[2] Dr. Edith Summerskill, Labour M.P. from 1938–61, Chairman of the Labour Party 1954–55, created Life Peeress in 1961.

"Politicians and Politics" by P.D.H.
Sunday Express, December 30, 1934

Commons School
Westminster

Dear Sir (or Madam),
I trust that your little boy (or girl) arrived home quite safely, happy and well for the holidays.

I am glad to be able to tell you that the school has had a good term.

Some parents say it is far too short. But you all know my views on that matter.

I think the dear children need all the relaxation and change they can have, so they can return to my loving care fit and eager for their daily round and common task at Westminster.

I enclose your little boy's (or girl's) Report. It tells you of the progress the little ones have made during the last twelve months.

Some have done well. Others have done badly. If your little boy (or girl) has done badly, try not to be too harsh.

Remember, we cannot all win prizes.

May I take this opportunity of wishing you and all your little ones a bright and prosperous New Year?

With best wishes,

Yours sincerely,
Peter Howard
(Headmaster)

Ramsay MacDonald[1]

Our head boy has been unlucky.

No doubt he would have made better progress if he had not been so long absent through illness. As it is, he has gone backward.

He has lost his influence over the school. I know it will sadden the public when I tell them that many of his juniors laugh at him.

He has had a great school career. But I can't help feeling it is a pity Ramsay did not leave us at the end of last term.

He would have left at the height of his prestige.

I think that perhaps when he goes out into the great world from this school he will rise to great heights.

He may even become a peer.
English Master's comment: Syntax and grammar definitely his weak subject. Composition. Style flowery, but lacks any sort of form.

[1] Prime Minister of Great Britain in 1934.

76

Winston Churchill[1]

A bad boy.

He is always making trouble. He is always fighting. He started a feud against young Sam Hoare[2] last term, and split the school into two camps.

He has great influence and a large gang of followers.

I think the boys are afraid of him. And they have reason to be. For Winston has a tongue, as well as cheek.

Geography Master's comment: His interest in this subject is extraordinary.

He has been devoting all his time and attention to a study of the British Empire, and to India in particular. Some of the opinions he forms are most controversial.

But it is refreshing for a master of a school like ours to have such a pupil who shows such sincere and able interest in such a great subject.

Leslie Hore-Belisha

The busiest boy of the year.

Capable of exercising the very greatest influence over the steps taken by all of us, masters and pupils alike.

Despite his industry, Leslie has been in a lot of trouble. In fact, he has spent a large part of his time doing lines.

Music Master's report: Not much of a voice. Leslie's best song is "I'm for ever blowing bubbles".

Nancy Astor[3]

She has struck up a friendship with Isaac Foot (Foot Major). She will be sad when Isaac leaves. And I fear he will not be with us next term whether he wants to or not.

No headmaster could wish for two better pupils. They use all their influence in the school against drink, smoking and betting.

I am sorry to say that influence is not great. Not even as great as it was at the beginning of the term. Next term I expect it to be even smaller.

Victor Cazalet[4]

I had thought of moving Victor up into the Lower Fourth next term. But I have decided not to do so.

Fourth Forms are not faggable. And little Victor is easily the best fag in the school.

House Master's report: An unpopular boy. But I can't see why. Little Victor has many friends among the prefects, and treats them generously at the tuckshop.

[1] Later Rt. Hon. Sir Winston Churchill.
[2] Later Sir Samuel Hoare, Secretary of State for India in 1931.
[3] Unionist Member for Sutton Division of Plymouth 1919–45.
[4] Unionist Member for Chippenham 1924–43.

Let us observe Mr. Robert Boothby.[1] Although only thirty-four, he has represented East Aberdeenshire in Parliament for the last ten years. He is an attractive personality. Good-looking, untidy and square. If anything too square, for he is putting on weight.

A few years ago many saw in him a future leader of our party. But his political star began to wane. For Mr. Boothby is a City man. And his City habits were a weakness in the House of Commons.

Sometimes he was a bull; sometimes a bear. He could never make up his mind about the values of the political stocks and shares.

But in the City he did well. He began to spend more and more of his time there. People began to say that his political career was over. And they said he was getting too fat.

Yet Mr. Boothby sent his star flaming up sky high at the end of last session. He made a successful speech on the motion for the adjournment.

I believe Mr. Boothby, if he gave up all his time and energy to it, could climb to the very top of the political ladder. But I doubt whether he will give up his time and his energy.

He is fond of good living. He does not care if a woman is a good looker, so long as she is a good cooker. And his favourite dish is herrings.

"I shall choose a wife who can cook," he declares. "And the peak of her art will be in the preparation of the herring.

"Good looks are of no importance whatever."

Howard developed a style of his own, often bringing his own name into the article. His style was not easily forgotten. It annoyed some and amused others, and lent itself to parody. Punch of July 11, 1934, quoted at length from his column, using it, ironically, as an example to young reporters. The quotation from "Politicians and Politics" ran:

It is said that while Mr. MacDonald is travelling, Mr. Baldwin[2] will spend a month at Aix-les-Bains.

That decision will give great joy to Sir John Simon[3] and to myself.

Sir John's joy will lie in the fact that he will be Acting Prime Minister while his seniors travel south and west.

My own joy is more difficult to describe. I can only say that Sir John's triumphs have always been a joy to me. He once refused to address a public meeting unless I was present. Don't assume that his decision was

---

[1] Later Lord Boothby M.P. for East Aberdeenshire, 1924–58.
[2] Prime Minister of Great Britain.
[3] Chancellor of the Exchequer 1937–40. Lord Chancellor 1940–45.

taken on account of my size, though I stand over 6 ft. 3 ins. There was no danger of disorder.

It was due entirely to the admiration of the Wadham double first for the Wadham Blue and International.

Punch added:

This is not taken, it is true, from a news report but from an article, in the form of notes, on politics and politicians.

I hope that the author will pardon me for borrowing it without permission. It is so good that many a young reporter might study it with profit.

With a model like that before him, his account of the Stepney fire should gain considerably in popular appeal:

I Attend a Conflagration and Receive Thanks of Fire Chief
(by our Best-Looking Reporter)

"An enormous crowd thronged the streets in the vicinity of Messrs. Battock and Slag's cattlefood warehouse in Stepney early this morning, and it required all the strength of a man who in his time was wrestling champion of Shropshire before I could thrust my way through to the scene of the fire that threatened destruction to the valuable consignment of linseed-cake stored in the huge building.

" 'A fire, eh?' I said, looking down at the six-foot five-inch Captain of the Stepney Brigade. Flames licked my boots. A lump of falling masonry crashed to the ground within six inches of where I stood.

" 'Come out of that, you fool!' called the Captain. 'No man can stay there and live.'

"A two-ton block of stone brushed my shoulder on its furious earthward career, but I did not move. A reporter has to take risks.

"For nearly two hours I held my ground in that hell of smoke and flames and splintering débris, while the intrepid firemen, advancing with reckless courage almost up to my own point of vantage, battled to subdue the flames.

"It was Sir Rollo Fitzhose, Chief of the Metropolitan Fire Brigade (East Division), who finally persuaded me to withdraw.

" 'Chris!' he cried to me above the roar of the fire that now curled and flickered about my knees — 'Chris, for the sake of our old association on the cricket field, come back to safety.'

"He was thinking of the time we used to go in first together for England."

Howard's politics had changed during his first year in Fleet Street. He supported Lord Beaverbrook's campaign for isolation and Empire Free Trade, and advertised it in his column.

"Politicians and Politics"
Sunday Express, June 2, 1935

Next Thursday evening at 8.30 at the Caxton Hall, Westminster, a young politician is speaking. Soon he will be leading a vast section of opinion in this country. He is Mr. Frank Owen,[1] who sat as member for Hereford from 1929 to 1931. I predict a fine future for him. Why? Not because he is well-known. Not because he is wealthy. But because he has returned to fight in the political arena armed with the most powerful of all political weapons — absolute sincerity.

He is a fiery and unforgettable orator. He commands a Welsh fervour. He has something of Mr. Lloyd George's flame. He preaches the gospel of peace. Wherever he goes, he wins proselytes for the cause of Isolation.

Do not be disappointed if, when you arrive at the Caxton Hall next Thursday, you find someone speaking without that unforgettable fire of which I have told you. For that will not be Frank Owen. It will be me.

I speak before Frank Owen. And, while I may not approach him in the force of my oratory, I equal him in the abundance of my conviction.

At the same time, he applied to stand for Parliament for the last time in his life:

"In those days my Tory convictions were much to the fore. When a vacancy occurred in a certain Parliamentary division, I put on my best coat and went to see the Chairman. I told him I would like to be a candidate.

"He informed me I was just the sort of fellow they were looking for. Then he asked, 'How much will you subscribe to the local association?' I answered that I did not wish to make money out of public life, but would give my Parliamentary salary, at that time £400 a year.

"He replied, 'I am sorry, Mr. Howard. We have already been offered £1,000 a year. If you can't do better than that, I'm afraid it is out of the question.'

"This was my first introduction to the power of money in the British democratic system. But I soon discovered that many good Tory seats were up for sale.

"On the Labour side also, a seat in Parliament was sometimes awarded, almost in the nature of an honourable pension and retirement, to those who had grown old in Trade Union service."

Howard returned again and again to themes of his earlier convictions:

[1] Frank Owen, Editor of the Evening Standard, 1938–41.

"Politicians and Politics" by P.D.H.
Sunday Express, August 4, 1935

I have just returned from a Distressed Area. Abertillery, Merthyr Tydfil, Ebbw Vale, Pontypool.

What of the politics in these Valleys of Despair? The miners were the Black Storm Troops of the Socialist movement.

What are they now? Socialists still. Storm Troops no more.

The spirit has gone out of them. They have gone beyond politics as they have gone beyond everything else in life.

They are the salt of the earth. The salt that has lost the savour of living.

It is better to wear out than to rust out. And these men are rusting out.

Now the concern for these unemployed should be the sole issue in public life. It should be the only question at the next election.

But will it give subject matter for speeches when the General Election comes on?

Not at all. Peace and war will be the big issue.

But his main task, which served both his beliefs and his ambition, was to scourge the politicians:

"Politicians and Politics" by P.D.H.
Sunday Express, September 16, 1935

Now Hitler has a friend in the House of Commons. His name is Sir Arnold Wilson.[1] He is the fifty-one year old member for Hitchin. Lantern-jawed, beetle-browed, Sir Arnold loses no opportunity of boosting Hitler's stock in this country.

"He has made an astonishing declaration. He says he will not go to war against an expanding nation unless we first have offered them a piece of British territory. To which expanding nation does he refer? Plainly to Germany.

Only a few days ago Dr. Frick, Hitler's Reich Minister for the Interior, said that Germany's need of expansion was greater than Italy's.

Why does Sir Arnold so concern himself with the interest of foreign countries? Such concern on the part of a member of our Parliament damages our interests. It does us harm, not good.

Sir Arnold was elected as member for Hitchin. He is self-appointed as member for Hitler. If he doesn't throw Hitler over, I hope and believe that Hitchin will throw him over.

[1] National Conservative Member for Hitchin (Herts) 1933–40.

81

"Politicians and Politics" by P.D.H.
Sunday Express, October 27, 1935
We stand a fine chance of losing both the Liberal Foots. Dingle[1] is sure
to go, and Isaac[2] stands a first-rate chance of defeat.

Isaac Foot, member for Bodmin, is fifty-five years old. Grey-haired and
severe, he is the leading Pussyfoot of Westminster.

His thirty-year old son, Dingle, member for Dundee, is like his father
in appearance and manner. Dry as dust, the pair of them.

Without its Feet, I think the next Parliament should be able to move
forward a great deal faster.

Sometimes Howard was right, sometimes he was wrong. When war
broke out Sir Arnold Wilson was to prove his courage by enlisting, at
over fifty years of age, in the R.A.F. as a bomber's tail gunner. He was killed
in a raid over Germany. Sir Dingle Foot was to survive to become Solicitor-
General in Mr. Wilson's Government.

Meanwhile, Howard made his mark: "I think I was feared," he wrote
later. "I am certain I was hated. I am sure that in the eyes of Fleet Street
I was successful."

[1] Later Rt. Hon. Sir Dingle Foot, Q.C. Labour Member for Ipswich.
[2] Liberal Member for the Bodmin Division of Cornwall. President, Liberal
Parliamentary Organisation 1947.

Chapter 7

"British Governments of the last few years have been much like a child with a button in its gullet. They have had to be shaken and banged by public opinion until they are on the point of destruction before they will yield the smallest item."

P.D.H. Guilty Men, July 1940.

Peter Howard did not always agree with Lord Beaverbrook. Sometimes he told him so to his face, but seldom or never in the newspaper. There he gave him almost unqualified support. That is what he conceived himself to be paid for, and that was what he did.

On many issues — on Beaverbrook's hostility towards Baldwin and his advocacy of rearmament, for instance — Howard's beliefs and his duties coincided. On such issues they both supported Mr. Churchill, then protesting in the wilderness.

"Politicians and Politics" by P.D.H.
Sunday Express, June 7, 1936

Mr. Churchill in his campaign for rearmament, lasting over three years, has now been shown by events to be right.

Mr. Baldwin himself has been compelled to acknowledge that on the question of German air strength Mr. Churchill was right and he, Mr. Baldwin, was wrong.

Now that the rearmament programme of the Government is moving too slowly for Mr. Churchill and too slowly to protect this country from the danger of sudden foreign invasion, Mr. Churchill is in duty bound to resort to any and every method within his power to drive the Government into effective and aggressive action.

"Politicians and Politics" by P.D.H.
Sunday Express, October 4, 1936

The sooner Mr. Baldwin hands over the better. For the world is full of crisis. Everywhere we face calamity in foreign countries. On all sides danger threatens.

This is not a time for Mr. Baldwin to fill the office of Prime Minister. He has talked in the past about the prerogative of the harlot, power without responsibility. Well, Mr. Baldwin enjoys that prerogative now. He has the power and he cannot undertake the responsibility.

He has been treating the country very badly. The absentee landlords of Ireland were bad enough, but the absentee tenant of Downing Street is much, much worse.

Beaverbrook entered fully into these campaigns:

"In the days when Beaverbrook and Baldwin were at each other's underbellies, complaints about what I had written would sometimes come by telephone from Sir Samuel Hoare, later Lord Templewood, who was a friend of both B's. I happened to be in the room when Hoare called Beaverbrook.

"Beaverbrook: 'Yaas . . . yaas . . . yaas. Now listen to me. I can't do anything with the fellow. No, I tell you. I can't do anything with him. Now listen . . . Listen. I tell you what I'll do. I'll have him down here and I'll roll him in the mud. Yaas. I'll roll him in the mud. Will that satisfy you? . . . Goodbye to you.'

"Then, replacing the telephone, he looked at me and a grin like a slice of melon cut across his face. He began to slap his hands on his knees and to laugh. 'Ha, ha, ha. Do it again, Peter. Do it again next week.' And indeed, I did."

"Politicians and Politics" by P.D.H.
Sunday Express, March 28, 1937

There is a campaign. It is directed against Mr. Winston Churchill. Politicians are whispering about him in the lobbies.

What do they say? That he has suddenly changed his mind about the Government. That he has stopped attacking it and has begun to praise it in the hopes of getting a job when the Cabinet shuffle comes along and Mr. Baldwin retires.

This is a strange accusation. For it is not Mr. Churchill but the Government itself which has changed its mind. Not long ago, when the Government stood firm against rearmament, Mr. Churchill attacked it on that issue. He urged the rearmament of Britain.

And now the Government has adopted Mr. Churchill's policy. It is busy rearming. And, at the same time, its supporters criticise Mr. Churchill as inconsistent because he no longer attacks the Government which has adopted his policy.

Will Mr. Churchill be in the new Cabinet? He should be. Some say that Mr. Chamberlain will be afraid to include him. Certainly the people of the country want to see him back in office.

But there were other issues where the views of Lord Beaverbrook and those of Mr. Churchill did not coincide. Churchill was at this time writing a weekly article in the *Evening Standard*, and the differences between the two men were often to cause difficulties in the *Standard* offices:

"Churchill sat all by himself in the moonlight, or almost, it seemed, in the sunset of a career which had somehow missed greatness. His war song against the Nazis was almost a solo. Just the same he sang it fortissimo in the columns of the *Evening Standard*.

"Meanwhile, my boss, Lord Beaverbrook, was advocating the cause of Splendid Isolation. He was coining phrases such as, 'There will be no war this year or next year either.' He was paying me a large salary to write leaders on the subject. And he was entirely opposed to Mr. Churchill's big idea.

"So Percy Cudlipp, then Editor of the *Evening Standard*, experienced something of the sensations of a football during a Cup Final. Fortunately, Percy has toughness, resilience and a sense of humour, which are qualities needed by any successful football.

"His phone would ring in the morning, 'Cudlipp? This is Lord Beaverbrook here. What's the name of that fellow who writes in your paper? . . . What's his name? . . . Yes, Winston Churchill. That's the fellow I mean. Now, Percy, I hope you're not paying him too much for his articles? . . . Good God, all that? You don't mean it. That's terrible, terrible . . . Well, anyway, I hope you're not tied up too long with him – how long does his contract run? . . . Good God, a year? Another whole year? Well now, see here, Percy, get him off the subject of the Nazis. He's obsessed by this damned fellow Hitler. Get him on to the Broad Home Theme, the great themes of the Empire, Unemployment, Agriculture – let him write on subjects like that. Anything else? Goodbye to you.'

"And Percy would find the telephone dead in his hand. Then he would ring up Mr. Churchill. The conversation would run something like this:

"'Good morning, Mr. Churchill. What will your article be about this week?'

"'Good morning, Mr. Cudlipp. I thought we should deal this week with the subject of the Nazis. We must awaken the country to the danger of this gang of criminals, and I feel we could profitably discuss the Nazi dreams of expansion in the Balkans this week.'

"'Yes, Mr. Churchill, that would be most interesting. But I wonder if perhaps this week an article on the Broad Home Theme might give our readers a change – some subject like Unemployment or Agriculture?'

"'Quite so, Mr. Cudlipp, quite so. And we will come on to the Broad Home Theme. But I think this week a strong declaration on the Nazis will be more timely.'

"And the telephone would again to silent."

Churchill read Howard's articles and was kind to him when he called at Chartwell:

"He used to read my political articles with care, though not always with appreciation. He helped me greatly with comments and suggestions which found their way to me.

"He took exception to the phrase, 'For why?' which I used from time to time. He would steam up to me in the Lobby of the House of Commons, looking like a formidable battleship pouting, 'For why? For why?' at me aggressively through the funnel of his mouth.

"One evening I had to go to Churchill's country home on newspaper business. I travelled straight from my work in Fleet Street to Chartwell. It was summer weather. I was wearing old clothes, and was hot and tired from the bustle and stir of the presses.

"Churchill was in his garden. He was dressed up in some ancient and subfusc costume which made him look like a genial Michelin tyre advertisement come to life. He was building a wall, and handling the bricks with an enthusiasm which I could easily detect and with a skill which I found it harder to judge – though the wall seemed straight enough.

"He had a party of distinguished guests coming to dinner. He insisted on my staying, a black crow among gilded birds of paradise, an inky journalist in grey bags among white ties and tiaras. Yet I was made to feel the most welcome of all the guests. Churchill has a great-heartedness, a warmth and simplicity in private life which explains the rock-ribbed loyalty of his friends.

"He fetched his own shaving tackle for me and stood over me in his private bathroom while I washed, brushed, scraped and made myself presentable. He showed all the comradeship and solicitude of an elder brother, eager for my sake, not his own, that I should appear to best advantage among his friends. It was a revealing sidelight on the character of this citizen of fate.

"At that period, Churchill was almost at the ebb of his fortunes. He was mellow, genial, philosophical and wise. Lord Beaverbrook, in writing of Churchill, has recorded his opinion that 'Churchill down' is the most charming of companions. But 'Churchill on the top of the wave' has in him the stuff of which tyrants are made.

"I remember that Lord Baldwin was on the point of retiring from the Premiership. Churchill had many reasons for being bitter with Lord Baldwin. He had been in the British Cabinet before Lord Baldwin entered Parliament at all. He had seen the older, slower, steadier man start from far behind, catch him up and outstrip him in the race for power. Yet Churchill was not bitter.

"He said to me after dinner that night, 'Baldwin is as clever as a Redskin. He will go down to Bewdley and on Friday nights, or whenever it is that he dances, he will prance around his wigwam pole with my bleeding scalp dangling at his belt.'

"He laughed without rancour. It was said with lightness and in tones which Lord Baldwin himself would have heard without taking offence.

"Later Churchill spoke of the things deep in his heart. He spoke with the smouldering fire of a visionary about the need to destroy the Nazis. He felt war was inevitable – and the sooner it was over, the sooner to sleep.

"This big idea had gripped him entirely, just as Hitler and Lenin had been gripped by their ideas. It stirred me to meet the explosive force of a master passion in an age when most Britons regarded enthusiasm with suspicion.

"As a result of that evening in his home, one thing became perfectly clear to me. I had doubts as to whether this simple and single idea, 'The Nazis must be destroyed', was adequate by itself to build a new world. But I had no doubt at all that as an organiser of victory against the Nazis, Churchill would be unsurpassed.

"I did not want war. I did not yet quit my hopes of peace. But if war had to be our lot and portion, I wanted Churchill. I can see him now, a sombre and brooding figure bidding me farewell from his doorway in the darkness of that summer night. Looked upon by the majority of his countrymen as a spent force, he was heavy with his own sense of impending destiny."

It was during the Abdication crisis that Howard had his first major disagreement with Beaverbrook. Beaverbrook was a passionate supporter of the King, not least because Baldwin was the King's principal opponent. The crisis had broken while Beaverbrook was on the Atlantic *en route* for New York. He took the next boat back, and led the King's campaign both privately and in the Press:

"When King Edward VIII, now the Duke of Windsor, was on the Throne and wishing to wed Mrs. Simpson and remain as King, it was bold to tell Beaverbrook that the plan was brave but bogus – it

87

could never work. When the local inhabitants began chalking rude messages about the American lady on the walls of the Highland stations, Beaverbrook did not want to hear it. He ordered me out of his house for telling him I did not believe the King could wed the lady, and keep his Throne."

Yet it was Howard who wrote the Sunday Express editorial, headed, "A Right that Belongs to All Men", putting Beaverbrook's view of the matter on December 6, 1936:

The British people face a constitutional crisis which tries to its utmost those qualities of political judgment and human sympathy fostered in this happy island through centuries of democratic growth.

The crisis takes on gravity and poignancy as it relates to the cherished institution of the Monarchy and the person of a King who has in the faithful discharge of heavy duties given and won love and devotion.

The King's intention to marry Mrs. Simpson is not the whim of a young and inexperienced man. It is the result of the ripe reflection of one who is mature in years and instructed in judgment.

In seeking to unite his life with the woman whom he loves, he asks for himself no more than he must wish for all his people.

In the clash of opinion which dismays our people, it has been suggested that the King might marry Mrs. Simpson in his capacity as Duke of Cornwall.

This proposal Mr. Baldwin has brushed aside. But it has yet to be determined whether the people, attached as they are to the person of the Sovereign, are prepared to endorse Mr. Baldwin's decision.

Whatever their views on marriage, they regard even the possibility of abdication with deep sorrow.

And they may ask themselves whether, in a world where our outlook on fundamental matters is changing so rapidly, it will be possible to impose indefinitely on our monarchs a code of restrictions which is not founded in law nor hallowed by the conscience of millions.

As soon as the crisis was over and the issue decided, policy changed:

Sunday Express, December 13, 1936

Today the whole Empire and all those who were embroiled in the recent tragic controversy are united in one single loyalty: a loyalty to our new King and his Queen, and a determination to strengthen and maintain with love and affection the man and the woman who take up their heavy burden of responsibility in such circumstances.

This item appeared in a second column called "The March of Time", which Howard had been writing since April 1936. His increasing salary enabled the Howards to live more comfortably. They had moved from Theobald's Road to a larger house at 25, Newton Road, Holland Park, in which they were to stay until the outbreak of war. On October 16, 1936, the Howards' second child, Anne, had been born.

In May 1937, Baldwin resigned the Premiership.

"Politicians and Politics" by P.D.H.
Sunday Express, May 23, 1937

Mr. Baldwin is not our retiring Premier. He is our retiring Prima Donna. The number of his farewells is growing.

Farewell Number 1 was in the House of Commons when he made his "Give Peace in Industry" speech.

Farewell Number 2 came over the wireless on Coronation Day. This time the theme was "Fair play for George VI".

Farewell Number 3 was delivered to the Youth of the Empire at the Albert Hall. And what was Mr. Baldwin's wisdom then? — "The League is bust".

Each one of Mr. Baldwin's farewells was better than the one before.

I'm bound to say that in his third farewell Mr. Baldwin was more like Melba than ever. It was not a speech but a song our retiring Prima delivered.

The language used by Mr. Baldwin at the Albert Hall was among the finest heard in this generation.

The phrase "brotherhood of man implying the fatherhood of God" was magnificent.

Never before has Mr. Baldwin made such copious notes for a speech. He read from them all the time.

The day of abdication is Friday. And no Prime Minister or Prima Donna has ever left the stage in such a blaze of glory as Mr. Baldwin.

"Envy itself is dumb, in wonder lost,
And factions strive which shall applaud him most."

Mr. Baldwin has never in his long career had so many fans as now, when he is quitting the footlights for ever.

"Politicians and Politics" by P.D.H.
Sunday Express, May 30, 1936

The Man we Need
Winston Churchill is not in. He is still outside in the cold.

In my opinion, it is a national disaster that at a time like the present the country is deprived of the services of Churchill. He is the man for the hour.

He has made mistakes. But no one has ever accomplished anything without making mistakes.

Never mind. Winston Churchill is only sixty-two. Five long years before he reaches the age of Mr. Chamberlain, who now becomes Premier for the first time.

One of Howard's principal targets through these years was the Government Chief Whip, Captain David Margesson.

"Politicians and Politics" by P.D.H.
Sunday Express, December 15, 1935

New members have been having an interesting time lately. The Chief Whip summoned them to a meeting.

I am told it was just like school again. The strictest of discipline. No talking, except by the Headmaster. And plenty of sound advice.

Captain Margesson warned his pupils not to wear top hats. Then he passed on to the subject of maiden speeches. He advised his flock to make them soon. Otherwise he said a disaster would befall them.

What disaster? Why, said Captain Margesson, that terrible fellow Peter Howard would write about them in his column and call them silent members.

Now I love helping Captain Margesson whenever I can. So I will reinforce his horrid warning by giving here and now the names of half-a-dozen Government members who, so far as I can discover, have sat in Parliament for the last four years without breaking their silence:

> Captain M. Bullock (Waterloo)
> Colonel H. W. Burton (West Suffolk)
> Lord C. Crichton-Stuart (Northwich, Chester)
> J. Despencer-Robertson (Salisbury)
> Major T. L. Dugdale (Richmond, Yorks.)
> Sir J. Edmondson (Banbury)

The names are in alphabetical order. From time to time I will continue with my list.

Now, come along, gentlemen, I shall be in the House next Tuesday. If some of you stand up then and speak, I promise to listen to you. What is more, I promise to write about you if your speech is worth it.

A friend of mine came up to me in the Lobby of the House of Commons and said in a shaking voice: "David wants you." "David who?" said I. My friend looked shocked. There was only one David for him. "David Margesson, of course," he answered.

Captain David Margesson is the great Chief Whip of the Government; M.P.s tremble at his name.

As I walked off for my interview my friends among them regarded me with sympathy, my enemies with glee.

But Captain Margesson could not have been more charming. He wanted to talk to me about Mr. Lipson, Conservative M.P. for Cheltenham, who won the by-election there against a Government candidate.

He said, "I read in your column last Sunday that I had walked out of the House of Commons when Lipson took the oath as a new member. I did so because I had to introduce another new member directly Lipson had finished. I should never be discourteous to a new member even if I did disagree with him."

"Do you disagree with Mr. Lipson then?" I asked.

"I have no quarrel with him," replied Captain Margesson. "Why should I? He fought the by-election supporting the policy of the Government."

"Then why doesn't he get the Government whip?" I demanded.

"Well, there is no doubt," said Captain Margesson, "that the difficulties which exist at present at Cheltenham will soon be smoothed away. That will be all right. Lipson will be taken in with us."

So Mr. Lipson and his friends in Cheltenham can sneck up. Chief Whip Margesson is quite ready to give Mr. Lipson the Government whip as soon as the differences at Cheltenham are composed.

.   .   .

By August 1937, Howard was writing regularly for the Daily Express and the Evening Standard, as well as for the Sunday Express. The pressure was enormous, but it suited Howard. At different times he wrote under many pen-names. There were serious articles from Adam Bothwell and John Hampden, a daily children's feature called "Pindar the Panda", illustrated by Low, in the Evening Standard and farming articles under the pen-name Brent Ely. One of the most notorious of these noms-de-plume was Captain Barnabe Rich:

"Rich was a colossal cad. He used to say all the things that people want to say but never do say. He was rude to all the people you had to be very polite to. Beaverbrook knew I was writing this stuff, but nobody else knew.

"Captain Barnabe Rich became the talk of London society. And everybody was trying to find out who this awful cad was. A great friend of Beaverbrook's was a society figure called Captain Michael Wardell,[1] who was right in the thick of the crowd Rich was writing about. So I used to go round the London clubs and drawing rooms and if anybody asked me who Captain Barnabe Rich was, I would say, 'Well, who on the *Express* would know all these people?' They would say, 'Well, Mike Wardell is the only one, I think.' And I would say, 'Well, I don't know who it would be, but Wardell knows them all.' It was hard on Wardell, but Beaverbrook and I enjoyed it.

"Then the time came when we had to say who Captain Barnabe Rich was. So I said to Beaverbrook, 'I know what we'll do. We'll print the photograph of Rich in the *Evening Standard*.' 'How will you do that?' he said. 'You leave it to me,' I replied. So next day we had a picture taken right out of the Moss Bros. advertisement of a very splendid fellow in a dashing suit and top hat. The caption read, 'Captain Barnabe Rich at the Races.' Everybody thought to themselves, 'I've seen that man somewhere.' But nobody could think where. And, of course, it was the Moss Bros. advertisement."

Partly to get away from the pressure of Fleet Street — or at least make it more difficult to recall him at weekends — Howard now began looking for a country cottage. With two children and a third on the way, he wanted a place for them outside London. But, more important, Howard himself wanted to get away from the "abominable nuisance of having to meet people". He chose East Anglia because at that time it was the most difficult part of England to reach. The travel arrangements were poor; the roads were worse; and nobody in their senses, he felt, was going to follow him there. He was also deeply drawn to the land. Perhaps in some forgotten corner of his mind the Howards of Meldreth pulled him towards his past. He seemed more at home in the countryside than he ever did in London, even at the height of his success. There was no explanation for this, except that the earth and its fruits were a part of him which he could never discard.

On August 30, 1937, Howard bought a small thatched cottage at Preston in West Suffolk. It was called Old Thatches. It was, in fact, three agricultural cottages rolled into one, with low ceilings, oak beams and three staircases. As a country escape it was ideal. There was enough land to provide an orchard, a lawn, a duck pond and a small paddock beside it for the children to play in. After this he became a weekend commuter, travelling to Suffolk early Sunday morning after the *Sunday Express* went to bed, and

[1] Later Proprietor and Publisher of the *Daily Gleaner*, Fredericton, New Brunswick, Canada.

back to London on a Tuesday unless summoned by Beaverbrook before. He would sometimes bring Fleet Street friends home with him, and the cottage shook to the bang of doors and men's feet. The small drawing room was filled with smoke and beer mugs. The children, who after December 31, 1937, included a second son, Anthony, were kept upstairs or outside.

Howard had a hot temper and did not like his weekends disturbed. He also had a warm heart, and would play riotous games, charging round the house with the children on his shoulders or throwing them high into the air and catching them again. His friends were by no means all journalists. Artists, politicians, writers and sportsmen, as well as some of the best French chefs in London, would spend weekends at Old Thatches. The food and drink were good. The talk lively. But inevitably the *Express* deadlines had to be hit.

1938 was the year in which Beaverbrook was to herald the cry, "No war this year, nor next year either." Howard still called for rearmament.

"Politicians and Politics" by P.D.H.
Sunday Express, June 5, 1938

One situation will have to be cleared up. That is the Hore-Belisha situation.

Our War Minister has made many pronouncements that our anti-aircraft defence services are in good order. He says, "Modernised three-inch guns are ready for immediate use in an emergency." He declares, with reference to the 3·7 inch gun, "Delivery is ahead of schedule."

Now, nobody doubts Mr. Hore-Belisha's word. But what is schedule? Schedule may be far behind our requirements.

Anxiety among the public on this issue has reached a very high pitch. The simple question is: ARE OUR DEFENCES ADEQUATELY EQUIPPED WITH 3·7 GUNS? None but the 3·7 guns will satisfy the people who know.

With 3·7 guns London can be adequately defended. But in no other circumstances. These guns are more necessary to our defence system than bombers or anything else.

The public has confidence in Mr. Hore-Belisha's administration at the War Office. It makes no complaint of his continued appeals for support. But at the same time, this particular matter can be left where it is no longer.

Mr. Hore-Belisha must clear up the position for his own sake as well as ours. If he does not, a storm may arise against him like the one which blew Lord Swinton away.

But he continued to badger M.P.s at sensitive personal points:

"Politicians and Politics" by P.D.H.
Sunday Express, June 19, 1938

It is surprising how often M.P.s mistake the date of their birth. The late Lord Carson's age was wrongly stated in *Who's Who*.

Then there is Mr. Henry "Chips" Channon, member for Southend. His reckoning is just two years out. It is said in the books of reference that he was born on March 7, 1899, making his age thirty-nine.

On the other hand, Mr. Michael J. Flynn tells me that Mr. "Chips" Channon was born on March 7, 1897, making his age forty-one. On the whole, I prefer to accept Mr. Flynn's version.

For why? Mr. Flynn is Clerk of Cook County in the State of Illinois, where Mr. Channon was born. And Mr. Flynn has backed up his story by sending me a photostat copy of Mr. "Chips" Channon's birth certificate.

Mr. "Chips" Channon recorded in his diary:

"June 19, 1938: The *Sunday Express* today published a most extraordinary paragraph to the effect that I am really forty-one instead of thirty-nine, and hinted that I had faked my age in the reference books. The awful thing is that it is true. Now I feel apprehensive and shy, as one does when one is in disgrace. Honour is being very sweet and loyal about it . . . I told her she would be a widow two years earlier."

In July 1938, Howard began writing the "Opinion" column in the *Daily Express*, and the *Evening Standard* editorials. His leader in the *Evening Standard* on September 15, read:

Today we walk in the sunlight: from our path has been lifted the shadow of the clouds which so long darkened our journeying.

It was the dread of war which cast the gloom upon us. It is the hand of Mr. Neville Chamberlain, our Prime Minister, which now removes that dread.

By his air journey to Herr Hitler, the British Premier reinforces and establishes the high position which he has already gained for himself in the hearts and affections of the people.

By November 27, he wrote in his column:

The old plan is dying with the old year. The leaves have fallen, and so have the dreams of Mr. Chamberlain.

Appeasement is dead. Appeasement with Germany is finished because of the Germans. They have ended it with their pogroms and their attacks on Britain.

At the beginning of 1939, Beaverbrook was still supporting appeasement. Howard wrote in support of it, but felt increasingly that it was a forlorn hope. That January he had an experience which pushed him further along that path. At lunch in Fleet Street one day he was asked to join the British Bobsleigh team for the World Championships at Cortina. One of the team had fallen ill. Would he take his place?

When Howard said he had never been on a bobsleigh in his life, his friend replied, "Never mind, you are the right build. You are not afraid of speed, and you know how to work with a team. You are just the man we are looking for." *The Express* gave Howard two weeks' holiday with pay.

Howard took Doë with him to Cortina, and she was a good deal more frightened of the event than he was. On one of the trial runs, the loudspeaker announced, "One man off" the British bob. Doë leapt to her feet, "I know it's Peter," she said. It was. But he was unhurt:

"The teams for the World Championship assembled at Cortina. It was an immense occasion for the Italians. The eyes of all the sporting world were upon them, and they made the most of it. Countess Ciano, then in the heyday of her power and glory, represented her father, Mussolini, throughout the four days of the races, and handed out trophies at the end.

"There were fanfares, flags and all the pomp and ceremony of a Fascist Fiesta. Teams came from most countries in Europe to compete – Rumania, Belgium, France, Switzerland, Italy and many more. There was a strong and fine team from the United States of America, under the captaincy of Jack Heaton.

"The Germans entered four teams, most of them officers from Goering's Luftwaffe. They had been told to win the World Championship at all costs, on the grounds that the prestige of the Reich would be boosted by victory. They set about this task with silent, sustained efficiency. They kept to themselves, spoke as little as possible in case they inadvertently gave away any secrets, and mounted a permanent guard on their racing bobs, fearing the rest of us might tamper with them.

"The American team were our strong allies. The Italians, on the other hand, cheered the Germans loudly from the grandstands and in public, and occasionally booed or whistled as the British team flashed by.

"At night, in the privacy of our hotel, some of the Italians came to visit us, and begged us with tears in their eyes to beat the Germans, as they thought we were the only team likely to do so.

"There were some strange interludes in this warfare. The Italians had built a wonderful racing track at Cortina. But it finished at the finishing post. They had forgotten that the bobs raced past that point at nearly one hundred miles an hour and needed at least a quarter of a mile of surfaced and uphill ice before they could pull up in safety.

"The result was that the most dangerous part of the race came after you had finished the course. The Germans found themselves quite unable to take the corner after the finishing post. They crashed there almost every time. By the last day of the Championship they had been reduced by injuries from four teams to one.

"They displayed a cold courage which startled and frightened us. One German team crashed badly. Two of the men were seriously injured and had to go to hospital. Another was cut on his thigh. The fourth, the captain, had a gash nearly four inches long on his cheek. As we ran forward to help, the captain picked himself up, surveyed his fallen and writhing comrades, then turned his back on them and marching to the timekeeper's hut said in German, 'What was our time, please?'

"The Belgians also crashed here. One of their team was injured and they had no reserve to take his place. They were doing well in the races and had one more descent to make to complete the course. That night they scoured the bars of Cortina, searching for some Belgian who would make the descent for the glory of his nation. Around midnight they found him. He was a charming, unassuming and above all unsuspicious young man who knew nothing about bobbing.

"Lobsters turn from black to red very swiftly when plunged into boiling water. Humans change yet more swiftly from pink to green when plunged down an ice track on a racing bob without knowing what they are in for.

"How they held him on remains a mystery. But they made good time and the young Belgian was rightly a hero of Cortina.

"After the first two days we made a united and vehement protest to the authorities about the dangerous state of the track. They went into conference and presently emerged with beaming smiles, saying, 'To-morrow everything will be all right.'

"Next day we eagerly visited the danger point before climbing the mountain to the start. The track was as it always had been. Evidently the job of reconstruction had been too heavy to undertake. But there was an addition to the amenities. An aged and lovable gentleman with long drooping moustaches had been stationed there. He had an open penknife in his hand. He explained that his job was to scrape the blood off the ice if there was a spill, so that the onlookers should not suffer from any feelings of distress.

"We had no reserves for our British team. So we provided ourselves with drugs in case any of us suffered injury. For, injured or not, we were resolved to get the bob down the track somehow or other.

"The first day of the Championships we made a bad beginning. We got the worst of the draw, having to race on a badly cut-up track after the sun had risen and a slight thaw had taken the bite and speed out of the ice. The Germans led us by over a second.

"On the three following days, the situation improved. We broke the world's record for the Cortina run on each occasion, doing better every day, and finally ended ahead of the Germans.

"It would be idle to pretend that this triumph gave everybody satisfaction. There was a sultry atmosphere as we moved into the hotel to receive our prizes.

"A band was provided. Unfortunately, owing to some misunderstanding or more probably because our victory over the Germans had upset previous arrangements, when the words 'Great Britain' were shouted and we advanced towards the Countess to collect our pots, the band broke into a loud and spirited rendering of *Deutschland uber Alles*.

"The Germans looked furious. We stood to attention with British phlegm. But the Countess, after giving the band a glance almost loud enough to drown their music, suddenly burst into peals of shrill laughter.

"Then she gave us our pots and we took our departure. We had a happy party with the American team that evening. We talked together of the Olympic Games which were to be held at the end of that fateful year, 1939, in Germany at Garmisch and at which some of us had been invited to represent our nations."

. . .

"The March of Time" by P.D.H.
Sunday Express, March 9, 1939

What will Hitler do now? That is the question each man asks his neighbour. And all the world waits for the answer.

In a situation so uncertain as the one which faces us today, confronted as we are by a man of power who has shown himself to be untrustworthy and unable to deal honestly with his neighbours, we have a duty to perform.

We cannot afford to let another week or day or hour go by. We must stimulate our activities and increase our vigilance in regard to defence.

For the warning bell is clanging. The red light shines forth. The signals are at danger. We have come to the point where now and here the nation must be mobilised.

The time has gone past when we can afford to pass our days discussing with our friends whether or not to volunteer for some form of National Service. As an essential measure of security, on which the future of all of us may depend, we need a register of our national resources of manpower. And that register must be compulsory.

"Politicians and Politics" by P.D.H.
Sunday Express, July 23, 1939

Last week an account was published in the columns of the *Sunday Express* of the political movement against our Prime Minister, Mr. Chamberlain. It gave a first-rate objective view of events.

But there you are. Perhaps I shall be thought prejudiced on this issue. I wrote the article myself. For it I find myself attacked and assailed in the leader columns of the *Daily Telegraph*. Why? Because the *Daily Telegraph* declares that it is not opposed to Mr. Chamberlain though in favour of Mr. Churchill.

That organ knows perfectly well that you cannot advocate the cause of Churchill without opposing the Premier.

Mr. Chamberlain does not want to bring Mr. Churchill into the Government. The *Daily Telegraph* desires to push Churchill into the Cabinet whether the Prime Minister wants him there or not. If that is not opposition to Mr. Chamberlain, then what is?

If I plan to try to push Mr. Churchill on to the board of the *Daily Telegraph* in face of opposition from Lord Camrose, would not that be an act hostile to Lord Camrose?

For my part I make no objection to those who say that they are for Chamberlain and for Churchill too. It is much the same thing as being a devout member of the Roman Catholic Church and at the same time going down to the street corner to make a confession from the midst of the Salvation Army circle.

It was during these three months before the outbreak of World War II that the first cracks began to appear in the Howards' marriage. Doë spent many weeks with the children in the country, while Peter stayed at his work in London:

"I began to wear a mask in the home. It was only a little mask, but it was a thick one. I discovered to my surprise that my interest in the freshness of lips, soft eyes and the beauty and admiration of other women had not left me. My interest was academic. But the margin between an academic interest and an actual interest was like hair on a bald man's head. It diminished slowly but steadily with the years.

"I told myself that there was little harm in what I did so long as Doë had no cause for grief. If she knew nothing, she could not feel sad on that account.

"In fact, as my married journey ran on, I found that the ideas propagated by gentlemen like Bertrand Russell were deep-rooted in my heart and desire. They had been covered up rather than cured by happy marriage.

98

"Sometimes I took an evening off from the home. I worked hard to earn money for it. And I felt that a man who worked hard was entitled to his relaxations, wherever they might lie.

"Doë thought, or at least was told, that I was on newspaper work on such occasions. And indeed I did pick up gossip this way around the town.

"Naturally, the following evening I would return home early, often bringing some small gift to Doë. I would devote myself entirely to her. We would go out together perhaps to some cavernous café in Soho to eat pungent-spiced continental dishes, to hear French talked and talk it together, to rejoice in the fun of each other's company. These were the best evenings of life. I found it hard to see while they lasted how I could ever want to spend them differently. And yet, and yet.

"So our marriage ran, Doë's and mine – a gay and rippling journey, like a Dartmoor stream, with light and shade, the sudden sharp and jagged rock, the occasional calm, still stretch of deeper water.

"And presently, before you can see why or how, the waters are divided – two streams run side by side where one travelled the heather before – the waters still chatter and laugh and run together for a time and then perhaps in different directions. In their shrunken and divided condition they tinkle still but lose the deeper notes.

"Doë and I found each had corners in our lives which belonged to ourselves alone and not to each other. We felt that normal. We found it the way to live. A wife has the right to her own friends. A man must have some privacy. That is what we told each other, with a spontaneity of the lips and a sadness of the heart."

But, although the marriage was no longer entirely happy, the division was still slight by Fleet Street standards, and money was plentiful. Howard decided to invest in a farm four miles from his cottage at Preston. In September 1939, he bought Hill Farm, Brent Eleigh, near Lavenham, for £10 an acre:

"Much of it was in a tumble-down state. The hedges marched out across the headlands and were tall with years of neglected growth. The fields were hungry, and in some cases starving. The land was hilly and awkward. The ditches were full and many of the drains blocked.

"We bought the farm in a fit of enthusiasm, and often afterwards thought it was a mad thing to have done. We had a romantic idea that the stream of money which for so long in Britain had poured from the land into the cities should be diverted back to the countryside again."

.   .   .

The second World War was declared on September 3, 1939. The Howard children were in Suffolk with their nanny for the summer holidays. Doë was in London. Peter persuaded her to load the car and leave London at once for Suffolk:

"When war broke out, my thoughts flew to my income. That was an immediate reaction to events.

"I began to keep a careful account of expenditure in my diary. Being fond of food and drink, I used to spend plenty on these commodities. They seemed to me the obvious things to cut down on. For a month I went on the water-wagon. I told my friends that I did this for the sake of my stomach. In fact I did it for the sake of my pocket. I was worried by the thought that my newspaper work might come to an end and that my money would be taken from me. Although some of us forget this now, many people shared this feeling at the outbreak of war."

The Howards' house in Newton Road was sold, and later hit by a bomb. Meanwhile, like all other men of his age, Peter Howard received his call-up papers. He was passed "not A.1." by the medical board on account of his lame leg. Also journalists were in a reserved occupation because their work was considered to be of national importance. The *Express Newspapers*, once war was declared, immediately put all their strength into backing the British war effort. In this Howard joined.

"The March of Time" by P.D.H.
Sunday Express, September 3, 1939

Twenty-one years. What a staggering change in our fortune has come about in that short space of time.

Twenty-one years ago we were swinging along with a shout of triumph and joy, convinced that never again would the civilised nations of Europe submit their quarrels to the awful arbitrament of war.

Today we prepare once more to dig ourselves into the mud, to sweat and toil and suffer, to see our husbands and sons and friends struck down in battle.

And, if the worst forebodings are realised, women and children, too, may be called on this time to face bombardment from the skies.

We have many advantages compared with our 1914 position. We do not expect easy triumphs. We know the Germans to be a strong and ruthless enemy.

We realise quite well that at any rate in the early days of the contest we may have to suffer and endure disappointments and setbacks which befall every nation marching into battle. We are ready to face them without dismay.

Above all, our cause is recognised as just by the whole earth, except **our** enemies.

At the outbreak of the last war, in many countries and especially in the United States of America, there was a substantial body of opinion sympathetic to German aims.

Today Britain and her friends carry into battle the hopes and prayers of every liberty-loving man and woman over the whole surface of the globe.

So we go marching on.

There was still much in a seeming lighter vein:

"Politicians and Politics" by P.D.H.
Sunday Express, December 17, 1939

I dedicate my article this week
       "To the tintinnabulation that so musically wells
       From the bells, bells, bells, bells, bells, bells, bells,
       From the jingling and the tingling of the bells."
The bells I mean are, of course, telephone bells. For the last three days my telephones have not stopped ringing.

I have made a careful note of each call. No fewer than twenty-eight of them have been from people anxious to give me an exact and circumstantial account of all which took place at the secret session of Parliament.

Were these people who rang me up M.P.s or noble Lords? Oho, aha. Like the young lady in the song, 'I will not say, yes. I will not say, no.'

But I will reveal to you that the details of all these accounts bore a striking similarity to each other.

My conclusion is this. No secret of any consequence should be disclosed by the Government at any secret session. That being so, secret sessions serve no useful purpose. None at all.

In the days of phoney war, Beaverbrook, who had to the last hoped that there would be no war, was still anxious that there should not be a big war:

"One evening late, I was down at his house with Brendan Bracken,[1] Aneurin Bevan[2] and Frank Owen. Beaverbrook turned to me and said, 'What do you think of the war?'

"I said, 'We've got to win it. We're in it. Politically it is impossible for anybody to withdraw. The British people would not stand it. We have got to beat Hitler.'

[1] Conservative M.P. for N. Paddington 1929–45. Minister of Information 1941–45.
[2] Labour M.P. for Ebbw Vale from 1929. Minister of Health 1945–51.

" 'What should we do with Chamberlain?' Beaverbrook went on.

" 'Chamberlain is not a war man,' I replied. 'He's a man of peace. His heart is not in the war. The only hope is to put Churchill in charge and get rid of Chamberlain.'

" 'Get out of my house,' roared Beaverbrook. 'Get out of my house. I don't want you in my house. Get out of my house.' He was shaking with rage.

"I went. It was one o'clock in the morning. I started to walk the two miles to my bed through the blackout. I had gone about two hundred yards when behind me I heard a scurry and a patter. There was Beaverbrook, a small asthmatic figure, coatless and hatless, trotting after me.

" 'Peter,' he said, 'forgive me. I shouldn't speak to you like that. You'll think no more of it?' "

It was by now apparent that the British preparations for war had been disastrously mismanaged. Howard and his friends, Frank Owen and Michael Foot, were becoming increasingly impatient. They blamed the Cabinet and all who had supported them, including Lord Beaverbrook.

"Right and Wrong" by P.D.H.
Evening Standard, February 6, 1940

Do you know of the Boothby technique? It is a political method of approach to problems, which gets its name from Mr. Robert Boothby, Tory M.P. for East Aberdeenshire. That gentleman has been right about every issue and wrong about every issue that has ever arisen.

For why? Because his mind is so broad, his opinions so liberal that he sees two sides to every question – and advocates both of them.

Some public men adopt the Boothby technique. Others, not so. You can never doubt for a moment where they stand or what they think.

Lord Beaverbrook, for example, is always decided and entirely cocksure that his views are right.

I am bound to tell you, however, that sometimes he is wrong.

He said in 1938, "There will be no war involving Britain this year." Quite right.

In the dark days he stuck by his prediction. When midnight of December 31, 1938, chimed away he was much praised for his sagacity and sound judgment.

He said in 1939, "There will be no war involving Britain this year." Quite wrong.

When the black hour of 11 a.m. on September 3, 1939, struck, he was much reviled for folly, optimistic bluff and wishful thinking.

Beaverbrook retaliated two weeks later:

Evening Standard, February 22, 1940

One of our contributors — Mr. Peter Howard — telephones to know why the "raid" on Liverpool is not included in the map on page seven.

The reason why it is not included is that it has never been established that it took place.

An airplane did appear over Merseyside, and was fired at.

A little later a British training machine landed, bearing traces of gunfire.

If Mr. Howard would give some time to reading as well as writing he would have known that the *Evening Standard* "Diary" published this fact at the time. And that would have saved him his telephone call this afternoon.

On May 10, 1940, Hitler marched into the Low Countries. Beaverbrook telephoned Howard at the *Express* offices:

"He asked me how the news was coming in and then said, 'You can record in your diary, if you have one, that today Hitler lost the war.'

'Everyone else in London at this point seemed to think that Hitler might win the war. His attack and its speed had struck an icicle of foreboding into the warmth of many a brave heart. Beaverbrook went on, 'Hitler's entry into the Low Countries makes the intervention of the United States of America inevitable. I do not know whether he will overrun France. I do not even know if he will attempt to invade this country. But sooner or later now America will intervene and when America intervenes you can be sure Hitler will be vanquished.'"

That same day, the Chamberlain Government fell and Winston Churchill became Prime Minister. Beaverbrook joined the Cabinet as Minister of Aircraft Production. This spelt disaster for Howard's political writing. For Beaverbrook was not so pleased for Cabinet Ministers to be assailed each Sunday, when he had to meet them in Cabinet each Monday. Howard did not know it then, but he only had until July 7 when his column "Politicians and Politics" was to appear for the last time.

"Politicians and Politics" by P.D.H.
Sunday Express, May 12, 1940

I need utter no words of praise of Mr. Churchill. Since war began he has been looked on by the public as the man they desire for their leader in war.

He marches forward with the confidence, the heart and the hand of the entire British public.

.   .   .

On Friday, May 31, 1940, the British troops were in retreat at Dunkirk. That fateful weekend thousands of small ships crossed the Channel to evacuate the British army from the beaches. Peter Howard, Michael Foot and Frank Owen sat in the offices of the *Evening Standard* that Friday afternoon discussing the news as it came in. They placed the blame for the disastrous retreat squarely upon Chamberlain and his colleagues, most of whom were still in Churchill's Government. They decided to write a book, in which they would pillory the wilful negligence of these men.

On Monday, June 3, Howard, Foot and Owen returned to London each with eight chapters written during the weekend. They called the book, *Guilty Men*. They wrote under the pseudonym "Cato", because it was Cato who cleaned out the sewers of Rome.

The book was finished by Tuesday, June 4. On Wednesday it was accepted for publication by Victor Gollancz. The only parts to be queried for libel were those written by Howard, and these were swiftly adjusted.

The first edition of *Guilty Men* was published in July 1940. It was regarded as unpatriotic to attack British leadership in time of war, and W. H. Smith and Wymans refused to sell it. The authors engaged a fruit coster with a barrow to wheel copies of the book up and down Fleet Street. This started an avalanche, for which Gollancz were ill-prepared. They had expected the sales to reach five thousand. Over two hundred thousand copies were sold in the next months.

Speculation as to who had written *Guilty Men* grew and grew. Some accused Beaverbrook, others suspected either Foot, Owen or Howard. None guessed that it was all three of them.

Michael Foot wrote his own review in the *Evening Standard*:

"A Mystery Here" by Michael Foot

Pamphleteering is a forgotten weapon, yet once it was perhaps the most potent in English politics. A pamphlet by Swift broke the Duke of Marlborough. How many other of the great names in English literature were associated with this particular art? Milton, Burke, Junius and hundreds more.

The weapon has now been drawn from its scabbard with a vengeance. *Guilty Men* written by a mysterious and bashful "Cato" (Gollancz: 2s. 6d.) promises to become the most sensational political publication of the war.

It is a searing, savage, but documented, attack on the men responsible for the failure to provide Britain with the armaments to fight this war. It is an amazing vindication of the foresight of the present Prime Minister, and it pays full tribute to the men who have intensified the war effort in recent weeks.

The story is told by one who appears to have watched the drama from the floor of the House of Commons itself.

Some of the judgments are unfair. It has some flagrant omissions. But, whatever verdict is passed on the whole, none can dispute that its total effect is terrific.

Who is this "Cato" M.P.? And why does he hide his fireworks under a bushel?

Howard wrote his review in the *Daily Express*:

I cannot do more than pay a tribute to the powerfulness of the indict-ment brought by "Cato", the mysterious author of *Guilty Men*.

He starts off with the Blood Bath of Flanders:

"One Bren gun and one hero against eight Heinkels" . . .

"Three bayonets and three heroes against machine guns" . . .

"Marching men against incessant bombers. Why? Why? Why?"

"Flesh against steel, an Army doomed before it took the field."

Then, going back into the history of the last few wasted years, "Cato" dramatises the blundering, the broken pledges and the unfulfilled pro-mises of arms, quotes the speeches and takes us behind the scenes of the most shameful of happenings in British politics for many years.

His epilogue tells of the new determination that came with Churchill's accession to power and the vigour shown by his three Supply chiefs, Bevin, Morrison and Beaverbrook, to make Britain a fortress.

"But," and these are his last words, "the nation is united to a man in its desire to prosecute the war in total form; there must be a similar unity in the national confidence.

"Let the guilty men retire, then, of their own volition, and so make an essential contribution to the victory upon which all are implacably resolved."

The publication of *Guilty Men* embarrassed the Government so much that Howard was called to the office of E. J. Robertson, the General Manager of the *Daily Express*. He was told that, so long as Lord Beaverbrook was in the War Cabinet, he could no longer write articles about politics.

Chapter 8

HOWARD was furiously angry about the General Manager's decision. His career and reputation were based on his political column. His entire outlook was geared to attack, and his power rested in the politicians' fear of his assaults: "When I punched, I punched to hurt." Now he could punch them no more.

He haunted the ante-room of the General Manager's office, complaining bitterly of his treatment and demanding a reprieve. There he came up against the General Manager's secretary, Mrs. Edith Ducé, whose task it was to guard E. J. Robertson from interruption:

"Edith Ducé was a middle-aged woman. For a long time I cherished a grievance against her. I drank too much at a party, and behaved badly there. Mrs. Ducé got to hear of this affair. She went around the office telling her friends of my misdeeds.

"I detested Mrs. Ducé for this malicious gossip. Day by day, for months, we greeted each other with the frigid and artificial grin of mutual repugnance. I regarded her as a dangerous and distasteful person. I felt I had to mask my emotion and smile at her whenever we met in the lift or passed in the passageway because, after all, she was the General Manager's secretary, and being as I knew both a tattler and an intriguer might do me some harm.

"Presently I noticed a most remarkable change in Edith Ducé. Instead of appearing acidulous, she looked out at life with greater benevolence. She seemed altogether more contented and happy.

"One day she stood still in the passage as I hurried past her with my determined grin, and called after me, 'Peter.' It was the first time she had used my Christian name in addressing me, and I was indignant that a secretary, even the General Manager's secretary, should call me 'Peter' inside the *Express* building. Edith Ducé asked me to come into her room. There, after some polite palaver in which I was on my guard and she appeared to be seeking for words to use, she told me that she knew that in the past she had tried to do me some injury by her malice and her tongue. She apologised for it and hoped we should be better friends in future. Then she said something like this, 'I am a different woman from what I used to be. I thought it right to tell you why. I made up my mind that the only way to lead my life was on a Christian basis.'

"This was said to me by Mrs. Ducé in a matter-of-fact fashion, without embarrassment on her part. Its effect on me was shattering. I mumbled, 'Thank you very much. Very interesting. Must tell me more about it some other time.' Like a chicken I bolted.

"I remember, as I went away, breaking into a run as I realised with ferocity that I had stumbled on a story about Mrs. Ducé which would make her seem far more ridiculous and contemptible in the eyes of my fellow journalists than her account of my drunkenness had made me appear in the eyes of her fellow secretaries.

"I went about the place telling everyone that Mrs. Ducé now suffered from religious mania. But she beat me to it. Many people had heard the story from her own lips already. In the language of Fleet Street I had been 'scooped'. For Mrs. Ducé was not a common-or-garden Bible-puncher. She had actually joined the Oxford Group, and was to be known until the day of her death as a Buchmanite.

"She received much abuse and some persecution because of what were casually called her 'pernicious doctrines'.

"I knew all about these 'pernicious' doctrines. That is to say, I knew everything that had appeared in the Press, or had been whispered down Fleet Street, about the Oxford Group.

"I believed a good deal of what I heard. For by this time my whole temperament was attuned to attack. I sought for weaknesses in the situation of any person or company, I was not on the lookout for strength.

"One day, as I stood in the anteroom where Mrs. Ducé worked, waiting to see the General Manager, I was treating her to my opinions about some fellows who in my judgment were impeding the war effort. I said these men ought to be shot, like any other individual who, when his country was in danger, proved obstructive and unhelpful.

"Mrs. Ducé stopped typewriting. She said, 'You are quite entitled to say that, Peter, provided you are doing all you can yourself to help.' I must have looked somewhat bewildered, for she then said, 'Have you yourself been as helpful as possible here lately? Do you ever ask yourself that question?'

"I replied that I thought I had.

"The next event was the ringing of the telephone on my desk at about midday one Thursday.

" 'Are you free for a moment, Peter?' said Mrs. Ducé's voice.

" 'Yes,' said I.

" 'Come down for a minute then, will you? I have something for you.' "

Mrs. Ducé suggested to Howard in her office that morning that he should meet a Mr. Garth Lean.

"I had no intention of getting mixed up with the racket. So I asked Mrs. Ducé, 'Who is Garth Lean?'

" 'He is one of my friends in the Oxford Group, and I think he'll be able to help you,' answered Mrs. Ducé.

" 'Very kind of you,' said I, 'but that's not my line of country as well you know. I am not a religious person. I am an agnostic and that sort of thing doesn't interest me much.'

" 'That's a pity,' replied Mrs. Ducé. I left the room.

" When I got upstairs to my own desk, a new thought, potent and attractive, stimulated my imagination. Here, after all, was the chance I had been waiting for. Already much of Fleet Street abused the Oxford Group, or Buchmanites as journalists prefer to call them, saying that they were racketeers, pro-German and all the rest of it. Nobody had yet dared to print the story in that form.

"If I could take advantage of Mrs. Ducé's offer to introduce me to Lean I might be able to expose the whole affair.

"I went downstairs again to Mrs. Ducé's room. 'I've changed my mind,' I told her. 'I'd like to see your friend Bath Green or whatever he calls himself, after all.'

"Mrs. Ducé arranged that I should lunch with Lean at a flat in the Temple that very day."

Howard's lunch with Lean was an interesting encounter:

"He did not impress me very favourably. Physically he is a shaggy-looking sort of fellow, with a head that is going bald, and a laugh which now amuses me, but which then irritated me exceedingly. I can see that two things more than anything else impressed me unfavourably about Garth Lean.

"The first was that he spoke about God with respect but without embarrassment. This prejudiced me against anybody. I loathed that sort of business.

"The second was that, when I spoke of my problem of having to start and rebuild my newspaper column, he was not particularly sympathetic about it."

Howard did not much like Edith Ducé nor did he care for Lean. His purpose with both was malicious and in certain ways dishonest. This must have been apparent to them. But surprisingly it did not discourage them, even though Howard presented Lean at this time with one of the early copies of Guilty Men inscribed, "This book is splenetic like me."

"That day at luncheon in the Temple, Lean told me he believed in God.

"I told him I did not.

"He asked me, 'Why not?'

"For some reason, I found it difficult (I, so slick of the tongue that I could hold my own with Cabinet Ministers) to provide a cogent answer to that simple enquiry.

"I swallowed a mouthful of food to take time for reflection. Then I said to him, 'Well, why do you believe in Him?'

"This man replied, 'It is as foolish to argue about whether there is a God as it is to stand looking at an electric light switch and arguing whether if you turn it the light will go on. One fellow says it will. The other says it will not. The end of the argument is to turn the switch and see.'

"I asked Lean what he meant. He told me that the way to see whether God was there was to put Him to the proof. He declared that God would talk to each person who was ready to listen and obey.

"I said this sounded far-fetched to me. But I knew he believed what he told me. He was living at a swifter pace than I, and he had in his eyes a peace I longed for but never had grasped.

"When I told him again that I did not believe in God, he smiled and said, 'In that case, you won't mind listening to Him, will you? For you won't expect to hear anything anyway.'"

Incredibly Howard agreed to try it. He did so because, "I knew Garth Lean would ask me if I had listened to God. And I wanted to worm my way into the full confidence of Lean and the others, so that I could find out the whole truth about them."

The lunch came to an end. "We parted. I meant to expose the Oxford Group in a dramatic newspaper scoop. I suggested meeting Garth Lean again."

Howard did meet Lean again. This time at the Oxford Group head-quarters in London. Howard's arrival there was greeted with mixed feelings. Some of Lean's colleagues had tried to persuade him to cancel the invitation. They felt, knowing Howard's record, that whatever he wrote was bound to be hostile. They found it impossible to believe that Howard's interest was sincere. In this they were right. To his credit, Lean persisted in having Howard received.

"One fact soon became apparent to me. You might dislike these people, but you could not, if you surveyed the scene with an open mind, distrust them. Sincere goodwill radiated every room and person in the dwelling. There was a stimulating air about the place."

For Howard, it was a surprise. He had expected to find evidence to support the rumours he had heard in Fleet Street. He found none. It cannot be said he did not search for it. He stayed several days and nights at the headquarters; he met everyone; he asked questions; he kept his eyes open; he remembered everything that was said. He left convinced that the Oxford Group was not for him, but equally sure that what he had heard about them was untrue.

That August William Hickey's column in the *Daily Express* four times attacked the Oxford Group. This column was then written by Tom

Driberg[1] who had first established himself with the *Daily Express* twelve years before by writing the first public attack upon Dr. Buchman and the Group. It was not Howard's policy to contradict his own paper, but he felt he could not let the matter rest after his new-found information:

"After reading what was said, it seemed to me fair that the other side of the affair should be written. I thought it best, in the interests of good journalism and of truth, that both sides of the picture should be presented and that the public should judge between them."

Accordingly, Howard wrote his "Reply to Hickey":

All good cider comes from stinking apples. And some good things appear even out of the war.

One clean thing emerging from the grime of this conflict is an increase of tolerance. Jews are no longer news in Britain. Anti-Semitic sentiment has faded. In addition, the hysterical hatred of all aliens which gripped the country not long ago is now relaxing.

Many people have had a share in this transformation. And among the leaders of this crusade for fair play for Jews and aliens stands William Hickey.

Much of the vigour of this man's mind, much of the fire of his voice and the fury of his pen have been turned to the defence of these afflicted creatures. As an apostle of tolerance he has won the gratitude of hundreds and the admiration of thousands, including myself.

So I am surprised and dismayed to behold him now entering upon a savage persecution of a section of our community on account of their beliefs. I refer to William Hickey's sustained attack on the Oxford Group, or Buchmanites, as he prefers to call them.

It seems plain that William Hickey has a set detestation of these folk. He makes black and bitter charges against them.

There is nothing new in these stories. Plenty of people in Fleet Street mentioned them to me. I passed on the tales myself. And I believed them.

But then I did something about them which, so far as I can see, few other people in Fleet Street have bothered to do. I made it my business to investigate them.

I sought out the Oxford Group. I went to its headquarters. I made friends with the people there. I did my utmost to establish the truth or falseness of the charges laid against them by eminent journalists.

Now William Hickey says that guileless simple people are deceived by the Oxford Group. That they "have put it over them".

So I must set out my qualifications for the task of investigating the allegations against them. I do not regard myself as either guileless or simple. For years I have earned my living by dealing with politicians. I

[1] Later Labour Member of Parliament for Barking.

have interviewed them in order to earn my bread. My whole business in life has been to drag the truth out of M.P.s and Ministers of the Crown reluctant to disclose it. I declare that as a result of my experiences with politicians I never begin any interview without expecting that an attempt will be made to "put something over me". I am on the lookout.

Having set down these facts, I must record that after several weeks of close investigation, by means of conversation, cross-examination as well as by asking for and being given access to letters and files, I have reached the firm conviction that there is no basis of truth in the allegation of pacifism or of pro-Nazism (conscious or unconscious) made against the Oxford Group.

If I had found proof of pro-Nazism I should have disclosed it in the newspaper and given details to the Home Office. Instead, I regard it as fair to set out the conclusions I reached.

Thousands of Oxford Group men and women belong to the fighting services. Many of them are in the fighter squadrons at present engaged against the Nazi bombers.

The Oxford Group people in factories engaged on war production are striving to lessen friction between employers and employed, to settle disputes by friendly negotiation instead of by strike action, and to increase production in their factories. In many cases they are succeeding in a remarkable degree.

It would be useless for me to present these facts to you as matters of hearsay or second-hand evidence. I have held in my hands and inspected confidential reports from factory managers, workroom stewards and ordinary craftsmen, some dated as recently as last week, testimony which in my judgment is beyond dispute.

I place on record my considered view that the Oxford Group are exerting all their efforts to increasing the unity, strength and abilities of the country. And they are doing it well.

Now the question will be put to me, "Hey — Peter Howard — are you a member of the Oxford Group?"

My answer is that I find the standards aimed at by the Oxford Group difficult of achievement by me. But I should like to achieve them. I shall try to achieve them.

Two of them are absolute honesty and absolute unselfishness.

I cannot believe these goals deserve the flouts and gibes of anyone. Certainly they do not get mine.

And it is a real sadness to me to see a man with the power and ability of William Hickey spending his forces in hatred of the Oxford Group.

To Howard's surprise the article did not appear in the *Daily Express*. Its Editor, Arthur Christiansen, frankly told Howard that he thought it better journalism to attack the Oxford Group (Moral Re-Armament) than to print both sides. Howard now found himself in a difficult position. He was certain that the MRA people were honest in their beliefs, and that if they were true, nothing else mattered so much. But he knew the hostility he faced if he admitted this was enormous:

"I was afraid of contempt or ridicule. It may seem strange to you that I should be ready to send in a written article to the Editor of the Express saying what I did, and at the same time shrink from speaking about it. But that was the case. I was like a spectator at a football match. I was ready to cheer for the unpopular side when I felt sure nobody was looking. I was even convinced that this side would have to win out in the end. But I was far too comfortable in my furry overcoat, with my flask of whisky and sandwiches in my pocket, to get into shorts and go out into the mud and clamour and join the game myself."

Peter Howard's articles continued to pour into the Express. There was, at first nothing different about their style, but there was a difference in his personal attitude:

Most human beings if they get the chance persecute those who differ from them. Certainly, I have had the chance of indulging in persecution in this column. And I have grabbed it. I have rampaged about the place kicking and cursing everybody, knocking the politicians down and beating them up. I am bound to add that at the end of it all my knuckles are unbruised and the heads of the politicians are unbowed. In fact, everything is much the same.

Now with the years, I am becoming less harsh. I dip my pen in honey not vitriol. My violence is abated. I hope to woo with the soft notes of the flute in cases where I failed to terrify with the big bangs on the drum.

And so it might have remained for Peter Howard. But there was within him a sense of urgency, a sense of destiny — call it what you will — which thrust him onwards. But that was not enough to transform an agnostic journalist into a passionate Christian revolutionary. Howard felt he was within reach of a great experience, which he could only achieve by a decision of the will. He made that decision, not in the rush of Fleet Street, or in the glamour of a mass meeting, but alone, in a small room in London:

"I went back to my little top-storey room in Northumberland Avenue. I read again through those four absolute standards of honesty, purity, unselfishness and love with the orders which someone, call Him God or what you will, had put into my mind so luminously that morning. I thought to myself, 'Well, try anything once. If it doesn't work out, nobody need know. There's no harm done.' Yet just the same there was that in me which said that if I did do it, things would never be the same with me again.

"In that room I got down on my knees. And I prayed something like this, 'God, or whoever you are, if you are there, I will do what you tell me if you'll give me the strength to do it. But I can't do these things unless you help me.'

"From that moment when for the first time in my life I decided to give God a chance, if He were there, to talk to me, to be really honest with myself about the things He said to me, my life has been transformed.

"Do I mean that from that instant I became perfect? Of course not. Far from it. I stumble and grope my way along the thorny, narrow path which is marked by the blood-stained footprints of history. There are plenty of falls and many difficulties. Paul and Bunyan and many others wrote about that journey, charting the road for us ordinary men.

"It is an exhilarating human experience to be granted a sense of destiny, to be offered a distinctive place in a great and growing army marching under God to remake the world. Yet each of us can have it."

The results of this experience in Howard's life were manifold. He apologised to his brother, John, for his jealousy, and repaid money he owed in Oxford and to the Education Grants Committee for not becoming a teacher as he had promised to do. He went down to Suffolk and was completely honest with his wife. It was the most difficult thing to do. Doë had, unknown to him, already encountered Moral Re-Armament through reading a book. Had it not been for her understanding and encouragement, there is little doubt that Howard would never have been able to face telling her the truth. He had already deferred the decision several times. It was on the way to the station one cold Monday morning that Doë turned to her husband and said, "Peter, whatever you have done, you know I will always love you."

Howard wrote later:

"Our marriage has been transformed. Our lives have been transformed. We have found together, after all these years of married life, a swifter and more satisfying adventure than any we expected or experienced as we strode forth across that gangway on to Dover Quay, a honeymoon couple with the flush and flame upon us, two days after our wedding.

"Today we know the answer to all those things, great and small, which can and do stain or shadow the happiness of marriage and of life.

"We have been given a unity which does not depend on looks or on wealth, on health, on moods, or any physical intimacy which the years might shred and stale.

"We know that God understands both of us and loves both of us more fully than we can ourselves. It is not God's plan that marriage shall be nagging, dull or tumultuous. His plan is for marriage to begin as a free joyful human relationship and for it to stay this way."

Although Howard often spoke throughout his life of the results of that decision he took in the Constitutional Club, they were not the most important part of his experience. Of that, he spoke seldom. Yet, it was that miracle of faith which mattered more to him than any other part of his life. It was that faith which was to hold him through the storms which were to beat more heavily upon him than any he had ridden through before. Garth Lean, who saw most of Howard at the time, described it this way:

"The change which transformed Peter Howard from a brilliant journalist into a no less brilliant leader of Moral Re-Armament mystified many.

"His was a simple, but far-reaching experience of Christ's power, comparable to that of Wesley in the room off Aldersgate, or of St. Ignatius in the sick room at Loyola: an experience which Howard was later to make possible for thousands of others in many countries."

This was the only possible explanation. How else could a young man of thirty-three who cared little for those in MRA, who had never met Frank Buchman and who had no belief in God, suddenly change so completely?

"I was always searching for something. Call it what you will. It is hard to put a name to it. I named it Happiness. Looking back, I believe I was in search of some master passion, some great ideal to which I could wholly give myself, which would provide a motive and force for my living and by which the world could be remade.

"I sought it in my work, my home, my ambitions. And though I received much from all these things, and gave much to them also, yet the fullness of my heart's desire remained unsatisfied.

"Now, I have the silly but satisfying feeling that I have made a new discovery. I feel like Watt when he saw the kettle lid hop off, or when Newton beheld the apple fall to the ground.

"The thing I have discovered, the truth about the meaning of life, the very heart of the whole body of creation, was there all the time — like the force of gravity or steam power. But I, I have got at the secret.

"Will other people believe my secret? Not all of them. But I have been touched by a hand which I know is there even if others deny it or refuse to see it.

"I have faith in the future of mankind. I believe that from this war, even during this war, new ways, finer and more splendid ways of living, can appear upon the earth.

"Yet I know now that there is no hope at all for a better future in the world unless this message is learned by millions of men and women over the earth's surface.

"Here is the only remedy for the ills of the earth. I believe these ills will be cured.

"Here is the only light, the only glint or glow of expectation for the future. There are many reflections of life, many moons of delusion and delight. Here is the only true, blazing sun. This great light is being tended. A minority watch over it, cherishing its flame.

"Presently that flame will spread across the whole earth, setting the stubble alight, blazing its swift path from continent to continent, warming the hearts and illuminating the dark corners of the spirits of men."

The reaction in Fleet Street, when news of Howard's decision began to leak around, was electric. "My God," Percy Cudlipp, then Editor of the *Daily Herald*, exclaimed to his informant, "who will be next?" Some were hostile, others incredulous, still more scoffed. "Howard's gone soft. The Beaver won't stand much more of this sweetness and light stuff." Others were pleased but few dared to say so.

At Westminster the reaction was more positive:

"A woman M.P. who disliked me and for years had not spoken to me, stopped dead in her tracks in the Lobby of the House of Commons when she saw me: 'Good heavens, Peter Howard,' she said, 'what have you been doing? You look ten years younger.'"

· · ·

At home in Suffolk, the effect upon Howard's family was no less shattering:

Doë to P.D.H.

Darling, I find it a bit difficult to get used to you. I had so made up my mind that certain things you did would go on as long as we – making fun of me in public, getting drunk three times a year, making your angry face when I asked for money – that I can't quite get used to losing them. It unbalances me. I had built up a technique to deal with them and this has collapsed and I'm a bit lost. Only don't be too kind to me now. I only became tidy because you were untidy. I mustn't get slack or pleased because you aren't there to force me into better ways by your ways.

Howard suddenly found time for his children. Instead of the usual tablespoon of beer on Sunday mornings, they were taken to Sunday school. There was a peace and happiness and joy which the children could feel and respond to, without understanding how it had happened. His writing in *Express* newspapers was different.

"The March of Time" by P.D.H.
Sunday Express, October 27, 1940

It is easy to give way to spleen and disappointment when we survey the present activities of our former ally France. It is easy to abuse the French as treacherous and cowardly when we perceive the miserable rulers of that fallen republic toad-eating at the table of their Nazi lords.

Yet remember this. We owe a debt to the French. For many months they fought hard in this war. We could never have withdrawn all our soldiers from Dunkirk if the men of France had not, at the moment of departure, borne back the Nazi onrush. While the last of our soldiers embarked, the men of France held the rear.

And we thought so highly of the part played by the French sailors on that occasion that we decorated the French Admiral in charge of the operation.

Every Briton whose relative or friend came away safely from Dunkirk should remember with gratitude France as she was yesterday.

Today, instead of abuse and foolish recrimination, we should study the reasons for the disintegration of France, so that we, in these days of test and trial, may profit from the lesson.

What caused the collapse into ruins of the whole fabric of France – that nation whose masonry seemed so solid and whose towers seemed able to withstand for years the onslaught of tyranny?

The reason was decay, insidious and prolonged, in the very foundations of the State.

"The March of Time" by P.D.H.
Sunday Express, December 1, 1940

Complacency is the Devil's drug. It produces the fatty degeneration of a people. Last winter our complacent attitude to events, the self-satisfaction with which we waited for the Germans to crack and collapse, without exerting ourselves to the limit to bring about that situation, lost us the Battle of France.

We must beware lest this winter we are caught a second time in the same snare.

The fact must be faced that as a nation we have a tendency to be over-complacent. This tendency is sometimes displayed by the over-optimistic Ministerial pronouncements or by the tones with which BBC announcers give the news of a success. It is to be seen in the columns of the newspapers, and it is to be heard in private conversations around thousands of family tables.

So let us never for one instant forget the huge nature of the task before us. While we may lift up our hearts at each success as it comes to us, let us refrain from dining out for weeks on every small triumph. Let us cheer but not jeer. Let us repeat to ourselves as we get up each morning and before we go to bed every night:

> "Love not to brag,
> Love not to boast,
> Grief comes to him
> Who talks the most."

"People I Meet" by P.D.H.
Sunday Express, December 15, 1940

Here let me say that during last winter I was guilty of offering a piece of fatuous advice to the public. Before the bombardment by air began, I advocated that the numbers of auxiliary firemen and other paid A.R.P. workers who at that time lingered in idleness about the streets of our cities should be cut down.

This was a short-sighted viewpoint. Fortunately for us all, the authorities disregarded it. Since Goering's flying gorillas began their work, the firemen and A.R.P. workers have behaved with splendid skill and courage.

"The March of Time" by P.D.H.
Sunday Express, December 22, 1940

What does Christmas mean to many of us? If we are honest we shall admit that in many cases the religious character of the celebration has been lost by us.

In many homes Christmas has come to mean cigars, champagne, turkeys, plum pudding, and mince pies — a lot to drink and too much to eat.

How should we celebrate this wartime Christmas?

The *Sunday Express* suggests that this Christmas every woman, child and man in the islands should celebrate Christmas by eating a little less instead of a lot more.

"The March of Time" by P.D.H.
Sunday Express, January 5, 1941

Britons never, never, never shall be wrong. That is the new slogan which we seem to have adopted for the duration of this war.

Many of us are obsessed with a fatuous complacency about our own infallibility, and tainted with the foolish belief that it is weak to admit that we have fallen into error.

Our minds are dulled by the stupid doctrine that since we always win the last battle, we can be excused slowness and incompetence along our road to victory.

Must we always wait until we have suffered, bled and been brought to the edge of catastrophe before we exert ourselves?

"People I Meet" by P.D.H.
Sunday Express, March 9, 1941

Political systems and schemes and dreams do not really settle anything very much. Will you agree with me that the only real cure for the condition of things in the world today is a fundamental change in heart and habits of great masses of people in every country in the world, including our own?

Nations will continue to bleed and perish until a nobler conception of their duty towards their neighbour is established in them. It can be done. It must be done, if any lasting benefits are to come to us as a result of this war we are waging against Hitler. Now there are plenty of folk in Britain who consider that a better spirit in this nation will be achieved if they can get rid of the people who at present rule us and take on the job themselves.

I can speak with authority on this subject. I used to buoy myself up with the conviction that our fortunes would continue to decline until the day when Peter Howard was given some position of power and authority in the councils of the nation. This Peter Howard party remained a party of one, and I am still at large.

Are we going to begin now to build a new Britain in the spirit of faith and toleration? Or are we going to go forward into an age of "reason" which makes no bones about it and declares that God is all a myth and that man depends upon his own efforts for salvation and happiness (the same efforts he has relied on for the last twenty years)?

During these months after he had run up his flag, Howard obtained a greater response from the public and a larger number of letters than ever before in his career:

"I set these facts down, as some people have foolishly suggested that in Fleet Street a man who adopts as his standards the Christian standards of MRA is automatically a less effective journalist. For months after I declared my association with MRA, my work continued to appear in the paper and received praise from the management. Naturally, I did not attempt to write about MRA, for I should not have been allowed to do so.

"These were difficult days. In my own paper, columnists wrote paragraphs with the innuendo that MRA was pro-Nazi. Secretaries in the office were told that MRA members of the staff would not be tolerated. Other people were warned not to discuss MRA with me.

"Of course, these attempts to create difficulties added salt to the soup, so far as life in Fleet Street was concerned. Most people laughed at these admonitions, as I did myself. Certainly nobody paid much attention to them.

"Now I come to the point when this campaign reached its peak. Part of my duty was to write the leader column of the *Sunday Express*. One Saturday my leader was praised by the Editor, who had himself suggested to me the subject for the column. My leader was set up in print.

"Hours later, and by chance, I discovered that the Editor had secretly written another leader. This leader began with an account of how, when the Germans entered Paris, the door of a newspaper office had been opened to them by a disloyal employee. It discussed the subject of quislings and fifth columnists and ended with a demand that MRA whole-time workers should be conscripted into the army.

"This leader contained suggestions which I knew to be false. I told my Editor about them. The leader went out to 1,500,000 breakfast tables next morning just the same."

Pressure was brought to bear from other quarters. An Editor and a Cabinet Minister took Howard out to lunch and told him they had information that immediately America entered the war, Dr. Buchman, the founder of the Oxford Group and Moral Re-Armament, would be arrested. Howard asked them to produce their evidence. This they refused to do. "It comes from too high a source," they said.

Howard knew that President Roosevelt had supported MRA's programme in America, so he discounted his hosts' innuendos.

"I decided to write a book setting out the truth about MRA. I asked permission from the *Express* to publish this book. The answer I got was one which the *Express* was legally entitled to make — namely, that I could write a book on any other subject I chose, but not on the subject of MRA. If I wanted to write about that, I should have to leave the *Express*.

"It was a big decision to make. But there was that in me which said that publication of the truth about a great world movement was of more importance than the fate of one journalist, even a journalist so important to myself as me. So, with regret, I picked my hat off the peg and said *au revoir* to Fleet Street."

The decision which made Howard leave the *Express* was not taken by Lord Beaverbrook, who was by this time fully engaged building aircraft for the Battle of Britain, nor by E. J. Robertson, who was away ill, but by the Assistant General Manager, Leslie (Dick) Plummer[1], who had long opposed MRA. Years later, Lord Beaverbrook told Howard that he was troubled by what had happened. Afterwards he tried to get Howard back. He never succeeded. At the end of his life, Beaverbrook did not want to succeed. He recognised that Howard was meant for a different job.

Howard's departure from Fleet Street startled his friends. His arrival within the ranks of Moral Re-Armament startled everyone. He brought with him a hurricane personality which swept accepted concepts before him. If Fleet Street thought that Howard had lost his dynamism as soon as he stepped out of the *Express* buildings, they were wrong. He increased that quality until the day of his death. But immediately, he had to think of how to provide for his family:

"When I left the *Express* building for the last time, I clattered downstairs and out into the Fleet Street traffic. I had lived, slept, dreamed and breathed for my work. Now, I was out of a job. I walked to Liverpool Street Station and climbed into a railway carriage and travelled to Suffolk. For I meant to farm the land.

"Our farmer friends told us that it would take five years before Hill Farm could be made to pay. But at that time my salary from the *Express* came rolling in. Now suddenly our whole circumstances had altered. My job and salary had vanished overnight. I knew a little of the theory, but next to nothing of the practice of farming.

"There is a big difference between a man in a highly paid job in Fleet Street who owns a farm and has plenty of money to spend on it, and an ex-journalist with an old farm which is losing money fast and which is the only means of livelihood for himself and his wife and children.

"As I travelled eastwards towards Suffolk in the corner of my third-class carriage, I felt the prickle of fear. I was up against the timeless, ageless, endless problem of man — how to wrest a living from the stubborn womb of the earth. Would the land be my master or my servant? Would the old farm break me, or would I break it? I knew one of these two things had to happen."

[1] Later Sir Leslie Plummer, M.P. for Deptford.

Chapter 9

In the dawn days of Suffolk
When horses went to plough,
Their breath twin trumpets blowing
My shoulders did not bow
Beneath the load, as now.

We knew the sun must tumble
From summits in the sky,
That autumn follows summer,
That what is born must die.
We laughed — and asked not why.

The leaves are off the hedges.
The frost is on the wing.
The winds are blowing stronger.
We laugh, we leap, we sing,
Whatever seasons bring.

Come winter, come wild weather,
Come envy of the foe,
Or friendships smile and stabbing,
Unfaltering we go,
The victory ours, we know.

                    P.D.H. 1963

It was Spring, 1941, when Peter Howard stepped off the train at Lavenham Station to come home. As he passed through the village and along the Brent Eleigh road he could see the first pale green buds bursting in the hedges. Here a primrose, there a wild violet, and everywhere the earth beginning to move with life. After the second hump-backed bridge he turned right, up the farm drive. The road was rough and holed, with gaping puddles and loose stones.

At the crest of the hill, he saw the first dark shadows of the thatched barns and the house itself:

"There was an atmosphere of vanished glory about the place, a glory which had disappeared from so many British farms and holdings during a get-rich-quick age which despised and neglected agriculture, a glory which could be restored.

"The farmhouse had the shadow of old nobility about it, though many of the rooms were covered with layer upon layer of garish wallpaper, concealing the oaken beams beneath.

"That evening in our farmhouse, with the children put to bed upstairs in a bare room with oak beams, Doë and I camped in the unfurnished kitchen, cooking stew on a primus stove.

"In the old Fleet Street days, we often dined at the Savoy at midnight amid the lights and perfume, the paint and wine and music of a rich and artificial age.

"Now we spooned stew into our mouths, with an oil lamp stuck on a deal table as our companion, an inquisitive mouse stuck his nose through a cranny in the ancient farmhouse wall and peeped at us. I hit at him with a tablespoon and missed.

"We laughed together, Doë and I, and moved upstairs, gazing down by the light of the lamp on our three children drawing the soft, deep breaths in sleep. What would they say of the decision we had taken when they were old enough to understand it?

"We felt a tug of fear at the heart and a throb of resolve also. Before we went to bed that night we knelt and prayed to God for strength and courage."

The Howards were to need strength and courage. Innocent Men was published that April. It sold 155,000 copies, but Howard received no money for it. As with all his books and plays hereafter, he gave his royalties to Moral Re-Armament.

The Fleet Street reaction was a mixture of amazement, fury and a certain grudging admiration. Beaverbrook asked Michael Foot and Frank Owen down to Cherkley for dinner. He had a copy of Innocent Men there, and they read it that evening. Foot and Owen were angry about the title.

Foot telephoned Doë Howard in Suffolk and gave her a piece of his mind. It lasted twenty minutes, but Doë was too paralysed to put the phone down. Foot and Owen met Howard for lunch in a Fleet Street pub and suggested to him that in the spirit of "absolute unselfishness" he might not wish to take any more royalties from Guilty Men — a suggestion taken up by Philip Jordan in his column in the News Chronicle. Howard assured them that he preferred the original financial arrangement. It was his only income.

Cassandra[1] of the Daily Mirror, lamented the departure of "a gifted cuss with plenty of Adam", now turned into the "Reverend Howard

[1] Sir William Connor.

122

throwing his soul on the counter where it stinks like a codfish that's been too long out of salt water". But the writer of the full-page review in the *Sunday Pictorial* commented, "He is a courageous man. I admire him for it."

The general reaction in Fleet Street was much the same. "Peter Howard is off his nut. He's got no money of his own. Here he is — worked for years to establish himself in the *Express*. Beaverbrook looked on him as one of his brightest boys. He would certainly have got an executive job before long. And he throws it all up and goes out into the cold because of this MRA, whatever that may be."

Others were more unpleasant. They accused Howard of treachery not insanity. They said he was pacifist, Communist, Fascist and dishonest. These newspaper accusations disturbed his family. His parents, who had been so proud of him, were now ashamed of him. His mother wrote:

> Wealden Way,
> Little Common.
> April 1941

We are both deeply distressed over you and your affairs. We have a strong feeling that you are worried and things are not going well. The Buchmanites have absorbed you, but before you are entirely lost, can we do nothing to rescue you? At a stage in world affairs so dreadful, do not let pride or anything stand in your way. We would be only too glad to help you gain control of yourself, which you seem to us to have entirely lost.

This letter is written in real distress, which has been eating my heart out. Our dear love,

> Mum

The only member of his family who seemed to understand at all was his grandmother, Gracie:

> 53B, St. Anne's Crescent,
> Lewes.
> Sunday, April 20, 1941

Dearly loved Peter,

Thanks for your book. I have read it. I will re-read it with deepest interest.

The idea is no new idea, of God's guidance and help. Surely we could not have lived without it these past years. It is real, and most vital to us. Perhaps you have received a special call from God, and if so you must obey it, and go wherever He bids you. It has come to many in past years, and what a privilege to be chosen in this way.

I wish we could meet sometimes. Today we are in Spring sunshine, leading to hope that the summer may not be far off, and that it may bring victory and peace once more.

Ever in my thoughts are you,

Grannie

With few friends to turn to and no money, Howard had to make Hill Farm pay:

"Because I knew no better, sometimes I used to tell the men to plough when the weather made the land unfit to plough, or order them to roll the young corn when it would have harmed the crops for them to do it.

"They would look at each other when these orders were given, but were too polite to make any reply. They would go off to the fields, and return to me after half-an-hour or so with the comment, 'Can't work it today, master.'

"The hedges had crept out on to the land, ten and fifteen yards in some places.

"We skirted them and sat doggedly on our tractors, from dawn till dusk, cranking the heavy engines with cracked and blistered hands as the first glimmers of light shone through the darkness, switching from petrol to oil as the engine grew hot after a few minutes' work, and chugging steadily through the day, our bodies aching with fumes and vibration, chilled by the wind and mizzle of rain which blows in from the North Sea, but cheered by the even furrows of good earth laid in neat rows behind us, where the wilderness had been before.

"In the evenings we worked to restore the old glory of the farmhouse. Sixteen layers of bright wallpaper were stripped off one room before we came to what lay beneath — a copy of a newspaper, dated 1832 with an account of how a bull ran amok at Bury St. Edmunds and killed a dog before it was mastered, and the iron-hard beauty of the oak beams with the marks of the mattock still upon them.

"We uncovered an ancient chimney-piece, and found in the corner of it the sign of the master-builder which he had scratched with compasses on finishing the job centuries ago.

"Doë and I had to set our hands to tasks we have never done before. We planned and built our first new building, marking and measuring its foundation with sticks and string on the soaking meadow grass one dark morning. We sunk the corner posts, sloped the roof, sawed the beams and weather boarding, our unaccustomed hands and minds being perplexed and bruised at almost every small operation.

"How that building rose at all, I cannot think. But it still stands. We made so many mistakes, Doë and I. But we learned from each one of them.

"We quickly learned the bitter lesson of the handsome cow, with shiny hide and swelling udders, which proudly faces the dealers and the auctioneers at the local market. You take it home – and a few days later discover why such a fine-looking animal was for sale.

"We planned to increase our herd of cows so they should fertilize the hungry fields, which had smelt little muck for a decade and were hilly and awkward to plough.

"We chopped and hacked and sawed down the jungle growth of a quarter of a century. We burned it up behind us, and the charcoal dust from the fires stuck in the sweat on our brows and hands.

"Steam engines came and broke up with deep cultivations the hard pan of clay, which years of shallow ploughing to the same depth had left beneath the surface of many of our fields.

"So many memories of those early days of our farming adventure come crowding in upon me – and most of them are of Doë.

"She had lived all her life in cities. Her clothes and hats often came from Paris, which was the European capital she knew best. Her hair was curled and cosseted, her nails a delicate and almost human shade of pink.

"She dreaded life in the country. She was afraid it would turn her into a vegetable.

"Life on the farm drew forth from its scabbard, where Fleet Street life had laid it, all the shining, unconquerable steel of Doë's spirit.

"I see her now, sweat dripping off her brow on to the baking summer earth, hoeing, hoeing, hoeing until the time came for her to prepare the evening meal.

"I see her in an old mackintosh, with a sack tied round her head and shoulders, her body bent forward like an arrow against the horizontal December rain, rescuing hens from the swamped hencoops and bringing home a handful of eggs triumphantly for our winter meal.

"I see her standing upright with one hand rubbing her aching back and the other sweeping away the hair which had fallen into her eyes.

"Best I remember her in the evenings, when the day's work was done, when new difficulties had to be faced and planned, when sometimes it seemed hard to continue, to know whether we should pull through, when the temptation was to sell the place at a profit, which we could have done, and to get clear.

"Doë never faltered. She saw steady, cool and straight from the beginning. She had the dauntlessness of heart and the confidence in God which makes it hard for others to keep secret their fears or to maintain them.

"Today Doë's hands are chipped, chapped and stained. Yet they are lovelier to me than in the days of expensive and fragrant manicures in the West End of London – lovelier in the sense of more to be beloved. For they are the hands of a mature spirit which has stood full stature through the grey days. She has fought and triumphed in the battle of adversity."

In that battle everyone took part. Philip, Anne and Anthony would lie in bed at night and listen to the steady scrape, scrape, scrape of a knife below, peeling the last piece of plaster off the oak beams. But in the mornings, or the hot summer afternoons, they would be out pulling thistles and charlock from the growing crops.

At first there were few helpers. There was Fuller, the farm manager, Fred, the horseman, and Tommy Beeton. Tommy had come up the hill on his bicycle and asked Peter Howard for work. Howard told him that he planned to run the place on the basis of absolute honesty between boss and worker. Tommy took the job. A few weeks later, he came to Howard and returned rope and other material he had taken. What he could not return, he offered to pay for out of his wages. Howard accepted. It was the beginning of a lifelong friendship:

"Tom's face and arms are tanned by the sun, washed by the rain and hardened by the wind of many seasons. He cannot write or spell as well as a schoolmaster, but he understands the living heart-beat of the earth, the nurturing of animals from conception, through maturity to market, to breeding and to death, the rhythm of every field from ploughing and seeding to harvest. He is accustomed to balance the sudden disaster of a day against the steady pattern of years and of centuries. In ways unknown to himself, he has part of the wisdom of God as instinct in his bones.

"Those hands of his are chunky and strong with the warm wooden feel of the bark of trees in sunshine as you grip them. They are able to snatch a great weight and lift it upon his shoulders, and to weave straw delicately together in a thatch even if the strong winds blow, to perform operations upon pigs and other animals swiftly, painlessly with his penknife, without mistakes and without anaesthetic, or to mend many kinds of red-hot machinery in open fields, may be in winter time and often alone."

From Tom, Howard learnt the secrets of the land. This was more valuable to him than any agricultural college. It taught him not just what to do, but when to do it. Gradually, Howard began to make his way. "Old Man Thorpe"[1] from Lavenham Park would send over two men and a load of turnips: "That young man is sure to be in trouble. You get over there and help him out," he would say. The generosity was great. No one said very much, but they all knew that Howard was up against it. They understood the worry and the work which would decide the future of Hill Farm.

In the summer of 1941, it was not easy to imagine how the war would end. In Suffolk, many supposed that the Germans would invade. All the signposts were removed. You could not ask your way in East Anglia, even if you were well known. Nobody was saying anything. The Home Guard had great support in Lavenham and Howard was a member of it.

[1] Mr. W. E. Thorpe, a farming neighbour.

Dr. Frank Buchman and
Peter Howard in
America, 1960

The Hon. John F.
Powers, His Eminence
Cardinal Cushing and
Peter Howard in
Boston, Massachusetts,
1964

Peter and Doë
Howard, Tokyo
1963

Howard and
Rajmohan Gan
summer, 1964

"We expected the Nazis to attempt an invasion. Men, women and children, all of us, meant to fight. Yet we had nothing to fight with. In our part of Suffolk we had seven rifles and 120 rounds of ammunition to defend a front of eleven miles long and four miles deep.

"Each night as Doë and I tucked the children into bed they would say, 'Mummy, Daddy, are the Germans coming over now?' We would look at each other over their heads and make some joke as an answer.

"Every evening after the day's work men and women met together all over the Eastern Counties and concocted home-made bombs out of tar, gas and cotton-wool. We had to light the cotton-wool with a match and then throw the contrivance underneath an advancing tank in the hopes that it would catch fire.

"We dug trenches and hiding places in the undergrowth beside all roads leading from the coast, so the Nazis would not see us before we hurled our home-made bombs at them.

"We arranged meeting places in the woods if our countryside was overrun.

"We hid food in places where the Germans could not find it.

"We planned to set fire to our haystacks and burn everything of use to the enemy in the line of his advance.

"All night long we kept watch on the church towers, at cross-roads and at every important point in case the Nazis began to drop on us from the skies by parachute."

The Home Guard often made Hill Farm the base of their operations. It was not unusual for the children to see a soldier emerge from a milk churn in the cowshed, "Ssh, I am a British soldier," or from a haystack with straw all over his face, "I am a German," which sent them running in terror to the house.

There was only one machine gun on a firing range outside Lavenham. It was here that the Home Guard would assemble for firing practice. Many of them were teenage boys, longing to "have a go". Howard and Pryke[1] were responsible for the targets. On a summer evening, when firing had stopped, they went to remove the targets. Suddenly the machine gun behind them opened up with a barrage of bullets. Pryke and Howard fell flat on their faces. The bullets missed them by inches. They heard the sergeant bellowing at the young boy on the gun, "What on earth are you doing?" "But you said I could have a go," the boy replied. "I said next week," the sergeant roared. Mistakes of this kind were all too common.

During the war the men and women of Moral Re-Armament entered the Forces. Only eleven men remained to keep the organisation going in Britain. These were classed as "lay evangelists" and were as such exempt

[1] Lt. Reg Pryke of Lavenham.

from military service. Mr. Ernest Brown, the then Minister of Labour, had created this category for all non-ordained religious workers because of the value he placed on their service to the nation.

After Mr. Bevin became Minister of Labour in 1940 he announced that he was going to call up the MRA men. This meant he would treat Moral Re-Armament differently from any other Christian body. The Archbishops of Canterbury and York, and the heads of all the Free Churches protested, but Mr. Bevin stuck to his opinion. The resulting "battle of the eleven men" was one in which Howard was immediately involved. He left the farm in Doë's complete care at a critical moment and went to London. For Doë the responsibility was enormous. She had no experience of farming, nor much of England.

P.D.H. to Doë   4, Hay's Mews,
                                                 London, W.1
                                                 August 1941

So far almost forty M.P.s are committed to our cause. The number grows each day. There is no doubt at all, whatever the result of the immediate issue, that a steady and substantial advance is being made in almost every part of the country.

Whether it is right or wrong, but certainly it is true, I often find myself missing you with real pain. At least it is joyful to be so deeply in love after so many years of marriage with many more to come. You have my heart and I live with you in thought and spirit, even though just now we are separated by distance.

The wireless said this morning that farmers could apply for harvest help to the local military commander. You would be the best person to do this, I think.

P.D.H. to Doë   London, W.1
                                                 August 1941

A farm is one of the very few undertakings in which a man and wife can have full partnership. Unlike almost any other enterprise, you and I can work as a team there on every decision and every operation on the place. Someone has to work out the new philosophy for the land, putting in rather than getting out. Service first and perfection in every detail.

I also feel, beloved Doë, for the first time that we have some great task which we can learn together from the beginning — the apparatus and knowledge needed to farm the land, how much wheat per acre to drill, how to manage the milking in perfection from beginning to end, etc. It will be great fun and for once we shall really be marching in step in equality on the same mission.

P.D.H. to Doë   London W.1
                                                     August 1941

The farm loss in our first year was £1,200. I had reckoned on £1,000.
The effect is that our debt to the income tax people of £500 is almost
exactly wiped out. Into the lays goes the £316 we spent on seed last year
and on which we are getting the benefit in this year's harvest. Clemetson[1]
reckoned we lost nearly £600 on livestock last year.

My expectation is that we shall get results this year.

In fact, the losses on the farm increased steadily. It was only in 1943
that the first returns began to come in.

P.D.H. to Doë   London, W.1
                                                  September 10, 1941

Thanks for your letters which greatly strengthen and encourage me.

I am sorry if you had the impression that I was worried about money.
I am now satisfied that by careful management we can live on the farm
profits. But, of course, we must be prudent. In any event, I will try and
earn something this winter by writing.

On Tuesday, October 7, 1941, Mr. Bevin took part in a two-and-a-half
hour debate in the House of Commons on the issue of the "eleven men".
One hundred and seventy-four Members of Parliament had signed a
motion supporting MRA. The debate was grave, passionate and, in some
cases, venomous. But Mr. Bevin had told the Cabinet that if he was
defeated, he would resign. The Whips were on the doors and Mr. Bevin
got his way. In the debate Mr. Bevin accused the "eleven men" of being
conscientious objectors as opposed to "lay evangelists". He said he
regarded the public protest on their behalf as "undemocratic pressure".

P.D.H. to Doë   London, W.1
                                                   October 8, 1941

I am enclosing a verbatim account of what went on in Parliament
yesterday. It is exactly as *The Times* carried the story this morning.

Of course, Bevin's line on the affair opens up an issue far wider than
that of the eleven men, calling into question as it does the whole work –
past, present and future. It is the most serious attack ever delivered upon
us. Yet, in a sense, it is an attack which in the minds of fair-minded
people can be easily defeated. For the work is known to multitudes of
people the world over. And while some may dislike the manner or
method, none would question that it is religious work on the deepest
spiritual level.

It is a grave thing when a British Minister expresses a view in public

[1] Howard's accountant.

129

which is recognised by millions to be based on misinformation. It is the more grave because it touches so many people like myself who owe their faith to a contact with MRA near the nerve of the heart. And we cannot ever be easy in our minds again until that judgment is reversed and in as public a fashion as it was delivered.

P.D.H. to Doë   London, W.1
                                                                   October 1941

Yesterday the Free Church Federal Council passed a unanimous and strong resolution in our favour. This body represents about four million people. An action of this kind now taken is bound to have an effect.

On the other hand, a letter has been received from the head of the Ministry dealing with this matter by one of our friends cast in terms of such obduracy and rigidity that it seems plain nothing but heavy pressure will divert him.

The Press had given wide coverage to this controversy. Much space had been given to Bevin and the critics of the "eleven men", but scarcely any to their opponents. At the time, Howard had replied to these criticisms, but his articles were never published. So he began to write a book which dealt with the issue in detail. It was eventually called, *Fighters Ever*, and sold over 330,000 copies. It was published in November 1941.

P.D.H. to Doë   October 1941

The book is going well I believe. It is hard and difficult work, yet on the whole the production is more mature and certainly as interesting as *Innocent Men*. As soon as it is in transportable form you will have to read it through and give me your advice and comments on it – 28,000 words which is just over half the size of *Innocent Men* and it will sell at 6d. At one point we thought it might be called *Dangerous Men*, but then that has been discarded, and the best to date I think is *Our Defence is Sure*.

One day together, you and I, will write a book. We will work on it in the evening time by lamp or Calor gaslight. We will take time over it and it will be a polished, vigorous and warming document.

David Robertson, M.P. for Streatham, rang me up out of the blue yesterday. It was simply to say that he had wanted to speak for us but couldn't catch the Speaker's eye. He was sad the thing had gone the way it had, and that Bevin had made the fundamental and fatal mistake of failing to understand how deeply many people felt on the matter.

My own feeling about the men in Parliament is that while a few weaker brethren have been puffed away by the hot air, most of our supporters have been consolidated by events. It is an odd thing to say, but the feeling I have is that we gained a victory last week, or whenever it was (I have lost sense of time these last days). I suppose the Apostles must have found it hard to see the Crucifixion as a victory. Yet it was so. In the same way, out of what humanly was a rejection by men, I feel advances may come as a result of the rough ride in the House of Commons.

Howard returned to his farm in Suffolk. Eight land girls arrived to help with the farm work. They lived in the house and became, through those later years of the war, part of the Howard family. Some of them lost their brothers, fathers or friends during those months. The work was arduous even for men on the Suffolk boulder clay soil, but for women it was desperately heavy. They became strong and weather-worn. The farmhouse swelled to cope with the extra numbers. In spite of the crush, the house never lost the sense of home or welcome which Peter and Doë Howard created.

The farm men who came early to milk would get their breakfast before they went home. Howard shouldered the burden himself. He would rise early, at three or four o'clock in the morning. If he wanted a job done, he would always be there half-an-hour before time himself, and only leave when the others had gone home. In the early morning darkness you could see him, a massive shadow, striding round the buildings seeing that all was well.

Later in his life, when he was rarely at home, he would offer to do a weekend feeding in order to give his men time off. It brought back to him the memory of those first struggling years when it looked as if he would never make ends meet. He found peace and direction among his beasts.

At the end of December 1941, a new development took place in wartime Suffolk:

"All the able-bodied men were called to the village hall. On the floor were large wooden boxes. From them each one of us was handed a rifle and twenty rounds of ammunition. For the first time since Dunkirk we felt we had something to hit back with if the Nazis came. Our hearts sang a new song. It is a feeling I shall remember all my days.

"These rifles were the first weapons to reach the Eastern Counties from the USA. It was as if a friend had suddenly put a weapon in our hands at a time when our backs were to the wall and we had nothing but faith left us."

In February 1942, seven American officers arrived in England to prepare for the coming of the Eighth Air Force. They built many of their aerodromes in East Anglia:

"Many of them were placed on the finest farming land in Britain. Parts of the Eastern counties of England grow heavier crops per acre than any other land in the world. And the surveyors sent by the Air Ministry to pick the bases chose land which was as level as possible. But the level land is the best farming land, easiest to cultivate with horse and tractor, and the best farmers occupy it.

"Farmers whose families had owned and farmed the same land for many generations found themselves suddenly dispossessed. They had to wait as long as three or four years for compensation from the Government, and when it came it was far below the market value of their holdings. But there was no complaint.

"Soon acres of concrete lay where the acres of corn had stretched before. As dusk fell, we used to drive round the deserted perimeter tracks in a car with sporting guns pointing out of the windows and shoot at the partridges as they came home to rest.

"The first American arrivals stared at us in amazement, as, looking like a load of gangsters, we rolled by in the gloaming.

"Few of us in East Anglia had been to the United States. But the United States came to us. We saw them come in our hour of desperate need — young men in tens of thousands, nonchalant, gay, confident and courageous."

For the children of East Anglia the peril of those months were barely understood. Instead, the excitement of the convoys of American servicemen, from whom with a shout of "Any gum chum?" you could get the odd packet of chewing gum, seemed far more important. The Christmas parties, the first any war baby had ever experienced, were given on the American air bases. Peter Howard's three children were among those who were fortunate enough to go:

"There was a huge tree, decorations, games, a present for each guest, any amount of candy, which the men at the base had saved specially from their rations, and above all large quantities of ice cream.

"When the jeeps and trucks came back to the villages in the darkness, the children tumbled out of them with their eyes shining like stars and their cheeks red as holly-berries with excitement. 'Look what our American uncles gave me. Oh, Mummy, it was wonderful.'"

For Philip, Anne and Anthony Howard, like all those children, it was hard to imagine that the great bombers that droned overhead towards Germany were full of those young Americans who had treated them the night before, some of whom would never return. The children would climb on to the great straw stacks in the stackyard and lie there counting the planes as they flew eastwards. Then when they heard the sound of the returning bombers, they would rush back to their straw hideout and count those which returned. Often there were crippled planes, with a wing broken or an engine cut — always there were some missing. It was with a heaviness and unexplained sadness that they would gallop home in the dusk.

Some of Peter Howard's friends urged him to send his children to the safety of Canada or the United States along with thousands now going there. This he refused to do. The issue had been decided for him in the first week after meeting MRA. At that time newspaper friends had offered to provide money for his family to cross the Atlantic. He had decided to let them stay where they were. Other people in his village were not able to get away. He had felt it was up to him to set an example. He still felt the same.

At the height of the blitz on London, the East Anglian night was filled with battles in the sky. Then came the bomber raids, with bombs and landmines tossed out of escaping planes on to an unsuspecting country-side. A landmine was dropped one hundred yards from the farmhouse and knocked out every window, but the old Tudor building just shuddered and shook and settled back again. Finally, there were the VIs, "Doodle-bugs or buzz-bombs", with their flashing lights and high-pitched whine. Sometimes the engines cut out before reaching London and they would drop silently through the darkness. More often they would stop and start again. In that eternal pause, the children would lie in bed motionless with fingers in their ears. Anthony Howard was the philosopher on these occasions, "It's no use crying now," he'd say. "It's gone bang and we're safe."

Howard did not avoid difficulty himself and he did not want his children to do so. There was in him a passion to face the reality of the fear, the poor food, the lack of hot water. He would invent magical names for some unattractive dish and so get his children to eat it. He sent them off to the Lavenham school each day in pony and trap, and they returned that way whatever the weather, often bringing a friend with them to add to the numbers already round the dining room table. The children washed and dried the dishes for fifteen after the meal and put them away before games were allowed. The discipline brought occasional grumbles but no regrets.

There was a gaiety about the house coupled with quietness. Howard enjoyed good fun, but intensely disliked loud noise, the banging of doors, the shudder of running feet in the house, or high-pitched laughter. If he heard it, he would march towards the culprit and give them a piece of his mind. The next morning he would mention it again, and it did not often happen twice.

Having been so unpunctual himself as a young man, he became extremely punctual. No meal was served until everyone was present. Those who were late incurred the wrath and indignation of the hungry. Howard himself was out of his working clothes and on time for every meal. The same applied to his appointments or wartime duties.

Yet those years, with all the shadows of war, brought with them much joy. The farm work was heavy; the loss on the farm in the first two years was £2,615, but he never showed his anxiety or worry to his children. He was a wonderful father. After work he would organise exhilarating games — "leopard hunts", "kick the can", "hide and seek". The energy with which these games were played was total. Howard did not believe in "playing to lose" for the sake of the children. He insisted that everyone must play to win, and they did. He must have been exhausted, but he never showed it. In racing competitions, he would hop on his good leg, while the children ran beside him. He was an expert in the art of hopping and could cover almost eight feet at a time. He could still win a hopping race with his children until they were in their teens.

On the long winter evenings he would invent and tell fascinating animal stories. The characters were all well-known on the farm. Later, when his children went away to boarding school, he would write these stories in instalments each week. And later still, he used them to write a pantomime for his grandchildren.

He combined being a strict disciplinarian with an unusual depth of understanding. He was easy to talk to, and yet he could walk for miles across the fields with you and say nothing. His love of the countryside was enormous, but he no longer wanted to escape into it:

"When I bought it the farm was graded 'C'. That is the lowest grade of farm in my neighbourhood — the grade at which farms are taken away from farmers and managed in the national interest by the War Executive Committee. But as I was a new man, they gave me a chance. They waited to see what I could do.

"One day some gentlemen drove up to our farmhouse door in a car. They were members of the War Executive Committee and had come to inspect our land. We walked together from field to field in silence. Sometimes they asked me questions about the cropping of the fields and made notes in a little book. Then they shook my hand and departed. A month later I received the following letter:

"Dear Sir,

"The Executive Committee, on the advice of the appropriate District Committee, are very pleased to raise the classification of your farm to 'A', and to express their appreciation at your efforts in bringing about this result.

Yours faithfully,
(Signed)
Executive Officer.

"Grade 'A' is the highest grade obtainable in this district. Doë and I looked at each other across the table. Well, we had done it. We knew that whatever became of us in the future, whether we lived on the land or in the cities, rich or poor, sick or well, things would never be quite the same for us again."

The experience Howard gained through this battle and eventual victory over the land was invaluable. It made him able for the rest of his life to give accurate and competent instructions to his men, often from a distance of several thousand miles.

In 1965, the year Howard died, the farm profits had risen to over £6,000. And two years later they had reached over £9,000. In 1943, Howard's main interest was that he could provide more food for Britain at a time when she desperately needed it:

"This piece of earth has wrestled with many generations before I came on the scene, and it will strive with many more after I have departed. It knows no rest, and those who serve it cannot afford to pause in their toil."

During the war years, hundreds of people visited Hill Farm. Some of them had read Howard's books. All had heard that there was a unique spirit on the place, and many of them caught that spirit.

The arrival of German prisoners-of-war to work on the farms in Britain created little stir. Countrymen are traditionally reticent. For the Howard children it was frightening. They had heard that the Germans were "enemies". And now they were coming to Hill Farm. When Rüdi and Willi were dropped off the truck at the bottom of the farm drive that first morning, they must have found those three small pairs of dark eyes which stared at them alarming. They worked silently and perfectly. On instructions from the prison commander, they were to be given no food, nor taken into the house. They spoke little English, and automatically thought nobody would want to talk to them. Instead, Howard set out to make friends of them both. It took many months. Howard wrote and asked permission to give them both a hot meal each day. It was granted. Willi and Rüdi were in need of food. They ate hungrily.

Sometimes on a spring morning while Willi and Rüdi were hoeing the long rows of sugar beet, the children would go and watch them. Suddenly the men would hear the sound of a German aircraft. They recognised it before anyone else did, for they were airmen. Swiftly, they would turn and grab Anne under one arm and Anthony under the other. "*Schnell, schnell*," they said and ran for the ditch. "Quiet," they would say. The children would sit motionless while the black shadow passed over the field. Then in wild relief, they would run laughing back to the job, while Willi and Rüdi followed shaking their heads and smiling. The irony of it escaped the children. But Howard was grateful.

On September 17, 1944, Peter Howard's only brother, John, was one of those in the Paratroop regiment who left for Arnhem:

"One autumn morning I trod my way to work along a secret, scented hedgerow path beaten into hardness by the clump, clump, clump, of generations of agricultural boots against the soil.

"I took my four-pronged fork and began to shovel black moist muck from the cattle yard into the tumbrils.

"I did not sing at my work that morning. As my back began to ache in the rhythm of the toil, my heart ached too with a sense of apprehension and foreboding. For overhead, hour upon hour, in steady formation, the tugs and gliders flew east towards Arnhem. In one of them was my young and only brother.

"I wondered whether John would look out upon the farm as he passed by. He knew the place and loved it. He had shot partridges there and tramped the fields with me. Only a few weeks before he had written asking if he could come and work there when the war was over.

"So gay and brave I pictured him, as I straightened my aching back in the cattle yard, and, resting on my fork, strained my eyes to watch the airborne cavalcade ride by.

"His eyes were green-blue and his hair was golden. All through the war he fought — a private in the artillery, commando raids on the Channel Isles and Lofoten, a commission to the Royal Sussex Regiment, wounded at Alamein, now a captain in the Airborne Division on his way to Arnhem. 'It will take more than a Nazi to get me,' he said last time I saw him.

"John never came back from Arnhem. Most of his company were killed. They were at the flash-point of the fighting. John was raged at the death of his friends. He was last seen by a British scout two miles outside our perimeter, hiding by himself in a ditch and sniping at the enemy. The scout asked him whether he would not return to the perimeter. 'I'm doing very well where I am, thank you,' answered John. So the scout gave him a few biscuits and a hunk of cheese and left him alone in his ditch with the enemy all around him.

"Hard it is to believe that someone so young and vehement can be so quiet and still. Many of us in so many lands today have simple and cherished recollections like this, pearls of great price threaded on the everlasting string of memory, about someone we have loved and lost awhile.

"To me the worst pain of such a parting is the thought of how differently I should have acted if we could have our times together again. If only I had not said that . . . If only I had not done this . . . If only . . . I loved the boy so much and often showed it him so badly."

Howard's sorrow at the loss of his brother was shared by Willi and

Rüdi. It was hard for them to say what they felt. But they did so in halting English, "We are sorry."

By the end of 1944, Willi and Rüdi had become a part of the family. It was a firm friendship. The war mercifully seemed to be drawing to its close. It looked as if German prisoners might soon be returning home. Howard wrote to the War Office and asked if Willi and Rüdi could be invited to spend Christmas Day at Hill Farm. It was an unprecedented request. After long delays the permission was granted.

For the Howard family it was the last Christmas they would celebrate together for two years. The preparations were exciting. Warm balaclavas and socks were knitted for Willi and Rüdi, the tree was decorated with red apples in the German style, and the children learnt the words of *Stille Nacht* (Silent Night). All the farm men and their wives were invited in, and the land girls came, the neighbours and all those whom the Howards had known during the war years.

The amazement on Willi and Rüdi's faces as they stepped into that warm farm drawing room was always to be remembered. It was hard for them to believe it was not some dream, as they sat awkwardly at table eating off china and silver, which they had long since forgotten. After dinner they sat by the tree and wrote their first letters home to their families in East Germany. Then they unwrapped their gifts, and listened to the carols. Slowly they began to sing in German. It was the first time the children had seen grown men weep.

Willi and Rüdi left Britain soon afterwards. They wrote twice when they got home, and then no more. But they told their friends, "There is a farm in England which is different from any other we know. It is the first time we have not felt like prisoners."

.   .   .

In May 1945 came V.E. Day, and in July the General Election in which Winston Churchill was defeated and a Labour Government came to power. Peter Howard had voted for Churchill. Had John Howard been alive he would have voted for Attlee:

"John set his political hopes for the future on Labour. And he told me why. He used to say to me something like this: 'At least I know what the Labour Party stand for. They stand for a square deal for you and me, with food, a house and a job for all who will do it. They stand for everybody having an equal chance and for more even distribution of the wealth of the world — not cigars at the Ritz and starvation at the Rhondda, not duck at the Berkeley and dole at Barrow. Whether they'll be able to give it to us, I don't know.'

"Then I remember he once said rather wistfully as he puffed at a pipe several sizes too large for him, 'There was a wonderful spirit out in the desert with the Eighth Army, you know. You felt a real comradeship in arms. That's the spirit we want when the war is over — but I suppose it is impossible in peace time.'

"Now Labour is in power in Britain, the party on which John's political hopes were set. That party, as the party in power, carries with it the dreams and hearts not only of the Johns who died for liberty in foreign seas and lands and skies, but also the Toms and Dicks and Harrys of every shade of political conviction who return home to build the new world we're wanting.

"A measure of cynicism is widespread among the British people, the belief that wars are perhaps inevitable, that we can never win the kind of world we long for our children to enjoy, that mankind is caught like some dumb beast in a trap, condemned for ever to endure a measure of uncertainty and despair.

"I do not accept this policy of defeat. I believe that British Labour has today one of the most golden chances ever entrusted to a party by the masses of the people, glittering opportunity at a time when the difficulties and dangers are as dark as ever before in our long history. But I do not think the fact that Labour is in power is by itself sufficient to usher in the millennium.

"No. Labour governs us — but what idea will govern Labour? Will it be Labour led by God to remake the world, or Labour led by the nose to remake the mess?"

In 1945, Peter Howard published two books. The first, Ideas Have Legs, had been written and polished and rewritten over the years at the farm, and was an immediate and lasting success. Countless people all over the world owed a new start in life to that book. The other book was, Men on Trial, a collection of portraits of political leaders as they faced the peace.

Howard finished Men on Trial in September, just in time to leave on his first journey to America. He went to encounter a man he had not yet met, but who had already affected his life more than any other human being. The man's name was Frank Buchman.

Chapter 10

THE AUTUMN of 1945 meant reunion for many thousands of families. For Peter Howard it was the beginning of twenty years' work, out of which he was to spend no more than a few months at home with his wife and family. This was not from choice. He hated leaving them. But it was his commitment. He would say, "My life is not my own." From henceforth his time and energies were given unceasingly to other people.

Howard set off for America with three friends — George Light, the Chairman of the National Trades Union Club; Roland Wilson, the Secretary of Moral Re-Armament in Britain, and Andrew Strang. They sailed from Fowey aboard the Liberty ship *David B. Johnstone*, which was carrying some thirty passengers and a cargo of china clay to Portland, Maine. Doë went down to Cornwall to see her husband off. For Doë the parting was costly. Conditions in Britain after the war were difficult. Most families at last had their menfolk coming home to help them. Doë had three children, and a farm to run on her own. Peter Howard was to write to her almost every day.

P.D.H. to Doë   Aboard ship
                                              September 1945

The sea is 2,000 fathoms deep beneath me as I write to you. It is easy to talk of 3,000 miles of ocean but hard to comprehend the vastness of it until you sail across it day after day. Birds have followed us all the way across from Fowey.

We sail on a route called the Great Circle which, on account of the roundness of the earth, is 130 miles quicker than a direct point to point route. We had quite a rough day and had to change course twice as the ship began to roll so badly.

The Captain still talks of you and thinks you are wonderful. So, of course, do I. No need to tell you how constantly I think of you. I live out each hour with you and am able to imagine the farmhouse sounds and sights and smells through every day. I shut my eyes and expect to see you walking across the deck towards me any moment.

My home is an infinitely precious place, and you have built such a wonderful one. Believe me, it warms your heart and makes you feel a part of it however far you wander.

It is a wonderful gift of God that with all the pain of parting you can be closer to those you love across 3,000 miles of ocean than many who sit at the same fireside together.

On this ship, of twenty-one soldiers returning home from the European sphere, five are going back to divorce their wives. Each night the purser comes to the cabin for drugs as it is his job to inject and dose the V.D. cases aboard. Judging by appearances there are quite a number of these. One man has been overseas for four years and two months and is returning with $1.30 in his pocket. All are computing the future in cash terms. They think of everything in terms of the dollar. Yet with all that they are most likable, young, vigorous and independent.

The casualty list of life lost has been lighter for the democracies in this war than the one before. But the moral toll has been infinitely heavier. Many millions no longer think wrong is wrong.

The Labour Party rose from love not hate. Its true battleline is love against hate, brotherhood against bitterness, God's plan against man's intellectualism, God-control against class control. Without change nothing will alter, except the pace with which problems multiply themselves and divide mankind. MRA stands for more rapid action, men radically altered and more resolute attack.

I think we will have to face the fact that in spite of kicking over dictator powers in the war of arms, democracy itself is in decline. There is less true democracy in the world today than at any time in the last hundred years. In war, Parliament was able to take swift, cogent, united decisions because danger was such that individuals and parties sank their self-interest. But peace has extinguished the spark of selflessness which danger kindled.

It is interesting how all would-be dictators offer to trade men's personal liberty for material well-being. This spirit of greed is fatal for democracy and the dictators know it and use it. Democracy is a way of life. It breaks down if there is anywhere a strong sectional selfishness endeavouring to better itself at the expense of the whole. When material well-being becomes the first aim of many hearts, liberty is all but lost.

The aim of Labour was power. Power is all that Labour has so far achieved. The Labour Government will stand or fall on whether or not they create a new moral climate in Britain.

The opposite to Moral Re-Armament is demoralisation. And demoralisation is hurrying on the march through Europe and the world. Nations will go down more swiftly before the march of demoralisation than they did before the march of armies. MRA is not just the difference between nice and nasty. It is the difference between life and death.

I am thankful for you, Doë. Your heart and home stretch across the world.

Well, we are very near to landing, so I must soon close this letter. Remember my parents and Pamela around September 17, the Arnhem anniversary.

.   .   .

Howard arrived in America on September 16, 1945. He went first to Mackinac Island in Michigan to meet Dr. Frank Buchman.

The meeting between Buchman and Howard was a surprising one. The two men were so utterly different in age, in background and in outlook. Buchman expected to find in Howard a young, brash Fleet Street journalist. He found a quality and depth he had not expected. Howard expected to find in Buchman a serious and sick elderly man, for Buchman was sixty-seven and two years earlier had suffered a stroke which had left its physical mark. Instead he found a wit, energy and reality that amazed him. Buchman put Howard to work at once. He stayed in Mackinac only a few days. During the six months he spent in America and Canada, he travelled to over twenty of the major cities.

P.D.H. to Doë   Montreal
                                                     September 1945

I have literally not had a moment to myself until now, since we arrived. It has been a wonderful time but the hardest work I ever did.

This land is one of amazing plenty. It flows with milk and honey. The second-rate provincial hotel puts on meals and service which you could not find anywhere in London today.

Portland, Maine, where we landed is rocky. They call it the rock-bound coast of Maine. Paradoxically, having listened to somewhat eulogistic accounts by the members of the crew on the topic of American weather, we were at anchor outside the harbour for a considerable time on account of fog.

It was fun sitting up all night in the train on the way to New York. We travelled through New England. All the names there were English names. Imagine how my heart went when we got to Haverhill, and I heard the porter singing out the name in the genuine East Anglian pronunciation. The carriage we sat in was almost exactly the same as the saloon carriages from Liverpool Street — only air conditioned and with hot water, towels and soap in the wash place which was a help. It is a little thing like this which makes so forcible an impression upon you as you first hit America.

New York is steely, stupendous and diabolic. The climate both there and in Washington is something you cannot imagine — steamy heat so that you wake up sweating and stay that way through the daylight hours. Most of the buildings are air-conditioned.

The top of the Empire State Building is like balancing at the pinnacle of the tallest tooth of all in the midst of some vast, open steamy mouth. There you understand the strength of Christ's temptation. All the cities of the world spread under your feet; the *Queen Mary* in dock looking like a little toy steamer; buildings two or three times higher than Nelson's column, like wee puny lamp-posts in the streets beneath; cars like a procession of disciplined ants moving and stopping in crannies of the dust, which are streets far wider than Whitehall. 'All the cities of the world for you if you will cast yourself down and worship me,' said Satan. In a sense, New York has done this. Wealth unimaginable but a metallic quality even about the architecture and about the faces of the citizens — drive, thrust, clash, cash. Above all cash. For those who want to worship mammon New York is their Mecca. It is the atom bomb of humanity. Its drive, energy, strength is colossal, almost unbelievable. In a way right now it is like a nightmare come true. But it could be a power-house to make the dreams of humanity come true.

The American people are wonderful — direct, vital, friendly. There is no nonsense about them and an intense shrewdness coupled with a most diverting ingeniousness.

I am sending a few gifts for the children. I suggest the conjuring set for Philip's birthday, crayons for Anne's birthday, and the Swiss bag and flag-building sticks as immediate gifts for Anne and Ant. I will be thinking of them.

P.D.H. to Doë   Washington D.C.
                                                  October 1945

Washington you will love when you see it. It is amazingly like Paris with its broad and beautiful boulevards and old white Georgian homes set back and widely spaced.

Canada is a different land, an astonishing land — limitless tracks of it still unexplored or at least unexploited. Eleven million people living in a land capable of supporting 250 million. Miles of virgin forest painted in great strips of ochre and red and gold by the frost from the autumn.

When you are away from your country you begin to love it and the people in it far more than you ever did before.

P.D.H. to Doë   Mackinac Island
                                                  October 8, 1945

I am in bed late at night sitting with the pad on my knee and my little light shining, snatching a chance to send you a word with a Frenchman who flies across on Thursday.

Typical of Buchman is that with 400 folk here on Saturday afternoon, and a group of people who may have to decide about the whole future, and with no clear ideas from anybody what to do with them, he said, "Peter, take the meeting." And turning to me briskly, "Everything depends

Howard and his
eldest son,
Philip, in Kenya,
1955

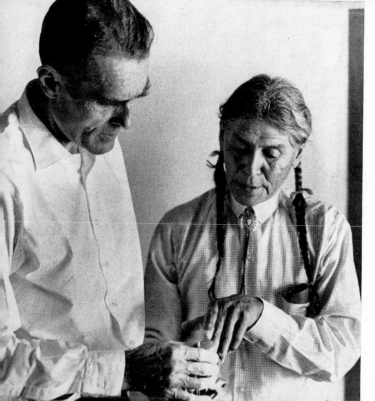

Howard meets
with American
Indian chief and
his people, New
Mexico, 1964

Howard addresses dock workers in the port of Rio de Janeiro, January, 1965

on how you handle it." Then he walked off. It was the first time I had been left with the whole baby on my lap for two hours on end.

This coming Saturday we have a big occasion at Grand Rapids. I am due to speak to 3,000 people in the City Hall. I am feeling tired for it is a pretty hectic programme.

Bless you and the children and all the family. I miss you a lot, as you know, every day.

P.D.H. to Doë   Mackinac Island
                                                       October 11, 1945

Buchman never wastes time tempering the wind to the shorn lamb. It does not interest him. His comments sometimes would make those who have complained of harshness go through the ceiling with chagrin, yet there is no harshness in them.

He is eager to meet you. He listens with closest care to every scrap I can tell him of you and the children. He came up to me the other day and said, "Well, Peter, you will be the Drummond of this generation for the nations." I said, "Frank, you must help me." He answered, "Yes, I mean to. I will." He is delighted with Men on Trial. He said, "Frankly, I was doubtful. I could not see how it would work out. I thought it must be just another book somewhere off there. But it is inspired. It is a treatise of statesmanship for nations. It is just right."

I went to a football match the evening before last. It was a high school game and we sat in the middle of about 8,000 teenagers, none of them was over seventeen, I would say. All of them might have been walking down Piccadilly at night — faces, full fathom five deep. Some with false eyelashes. The boys, many of them only our Philip's age, were wild as hawks. Several of them were drunk. The younger crowd here have slipped very fast — sex, drink and even drugs, I am told. Yet their freshness and eager spirit is poignant as you sense it underneath. They are so wistful and so hungry for love and direction from an older generation which has lost its way.

Peter Howard wrote to his mother for her birthday and sent her a copy of his book Ideas Have Legs, and a poem he had written for her. There was still no definite news of his brother, John, but he was presumed dead.

Evangeline Howard to P.D.H.   Wealden Way,
                                                       Bexhill-on-Sea
                                                       November 11, 1945

Your beautiful poem gave me much happiness. I don't suppose any other mother has had such a lovely tribute and, I fear, not deserved, but never mind it lifted up my heart.

Today is Armistice Day, but I just cannot bear to listen to all the services, so I shall write to you instead. John is never out of our thoughts, but we never speak about it. I think of him all the time, but if he is gone on before me to the next world, it will be lovely to be met. In any case, I believe, and I always have been sure that whatever is, is somehow for the best, but how one rebels against this best sometimes.

The book, which I have read twice, is far and away the best you have ever done. Your father agrees with me. It is a wonderful book, and I think will do a lot of good. It should do so. I will not in any case lend our own copy with your precious inscription, but I will buy three copies and lend them round.

I am with you heart and soul over doing everything to save the dear children from another war. What good has our dear John's death done? But I wonder if he is spared a good deal of trouble. The world is in a terrible state. Never mind. Spring will soon be here.

Our dear love,

Mum

This letter brought Howard great joy. Since 1940, his mother had been trying with all her influence to wrest her son away from his commitment to MRA. When he and Doë visited her at Bexhill, she was so violent about it that Howard decided for a time it would be better to make a break and not to visit her. He never lost his deep love of her, but knew that no peace was possible until she accepted that his commitment to God came before his commitment to her. In time, she had accepted this.

Evangeline Howard, who had often believed the criticisms made against her son, was encouraged to change her mind by a letter which appeared in The Times on December 29, 1945. The signatories were Lord Ammon, Deputy Leader of the House of Lords; Harold E. Clay, Chairman of the London Labour Party; Lord Courthope, President of the National Union of Conservative Associations; the Bishop of Lichfield; Sir Lynden Macassey, Chairman of Reuter's; Sir Cyril Norwood, President of St. John's College, Oxford; and Sir David Ross, Provost of Oriel College, Oxford. The letter described a secret report compiled by the head office of the Gestapo in 1939 and issued to all Gestapo units in 1942. It warned Gestapo members against the work of MRA in Europe. This report had been captured during the Allied advance in Alsace.

"The whole report," wrote the authors of the letter, "finally dispels the widespread misrepresentations which have been circulated against this Christian movement."

In the light of this letter, Evangeline Howard was willing to admit that she had been wrong.

On December 5, 1945, a memorial service was held at Somerby, Leicestershire, for the men of the 10th Battalion, the Parachute Regiment, who had fallen at Arnhem. This tiny village had been the place where the men had trained before going out to Arnhem. Peter Howard could not be there, but his wife, Doë, represented him.

Doë to P.D.H.   Hill Farm
                                                December 6, 1945

I wanted to get this to you by December 17. A strange way, perhaps, of celebrating a wedding anniversary. But it seems to me this year, separated as we are, our wedding day is not so much an occasion to rejoice, as a time to pledge ourselves to use our bond for the world's families, the broken, the bereaved, the homeless. John's sacrifice is a constant spur to us both to give all.

I was proud to belong to your family as I watched the faces of those who had fought with him. And they were proud of John and all the others.

As we drove up to the little golden stoned church, a procession of the relatives of the fallen men who had arrived by special charabancs were just walking in. They had come from every part of the country. Mostly in black, rich and very poor, some carrying small wreaths and bunches of flowers carefully wrapped in paper. Men of the Parachute Regiment in their wine-coloured berets were lining the way. Within a moment there wasn't a seat in the tiny church with its beamed ceiling and carved heads at each beam-end. In the outer aisle, the men of the regiment sat all together. During their training in the summer of 1944 they must have come here Sunday after Sunday and sat in the same seats. John must have come here.

We stood for the National Anthem. And then we sang the hymns. Then Major-General Urquhart walked to the side of the church, as we all turned to face it, and pulled the Jack off the tablet. Just a gold Cross on black and the Parachute emblems. Some day you must see it. It is a simple and lovely thing.

The door slowly opened and the "Last Post" sounded. And every heart in that filled church broke. You could hear the sobs and you could just feel the pain and the cost. Somehow the whole place seemed too small to contain the sorrow. Some faces stand out. A tall, grey-haired fine looking father, erect, staring straight ahead, not a tear in his eye and yet the agony of a dead child on his face. A young Parachute officer with curly hair and his chin half shot away, holding on to the back of the bench for strength. A young boy of twelve with flaxen hair, a long black coat, not crying either but a wounded look, a deep misery in his eyes. And next to him his mother, a wealthy woman in black and furs, oldish, stout and crying without bothering to wipe away her tears. The trumpet seemed to go on for hours. And then we prayed and sang "For all the Saints". We walked out shoulder to shoulder with people moving to the side to put their wreaths under the tablet.

I feel sad we shall not have our Wedding Day and my birthday and Christmas and young Ant's birthday and our own special New Year Eve together, but with it all I feel strangely close and tremendously grateful.

December 17 was the Howards' 13th wedding anniversary. It was impossible to send very much in the way of gifts from Britain to America, but instead Doë wrote a letter – "To a husband away fighting a war":

"When I didn't know you, England meant a lot to me. But not the same as she means today.

"England, in my early days, meant above all, Nursie, slight and London-born, with her Cockney accent which, for some unexplained reason, we never caught. She would have thrown herself under a train for us. She slapped my sister's face a month before her wedding, and mine the day after I had met you. Yet always she was at the very centre of our hearts: a rock in time of trouble with the guts of a Highland Division and the steadiness of a Convoy Commander. Thirty years of giving your life to someone else's children. That is a part of England.

"Then England meant P. & O. passengers passing through our Marseilles home. Fair women in slim canoes for shoes, pale grey voile drapes, pale eyes, pastel effect all over. The men tall and tweedy and comfortingly unsuave. They seemed so sure of what they were in the world for. And at peace because they were doing what they felt they were meant to do in life.

"England meant also filthy Channel crossings when you were quite sure it wasn't really worth that much misery to spend a month in the rain on a cold beach ... and canters in Rotten Row, black bowlered, ageless and at ease, I, the nth generation of little girls to bounce and pant at the other end of a leading rein.

"Then later I grew up. In my student days I was not very pro-English. With others I made fun of backward, ball-pushing English youth. 'Why, at fifteen we passed exams they just managed to get through at Oxford. The mind was the thing. The lucidity of the French mind. Not games. What use were they?'

"(I remember during Dunkirk praying – I who didn't pray – that the teamwork, the guts, the character that had been born in those English boys while they played those despised games, would pull us through and save me and my children from worse than death.)

"That was some of England once.

"And what does England mean now? Our home is England, with its oaken beams so strong and shapely, its great Tudor fireplace where we have so often sat. And around which now we have learned to pray, and ask God's direction on the way to go.

"England, too, is the rolling Suffolk fields with the dark brown of plough and the silver of stubble, the green of beet and the golden of corn.

"England is every corner of London we have ever been in together, and that is most of that much-loved city.

"And, such a short time ago, and yet it seems centuries, V.J. night in front of the Palace, my arm in yours, and that sound family, beloved and binding an Empire together, on the red-draped balcony, waving, and every wave making us surer still that here, in a united family, and in millions of families like it, lies the hope of the world.

"Then our three children are the best of England to me, with their dark eyes and their pink cheeks, their fun and freedom. Philip with his feel for the classics and his sense of fairness. Anne, her heart out to the weak and helpless, her passionate feelings for every lost cause. Anthony with his love of the soil and of all the crafts of farming, his bull-doggish determination never to give up a job or a race until it is through.

"Above all, you are England to me, with your strength and your steadiness, your loyalty and your courage, the way you have set your hand to the plough and will never turn back. May your furrow be ever straighter, ever deeper. And as you become day by day the man God wants you to be, may England become the nation God wants her to be.

"You are England, you that I love. And England has become for ever more the very fabric of my heart and being."

Peter Howard spent Christmas in Los Angeles. On Boxing Day, he went with Frank Buchman to meet six MRA men returning from service in the United States Forces. Howard later described that reunion:

"Frank Buchman stood at the American airfield as they flew in. He stood there with a crowd of his friends in the glare of the searchlight and the shadows of the moon. Across the concrete runway they came towards him, and there for a full minute they stood in stillness together. Hardly a word was said.

"But the tears rolled down Frank Buchman's face, and he was not alone in that. Then he turned towards the waiting cars saying, 'Well, you're home. And now let's get on with the fight.' "

P.D.H. to Doë

Los Angeles
December 30, 1945

I am setting to work tomorrow to write a book, to be called *That Man Frank Buchman*. It is not to be an exhaustive biography. Humanly, I feel inadequate and the circumstances are extremely difficult. I have nobody to work along with me, no secretarial help that is either regular or adequate and no quiet room. The place is like bedlam for eighteen hours of the twenty-four.

I need to learn the lessons of life, preferably from God. If not, then by mistakes, but I must learn them humbly, eagerly and remember always that so long as I am in this world there will be infinitely more to learn than I already know.

Yesterday I went to the Los Angeles Breakfast Club. It was a burlesque of a bump supper and rowing breakfast at Oxford. There were 600 men and women present. Also a crowd of scantily clad chorus girls wearing pink roses, as well as a chaplain who told comic and vulgar stories about the Church over the microphones. He then gave large ladle-fulls of uplift about the old school songs after you have been licked on the football field, representing the true feeling of friendship and love. There was a crowd of old gents who call themselves "The Roosters" who sat together and barracked all that went on and threw grapefruit at people. There were two nude dancers. Try them at breakfast with ham and eggs. There was a man playing a xylophone and a girl playing the concertina. There was a male voice choir; the President of California University also giving uplift, and two men being initiated into the Breakfast Club. They were blind-folded and then made to plunge their hands into a plate of raw eggs while a piece of cooked ham was placed on top of them.

On January 16, I am billed to speak there and if "The Roosters" throw something at me they will be surprised what they get back.

Yesterday Buchman suddenly said, "Peter come." So I put on my coat and went. We arrived at a symphony concert where Rubinstein was playing. He certainly caught that piano some almighty cracks. Once he literally left the ground and landed with both hands at the keyboard. I think I should be a good pianist if I could only land my hands on the right place.

P.D.H. to Doë   Los Angeles
                                                 January 3, 1946

I am working hard at the book. I rise at five o'clock and work until eight. It is the only time of day when the house is reasonably undisturbed. I go downstairs to where I have found a gas fire which I light and work away. I am doing about a chapter a day and hope to finish a preliminary draft by about January 22.

Buchman is entirely impersonal in his corrective. You never feel that he has any personal handle in the matter, but he is utterly outspoken on what he feels. If people speak too long he tells them. If they do it again he just doesn't have them speak any more.

One of Buchman's favourite expressions is, "Now he can damn well go to thunder." He adds, "If I didn't say 'damn' sometimes, Peter, they wouldn't pay any attention to me."

We still lead a fairly busy life. A luncheon for the City Council today, at which I spoke. Tomorrow I am spending the morning with Flannery, who wrote the book *Assignment to Berlin*. He is going to interview me for the radio in the afternoon.

On January 1, Buchman and all of us breakfasted at six-thirty and left at seven-thirty in cars for Pasadena, where the New Year's Day Rose Parade began at nine-fifteen. Then on to the great Rose Bowl football match between Alabama, the best team of the East, and the University of Southern California, champions of the West.

One fellow would have delighted you. He weighed 300 lbs. according to the programme. He did nothing at all except leap into heaps of men when one scored and wave his legs in the air. Old Father Time came out at half-time and the crowd ironically yelled, "Here's the new half-back for Southern California," who were getting beaten. It was more like a theatre than a game.

It brought out a metallic commercialism. Here there is no fun any more except in bottles of liquor, or in battles for dollar or dominion. You have a sense of a mighty people on the slide. The second generation aristocracy is either too soft or too hard. We shall have to raise a new aristocracy.

P.D.H. to Doë

Los Angeles
January 8, 1946

The last half-mile of a race is sometimes the going which brings the best out of a thoroughbred. You are a thoroughbred if ever there was one and we are in the last half-mile of the race. We were set to run when we said goodbye at Fowey. You with your grey dress and your deep eyes that I love so well. It has been a well-run race, and now we are so near to reunion.

Personally, I am far spent both physically and spiritually. This writing which now goes forward is Custer's last stand. I sometimes feel as if a giant had put a straw into my stomach and been sucking the guts out of me steadily for the last months. You do not always find over here the refreshment and rebound which so wonderfully revives you at the farm.

The interviewer in the radio broadcast suddenly said, "And Mr. Howard, just what is Moral Re-Armament?" I had to answer on the dot and said, "Well, it is democracy's answer to totalitarianism of any kind. It is not an organisation, but an organism effectively at work all over the world spreading like yeast through the bodies of sixty nations to lift the living and thinking of the people. It is giving democracy what it lacked between the two wars — an inspired ideology. Some people think it is a new religion. It is nothing of the kind. In fact, it is a new force which at last gives legs to the ideas we know are right and sets them marching. It enlists all people of goodwill to change, unite and fight for a free future."

I had supper the other night at a place where they say if you are not delighted you need pay nothing – pay what you think the meal is worth. As you leave there is a large notice which says, "Food for the soul is also important." There are coloured lights, a wishing well, which elderly ladies patronise at five cents a time, artificial rain which falls on the roof every five minutes to make you feel you are out-of-doors, a chapel where you can meditate, and an organ which plays juke music and "The Old Rugged Cross". The interior décor is of palm trees and parrots. The proprietor when I met him said with pride, "You've never seen a place like this anywhere, have you?" I had to admit I had not. He remarked, "There's nothing like it in the world." Then he took 50% off my bill.

P.D.H. to Doë   Los Angeles
                                               January 15, 1946
    England needs more friends today than ever before in history and has fewer. It has been quite salutary out here to discover how many people hate and despise us. When she was all-powerful many dared not express their feelings, but not so now.
    The book is going fast. How well is another matter. By the time you get this I shall have finished the first draft. It is short, about 25,000 words so far written, and different from anything attempted before. It is almost a straight factual news story.

P.D.H. to Doë   Los Angeles
                                               February 1, 1946
    Sometimes in the past you have indicated to me that my behaviour at symphony concerts is not all it should be.
    Well, last night I went to the concert with Artur Rodzinski[1] and made notes of how to behave so I shall do you more credit in future.
    We sat in the middle of the orchestra stalls. The pieces were: suite from the incidental music to Maeterlinck's play "The Betrothal". Rodzinski got a fit of sneezing half way through this and held up his hat and sneezed into it loudly several times, and then roared with laughter so everyone said, "Ssh, ssh." At the end he remarked, "Well, this can be said – such music will not actually harm anybody."
    The next piece was Chausson's symphony in B flat major. Rodzinski says it is very difficult to play. He conducted from his seat with much violence and encouraged the orchestra with quite loud cries. When the trumpeter was playing a sombre solo, he remarked in an audible voice, "I would shoot that trumpeter were he mine."
    The piece that followed was Tchaikovsky's concerto for violin and orchestra in D major. The fiddler was Isaac Stern, who is a boy protégé of twenty-five. "Fiddle-de-dee, fiddle-de-dee, fiddle-de-dee," said Rodzinski loudly in tune with all the solo passages. He told me just how much

[1] Conductor of the New York Philharmonic Orchestra.

longer there was to go. "Five minutes more, my God. Two more minutes. Forty seconds, pom, pom, te pom. Twenty seconds. Four seconds. Finish."

When he met the orchestra and soloists behind the scenes they all shouted in different languages. I told him about a musician who had retired ten years before. "Such a man has nothing to retire from and makes a mistake in returning from retirement. What a death's head. He has nothing in him," were Rodzinski's comments.

The draft of the book has gone to the publishers. I feel pretty well disembowelled and long to get away for a few days. The ship will be like heaven.

Last Sunday I was sitting in the sunshine on the porch dictating a letter or two. Buchman was beside me. Some boys came past playing football. "My, I can remember doing just that as if it were yesterday," said Buchman. "Did you like football?" I asked. "Yes," said Buchman. "You know, I have loved my life."

P.D.H. to Doë   In the train to the East
                                                    February 12, 1946

I shall post this in Chicago which we reach tomorrow. The last days in Los Angeles were exceedingly hectic. Sunday was the day of parting with Buchman. Wood[1] helped me to pack in the morning. We will cross together on February 28, the first convenient ship we can get.

Buchman gave a lunch party for me the last day. He was very generous in what he said, "Born of the Spirit and living by grace abounding. It takes something exceptional. I can say I have learnt something new myself since Peter joined me of the meaning of living by grace." Later, at a large meeting in the main lecture theatre of the university, he said, "Peter Howard has brought the conception of ideology to birth in America. It is hard to put into words what the country owes him. He has carried with him everywhere a living experience of Jesus Christ."

He came with a crowd to the station to say goodbye. For the last three months I have been scarcely away from his side. I think we have had almost every meal together. I have come to understand him and love him a lot. He is by no means a saint in the pious sense of the phrase. Some of his words and ways would be quite a shock to some of our friends. It is a curious thing that Buchman's personality, as such, is not always pleasing, but he is a living example of how the dominion of the Holy Spirit transcends human personality.

At the station we sang "Auld Lang Syne" and I stood in the window of the train much moved. It is strange because there is nothing in the world I have so much wanted in my life as to see you again.

[1] Mr. A. Lawson Wood of Aberdeenshire; later Assistant Secretary of Moral Re-Armament, Great Britain.

I set off on this trip towards you even more eagerly, indeed far more eagerly, than I did on my wedding trip to Marseilles. That's a wonderful thing after thirteen years, isn't it? These months away from you have made me realise how vital a part of my whole make-up and spirit you are.

I feel that no Englishman has seen America before, the way I have seen it. Buchman has opened up the homes of all his friends everywhere. He has from the first trusted me and taken me on the inside entirely. If ever I asked him what I should say on any occasion — and I must have made at least 150 speeches since I came to the States — he replied, "I would never try and make your speech for you."

Howard visited Washington again en route for England and was received by President Truman at the White House. He was one of those of whom Howard had written in *Men on Trial*:

"Some say Truman will be outweighted in his dealings with men of the international stature of Churchill and Stalin. I am not so sure. I predict that Truman will be a statesman formidable beyond expectation. For he has an immense source of strength. He is a man of unyielding principle.

"His recent history offers a first-rate example of his constancy and courage. During his investigations into the state of American industry he came in contact with the workers for Moral Re-Armament. He came to the conclusion that 'there is not a single industrial bottleneck which could not be broken in a matter of weeks if this crowd were given the green light to go full steam ahead'.

"Certain sections of the American press began a smear campaign against Moral Re-Armament, and every inducement was made to Truman to withdraw the endorsement he had given to that work. Instead he called the American pressmen together and issued a statement, part of which said, 'I have given much time and thought to this matter and have come to the clear conviction that the problems to which the Moral Re-Armament programme is finding an effective solution are the most urgent in our whole production picture.' The easier course would have been to stay silent.

"Now Truman has the harder task of showing the victorious nations that they may themselves, after victory, be saddled with totalitarian systems they went to war to beat. He has not only to help build the new machinery of national and international harmony, but also to get public opinion to the place where it sees that without a new spirit in the engine there will be further breakdowns."

President Truman listened to Howard with lively interest. Howard sailed for England at the end of February aboard the *Queen Elizabeth*. At Southampton, Doë and his two younger children were there to meet him.

It was a misty March morning as the shadow of that enormous ship appeared off Southampton. The joy of meeting again was unspeakable. Anne and Anthony were given the first banana they had ever seen. They tried to eat it with its skin on. On the journey to London in the boat train, there was so much to tell, and even more that words could not express.

But Howard was not to be long at home. In the summer of 1946, Frank Buchman came to Europe for the first time since the war. The preparations involved for the visit were vast and took Howard all over Europe for many months.

In the Autumn of 1946, Anne and Anthony were sent to boarding school, Anthony to join Philip at Cheam School, and Anne to a junior school in Bexhill. The school in Bexhill was not a success, and Anne wrote unhappy letters home asking to be taken away. Early in 1947, Peter Howard went down to see her. He was about to leave once more for America, this time with Doë. In the car as they drove back to the school, Anne explained that she could not face being left there, with her parents abroad and very unhappy. For Howard it was a difficult decision. He said, "We made a mistake when we sent you here. I am sorry. But if I take you away from this, you will run away from everything for the rest of your life."

It was the beginning of three miserable years for Anne. But it was a wise decision. When the Howards left for America they wrote regularly to their children. Every week an instalment of a story would arrive for them at school. There was nothing unusual about Philip, Anne and Anthony. Although their parents' letters from America were full of interesting places and people, the replies were typical of school children everywhere:

Anne to P.D.H.   Bexhill-on-Sea
    I am sorry I was so unhappy when you left. It must have been awful for you. It was lovely to see you. I think of you every night.
    I am tenth in my form and at a desk. Tell Mummy and show her this letter. I have made friends with nearly all the people in my form.
    I have your picture and look at your face every time I write.
    Much love,
                            Anne

Anthony to P.D.H.   Cheam School
    You will be glad to hear that the mice are dead. Philip is bringing his hen home with him. I am bringing a cat.
    I hope you sometimes get some Yorkshire pudding.
    With love from,
                            Ant.

Philip to P.D.H. and Doë   Cheam School
   I was fifth in Latin out of nine, and third in maths.
   We had a battle de luxe yesterday though the result was indecisive.
We entered the enemy fort but were recalled as the Black Shadows were
attacking in the rear. I am in command of a battery of guns.
   We had a lecture on diving yesterday. The lecturer brought all his diving
kit with him, and several sticks of dynamite and other explosives. He told
us how at a school in Kent, where he had given a lecture, he had dropped a
stick of gelatine (which has twice the explosive power of dynamite), but
this did not seem to put him off and he kept on throwing the gelatine
up in the air and catching it.
   I have not got any jams or sweets left.
   More than half the school had visitors yesterday. One boy who had
visitors gave me a chocolate ice cream, while another took me out to tea
with his mother and father.
   Love from,

                              Philip

The Howards spent Christmas 1947 in Richmond, Virginia.

P.D.H. to his children   December 1947
   We crossed the narrow strip of West Virginia which thrusts up between
Ohio and Pennsylvania. They call this the Panhandle country because it is
like the end of a frying pan. Here the industry is opencast coalmining. For
miles and miles along the roadside the earth has been ripped open by
great machines and you can see the coalseam about twenty feet down and
three feet thick, with trucks carrying it away to Pittsburg. We drove
through Pittsburg. It is one of the great steel cities of the world. We came
to it as dusk fell. For more than fifteen miles outside the city the trees and
fields were covered with a film of dust and soot from the furnaces. The
flames rise way above the chimney tops in billows and waves. Their
reflection is cast back in the oily dark river surface and it seems as if the
whole place is on fire.

P.D.H.   Washington D.C.
                                                          January 1948
   America is the land of freedom. The root of freedom is the choice to do
what is right. For the choice to do what is wrong does not issue in freedom
but exploitation, and finally in enslavement. I believe that compromise
with moral standards is the mortal enemy of freedom.

Chapter 11

I N the immediate post-war years, much of the work of Moral Re-
Armament in Europe was concentrated upon France, Germany and
Italy and included conferences at Mountain House, Caux-sur-Mon-
treux. Chancellor Adenauer[1] was later to say that this work had saved the
Ruhr from Communism, and both he and Robert Schuman[2] stated that
MRA had played a major part in reconciling their two countries. De
Gasperi[3] of Italy also paid tribute to its part in reuniting Europe. Peter
Howard spent much of his time from 1946 to 1950 working in these
countries.

During these years, relations between Buchman and Howard underwent a serious change:

"From one day to the next Buchman bolted and barred every door and
window in our relationship. Nothing I could do was right. Publicly and
privately, in and out of season, I was rebuked and assailed. Buchman was
determined that I should turn to God alone and to no human authority
for my foundation in life.

"Once at a meal to which many important guests were invited, I was
asked to sit at Buchman's table. When Buchman arrived and saw me there
he at once and in a loud voice said, 'Take him away. I will not sit down at
table with him. I do not want him among these people.'

"This incident was typical of our relationship at that time, and things
continued so for nearly four years.

"Once I asked Buchman, 'How long shall I go on in this state of darkness and despair?' Buchman replied, 'I just don't know. It's your decision
not mine.' "

They were, for Howard, active years, but years in the wilderness. Buchman did not invite him to be with him and even questioned whether he
should ever write again. Few men, perhaps, would have lived through
those years and remained faithful to their calling. As it was, Howard
passed through many moments of despair. Without Doë's faith and support, it must have been the end of his life with MRA.

[1] Chancellor of the Federal Republic of Germany 1949–63.
[2] Successively Premier and Foreign Minister of France.
[3] Foreign Minister, then Prime Minister of Italy.

The apparent harshness with which Buchman dealt with Howard at this period was, in reality, a measure of his trust in him. Buchman was a genius at reading and understanding men. Howard had asked him to help him. He saw in Howard the possibility of great leadership, coupled with weaknesses of pride, conceit and a dependence upon man's approval. Buchman was out to produce a man whose blade was sharpened and whose life was freed from every human attachment.

For Buchman the risks he took with Howard, and the pain he caused himself in doing it, were great. He accepted it as a normal part of life. "I have had to be ready," he once said, "to risk every relationship in life, day and night, seven days a week, for the last forty years. Otherwise, our work in the world would not be where it is today."

The break between Buchman and Howard was to last for four years. Later he was to say to Howard, "Peter, I rely on you to give me the corrective I need. I am just like everybody else. I need correction every day in my life, but too few people have the care and commonsense to give it me."

Those who knew Peter Howard in the last years of his life will understand that these four bleak years with Buchman made the achievements of the future possible. As Howard himself often quoted, "There is no Crown without the Cross."

P.D.H. to Doë   Mountain House, Caux
                                                        1949

Yesterday I thought of you through the day and that your meeting with the children would be overflowed with happiness. I do rejoice you are together and it will be a wonderful time.

The clouds came rolling over the lake and it was raining here. The other side of the lake looked like breakers against a cliff wall with the winds swirling the clouds against the sides of the rock walls. It is not your kind of weather, but I found a refreshment in it.

I do feel so sorry that I made our goodbye a sad one. I simply could not bear the idea of being left alone here and not seeing the children, and spending the rest of my life on a routine which humanly, as you know, does not delight me.

My heart is fully at peace and God is using me quite deeply in the lives of people. Yet it is true that my fears so often overlay my hopes. My expectancy of the future is imprisoned by my experience of the past and I feel the creative force within me slowly ebbing away as the months go on.

I am under no illusion that apart from God, I can do nothing with my life now. I know, for example, even if I went into newspapers or politics again, the old flair and fight is gone, and rightly gone. I have a dominating personality and need a strong mastery of the Spirit.

Howard's old friends were not unaware of his condition. Christiansen and Robertson of the *Daily Express*, on Beaverbrook's advice, invited Howard to the *Daily Express* offices.

P.D.H. to F.N.D.B. London

To cut a long story short, they offered me £2,000 a year for one article a month in the *Daily Express* about the land. In addition a profile of one of the statesmen in the *Sunday Express* once every two or three weeks, and an article on world affairs in the *Evening Standard*. Robertson then said, "I am going to tell you something which I didn't mean to tell you when you came in. Have you ever thought of being an editor?" I said to Robertson, "Don't talk that way. You will make Chris nervous." (Christiansen was at that time Editor of the *Daily Express*.) Robertson then said they want someone to take over the *Sunday Express* in a year or so's time. And that seems to be what is in their minds for me.

Later Lord Beaverbrook invited Howard to Cherkley.

P.D.H. to F.N.D.B. London

Beaverbrook's proposition was £2,500 a year plus £500 free of income tax for a weekly article in his newspapers. He said I could have complete liberty of expression, except there was to be no libel and that there must be no continuous propaganda for Moral Re-Armament. "I want you to understand this, Peter," he said. "I am wholly in favour of Moral Re-Armament. You may find this hard to believe but it is so. I wish it a great success, but I do not want to become a propagandist for Moral Re-Armament or the Catholic Church, or Communism, or Socialism, or Conservatism, or even the Presbyterian Church, to which I belong. I regard Moral Re-Armament as highly as I regard the Presbyterian Church, except that I think Moral Re-Armament is run far better."

In the course of the afternoon he showed me his farm at Cherkley. He took me in his car to see his hayfield. Before parting he said to me, "Yours is an amazing story, isn't it, Peter?"

Howard was tempted to accept Beaverbrook's offer. But he did not. The money would have been useful enough, the friendship at that time would have been golden. But Howard was held by a destiny he neither fully understood or even, at that time, believed in. He was also held by the changes he had seen taking place in other men and situations.

Howard wrote in 1950:

"One cold winter night a veteran Communist leader, Max Bladeck, took the chair at a trade union meeting. He is a small man, every inch a fighter, with sharp eyes, and intellectual forehead and a chest racked by silicosis. He is head of the works council of one of the largest collieries in the Ruhr, and has been twenty-five years a member of the Communist Party. The meeting was in a beer hall.

"When the Moral Re-Armament men arrived, amid the smoke and glasses and the lights, they found that Bladeck had arranged for some of the most skilful Communist speakers in his district to demolish them. Six of them spoke one after the other.

"They went on the attack. They spoke for an hour on the theme that in the heart of every capitalist is a Fascist and that Western nations are preparing the next world war. They quoted Marx on the need to change the system, and Stalin's dictum that the bourgeois had never yet put principle before profit. Pointing to the history of the Churches, they declared that Christianity had tried for 2,000 years to build a new world — and failed. Now it was their turn.

"At this point the MRA men took the floor. One of them, a worker from Lancashire, began by admitting that his own country, Britain, had sometimes made mistakes. The Germans' interest was caught.

" 'Everybody,' added this man, 'wants to see the other fellow change. Every nation wants to see the other nation change. Yet everybody is waiting for the other fellow to begin.' They were listening now, and there were cries of 'Hear, hear!' all over the hall.

" 'But,' the spokesman continued, 'the best place to start is with your-self. Why not start with our own class, our own race, our own nation, and then carry it to the world?'

"Through the smoky air, amid tense silence, a shipyard worker from Clydeside declared, 'Labour has never been so powerful and never been so divided. We have learned to split the atom. But we have not learned to unite humanity. The Labour movement has within it the seeds of its own defeat — unless it learns to change human nature. Human nature can be changed. It must be changed on a colossal scale.'

"A Canadian industrialist was introduced. His changed attitude to-wards labour amazed the Communists. The meeting lasted for four hours. Not a man had left the hall.

"Battles like this were fought daily in the Ruhr. Week after week for months on end the MRA men met the miners in their homes and in the pits. As a result hundreds of workers and their leaders went to Caux where the World Assembly for Moral Re-Armament was in session. Among them went Bladeck and another veteran Communist, Paul Kurowski.

"At Caux these men saw a living demonstration of an ideology based on change, change not for one class but for every class. 'For twenty-five years I have sung the Internationale with all my heart and strength,' said Kurowski, after some days there, 'but this is the first time I have seen it lived.'

"They began to change. But change is never comfortable, whether for a

Communist, a capitalist or anyone else. It means facing absolute moral standards. It will involve being different at home. It may call for a break with personal habits or long-cherished points of view.

"Bladeck and Kurowski talked far into the night. They fought back with every shot in the Marxist locker. But always they were held by the affection of their new friends and by the relentless logic of the MRA ideology.

"Finally Kurowski stated their conclusion, 'Anyone who will not follow the absolute standards of honesty, purity, unselfishness and love is a traitor to his class and to his nation.'

"Meanwhile, back in the Ruhr, reports were received by the West German Communist Party that Bladeck and Kurowski were beginning to accept the ideology of Moral Re-Armament. The Party became alarmed. They sent one of their most trusted members, Willi Benedens, to bring Bladeck and Kurowski home.

"Benedens was a district political secretary of the Communist Party. He had been removed from Hitler's air force because his convictions became suspect and had been sent to the Eastern Front where he lost both legs.

"What happened when he came to Caux? It can best be described in his own words, 'I fought bitterly against my friends who went to Caux and who were officials of the Communist Party,' said Benedens. 'But when I came there I found the thing I had for years fought for—the classless society.'

"Benedens, Kurowski and Bladeck returned to the Ruhr together. They were called before the Communist Party Executive. They gave a simple explanation. 'We have found,' they said, 'an ideology greater than Communism.'

"The West German Communist Party was in a dilemma. For years the Leninist doctrine has been for Communism to infiltrate into the structure of society and change it. Yet here were men, not weaklings but the hard core of the Party, who went to Caux and themselves were changed.

"Meanwhile, the three men had called a meeting of the Party stalwarts. In a description of this meeting they wrote, 'The going was hot. But the longest speech has to stop sometime. Ten men can sing together, but they cannot talk together. When ten men talk at once, you cannot tell what anyone is saying. When we spoke of Caux the loud voices became quieter. Soon they were all listening, silent and thoughtful.'

"The official Communist newspaper in Western Germany, *Freies Volk*, on October 6, 1949, came out with a major article written by the chairman of the Ruhr regional committee of the Party, Hugo Paul, on Moral Re-Armament. It said, 'The dangerous activity of Moral Re-Armament has been under-estimated by the Regional Executive of the Party. These men from Caux have been recommending the Party to make itself conversant with world-revolutionising new ideas.'

"The men from Caux stood firm. From Essen, Dortmund and other parts of the Ruhr seasoned Marxists joined them.

"Meanwhile, Bladeck, Kurowski and Benedens had won re-election to their works councils with increased majorities in the face of bitter attack."

In May 1949, Howard left home again to help with the work in Germany. This time he travelled through Holland.

P.D.H. to Doë
Cologne
May 1949

Thank you so much for the love and care of your packing and also for the food. It is worth more than rubies here. I came happily in the train all yesterday. I had a second-class non-smoker to myself all the way from the Hook to here. As we approached Cologne, I stuck my head out of the window to see the Cathedral.

The Berlin trip is now on. We fly from Frankfurt tomorrow morning. We stay in Berlin a week.

I loved the train journey through Holland. It is amazing to see how well the Dutch have cared for their soil. In most places, where the surface is scratched more than a few inches, you can see sand underneath. There are trees and reed fences put up everywhere to prevent wind erosion.

There were scores of acres of tulips and other flowers — rivers of colour flowing across the landscape. The windmills were rolling and waving everywhere, and it interested me how much they use windpower for quite small jobs of haulage. I often saw windmills with the height of only seven or eight feet throbbing away in the corner of some field to lift water into a trough for cattle or something of that kind.

The Dutch fields bear everywhere the mark of shrewd and hard-working husbandry. I saw one man on a field of about three acres. He was going up and down, toe to heel in his clogs, with his hands behind his back. He did not want heavy horses or tractors on his land for that job. It was ten o'clock when I passed him and he never glanced up as the train went by. He had covered about a third of an acre.

The centre of Rotterdam has gone, but it is not to be compared with places like Gladbach or Cologne which are 60% flat.

Cologne Cathedral is stupendous and a dream of beauty. Bombs have smashed the pinnacles of it, and hundreds of feet up are holes through which heaven stares. The bombs have also smashed the floor of the cathedral and opened up vaults and foundations which nobody knew were there.

This morning I pushed open a locked door and walked the floors which Charlemagne trod. Our young waiter at this hotel was four years a prisoner-of-war in England, a nice boy who talks good English. He told me, "I want to get back to England. All the dreams I had for my own country are smashed. I want to be rich but there is no money to be made here and no future except as a landworker. People get rich who work with their heads not with their hands."

When I went up to my room last night I found the chambermaid with all my food out on the floor going through it.

The will to recovery is tremendous. The British are causing much bitterness with their dismantling policy, which the Germans feel is based on fear of competition. Thousands of men are thrown out of work by this procedure. But while the Allies steadily pull down plants and buildings, they are allowing the Germans to build new plants and buildings because they are not on any list in Whitehall or Washington. The result, as Jung, the second man in I. G. Farben pointed out to me, is likely to be that after a few years of misery, Germany will be equipped with an industrial plant so up-to-date that it can knock spots off other plants in the world. The Marxist trade unionists blame the democracies for not helping them more effectively in their struggle against Hitler. The employers think they have done more for their employees than the Americans.

The popularity of the Occupation authorities is Americans first, the British and then the French. The French live off the country. The British are cold and correct. The Americans soft and lavish.

P.D.H. to Doë   Berlin
                                                  May 16, 1949
We flew in from Frankfurt. The trip was a little bumpy and it was the only time since I left you that I was glad you were not with me. We landed at Tempelhof Airport, so full of memories. The vast square outside built in 1936.

We are staying at a magnificent house which looks out across the lake. It belongs to the Finance Minister who is at present in gaol. It is quite an eerie feeling to be in his home, with his pictures, books and carpets, and peopled by the ghosts of Goebbels, Goering and even Hitler himself, who were often in these rooms.

Being in the charge of the Americans we were greeted at Tempelhof by a Captain Lake, who escorted us through the customs as V.I.P.s and brought us here in military cars. We are in no hardship.

Berlin, strangely enough, is a more winning city than before. It has more heart even though it is a broken heart. The destruction is too big to grasp. Since the war, one new building only — a ladies' department store — has gone up. They lost 250,000 in two nights' bombing in Dresden. But here there was street fighting as well, and three-and-a-half million people are living in a dead and haunted city. There are 50,000 women engaged in shifting rubble in Berlin.

We were driven around by an unrepentant Nazi. He hates the Russians.

He hates the Allies. He hopes only for the vision of a newly risen Germany. He did say with passionate conviction, "Germany will never make another war." But when we passed the wrecked Chancellery, I said, "Is that where they found Hitler's body?" He shrugged his shoulders and said, "If they did find it. If he is dead." There are millions like him here. The youth of Germany is nihilistic. If we do not capture it, some new Führer may, or a strong minority group will.

Goering never rebuilt the burnt-out Reichstag. He left it as a shell in Hitler's favourite city to remind men of the futility of democracy and the wickedness of the opposition to the Nazi régime. That shell of the Reichstag still stands today and it is about the best preserved building in the area. The houses stand like skeletons for miles on end. When a strong wind blows, fresh pieces of masonry tumble down on to the heaps below to bury yet more deeply the dead who still lie there.

Yesterday was May Day. Across the Brandenburg Gate the Russians had hung a huge banner which said, "We do not want Berlin to become a sacrifice to those warmongers who talk German but think in terms of atom bombs and dollars."

We drove along the autobahn where the mass rallies used to be held and were taken to the Olympic stadium which is untouched. It is a colossal arena, built in a year and seating 100,000 people.

There has never before in history been anything so swift as the rise of Hitler's dynasty and so mighty as his fall. Here in Berlin you can see the sowing of the wind and the reaping of the whirlwind.

P.D.H. to Doë   Berlin
                                                                      May 1949
This has been a staggering trip. I wish with all my heart you were with us. The response at the highest level of the nation is something I have never seen before. We have been received by the Cabinet, the top Civic authorities, the heads of the trade unions, the Catholics and the press. We had a press conference arranged by the Germans at the Press Club. First-rate articles in all the newspapers.

At a party lasting until two in the morning came the executive of the SPD (the powerful Marxist-Socialist Party of Germany) and the actors and actresses of Berlin.

We went and addressed the SPD youth at their training school. It is a vast gloomy Victorian abode where Himmler used to live. At the end of our session, the Chairman said, "I doubt the class warfare. Socialists must put the whole of life on a fresh basis. Moral Re-Armament contains the great truths of humanism, Christianity and Socialism." The students were enthusiastic and they have asked us back again. They had had a large group of youth from the Russian Sector brought in to hear us.

Last night the first letters I have had since leaving you finally caught up with me. Among them was Buchman's from Caux. Your trust through the years has been a girder to my living and where I should be without it today, God knows. But you need not fear for me. My first reaction to the letter was a certain numbness as of a pig at Elmswell when the shears are clipped around his head, but this passed in a few minutes and both last night and this morning I have true peace of heart. I sometimes feel, "Well, I am no damn good to man or beast. I am through with anything worthwhile anyway and the sooner I die the better."

The letter from Buchman bluntly pointed out some of Howard's faults. Elmswell is the bacon factory near Hill Farm.

P.D.H. to Doë   Berlin
                                                 May 1949

The sky is clear blue and through it, night and day at intervals of two minutes, roar the huge planes of the Airlift.

My heart has been much with you thinking of dear old Ant and Anne going back to school. Anne will enjoy this last term. Little old Ant is just cracking through the shell from childhood to boyhood. It is painful but joyful for him. I often long to spare my children some of the crunches of life, but of course one cannot do it.

They have been fascinating days here. We have been working almost entirely with the workers and the trade unions. The Lord Mayor is Reuther. He talks four languages and was Lenin's first Commissar in the Volga area. Lenin denounced him as too independent. Reuther, who gave a reception for us yesterday, admires Lenin tremendously but thinks Stalin is a poor fish. He is optimistic and no fool. He thinks the Kremlin façade is very thin and that there is real prospect of a sudden crack up of the whole front. Personally, I don't see this at all.

We met the head of UGO, the trade union, who has been agricultural worker, policeman, sailor and M.P. One of his first remarks was, "I don't want Wesley from Britain or Father Divine from America." These men hate religion because they don't know what it is. They respond at once to a quality of heart and life and to absolute standards. They get an ideological concept. This man ended by asking. "How can I find in my heart the peace to discern what is right?" He pulled a twenty mark note out of his pocket to give to us.

It has been interesting on this Berlin trip that while the response has been colossal and the Germans have responded very much to the words of Irène Laure about France's faults, and to Jaeger's[1] words on Britain's shortcomings, there was not one whisper from any German of any sense of responsibility for the past or present. Many of those we saw had

[1] Mr. William Jaeger, for thirty years worked with world labour and industry for MRA.

163

themselves suffered under Hitler and felt they had done more than most of us. Others felt Hitler had gone mad and brought them to disaster, but the fact that he had failed was their main criticism of him. One man found it unreasonable that the Dutch four years after the war were still sore about the rape of their nation, and said that the Germans might have to take trade to other countries if the Dutch persisted in their attitude. It is a battle to break the core of pride in every nation, I suppose.

Madame Irène Laure, who was in Berlin with Howard, had been for many years a Member of Parliament for Marseilles, a member of the Socialist Party executive, and head of the Socialist women of her country. During the war, she was a leading figure in the French Resistance. Howard wrote:

"Her son was tortured in order to force her to disclose secrets of the Resistance. She refused. But her heart broke and hate took its place. 'I had only one wish – to destroy all Germans,' she said.

"She was invited to Caux. She went with scepticism but thinking that it would be a nice holiday for herself and her son. On her first day there she heard some Germans addressing the Assembly, but these Germans were honestly facing the mistakes of the past and their own nation's need of change.

"The French woman was in turmoil. For three weeks, as she says, 'I tried to find the flea in the straw.' There was no flea. It was reality. The iron of hate melted. She changed. She went to Germany and lived in the homes of the Germans and spoke to millions on the radio and at mass meetings. She spoke in seven of the parliaments of the West German states.

"Irène says, 'Can you think what it meant in change for me to go to Germany? In my heart I had willed the ruins that I saw there. I am a mother and a grandmother, I am a Socialist and all my life have talked about fraternity, yet I had longed for those ruins. I had to ask forgiveness for my hatred from those people who were living in the ruins. I had to ask forgiveness from those 50,000 women whom I saw grey with fatigue, clearing the rubble in Berlin.

"'I do not forget the ruins in my own or in other countries that the Germans invaded. Not at all. But the thing I could do was to face my own hatred and ask forgiveness for it. Change in me brought forth change in many Germans.'"

In Berlin a cable arrived inviting every member of the party, except Howard, to join Buchman in Switzerland. Howard went home. In the holidays he camped on the farm with his children.

P.D.H. to his parents:

Dearest Mum and Dad, I have been doing for the last four days something that I had not done for twenty years. I have been sleeping out in the open air in a tent with the children.

Twenty years ago I used to sleep like a dog all night long in the open. That is not so now. But I rest with deep peace in my heart, listening to the sounds of the night around me.

Up at Abbott's Hall[1] there are many nightingales. They sing all through the night, and when the wind is silent you can hear the throb of their deeper notes, and understand the force of the body that a small bird uses to sing so loud and varied a tone.

Somewhere far away, I think maybe in Waldingfield, you can just hear a church chiming the hours. Otherwise, there is nothing except the flap of the canvas in the breeze, the footsteps of the rain, and the wind plucking the strings of the trees.

My heart travelled many years and miles as I lay out there in the night. I remembered the Cherrybrook and the Dart, and Dad's trout, red and silver among the reeds at the end of the day. I remembered old Farmer White and Miss Redstone playing you both at whist, and accusing you of cheating when Dad twiddled his forelock. I remembered long waits with mother beside kettles that refused to boil on damp wood before Daddy came striding over the heather, only an hour or two after he had been expected.

I remembered so many days of intense happiness together in Cumberland, Dartmoor, Scotland, Wales and even in less wild places like Brighton or Bexhill-on-Sea.

As I get older I do not feel the tremendous surge of happiness at the smells and sounds of the river, and at the colours of the mountains and the moors. But in a strange way the times we have spent in these places bring deeper contentment now than ever they did.

Lying out there in the night time, many things seemed to fall into place. I was thinking much of old John, and he seemed very close to me at times. Under the stars there seems somehow more space and certainty than during the daylight and business of daytime, and I felt more and more sure that these years here are a small part of a big story.

Youth and age, failure and success, nothing much matters except that God is there and loves us, and forgives fellows like myself, even as we forgive each other.

In the mornings I left the boys asleep in the tent and came out each day into sunshine. The rabbits went scuttering away in front of me leaving wakes of green grass behind them in the silver of the dew. Up on the top of the elm tree an old cuckoo sat shouting at me. I fed the bullocks, and

[1] One of the Hill Farm houses.

165

came back to the camp to blow the fire into life and cook the breakfast before the day's work.

.　　　.　　　.

It was not until February 1950 that Peter Howard heard from Frank Buchman again. He received an invitation to join Buchman in Rome. He went via Lille and Paris.

P.D.H. to Doë   Paris
                                                   February 18, 1950
The time in Lille has been wonderful. We had a unique press conference, about the best in results I have ever known. Forty journalists and their wives were there, and we had positive reports in every Lille newspaper, except the Communist one this morning.

We went on from there to be received by the Cardinal at his Palace. He spoke for about twenty minutes, ending up by saying, "I am glad to be able to tell you that I approved of your work and am going to ask God to bless it."

P.D.H. to Doë   En route to Rome
                                                    February 1950
Where in the world do you think I am? I am sitting in my dressing gown in the spare room of Tante Marie's[1] apartment at Monte Carlo with the early morning sun streaming in through the window.

As we got closer and closer to Monaco, I could not for the life of me remember the address. But when we reached Nice at one o'clock yesterday, I looked in the local book and, praise God, her name was in it. I rang her straight away. She could not believe it was me and asked frantically after you. Then she bade me come at once. So I took the bus over the upper Corniche. Tante Marie was there at the bus stop to meet me, and she and Audrey (the companion) — they have altered very little — have given me a royal time.

We have never been back to your home since we have been married, and I couldn't help remembering as I drove without you through Provence how very much I had longed to build the perfect life with you when last I came there to get married to you, and how much I planned and hoped to do with you and for you, and how often I have failed to do it. But to me these years with all the faded dreams and broken hopes have been a pageant of unending adventure which has brought me happiness beyond anything I ever expected when we set forth. And indeed I do thank you with the whole of my heart. You are a wonderful wife to me, and the future is full of joy with you to share it.

[1] Doë's aunt whom the Howards had not seen since before the war.

Here we are living in the old Italian Military Academy just beside St. Peter's.

There is still great wealth and much smartness in Rome. The poor are very poor and the rich are very rich. But there is little sign of a conquered nation until you get into the devastated countryside which was shattered during the German retreat north.

Last night we took a car and went to see the Coliseum in moonlight. It was strange to stand in the places where they kept the lions and also the Christians. There were seats for over half-a-million people and they could all get a better view of what was going on than most folk at a modern football match. We also stood outside the Vatican and saw the lights burning there. They are in the midst of excavations under the altar of St. Peter's. It is said they have found the Saint's bones there.

Eerie to stand in the great square where Musso used to make his speeches and look up at the deserted little balcony from which the thunder of that man of power would roll, echoed by "Il Duce. Il Duce," by the crowd. Now it is bare and shabby. Crowds pass without an upward glance. It is interesting how quickly these power-men can fall. Musso dominated this scene as fully as any dictator dominates any nation today, but now he has gone in a puff of wind and we are still at it.

It was in Rome that Howard was to find a liberty and commitment which he had searched for over four painful years:

"I could not build friendship with Buchman by trying to do what I thought would please him. He fought strongly, with a fierceness that seemed unreasonable but which worked, against the weakness in those who tried to put their trust in him as a man. But if I was giving everything in a battle, I found myself in natural and spurring comradeship at his side. He believed this to be the normal link of all who love God. I could not earn his friendship. He gave it freely to fighting hearts around him. Right or wrong, he would say what he felt, and expected all to do the same.

" 'Salted with the fire of the discipline,' was a phrase he loved and repeated. He quoted William Penn's words that ring down the ages: 'Men must choose to be governed by God or they condemn themselves to be ruled by tyrants.' He knew this to be true not only for nations struggling to keep their freedom, but also for every man who wants to be free from the tyranny of dictatorship in the home, or the thraldom of defeat by vice or habit."

That Easter in Rome, Howard had two clear thoughts, "Live absolute purity for God's sake. The heart of this idea will be your permanent home for the rest of your life."

"This represented for me the same cutting of all human security which Buchman faced when he gave up his paid job. It might mean never going back to my home or my country again. It meant being ready for anything and everything God demanded."

P.D.H. to Doë   Rome
                                               March 1950

For many days now quite vainly I have been trying to sit down at my typewriter and send the account of our time in St. Peter's, when we saw the Pope carried in glory on his Throne, our visit to the Catacombs and to Villa d'Este, but life has been a non-stop affair from five-thirty until midnight most days for me.

This trip has in some ways meant for me something like the experience Buchman had in the Lake District. And while it has not given me his qualities, it has given me his level of commitment. Hold me to that.

Thinking of the future I know that an experience of the Cross is the only cement of our work. Any splits in our own or any other work have come through a refusal to face it. It ends fear and favour. We need men now who will do nothing except provide a nucleus for God for the rest of their lives, men who will do everything together and nothing alone.

One thing clear to me is that if we are not winning men to the deepest experience we are not living an ideology. It does not mean you can take everyone there all at once, but that some get there with you all the time. Buchman is very direct and down-to-earth and he is not daunted by those who don't like it.

I have been thinking a lot about youth. My heart is very much with them. I feel that many of them, if not most, have never known this deeper experience of the Cross where their self-will is handed over. What you get is a steely philosophy, garlanded and rendered charming by the attraction of youth which has made up its mind to have its own way on many points and yells "dictatorship" if anybody tries to stop it. Adults must not be allowed to stifle, smother or stereotype youth. Equally, we must change this spirit in some of the young who think it is rendering the world a pioneering service by rebellion and brashness.

P.D.H. to Doë   Rome
                                             March 1950

My main work is with youth. They are as charming as heaven and as selfish as hell. At the drop of a hat they are off at night — women, smokes, drinks. The young people are hungry for fun and also for the deepest spiritual truth you can give. The thing which holds them is not what is said but a quality of life — absolute moral standards all the time. You cannot afford one word or moment off parade. If you do, you lose them. It is interesting that the folk who chaff them up, horse along with them and crack the kind of bluish joke for fear of being thought pious, lose them in the end.

For Howard this marked a watershed in his life. It also brought him back to Buchman's side: "I was walking along a passage and Buchman's voice said, 'Just like old times, isn't it, Peter?' That was all."

P.D.H. to Doë   Rome
                                                        March 16, 1950
In the last days at Rome I have had the best times I ever have had with Buchman. There has not been anything dramatic about it. I have talked out in the fullest and simplest terms with him the whole future of the work. The way in which he has moved to the heart of the situation here is an education. He is so funny. "Halleluja," he said the other day. And when one of the young Americans looked blank, Buchman added, "That is our college yell."

P.D.H. to Doë   Rome
                                                        March 17, 1950
After tea yesterday all the crowd went to a cinema while I stayed to look after Buchman. We talked over all the past. I told him that I felt it was my fault I had not lived at his side and had run away from him. "Yes, I felt you did that," said Buchman. "I think it has been all as much my fault. I could have made things easier for you. I could have talked to you early on, but I lacked the strength or may be it wasn't the time." I said sometimes you came to the place where without conscious sin you just did not know where and how to turn. "I understand that," said Buchman, "and I felt it in you but always and always knew you would change."

Buchman feels that some young people have come to think they are the whole business, that they know all the answers, and that their job is to help us by rebelling against the authority of the senior people as publicly and frequently as possible. To one centre he sent the following cable yesterday, "Youth is not the whole thing. If they won't work like everyone else, send them home. With my best compliments, Frank."

Those days in Rome were the beginning for Howard of eleven years of strenuous work with Buchman. There was God at the centre of the relationship and no false loyalties to man. This experience was not just a personal one. It freed Howard for a leadership which was to impact many nations as well as countless individuals. He had none of the glamour of personal power. He was in charge of no country. But he became a potent and lightning force in the battle for good against evil, for Almighty God against almighty man.

Spring, with her colour, warmth and scent,
Season of budding and rebirth,
Heralds the harvest for the earth.
And just as God drew in the sky
His bow of mystic symmetry —
A covenant of majesty,
That men no more need dread a flood
As symbol of the wrath of God —
So year by year He sends the spring,
Promise and pardon mingling,
While Christ eternal from the Cross
Bounty bestows from utter loss.
The broken, cold and stagnant earth
Quickens with miracles of birth,
And spirits, broken, contrite, cold,
Are healed with blessings manifold,
While hopes and hearts and harvesting
Stir with renewal in the spring.
At Eastertide the power, the joy,
Runs barefoot like a little boy
Across the land in revelry.
At Eastertide the joy, the power,
Rises like sap. O magic hour,
When hope grows warm with certainty
Of miracles that we shall see,
Of harvest in the fields again
And harvest in the hearts of men —
God's Kingdom after sweat and pain.
Yes, death becomes a wondrous thing
'Mid Cross and crocus in the spring.
Beauty is free to walk abroad
And spread the glory of the Lord.
The stiff white collars of the frost
Melt from the hedgerows, and, embossed
With cowslip and anemone,
The robes of Easter warm each day.
Spring touches with her garment's hem
The thickets as she garlands them;
With green and blossom cloaks the thorn
That crowned a King one bitter dawn.
The robin, with his breast as red
As streamed the blood from that bowed head,

With beak and claws his tiny loom,
Weaves and reweaves his simple home.
Skeleton leaves and horses' hair
The fabric and foundation bear,
With craftsmanship his perfect prayer.
The stackyard ricks rise 'mid the hum
And bustle of the hungry drum.
The slender, silver straw of wheat,
Like ash-blond hair about your feet,
With oatstraw gold and beanstraw brown,
To build the thriving stackyard town.
While from the drum the sacks are filling
With grain for cattle and for milling —
The self-same kernel of the corn
Which Jesus ate one Sabbath morn.
And ever since the time, 'tis said,
A Baby in the wheat is laid.
Swaddled by chaff, in every grain
You see Him rise from death again.

In spring the horseman drives his plough
And lays the furrows row by row,
Like ripples of a rising tide
Across the arable they ride —
Then crooms to kill the tares and weeds,
With drills to sow the swelling seeds.
And some will fall and never grow,
Snatched straightaway by rook or crow.
And some will fall on stony ground;
So, rootless, withered will be found
In the sun's blaze. And some will choke
'Mid thistle, devil's claw and dock.
And some will gleam with harvest gold
An hundred and an hundred-fold,
Just as two thousand years ago
The Son of Man foretold it so.
He walks the land round Easter Day,
Life-giving in fertility.
In spring the sea obeys the will
Of Him who whispered "Peace, be still."
The wrinkled ocean kneels and crawls
Against our towering island walls,
And seagulls sickle through the sky,
Plying their ancient husbandry

To glean sea-fruit among the caves
And pools o'erbrimming with the waves —
Crablings and shrimps and fish in shell
From each enamelled, twisting cell.
The sounds and scents and mystery
Which made them hunger for the sea,
Those fishermen of Galilee —
And on the seashore Christ appeared,
While Peter fished and others feared
That first unfailing Eastertide,
Which told the world Christ had not died.

O, heaven is earth and earth is heaven
To know that Christ the King is risen,
To know the Easter tale is true
That Jesus maketh all things new —
Earth, ocean, men and nations too.
    Christ is risen
From tomb on earth to throne in heaven.
The world is new, our sins forgiven.
    Alleluia!

Chapter 12

FROM 1950 onwards, Peter Howard worked at Buchman's side. He was with him at Caux that summer when the first representative group to leave Japan since the war arrived there. He wrote at the time:

"The party of seventy-six included the Governors of seven Prefectures; M.P.s of all parties; the Mayors of several cities including Hiroshima and Nagasaki; businessmen; trade union leaders; and leading educational, press and radio personalities.

"Before they left, the Prime Minister, Mr. Yoshida, told them, 'In 1870 a representative group of Japanese travelled to the West. On their return they changed the course of Japanese life. I believe that when this delegation returns, you, too, will open a new page in our history.'

"At Caux the Japanese began to pattern among themselves the secret of unity for their nation. One of the delegates was Mr. Eiji Suzuki, the chief of police of Osaka. His wife said that she never knows when he leaves home in the morning whether he will get safely back at night. He is a big man with a mask of toughness which his job demands. One of his bitter enemies was another member of the delegation, Mr. Katsuji Nakajima, a leader of the Metalworkers' Union of Japan.

"Nakajima is little more than half the size of the chief of police, but full of fight. He was in Hiroshima when the bomb fell and bears the marks of it to this day. He loathed the chief of police so much that all the way in the aeroplane he would not speak to him.

"His eyes spark with fire behind his spectacles. But the water of tears quenched the fire as he went to see the chief of police one day at Caux and begged pardon for his hate.

"Next day the chief of police begged the pardon of Mr. Nakajima for his hatred of the Socialists and Communists. He said, 'I have been overcome by your tremendous spirit.'

"Someone from another country, who had lived for years in Japan and knows the great reserve and proper pride of her people, said that if he had not seen this with his own eyes he would never have believed it possible. One of the members of the Japanese Diet described it as 'the greatest gift that could be given to Japan. It answers the hatred that threatens to tear Japan with civil war.'

"The Japanese summed up the significance of their journey in a statement which appeared in *The Observer*. They said, 'Russia has advanced in Asia because the Soviet Government understands the art of ideological war. It fights for the minds of men. We appeal to the governments and people of the West to do the same — to make themselves expert in the philosophy and practice of Moral Re-Armament, which is the ideology of the future. Then all Asia will listen.' "

When the Japanese reached Washington that July, they were the first Japanese in history to address the two Houses of Congress. Howard wrote:

"Mr. Kuriyama's[1] speech was interrupted by loud applause. The Senators rose to him as he finished his speech. He said, 'We went to Caux in search of the true content of democracy. We found the ideology which will feed democracy in Japan.' Then he continued, 'We are sincerely sorry for Japan's big mistake. We broke almost a century-old friendship between our two countries.' The Senate and the galleries sat in dead silence, deeply moved by his apology.

"*The New York Times* commented: 'Peace and goodwill can return, even after the most terrible events. The Mayors of Hiroshima and Nagasaki were among yesterday's visitors to Congress. If they felt that they too had something to forgive they had achieved that miracle. For a moment one could see out of the present darkness into the years when all men may be brothers.' "

.　　　.　　　.

In the next two years, Howard spent many months in America. The pain of parting from his family grew no less with the years. His son Philip, won a scholarship to Eton. Then to Oxford. But his father was seldom able to visit him. He missed all the events of Philip's last Half at Eton and the subsequent terms at Oxford. It was much the same for Anne and Anthony. And, above all, for Doë, who cared for the children, and gave her support and encouragement across three thousand miles of ocean.

P.D.H. to Doë   U.S.A.
                                                                              1951
It is always hell to say goodbye. I must say I found myself close to tears when I saw Ant weeping. He is a dear lad and I only wish I could have done more with and for him. His heart like my own hates to say

[1] Mr. Chojiro Kuriyama, Member of the Government Party of the Japanese Diet.

goodbye to those he loves. For some reason this parting from you all has been hard. I realise that another holiday has come and gone with only the briefest of times as a family.

Howard was in America with a second Japanese delegation.

P.D.H. to Doë   New York
                                                                                    May 3, 1951
We have just been in Washington with the Japanese delegation. They gave us lunch in the room where they entertained MacArthur. The place was so full that Joe Martin, the Speaker, could not get a chair when he arrived late.

P.D.H. to Doë   New York
                                                                                    May 1951
I rang Beaverbrook this morning. He had just landed from the *Queen Elizabeth*. I heard he was there so telephoned the Waldorf. B. was dumbfounded that I knew so soon he was in the city. I told him about Mackinac and he said, "Wherever I go I hear of your doings." He mentioned Kerr-Jarrett, who is the Custos of St. James, Jamaica, and was at Washington. "Do you know what a Custos is?" he asked. "Lord High Executioner," said I. He laughed loud and long. "I want to see you and shall be looking for you," he said.

P.D.H. to Doë   Mackinac Island
                                                                                    June 1, 1951
The *New York Times'* man arrived at crack of dawn yesterday and Buchman was great with him. His opening line was, "I am paid to be cynical." Whereupon Buchman on introducing him to everybody or anybody remarked, "Now don't give him anything positive. Give him the negatives. That's what he wants." The fellow was much captivated by all this.

The I.N.S. telephoned from Detroit in the course of the day and made me their paid correspondent for the Assembly. It is the first paid job I have had since Beaverbrook. I have to file 250 words morning and evening, which is not too desperate, and they will give me £100, which is poor I'd say. But how much is bread worth when you have no wheat? The A.P. want 150 words and this also falls to my lot and portion unpaid. The A.P. woman on the island gets the dollars and we do the work, but at least it reaches millions of people.

It is a joy and also a lesson to have the chance to see Buchman as he sets up an Assembly like this. The night before last he had very great pain. He was in real agony for a time. His only comment was, "I always get something like this just before the big events. It is to make me utterly dependent on God, I suppose." His prayer that night was, "Make me a better man. And thank you for pain which purifies and strengthens. Amen."

The lilac is just about to bloom here. The spring comes late.

P.D.H. to Doë   Detroit
                                                               June 23, 1951

I came unexpectedly overnight to Detroit and saw a remarkable sight on the platform when we disembarked. John L. Lewis, who hopes to amalgamate the local 600 Union of Fords (membership 75,000) with his own, was arriving to address them. There was a brass band and a milling mob of unionists, most of them wearing hats with "solidarity" written on them, already there to welcome the great man. When he arrived they all sang to the tune of "Glory, glory, Alleluja" the words of "Solidarity for Ever. The union makes us one."

John L. is a jaded man, pale faced, much smaller than I had pictured him and a typical Welshman. He might have come straight out of the Rhondda. He was stimulated by the welcome, but looked rather like a lonely little yellow lion out of a children's book.

We are now at the airport where we are waiting for a plane. What happened was that Eddy Rickenbacker[1] has a meeting of 200 of his executives from 87 cities in Miami tomorrow and they telephoned asking us to speak to them about MRA.

The interest in all the airlines based in Miami was intense since the surprise settlement earlier that year of the dispute in National Airlines. Howard wrote at that time:

" 'At the start of 1951 you could have bought the goodwill of our airline for a thousand dollars,' said one of the Board of National Airlines. 'Today you could not buy it for millions.'

"A feud which had lasted years caused one of the longest strikes in airlines history, and was about to cause another one 'was brought to a screeching halt as the result of Moral Re-Armament'. So says W. T. 'Slim' Babbitt, Vice-President of the Air Line Pilots' Association of America (ALPA).

"Two men were at the heart of this feud. One was Babbitt himself, the other G. T. Baker, President of National Airlines.

" 'We were two deadly enemies,' says 'Slim' Babbitt.

"Baker is tough and square, a man who has fought his way up from the ground to the top of a large industrial enterprise. In that struggle he became ruthless.

" 'Slim' Babbitt is a shrewd, down-to-earth character. He is skilled in the

[1] President, Eastern Airlines.

art of industrial negotiation and has fought without fear or favour for the interests of the pilots.

"The trouble began many years ago, and distrust, fear and hate mounted steadily. Matters came to a head in February 1948, when Baker fired a pilot without, as the pilots believed, giving him a fair chance to state his case. The National pilots went on strike. Baker tried to keep going by introducing non-union pilots.

"The union pilots struck back in many ways. Streamers were drawn by planes over Miami saying, 'Don't fly National'. Match books were distributed in hotels with the same slogan. The offices of National Airlines were picketed and passengers were warned that National's aircraft were unsafe.

"Baker filed a £5,000,000 claim against them for defaming his company. After ten months the Civil Aeronautics Board stepped in. They ordered an investigation to consider the dismemberment of National Airlines and the dividing up of its services among other airlines.

"Finally Baker agreed to put the ALPA pilots back to work. But, in fact, the period between 1948 and 1951 was, to quote 'Slim' Babbitt, 'much worse than the actual strike'.

"Babbitt says that in that period the Pilots' Association spent hundreds of thousands of dollars in their efforts to ruin Baker.

"Baker comments, 'That is duplicate for me.'

"At the end of 1950, Babbitt and the pilots decided to put National Airlines and Baker out of business forever. The dismemberment order by the Civil Aeronautics Board was still pending, and in December 1950, Babbitt called the pilots of National to a strike vote, which in his mind meant the end of the airlines.

"It is at this point that Moral Re-Armament enters the story. A businessman in Florida, who knows Moral Re-Armament but did not know Baker, decided that the two must be brought together. Executives in the airlines told him it would be impossible for him to see Baker. But the businessman was undaunted. He went right to Baker's office and persisted.

"Baker said later of this interview, 'I was waiting for the gimmick, but it never came.' That afternoon Baker went into the office of his Vice-President every fifteen or twenty minutes. His mind had begun to move at a new level. He said, 'We haven't been honest. I always thought I was an honest-to-God sort of a guy – but absolute honesty, that's something different.

"Word reached 'Slim' Babbitt of a new attitude in Baker. He did not believe one word of it. He sent some of the negotiating pilots around to see what was going on.

"They arrived, not expecting to see Baker, but as soon as he heard they were there he sent word to bring the pilots up to his office. They had never been there before. Presently one of them telephoned Babbitt and said, 'Where do you think we are? Baker is out of the room at the moment but we are in his office, smoking his cigars. We are four feet off the ground and Baker's on the ceiling and we can't get him down.'

"Baker proposed to Babbitt that the mediation on the pending strike, fixed for January 2 by the National Mediation Board, should be postponed until after the Moral Re-Armament Assembly which was being held in Washington during the opening days of January 1951, and that Babbitt and some of the pilots should attend the Assembly with Baker and some of his senior executives.

"Babbitt was suspicious. But finally he agreed. 'I went strictly to case the joint,' he says. He would not stay at the same Washington hotel as Baker and the other delegates.

"But they met after the performance of one of the MRA plays. Except in the courtroom, this was the first time the men had met personally. They went to a hotel room and talked. 'We got further in three hours than we had in the three previous years,' they later said. Babbitt and Baker began to talk about the world situation. Then there was a pause. Baker suddenly said, 'I have been wrong.' He began to tell Babbitt of the places where he felt he had failed to do the right thing in his dealings with the pilots. 'He did not blame the pilots once,' said Babbitt, 'on any point at all.'

"Babbitt admitted to Baker that he had 'dreamed up' many of the thirteen strike grievances that were at issue as part of the campaign to ruin Baker.

"Baker and his executives, Babbitt and the pilots flew back to Florida. Babbitt wired the Moral Re-Armament Assembly at this time, 'We are now busily engaged in the mechanics of cutting the ropes which have retarded National Airlines as well as its pilots so the two will be free to go forward as a team to build an airline with unlimited potentiality for both parties. Until I get more information, I shall refer to MRA as a wonder drug that makes real human beings out of people.'

"In March they announced their settlement to the press. The Civil Aeronautics Board withdrew its pending dismemberment order. The banks, which for years had been reluctant to advance money to National, loaned enough to buy a number of new planes.

"These events made front-page news in America. The *Miami Herald* headlined its story: 'Moral Re-Armament Ushers in Era of Understanding'.

"The settlement of the feud between Baker and Babbitt did not, of course, mean that all grievances were ended for all time in National. It did mean that an industrial bottleneck which was killing the line was broken.

"D. W. Rentzel, Chairman of the Civil Aeronautics Board, issued the following public statement, 'To those familiar with the long history of bitter and acrimonious dispute the transformation in the attitude of the parties has been little short of miraculous.' "

P.D.H. to Doë   Columbus Hotel, Miami
                                                        June 25, 1951

We were with 250 of Rickenbacker's executives for two-and-a-quarter hours. At the end they all stood up and cheered like billyo, which in this heat was probably pure relief the thing was over.

Your encouragement and thought over my writing mean and have meant so much. To be honest I always feel there is better writing in me than ever gets out. To write at one's best does take time and sweat. It is hard to do on a hit and run basis. Somehow I need to plan my life where every day I write for an hour or so. On the road it seems impossible, but we will contrive it together one day.

P.D.H. to Doë   Chicago
                                                        June 27, 1951

We went to an early lunch today with Professor Moon. He is one of the nuclear men. He entertained twenty-five of us in the same block of buildings where in 1942 the first chain reaction of nuclear energy was produced. His guests were mainly Japanese, some of whom had lost everything at Hiroshima and Nagasaki. Moon spoke. Likewise the head of the student body of Osaka University and three Chicago University professors. Also your humble husband and the head of 300,000 textile workers in Japan. Then we went on to be received by the Mayor. We were later on television. At five this afternoon we go off to an early dinner at a modern factory on the north side. Then to a public meeting, to which the press are coming. Then bed I hope.

P.D.H. to Doë   Detroit
                                                         July 1, 1951

It was really hot last night in Detroit, 96 degrees. I was tired, Barrett[1] was flying home and you were a long way off. I got really lonely all of a sudden. Then on to the bus that goes from the air station into town clambered a little Negro boy of about eight. He sat down beside me. He had flown from Hotsprings, Arkansas, where he had been in hospital since January. He was all excited to be going to see his mother again. To tell the truth he reminded me terribly of Ant with his ways. When I asked his name he replied, "They call me Gee-wizz." Anyway this child chattered away. He cheered me up considerably.

P.D.H. to Doë   July 17, 1951

I am gaily sailing in a train back to St. Ignace. On the plane today was most of the Board of the Chicago and Southern Airlines which is just merging with Delta. They asked me forward to the cabin near the pilot's place where they were sitting. They began by saying rather rudely that they were not fully sold on MRA. I replied with equal vigour that I

[1] Mr. R. M. S. Barrett of Edinburgh. Worked with MRA since 1932.

179

was not at all sold on C. & S. Airlines, but that at least I was trying it to see how it worked. We then had a valuable hour.

The train has just passed a marsh from which a cloud of wild duck rose and flew like arrows as we drew level. Then a tragic sight, a place that once must have been a magnificent ranch, hewed out of the vastness of the forest, of at least twelve buildings and a fine house, which had been deserted. The roofs of the buildings have just collapsed like hats on top of the ruin. You can see where once the fields and fences were. But now the forest is racing in again and in a few years, I suppose, that will all be gone.

P.D.H. to Doë   Miami
                                                              January 1952
A great thing happened in the bus strike here. Pawley[1] telegraphed from Portugal, where he flew with Lovett[2] for the NATO meeting, asking myself and Newton to accept and pass on to others his thanks for the 'magnificent help of MRA in helping to settle the Miami transit bus strike'. Insofar as human credit can be taken, it belongs to Buchman, who had the whole idea and fought to fulfil it. God has worked His wonders.

Buchman is to have his operation. He goes into hospital today and is operated on the day after tomorrow. He said to me, "Thank you for everything. I shan't see you for a few days and if this is the end, why, what is that? There is life after death."

Tonight we have another training meeting for which I am responsible. I have never been more physically exhausted. Our people here need to learn that MRA is not an idea that one promotes. It is people with a revolutionary passion to put right what is wrong – a revolutionary passion as all-consuming as the revolutionary passion of any of the isms, but bringing change through change in human nature – not up in the sky and airy-fairy, but down-to-earth and dealing with the actual problems of the hour.

P.D.H. to Doë   March 7, 1952
I have just come in from having my hair clipped by a Greek barber. He wanted to clip my eyebrows, too, but I stopped him. He said to me in a strong Greek accent, "Brother, you are sure losing your hair." I thought he was going to sell me some hair tonic, but instead he told me to brush it three times a day with a stiff brush. Pointing to his own bald head he added, "I did not do this."

He left Corinth thirty years ago as a young man of twenty-four. He had saved up enough by 1930 to travel home when the crash came. He

[1] Mr. William D. Pawley, Sr., President of the Miami Bus Company, and American Ambassador to Brazil and Peru.
[2] Mr. Robert A. Lovett, Secretary of Defence.

lost everything. He was in hospital a month because the shock nearly sent him out of his mind. "I sometimes wonder if I am really O.K. yet," he said grinning and waving a cut-throat razor at me. He has never been back. His father died. His mother is eighty and longs to see him before she dies. He sends her cans of butter and hopes to go back this year.

The one sadness I have is about Philip's last Half at Eton. I would give my back teeth to hear him speak on June 4 and all the other things associated with the climax of his Eton years.

P.D.H. to Doë   Miami
                                        March 18, 1952

We still have to fight a deep-seated organisational mentality. There is a curious conviction that by organised activity people will change and nations will change. If organised activity would do it, why the UN would have been effective long since. Of course it is a far cheaper procedure than the Cross.

I was walking last night on the golf course. I actually played two holes with Campbell[1] with a number four iron as dusk fell and saw a pair of cardinals, deep red with little crests. Also a vividly-coloured woodpecker.

It is nice to sit with you for a spell. I can almost believe that if I speak you will answer me.

P.D.H. to Doë   Allentown (F.N.D.B.'s home)
                                          April 7, 1952

We got in yesterday after a pleasant six-hour train journey. The prices on the railway here are wicked — $3 for an indifferent dinner and $1.65 for tea and a sandwich.

Buchman was talking about his mother and father this morning. It is moving how much the memory of his family still means. He said, "Father was a strikingly handsome man. He retired at forty-one and died at eighty-one. He was a great horticulturalist. Some of his apple trees are still left. My grandmother, Greenwalt, wore her own imported silks and corsets. That was the equivalent of riding in a Cadillac today. Their place in the country was the place I slept best in all the world. Once I would have liked to retire there but not now." Then looking at his mother's photo he remarked, "Leave on the light. I like to look at her."

P.D.H. to Doë   New York
                                          April 1952

My heart is full of you all, and I walk beside you through the days. It must be beautiful at home now. Please send me a brief word of progress with the pigs, pence and sheep.

[1] Dr. Paul Campbell, on the staff of the Henry Ford Hospital, Detroit, 1938–42. Later Dr. Buchman's personal physician.

I am in my life's work, though I came late to it. It is the wonder of the world to be called to serve God in its remaking. We are faced today with a breakdown in civilisation. It is not a national problem. It is the problem of men who will not sacrifice their selfishness, plans and viewpoints because they are compromising in their own lives.

One thing that makes some people shear off from Buchman is his wholehearted uncompromising attack on evil. He never lets one thing pass, whether in the kitchen or a conference. I cherish that quality for myself.

P.D.H. to Doë   New York
                                                        April 21, 1952

On Friday a lady arrived with a large box of candy for Buchman and another for me. Buchman said, "Don't open yours. Keep it for Doë." So I have.

Buchman is in great form. Someone went to him yesterday and wept bitter tears at what they had seen about their failures of the years, and of how they felt they had betrayed the trust Buchman had in them. But all Buchman said was, "Oh, I am a hopeless failure. I have not done the things I should with you all, etc." This made the person concerned worse than ever. Buchman's prayer afterwards was, "God forgive this old hypocrite. Goodnight."

He also said, "Unity grows where men have a common purpose which means more to them than their own selfish plans and aims. There are in Washington so many special rules for special people. That is the heart of the philosophy of corruption there. It often starts with ambition but it ends in exploitation. The wages of sin is death for the other fellow, as opposed to the liberty of the Cross which is the death of self. The men who have led the nations furthest astray feel most keenly how lucky the nations are to have them. We need a new concept of leadership."

The plain fact is that we are fighting a battle for America. Some think only of results. It is the mistake so easily made by men who are accustomed to mass movements. No organisational success is an adequate substitute for a living experience of God.

P.D.H. to Doë   Allentown
                                                        April 25, 1952

Yesterday I drove past the house in Pennsburg, now a little general store, where Buchman was born. It is not unlike the Maidenhead house, where a more disreputable character first saw the daylight. We also saw father Buchman's hotel, an old-style, five-floor square building right by the railway station.

P.D.H. to Doë   Chicago
                                            May 21, 1952

We got in to Chicago yesterday morning after a good but rather bumpy night on the train. I am staying with Colonel and Mrs. Robert McCormick of *Chicago Tribune* fame. I am sitting up in bed writing this to you in a room which bears a large plaque of brass on the door "Winston Churchill". It is the room where the great man convalesced after being knocked down by a taxi cab before the war. Mrs. McCormick is a delightful lady and talks a lot about her husband to whom she refers all the time as "The Colonel".

The Colonel was educated in England at Ludgrove prep school. He later went to Groton and Yale here. He said the English taught him the secret of patriotism. His fancy for the Presidency is Taft. Hers is MacArthur, whom they have known well for a number of years. "It's true he's old," she says, "and so is Churchill. Churchill after all is a very heavy drinker which MacArthur is not." Then she added, "Don't tell 'The Colonel' I said I favour MacArthur or he'd cut my throat from ear to ear."

P.D.H. to Doë   Mackinac Island
                                            May 27, 1952

We have been hard at work. Buchman has been running over his broadcast. I have been writing a thousand words for the *Chicago Herald American* on the subject of Buchman. The Editor of the paper was at the Chicago dinner. He is a sharp, wise character named Harry Reutlinger. He came up to me before the dinner started and said, "I want to tell you one thing. If I don't like this dinner I'll leave." I said, "I want to tell you another thing. If I don't like it I will leave too." For some reason he liked this and told Campbell later that he regarded me as his blood brother.

In July 1952, Howard was in Washington with a British docker who had been formerly one of those to plan the "Beaverbrae" strike of 1949 which was estimated by *The Times* to have cost Britain £217,000,000. They were at a private meeting with Senators and Congressmen:

"The Senators asked the English docker what had made him into a Communist. He replied, 'I had a daughter. She did not get enough to eat because we were too poor. She died. That evening a priest came to my home and prayed with me and said that the girl would be buried without charge. Later that night the Communists came to my home and said, "Stick with us and we'll smash the system." I joined the Party that night.'

"The Americans then asked him about his training in Communism. He told them he had been taught how to provide men with women if they wanted women. How to find money and use it to corrupt and win individuals. How to promote jealousy, hatred, frustration and division and to separate men of goodwill from each other through pride or their private indulgence. Then he told how he had changed, and what he was fighting for. How he and all his family which had been reunited returned to the Catholic Church.

"At the end of a long evening the Senators said, 'Good night.' The docker replied, 'Just a moment. You have asked me many questions. Can I ask you one or two?' The Senators were surprised but agreed. The docker then said, 'You have all talked a lot about Communism tonight. How many of you have ever sat down with one Communist and changed him?' There was no answer. He then said, 'How many of you know how to sit down with a difficult person who is not a Communist and change him?' Again, there was no answer. The Englishman said, 'When democracy learns that secret, democracy will win the world.' "

In September Howard was in San Francisco with Buchman and a large group. The Japanese Peace Treaty was to be signed there, and five of the seven Japanese signatories dined with Buchman the evening before the conference opened. When Robert Schuman, who was representing France, heard that the London docker was meeting Harry Bridges and his long-shoremen, he said to Buchman, "Ah, the world is not big enough for you." And added, "You made peace with Japan two years before we signed it."

P.D.H. to Doë   San Francisco
                                                               September 9, 1952

Each day I breakfast on fruit, fresh raspberries, black figs, grapes, peaches. It brings our wonderful trip through France very close to me, and then we have a brief conference with Buchman and go to the Assembly meetings with the Peace delegates. We have really been the only ones to care for the Japanese. Their views may be summed up by Suzuki, leader of the Government Party in the Upper House, who said yesterday when the Treaty was finally signed, "What I have heard about MRA this week is much more important than the Treaty. It will be the basis of my report when I get back to Japan."

Pearson's[1] speech at the Assembly was the only one which showed any understanding of what the Japanese are really feeling. He said, "We must not forget that the Japanese themselves have suffered very greatly." He said it with warmth. And that afternoon Yoshida called upon him. It is amazing what the simplest piece of constructive action does.

Senator Wiley, who is one of the US signatories to the Treaty, and who spoke to the Commonwealth Club in mid-week, when he saw me sitting a few tables away called me up, asked for a copy of The World Rebuilt (by P.D.H.) and spent the first five minutes of his speech talking

[1] Lester Pearson, Foreign Minister and later Prime Minister of Canada.

about the book and MRA. He said, "We must deal with reality. I have talked in Europe with Eisenhower about MRA. This force is changing the tide of Communism and building unity between classes and nations in the world."

The City Council of San Francisco sent a copy of The World Rebuilt with a letter to every delegate at the conference. This angered men like Younger,[1] the British Under-Secretary, who said, "I do not like Howard. I do not like MRA."

Some things stick out from the conference. Most of the statesmen are ideological babies, and some of them also have a vested interest in their own selfishness. It is a significant but hardly believable fact that at the first banquet last night, neither Acheson,[2] nor Spender,[3] nor Governor Warren,[4] who all spoke, even mentioned Japan, though Yoshida was the final after-dinner speaker and all the Japanese were keenly feeling their first reception into the family of nations. Acheson made a speech about dirty underwear. Spender, the Australian, is a better man, but the whole performance was shoddy.

Gromyko[5] spoke here with much passion and plain sincerity, but his line was almost entirely to deal with territorial acquisitions and power politics rather than the bid for the minds and wills of men, which was the genius of Lenin.

Another thing you feel is that the free nations are as much in rebellion against the will of God as the Communist bloc. They think that do as you please is a good answer to do as you are told. It isn't. And in cold, clear, objective terms the demoralised philosophies of the West have caused as much human suffering and grief as the militant philosophies of the East.

P.D.H. to H.   San Francisco
                                            September 10, 1952

Buchman saw Alger Hiss,[6] one of the Americans, crossing the lobby of the Mark Hopkins Hotel. He is the blue-eyed boy of all the Allied diplomats. Buchman turned and said with passionate conviction, "Watch that man. Have nothing to do with him. There's something very wrong with him."

[1] Kenneth Younger, Labour Member for Grimsby 1945–59; Minister of State for Foreign Affairs 1950–51.
[2] Dean Acheson, US Secretary of State 1949–53.
[3] Sir Percy Spender, Vice-President, Japanese Peace Treaty Conference 1951; Australian Ambassador to US 1951–58.
[4] Governor Earl Warren, Governor of California 1943–53; Chief Justice of US from 1953.
[5] Andrei Gromyko, Soviet diplomatist, later Foreign Minister.
[6] Alger Hiss, Secretary-General of the San Francisco Conference.

These were strenuous years for Howard. Buchman was ill much of the time, and Howard travelled to and fro, often alone and with little money, landing in a different city each day to speak and meet the press or radio. The friendships he built during these years lasted him a lifetime.

Peter Howard was not what most Americans imagine as typically British. He was far too outspoken and lively for that. He was strong, sometimes painfully so, in his diagnosis. It was matched with an even stronger belief in cure. He made many mistakes, but he learned from them without rancour. He was impatient, but he learnt to turn that impatience into a passionate pursuit of good, rather than an irritation with people.

He came to understand America's strengths and weaknesses – and to love her people, regardless of both.

Chapter 13

THE TAJ MAHAL BY NIGHT AND DAY
On our 20th Anniversary

Pearl in the mist, you sleep against the moon
    So vast, so cold, so ancient in your dreams,
Shell-like and delicate, at heat of noon
    Your snow-smooth dome yet gleams.

A marble memory of love gone by,
    Of laughter that the climate of the years
Has frozen into stone — against the sky
    Your diamonds shine like tears.

And twenty thousand men moulded with sweat
    For twenty years that marble into leaf,
A foliage of love, lest men forget
    Through centuries your grief.

No marble and no moonlight mark our days.
    For us the timeless trail where all is loss
Of diamonds and delight, of pearl-strewn ways —
    And gain, the eternal Cross.

But in this fleeting second of our life
    Look down your stars as I my pledge unfold.
I would not trade one moment with my wife
    For all the Taj — in gold.

In October, 1952, Howard went to Asia for the first time, where he travelled for seven months with Buchman in Ceylon, India and Pakistan. The invitation had come from leaders of those countries[1] who knew Buchman and his work. The invitation to India read in part:

[1] The invitation to Ceylon was signed by the Prime Minister, Mr. Dudley Senanayake, four of his Cabinet and other representative leaders. That from India was sent by eighteen leaders, including Mr. G. L. Nanda, who later acted as Prime Minister on two occasions, Mr. J. R. D. Tata, aud Mr. Khandubhai Desai, President of the National Trades Union Congress.

"We are convinced that the true hope for bringing lasting change in social and economic conditions and for bringing peace to the world lies in multiplying such practical results as we believe to have been achieved by Moral Re-Armament — the giving of a new incentive to industry, the change of heart of capitalist and Communist alike, the replacing of mistrust, bitterness and hate between individuals and groups with understanding and co-operation. We consider that such moral re-armament of the nations is the need of the hour and the hope of the future."

Buchman had been advised that twenty or thirty people were all who could conveniently travel together on the sub-continent. Characteristically, he decided to take two hundred people and three plays with him. To Howard fell much of the practical organisation of the tour. He went first to Bombay, while Buchman and the main party proceeded to Ceylon.

P.D.H. to Doë   Bombay
                                                October 13, 1952
Last evening we were taken in a car to Juhu Beach, about five miles north of Bombay, and as the sun set went swimming in a sea that feels just like a warm bath. On the beach were men cracking whips and small boys turning cartwheels and tumbling; a band of percussion instruments; mothers with squads of children building circles in the sand for them with coloured flowers; and people riding horses. It was as crowded as Brighton beach but far more full of life and laughter. It is extraordinary to feel the warmth of heart of these people.

They welcomed us with bunches of flowers at the airport, and we are staying in the home of your friends, the Gandhys.

On the beach little boys sold coconuts which they cut open and which you drank — lovely warm stuff, quite unlike anything you get on Hampstead Heath. In the middle of this teeming city with its trams, cars and buses you see vultures perched on a tree.

P.D.H. to Doë   Bombay
                                                October 14, 1952
Everyone in this country is immensely willing but nobody is committed. The leadership of the city has set up various committees — reception, finance, recreation. The President of the Scindia Steamship Line presided over the meeting of the arrangements committee in the board room of his company last night.

Someone said to me sadly at lunch, "It used to be Bombay, the beautiful. Now it is Bombay, city of dirt and disease." Over one million people live more than ten in a room here and in tropical heat. You step over mothers and children asleep in the streets. Parents, so the head of the Untouchables told us, deliberately mutilate the limbs of their babies so as they grow older they may, by their pathos, be better able to beg.

This is the land of negatives. Everyone seems to know thirty good reasons why he won't and why this can't be. Activism coupled with inertia, once the arrangements have been made, seems a characteristic in India. The answer is to change men.

P.D.H. to Doë   Bombay
                                                          October 16, 1952

Our Anne's birthday. How abundantly good God is to us.

I had lunch with Tata's Board of Directors yesterday, and an excellent interview with Frank Moraes, Editor of *The Times of India*. When I walked in he said, "I was at Oxford with you. The first friendly word I ever had in England was your report of my speech in the Union."

At a party last evening, Gandhi's personal physician said, "I see you are not making plans but trying to fit yourselves and everybody into the Plan."

P.D.H. to Doë   Bombay
                                                          October 17, 1952

We are in the air *en route* for Colombo. The central plain of India is a magnificent sight from the sky. Every inch of the earth seems to be cultivated. I had expected mostly jungle but there are fields, very tiny fields.

Everything has worked wonderfully in Bombay. We have the prospect of a first-rate theatre seating 844 people, a special train to take us all over India, and a finance committee which really seems to expect to finance everything.

P.D.H. to Doë   Colombo
                                                          October 30, 1952

Yesterday I was off and gone at crack of dawn and did not get home till midnight.

We were the guests of the Minister of Agriculture at a demonstration of transplanting paddy. They had a thousand women knee deep in the soft mud of the fields planting rice by hand. It increases the yield by 50 per cent, but because of the toil and time most farmers have stopped doing it. A thousand women did fifty acres in a day.

We drove sixty miles through the most beautiful country imaginable — palm trees, tea bushes, rubber groves, tumbling rivers, and all the time the deep living green of the young paddy. We were in a car with the Minister and stopped at 8 a.m. for breakfast with a planter, including the most delicious homegrown tea. Then we drove to the demonstration.

There was an arch of welcome for us. The procession was headed b
twelve elephants wearing panoplies of many colours. Then came thirty-si
Kandy dancers with glorious silver headdresses spreading up from th
head like a peacock's tail and with a loose thong of leather, about tw
yards long, which whistles and lashes in the wind as they dance. The
wear underneath what seemed to be long white woollies. They have bell
tied to their toes. They dance and dance and dance, savagely, rhythmically
frantically. They dance of the hare and of the leopard. They danced i
front of us, amid literally thousands of villagers who had turned out t
see us, for nearly a mile on the dusty sun-soaked road. They were accom
panied by a band of boys dressed like the pirates in Peter Pan with hug
long leather drums which they walloped with their hands. And as the
beat they sing wild songs and with such hands as were free they shoo
castanets in the air.

Buchman spoke over the radio to the thousand women working in th
fields. He said, "There is enough rice in the world for everybody's need
Ceylon is a free nation. I congratulate her on her freedom. She can shov
the whole of Asia how to stay free. Empty stomachs will be filled witl
food. Empty hands with work. And empty hearts with an idea that reall
satisfies." The workers loved it. So did the Cabinet men. We then wer
given lunch wrapped in banana leaves – curry so hot that it made yo
think you had taken a chew on the wrong end of a cigar, and coconu
milk fresh from the nut.

Seven Cabinet Ministers were at the opening of the play last night. Th
head of the Bombay Waterfront Workers said, "That play could chang
every worker in India." The response is overwhelming. We are having t
double-up on Friday, Saturday and Sunday and put on two shows a day
which is an effort in this heat.

P.D.H. to Doë   Colombo
                                                 November 5, 1952
     We are addressing the dockers this afternoon. The men here ge
paid 80 rupees (about £6) a month. They have to keep their familie
on this. They are born in debt, live in debt, die in debt. But they have
really open hearts. Our battle is to focus our work all the time on the
men and situations that will actually affect Ceylon and Asia ideologic
ally.

Buchman had visited India many times, the first time being i
1915 when he became friends with Mahatma Gandhi. The Mahatma
said that MRA was "the best thing that has come out of the West"
Buchman spoke of his friendship with Gandhi when the party arrived ir
Bombay.

Howard greets Chancellor Konrad Adenauer on his birthday, 1963

Howard arrives in Rio de Janeiro, January, 1965

Howard during his tour of American Universities, 1964

P.D.H. to Doë   Bombay
                               November 15, 1952
When we docked there was a huge sign, "Welcome MRA", and half
the town had turned out to meet us – the Mayor, the Sheriff, Tata and
hundreds more.

In the afternoon the city gave Buchman a public welcome in the
Hanging Gardens of Bombay. It was beautifully done. The panorama
was magnificent. The Hanging Gardens are on Malabar Hill and the
Bay stretches gloriously away into the russet and gold of a tropical evening.

Buchman described how Gandhi and he walked into the sunset.
"It was like walking with Aristotle. His was a great spirit. He lives and
will live for ever. Something more now is needed." There was a dead
hush as he finished. The Mayor said, "MRA is the spearhead and sheet
anchor of all human aspirations."

We had the play in the evening. Just as we were due to start the music
failed. So I had to go and speak not knowing how long for. After five
minutes, to my mighty relief, someone whispered through the curtain,
"All is well." The Chief Minister of the Province, Desai,[1] spoke at the end.
He was magnificent. He said, "When you are firmly convinced you are
right you have to watch that you do not become self-righteous and so
make it difficult for others to change."

P.D.H. to Doë   Bombay
                               November 18, 1952
We dined last night after the play on the hill outside the city where
your family lived. It is beautiful. We dined with the man who owns five
big cars. He is of fabulous wealth. He lives with four brothers and all
their families in a house big enough to have 112 people live in it, which
is the number who do live there. Narayan,[2] the great Socialist, was also
there. He told us towards midnight that he is convinced economics will
never answer Communism. He was trained on a Californian fruit farm.
He was recently on a hunger strike because he believes Nehru's government has broken its word to the Socialists. Nehru wrote him a letter of
apology after ten days.

Most people here do not understand ideology. They are convinced
that no Hindu country can ever become Communist. There is also a
monumental self-righteousness, which the Western world has to pedal
hard to beat. They are so sure – and so thankful – they are better than
other men.

---

[1] Morarji Desai, later Deputy Prime Minister of India.
[2] Jaya Prakash Narayan, Founder of Indian Socialist Party.

P.D.H. to Doë   Bombay
                                              November 23, 1952

Yesterday was a special showing of the play for Tata's. The Board of
Directors sat in the front row. In the evening J.R.D. and his wife gave a
dinner party for Buchman. They live in a house called "The Cairn". It is
perched at the very summit of the city, and way down below you can see
the marvellous sweep of the Bay and the city lights twinkling and glim-
mering.

One of the industrialists there summed up the situation in this way,
"Nehru is the only man who holds the Congress Party together. If anything happens to him there will be at least ten years of splinter group
politics in India. Each group will represent some man's personal ambition.
After that we may grow up. The fact is that we obtained our freedom very
cheaply here. I used, as did my friends, to revolt and demonstrate in order
to get the British out of India. But we took over a magnificent going
concern. That's the truth."

I give this view because it is a common one. There is no doubt at all
that if England gave an answering ideology as her avowed national policy,
India would accept it. There is also no doubt that the post-war policies of
Britain have not won India any more than the pre-war policies did, though
the Labour Party is still regarded here as the great liberator.

P.D.H. to Doë   Bombay
                                              November 25, 1952

The mass meeting was a success. There were 7,000 squatting on the
ground with Buchman garlanded on the platform – the white linen of the
thousands against the brown red earth, the stars and an early half-moon
sailing out of a pale sky, kites wheeling in circles overhead, the green
trees and the houses surrounding the ten acres of public park where the
meeting was held, with heads poking out of every window, squads of
children stacked up against the platform at the very front and their
teeth gleaming in the darkness as they laughed and appreciated the
singing.

P.D.H. to Doë   Bombay
                                              November 27, 1952

Spyros Skouras came to the play last night. When he heard I was
married to a Greek his delight was unbounded. "You must learn to
make love in Greek," he said. "It is the most wonderful language for
love-making in the world." He sat in the front row, absolutely entranced
and gave all the money he had on him.

P.D.H. to Doë   November 29, 1952
                                                 St. Andrew's Day
    This morning the *Chronicle* and the *Free Press* came out with six-page
supplements on MRA. Frank Moraes came to see Buchman. He talked
about listening to God and said very simply, "I don't know why, but I
do find a sort of resistance to MRA." Buchman said, "Why keep your
resistance? You will learn from it." Then Moraes said, "They have magnificent plays in China. I could never discover what was behind them. What
is behind your plays?" So he is coming to the theatre tonight to see.

P.D.H. to Doë   December 2, 1952
                                                 On the train
    In a minute the train will start with a jump and a jerk, so make the
best of my writing if you can. We had a magnificent day at Ahmedabad.
The send-off from Bombay was vociferous. The dockers, businessmen,
workers all turned out, and Buchman was so loaded with garlands that it
was difficult for him to walk.
    At six-thirty at Ahmedabad all the excited Indians were banging on
Buchman's carriage door saying, "Get out. Get out." We had breakfast in a
palace. It belongs to a cotton king. His sister is head of the workers'
union. When they had a savage strike Gandhi got them both to the Ashram
and settled it. A union was built which is a pattern for India. After
breakfast we spoke to the men massed in the union hall. Then to Gandhi's
Ashram and the river, along which Buchman and Gandhi had walked. All
his books, papers and mats are still there.
    In the evening singing flocks of wild geese flew past overhead against
the moon. It was a wonderful sight.

P.D.H. to Doë   Taj Mahal, Agra
                                                 December 3, 1952
    Last night we saw the Taj Mahal by moonlight. It is as fresh as cream
cheese. It looks as if it were finished yesterday. It is hewn out of solid
blocks of marble, and in its original state was decorated with diamonds and
gold. Through the centuries (it was finished in 1631) the kings removed
the diamonds and replaced the gold with brass. It took 20,000 men
twenty-three years to build. The architect and masons were killed at the
end so they could not repeat the performance. It is the memorial to a
much-loved wife. She lies buried in the vault under the central pinnacle of
the dome. The king planned to build a similar monument to himself
over the other side of the river, but their son appalled at the expense put his
father in gaol where he finally died. Then the son buried him in the Taj
Mahal beside his beloved spouse.
    Buchman was in a state of real rage yesterday when he saw a large
number of our people walking in the sun without helmets in spite of

manifold warnings. Buchman turned on me as I happened to be nearby and tore several large strips off my hide, also cursing me for not resting. "You will get over-tired," he said. As we have been going steadily from 6 a.m. until past midnight and as, largely on his say-so, I have been leading a lot of the meetings, I felt I had already arrived at the point of his prediction. He said an interesting thing to one of the British who was hatless, "You condone what must not be condoned. It is British."

P.D.H. to Doë   Delhi
                                          December 5, 1952
We are at Jaipur House, one of the great palaces that has been taken over by the Government. It had not a stick or stone in it, but Nehru gave the order and it has been furnished and put at our disposal.

Buchman addressed Parliament last evening. 550 turned up to hear him.

P.D.H. to Doë   Hotel Cecil, Delhi
                                          December 8, 1952
This morning early came a summons to see the Prime Minister (Nehru). He wore a tall grey robe, pink rose, Gandhi cap and white trousers. We gave him, I would say, exactly what he did not expect. He is as solid as a handful of eels, but he put himself out to be more than polite. The people around him are as scared as schoolboys of the headmaster. It would be comic if this were not so great a nation. He asked, "How are you getting on?" We told him that the response, especially by the workers, is overwhelming, but we are here to learn from a nation that may have to give leadership to the world. He was silent. Then he said, "When people say that kind of thing it frightens me." We said, "It may be frightening but it can be true." He said the trouble was that all the people who talked about Gandhiji did not live up to his principles — they complied by talk with small living. Not that they are hypocrites, except the normal hypocrisy of politicians, he said quite seriously. He then told a long story of how when Alexander the Great left North India there was war. A general managed to disperse the rival armies by shrewd diplomacy and then sent for his defeated rival, gave him every honour and handed over to him all his own territory as well as his rival's territory. This story is ominous, especially as the press here today is full of the news of the big new motor roads which the Chinese are building in Tibet. Only six motor cars are known to be in Tibet.

In Parliament today there was a motion to make a big new road from Delhi to the Tibetan border. National route number one. "Victory," said Nehru, "is not necessarily the ultimate aim of war. You may miss your aim after victory or you can gain it after defeat. A moral force only means long-term intelligence in self-interest." On this basis India in a few years will be Communist or a military dictatorship.

P.D.H. to Doë   Delhi
                                               December 10, 1952

Lady Cripps[1] came to see Buchman at tea yesterday — just the three of us there. She said to me afterwards, "I wanted to see for myself. There is not an ounce of vanity in that man. It is a very rare thing. He is gentle."

P.D.H. to Doë   Delhi
                                               December 12, 1952

Mrs. Laski[2] came out at her press conference at Ahmedabad with the statement that MRA is a rich man's movement and the enemy of the working classes.

This morning Buchman took six of us to be received by the President of India. Buchman told him of his first guidance with Gandhi. Then we went to sign the books in our various Embassies. The Thai Ambassador said to Buchman, "I feel in meeting you I meet a new Buddha." Buchman replied, "I am just an old sinner come to life."

P.D.H. to Doë   Delhi
                                               December 13, 1952

We had lunch just now with the Minister of Health and several M.P.s from the Madras area. They talked of Mrs. Laski's statement, at which our Labour men nearly hit the roof. One of the M.P.s raised South Africa in these terms, "One criticism of MRA is that you have worked for so long in South Africa, but look at the racial disorder there was." I said, "Gandhiji was one of the great men of history. Would it not be damnably unfair to say that because India today was not fully united that Gandhiji had failed?" At this there was such an uproar that I literally crawled under the table, which made them roar with laughter. Incidentally, it was the first time, in the heat of the moment, I have heard Indians being really honest about the state of their nation. Nehru was honest about the gap between tradition and actuality, but his own life, I fear, is part of the problem.

In December 1952, Frank Buchman was decorated by the German Government for his work in uniting France and Germany following the war.

P.D.H. to Doë   Delhi
                                               December 18, 1952

The honour Buchman received — the Grand Cross of the Order of Merit — is the highest the Republic can award bar one. Going back in the car very weary, Buchman said, "Well, this is my Christmas gift to all our

[1] Widow of Sir Stafford Cripps.
[2] Mrs. Harold Laski.

people." It was a humble man accepting a decoration for his friends and giving the glory to God.

Jaipur House looked magnificent. The German Chargé d'Affaires spoke well. Buchman accepted the honour. Then the French Ambassador spoke. Then the Deputy Speaker of the Indian Parliament sprang to his feet.

The Burmese, Japanese, Thai, Finnish, Afghan, Pakistan, Danish, Nepalese, US, UK, Ceylon and other Embassies were all represented at the ceremony. Many distinguished Indians were there, including the head of Intelligence, Cabinet men and Labour leaders. All the waiters at Jaipur House came filing past to pay their respect to Buchman. One said, "You are so like our father Gandhi."

Peter Howard's twentieth wedding anniversary was on December 17. He was in Delhi.

P.D.H. to Doë   Delhi
                                                         December 19, 1952
This morning looking very battered and damaged in the post on the outside, but unchipped and beautiful within, my dear little mouse turned up. I love him so much — our china wedding. Thank you a million times. I keep on looking at him and he is watching me from the corner of this letter. He is a thing of beauty and a joy for ever. They certainly know how to make china — those Royal Danes.

Tomorrow my birthday — forty-four. God promised on my fortieth that the greatest years were at hand. So far it has proved wonderfully and mountingly true. I am sad, to be honest, that I have missed every blooming anniversary — yours, ours, mine, Philip, Anne, Ant twice, Easter and Christmas. But I feel so near and so part of you all.

P.D.H. to Doë   Delhi
                                                         December 26, 1952
We had a wonderful Christmas. On Christmas Eve there was a party at Jaipur House as soon as the play was over. We had turkey and plum pudding. What a treat and the place had been beautifully decorated. There was a Christmas tree and Crib. After the meal we had carols. I must say that as the candles softly glowed and outside the Indian stars shone clearly, I thought of the time it was at home (5.30 with you and 11 p.m. with us) and wondered if you would be singing also. At 11.58 the French Ambassador arrived to wish Buchman a merry Christmas.

We were up at crack of dawn on Christmas Day to prepare a full-scale presentation at the theatre — Christmas carols and finally "The Cowboy's Christmas". The place was packed out with Hindus, Moslems, diplomats and M.P.s. One Hindu said afterwards, "It gave me an absolutely fresh idea of what Christians are meant to be like." At the end of "The Cowboy's Christmas", although the curtain was down, they came backstage in hundreds and filed past the Crib for twenty minutes.

India's Five Year Plan for 380 million people if it succeeds will turn the whole of Asia in a new direction. Nanda, the Minister of Planning, told me last evening, "Unless we find an answer to corruption, division and confusion, we shall fail with our Plan."

P.D.H. to Doë   Delhi
                                        December 28, 1952

We have a double-page supplement in The Hindustan Times this morning.

The Deputy Minister of Posts and Telegraphs said quite seriously to me at dinner last night, "One of our Cabinet is behind the Iron Curtain (Minister of Health). He gave me a hint that he found evidence of a lack of full liberty there. It surprised me because they talk so much about democracy."

One very great asset here is the heritage of spiritual expectancy that Gandhi has left behind. But one colossal drawback is the fact that the Gandhians themselves have not produced in terms of unity or social and economic reforms the things Gandhi stood for. As a cynical newspaperman put it yesterday, "We had here for forty years a man who is perhaps the greatest man of the century. He talked about the things you talk about, but only one capitalist, Bajaj, changed. (Many of the capitalists who supported Gandhi are thorough-going ruffians.) We are not ready to wait any longer for the drastic economic revolution that is needed."

It is a point we need to ponder in view of the future of our own work — how to multiply the depth of change, particularly in the rich. They have a world message once they no longer worship money.

P.D.H. to Doë   Lucknow
                                        January 11, 1953

We ended up gloriously in Delhi. The President of the Punjab National Bank apologised before all his trade union leadership for the unjust way in which some of the rules of the bank have been enforced. The trade union leaders said they wanted to make MRA the basis of their dealings in the bank. The Manager of the main branch in Delhi was cynical. Next morning a number of his own employees arrived in his room with money which they had stolen and handed it back. He came to lunch at the Cecil with his pockets bulging with rupees.

Last night on the Delhi platform the leaders of the union were there to say goodbye. They told us that that day one of their men had done something which deserved instant dismissal. Instead of trying to cover it up he had admitted it. The President sent for him, told him he had made a few mistakes himself in his time, and sent him back to his work.

P.D.H. to Doë   Hyderabad
                                                 January 15, 1953
    The situation in India is desperately grave – nepotism, corruption,
confusion, division. The Communists have dug in far more deeply than
the rulers here are willing to admit. They are vigorously exploiting
communalism – the demand for separate states for each separate language
which apparently has long existed. They have already succeeded in winning
a separate Andhra State around Madras.
    The masses loved Gandhi who was their symbol of freedom, but are
rapidly falling out of love with his followers who use weapons to quell
violence and who certainly do not live the life.

P.D.H. to Doë   Hyderabad
                                                 January 16, 1953
    Last night the play was shown in the Pandal – a big open earthen space
walled with mats, and a roof supported by sixteen foot poles of bamboo
every few yards. All day long the annual meeting of Congress is in
session here. To give you the best summary, the Congress organiser said
after the show, which ended at 11.50 p.m. "There were 15,000 in the
Pandal. Many people came to your show who do not come to Congress
meetings. The cream of Hyderabad State were there."

P.D.H. to Doë   Hyderabad
                                                 January 18, 1953
    This morning we went out to the last plenary session of Congress.
We called at 7.30 on Nanda.[1] He described Nehru's attitude to us as at
first suspicious, then tolerant, now positive.
    You have to pay a thousand rupees to sit in the front seats of this
Congress, but we were put on the platform where we squatted for three-
and-a-half hours within a few yards of Nehru. When he saw us he left his
chair and came to within a foot of us and furiously drove off the newspapermen and photographers who were clouding our view so we could
see better. From then on he translated each introduction he made into
English as well as Hindi.

P.D.H. to Doë   Madras
                                                 January 23, 1953
    Gandhi once said, "How can I hope to unite a nation if I cannot
unite the thirty people who live with me?" A sound point which has
proved true since his parting.

P.D.H. to Doë   Madras
                                                 January 27, 1953
    Yesterday we were all asked to the Governor's reception. A glorious
[1] Gulzarilal Nanda, Minister for Planning, Irrigation and Power 1952–57.

event with white cloth tables, servants in scarlet and cloth of gold, and a band playing gay music under the trees.

To my amazement as I was quietly sipping tea under a tree, I saw the crowd parting left and right and Rajaji,[1] the Prime Minister, coming straight towards me. "Let's sit down. I want to talk," he said. So we found chairs and sat. We covered many points: Frank's age, why Communists do not like us, what exactly is our programme in the city. He said, "Someone is trying to undermine you in Delhi. You may think it best to go right ahead and pay no attention. But if you could get them straight on what you are really doing, it would be much easier." He asked about the play. Out of the corner of my eye I saw Sir R. K. Chettiar, Vice-Chancellor of the University, and earlier one of India's first Chancellors of the Exchequer after liberation. I suggested that Rajaji ask him. He did so and without any hesitation Sir R. K. said, "An excellent play. It has the answer to all our industrial difficulties in India." Then after a pause, "It has the answer to our divisions in India."

Then the moment came for a display of Indian dancing on a stage specially built. Servants called, "Rajaji," and I bade farewell. "No, come I want to talk some more," he said. So we walked slowly through the crowds. Then he insisted on taking me to the front seat with him where we sat through the performance of one-and-a-half hours. He talked of the dances. "They are supposed to be three thousand years old, but we seem to live in a bad age. The good things are going backwards," he said. "Not so," I said.

P.D.H. to Doë   Madras
                                                 January 28, 1953

The film studios have now taken us up in quite a big way. Vauhini Studios built a full-size stage for us in a studio where we can seat a thousand. It costs them 4,500 rupees a day not to shoot on the set which they made available to us. The director said, "The need of change is urgent. That is why we are doing it."

P.D.H. to Doë   Madras
                                                 February 3, 1953

I spent the whole morning with the Gandhians. Gandhi, incidentally, on landing in Europe and being tackled by the press about his clothes (this was the occasion when Churchill referred to him as a "naked fakir", a remark which is still remembered and quoted here) made a good crack. He said, "Over here the fashion is plus-fours. I prefer minus-fours."

P.D.H. to Doë   Madras
                                                 February 8, 1953

Last night I spoke to the press. We started at 6 p.m. I talked for twenty-five minutes. They said they had to go at seven, but in fact left at eight-thirty-five. Some of the Communists were there. One of them,

[1] Shri C. Rajagopalachari, first Governor-General of independent India.

secretary to Goenka,[1] the proprietor, said, "You talk about honest reporting. We have news of a man who is in hospital after being brutally handled by the MRA. Should we suppress this news?" I said, "News of the truth should not be suppressed, but a reporter who gave a story like that to the paper without checking it should be fired for inaccuracy and incompetence." He was really angry and said the assault took place in the presence of police and reporters, at which a rather dry old stick in the corner remarked, "In my experience assaults of that nature do not take place in the presence of police and reporters."

Later when I spoke of the responsibility that press men like myself had for the state of the world, the Communist stood up and said, "This is the first time I have heard a Western newspaperman talk that way. They all come here to tell us how right they are and how wrong we are." He wrung my hand and has a date with me tomorrow. So we will see.

P.D.H. to Doë   Madras
                                                   February 10, 1953

The Communist fellow at our newspaper meeting two nights ago sent me a letter this morning with a really unusual photograph of Gandhi. He says, "Your talk was enlightening and ennobling and greatly touched me."

P.D.H. to Doë   Madras
                                                   February 14, 1953

Reddi, the head of Vauhini Studios, came to the hotel at four with a scriptwriter. They began to talk. It was clear they were planning to trim MRA to suit their requirements. Suddenly Buchman burst out, "You are all wrong. You think you know about it, but you don't. I came here with hope. You leave me with a question mark. It is all watered down." When Reddi explained that his scriptwriter had been a school teacher, Buchman said, "But you didn't do it. How many people did you change at school?" "None." "I thought not. That's exactly it. You mean well, at least I think you do, but you can't give it. You haven't got it." It is illuminating how forthright under conviction Buchman can be and equally how forbearing. I would say that in these days forthrightness is to the fore.

P.D.H. to Doë   Madras
                                                   February 17, 1953

We had Ramnath Goenka to lunch yesterday. He told me afterwards that until 1947 he had fought like hell to win freedom for India. He said "bloody hell". "We taught millions to cheat, starve, disobey," he said. "But now we have our freedom they have remembered the lessons. We must have a new national philosophy or we shall go Communist."

[1] Shri Ramnath Goenka, newspaper director; Managing Director, Indian Express Group of Newspapers.

P.D.H. to Doë   Mysore
                                                 March 2, 1953
Yesterday we had a marvellous day. We drove up here, went into the
jungle and saw samba, deer and peacocks. We are the guests of the
Maharaja of Mysore. I am invited to tea this afternoon and have just
returned from a ceremony that is unique in a lifetime.

A few weeks ago an heir was born to the Maharaja. It is the first time in
eighty-eight years this has been so. This morning at a State ceremony in
the great Durbar Hall the babe was presented to the people. We were the
only Westerners present. We sat in the special gallery. It is a Hindu
religious ceremony so we all removed our shoes. You pass through a vast
vaulted marble gallery, positively a hundred yards long, looking out into
the blazing sunlight. Two giants 7 ft. 6 ins. tall, escorted us — guards
of the Maharaja in red uniforms and white turbans, holding naked
swords.

The crowd all squatted in their turbans of many colours and gorgeous
garments, gold, white, silver, saffron, red, green and a shining grey. The
priests came half-naked with ceremonial bowls and towels. The court
perfumer scattered incense. Musicians played their wild, throbbing, wailing
tunes.

Behind the curtained galleries you could see the glinting eyes of the
ladies of the court peeping. Finally the Maharaja himself disappeared and
after a pause brought out the babe and presented him to the people with
his two small daughters trotting by his side. All the crowd rose and
cheered. A forty-two gun salute began to fire outside the palace and
presently the scene was over. It lasted one-and-a-quarter hours.

P.D.H. to Doë   Madras
                                                 March 5, 1953
To tea with an editor yesterday came an Indian who had acted as
Buchman's personal secretary when he was out here in 1916. He is now
an Anglo-Catholic priest, a rope round his middle and a lot of fun. He
said when the editor talked of parasites who do not earn their daily
bread, "Parasites, parasites. You don't get into your office till ten, you
write until eleven. Then you go out and do not come back. You spend the
rest of the day drinking and you draw large sums of money for doing it.
Parasites." At which the editor roared with genuine laughter and said,
"He's got me in a corner."

P.D.H. to Doë   Calcutta
                                                 March 15, 1953
The Governor came to the show last night with much pomp and
circumstance. Then to an open-air supper at the Nizam of Hyderabad's
palace here. He has never even stayed one night in it, and it has been

taken over by the government. The Governor said to me at supper of Nehru (who has apparently warned him off making any public fuss of us), "He is so straightforward a man that if he gets a wrong idea into his head it takes a long time to put it out again." He said of Foss Westcott, the old Metropolitan, "If there had been a hundred Englishmen like him in India, India would be a dominion today." He said to the editor of a newspaper here, "I have heard the songs and speeches and seen the play. Crowds flock to MRA because it gives them the thing people are hungry for and they keep it simple." He added, "This is the only way to save India. We have a Bengal saying which says however much ointment you spread you do not cure the disease. We give a bit more rice here, a bit more legislation there, but that is only ointment. MRA really cures the disease."

P.D.H. to Doë   Calcutta
                                                March 19, 1953
Last night we dined with the Metropolitan, an Indian called Mukerjee.[1] He is a warm friend and said, "If the British had lived this faith, India would have changed. There is no doubt about it." When independence came the church here had ten million rupees a year cut off at once from their State income. The Vice-Principal of the Scottish Union College, who was also at dinner, said, "Of course, twenty years ago we used to have people being converted, but this does not happen any more. Economic circumstances have so altered."

P.D.H. to Doë   Calcutta
                                                March 20, 1953
Today we went to the students' college. A missionary in charge said, "There is no Communism in my college." We were greeted by a mob howling, "Go back MRA", and waving red flags with painted slogans saying we were pro-Hitler, Franco, Churchill, Ike, old Uncle Tom Cobbley and all. We got into the hall and the mob surged in. I had to kick off so started by saying, "I understand all the yelling. It makes me feel quite at home. I earned my living for years doing the same thing." This was a shrewder thrust than I knew, as it turned out later that many of the mob had been paid to break up the meeting and came from other colleges. Then I asked them if it were likely that the French Government plus a German Government, almost all of whom had been gaoled under Hitler, would decorate a man who was pro-Fascist. It got under their hide and they shouted and screamed. But I have a strong voice as well as firm conviction and I used both to the full. They were stirred at the end and silenced.

[1] Most Rev. Arabindo Nath Mukerjee, Bishop of Delhi 1947–50; Bishop of Calcutta and Metropolitan of India, Pakistan, Burma and Ceylon 1950–62.

P.D.H. to Doë   Calcutta
                                              March 21, 1953

We have a very full programme – tea with an Indian and a cocktail party with the British. It is interesting about the British cocktail party; Buchman is not invited. He laughed about it but it hurts him. I didn't want to go, but he told me to. He said, "They are always the same. They never have me meet any of their friends."

P.D.H. to Doë   Calcutta
                                              April 9, 1953

An English lady asked me at tea yesterday why I thought she had never changed her friends in England. I said, "Because you cannot cook cold codfish by pouring lukewarm water over them."

The Flame of the Forest is out. Isn't it a wonderful name? It is a tall tree with delicate green leaves that suddenly burst into a mass of scarlet blossom. Seen from afar through the shimmer of the sun haze, it really looks as if the jungle is on fire.

P.D.H. to Doë   Calcutta
                                              April 11, 1953

Just had lunch with two book publishers. One was fat and pious. He said that Communism is no danger in India. He quoted André Gide. I said Gide had lived crooked all life long, and when I did that I found it hard to see straight. He retorted by saying that India is certainly the most honest nation in the world today. I replied that I wholly agreed and as Mr. Nanda told us in Delhi that his Five Year Plan is liable to be wrecked by the corruption of the people, it showed where the rest of the world lives.

The other one got the point. He quoted an old Bengali proverb: "He who steals money, then goes to gaol." He said the up-to-date version is, "He who has been to gaol now steals the money." This is a reference to those who were in gaol during the struggle for independence.

P.D.H. to Doë   On the train
                                             April 13, 1953

We pass through grey-brown countryside, mile after mile. We see the oxen kneading the grain, two camels crossing a river, water buffaloes, peacock and the swarming, sprawling life of the villages.

One of the men who came to see us off in Calcutta had tears rolling down his cheeks which splashed in the dust as he said goodbye. One of the young Indian industrialists said he had lost his bitterness towards the British, got honest with his father, put right a wrong relationship with a girl and given a month's pay to MRA. "And that is only my beginning."

P.D.H. to Doë   Kashmir

April 16, 1953

We must learn to plan to reach the millions behind the Iron Curtain. Like it or not, Russia and China are the only nations today which have filled the hearts of millions with a sense of participation in building something new. What other nation even makes the attempt to do that?

The challenge of Communism may yet be recorded as the greatest blessing of the early twentieth century, because it challenged the sleeping will-power of the West and of the world. They had to sustain hatred and class conquest in order to keep the revolutionary fire burning, but they do not try to meet men's deepest needs.

Democracy's one sure hope is to enlist the whole world in the remaking of men and nations. The Communist masses might be the first to respond to this concept if they saw it was a reality in the lives of the leaders of democracy.

P.D.H. to Doë   Kashmir

May 1, 1953

They will be tossing their caps off the top of Magdalen Tower this morning, just as they did when I was a lad. Even the mention of May still gives my blood a tingle, but that's probably because with luck and an aeroplane, we may meet again in the merry month of May.

Indeed, Howard did return to Britain in May. He was in London with his family for the Coronation on June 2. The journey to India made him re-think every old idea he had ever held. It was to affect his life and his writing for good.

Chapter 14

"Next to losing the sense of a personal Christ, the worst
evil that can befall a Christian is to have no sense of anything
else. To grow up in complacent belief that God has no business
in this great groaning world of human beings except to attend to
a few saved souls is the negation of all religion. The first great
epoch in a Christian's life, after the awe and wonder of its
dawn, is when there breaks into his mind some sense that
Christ has a purpose for mankind, a purpose beyond him and his
needs, beyond the Churches and their creeds, beyond Heaven
and its saints—a purpose which embraces every man and
woman born, every kindred and nation formed, which
regards not their spiritual good alone but their welfare in
every part, their progress, their health, their work, their wages,
their happiness in this present world."

> Underlined by P.D.H. in his copy
> of The Greatest Thing in the World by
> Henry Drummond.

Peter Howard's first visit to Asia made him increasingly aware of the need
to answer the vast problems of continents. These were not just material
problems, but the deeper ones of division and corruption at the heart of the
nations he had visited. This, he realised, would require a larger action than
he had foreseen:

"A very small number of people around the world live to shift the
thinking of nations and continents. We are at the launching stage of a
world advance. It depends on whether we grasp the thinking and living
which will make what we do the most relevant thing in the statesmanship of Cabinets."

The expansion in Howard's thinking at this time led him to begin
writing for the theatre. He had never attempted it before. He wrote his
first play in 1953—a newspaper play, The Real News. In the next twelve
years he had written fourteen plays. He said of them:

"Some write for money. Some for fame. Some, though very few, for art. They feel beauty in their guts which they have to display to others with paint, and the performance of skilled professionals on stage and screen. Some just write for fun.

"These reasons are not mine. My ink is sweat. I do not find dipping in that pot funny. Fame is not for me and I do not take royalties from my plays. All winnings are given to charity.

"I write to preach. I write for the sake of propaganda. I write with a message and for no other reason. Do not believe those who say the theatre is no place for a man with a message of some kind. Some writers give their message without knowing they do it. A man who writes as if life had no meaning is the man with a strong message.

"My plays are propaganda plays. I write them to give people a purpose. The purpose is clear. The aim is simple. It is to encourage men to accept the growth in character that is essential if civilisation is to survive. It is to help all who want peace in the world to be ready to pay the price of peace in their own personalities. It is to end the censorship of virtue which creates vicious society. It is to enlist everybody everywhere in a revolution to remake the world."

Howard described his work as a "challenge to a perverse but fascinating generation". Harold Hobson[1] recognised this in its most literal form when he wrote during the run of one of Howard's plays at the Westminster Theatre: "I do not believe that there is today any theatre in London, the Westminster honourably excepted, which would *dare* to suggest that homosexuality is a sin. They would all, from Temple Bar to Sloane Square, be afraid of the derision with which such an unconventional judgment would be greeted."

Abroad, there was often a readier awareness of what Howard was aiming to do. Gabriel Marcel, the French philosopher, critic and playwright, wrote: "The many dramatic works which Peter Howard produced were for him the most effective means of renewing and resurrecting the inner life of the individual. In this sense his work can be compared with that of Brecht, for both it is a matter of forming a new type of man, the one Marxist, the other trained to the dictates of a Christian conscience." Egon Karter, the distinguished Swiss Director of the Komedie Theatre, Basel, added: "Peter Howard has shown how a real theatre of the people can be created. He has left behind the psychological drama of Ibsen and Sartre and has made the stage a platform not for a discussion of self-realisation, but to hold up a mirror in front of man so that he sees himself clearly. It is a shock therapy for the human reason and the human heart."

Howard's plays were not aimed at response, but at the changing of

[1] Drama Critic of *The Sunday Times* since 1947.

Howard escorts Dame Flora MacLeod to his daughter's wedding, June, 1962

Howard talks with students following his speech to the Royal Commonwealth Society, London, 1964

Doë and Peter Howard, Dame Flora MacLeod, Patrick and Anne Wolrige
Gordon in California, January, 1964

definite people and situations. "The Secretary of the Mineworkers in a pit in Northumberland came to see Howard's *Music at Midnight* in 1962," writes K. D. Belden in *The Story of the Westminster Theatre*. "His pit was in a critical condition. A thousand families depended on it for their livelihood, but it was threatened with being closed down because it could not pay its way. Only 1,700 tons of coal were being raised each day, and it was losing 39s. 6d. a ton. The miners' secretary was impressed and moved by the philosophy of the play. He went back and thought about it. Then he decided to apply it in his pit. Instead of maintaining a state of running warfare, he called together every element in the pit to co-operate to raise production, reduce absenteeism and improve quality of work. By the time *Music at Midnight* reached the Theatre Royal, Newcastle upon Tyne, on its tour a few months later, he was able to invite some of the cast down to the coal face on the day when production reached 2,500 tons a day. Some months later it topped 3,000 tons a day, and the pit is still in production."

The plays began to meet the need which Howard had seen in India – the need to challenge and inspire Communists and non-Communists alike. When *Through the Garden Wall* – a story of two families, representing the Communist and non-Communist worlds, living either side of a wall which only existed in their prejudices – was shown in Italy, it was noticeable that the Communist press was as enthusiastic as its Catholic counterpart. *L'Unità*, the Communist daily, wrote:

Peter Howard is up to his neck in the reality of our time and committed in an intense battle to bring about an easing of international tension. At first, in Rome, the audience was composed of the usual habitués of the theatre, the bourgeois frequenters at every first night. In fact, gradually as the days went by the Roman public became more selective, and more and more workers appeared in the theatre.

So for the first time in Italy the company decided to give special attention to the workers. In Rome one whole evening was given over to democratic organisations, and the same principle was repeated in Tuscany, in Umbria and in Emilia. Everywhere the workers responded to the theatre's appeal. A popular play and a popular success.

At the offices of *L'Unità* a limited number of tickets can be obtained for the two performances. The newspaper is keeping them for its readers and subscribers."

In 1955, Howard wrote a musical play called *The Vanishing Island*. With 244 people from twenty-four countries it travelled over 80,000 miles through America, Asia, Africa and Europe. It was the first time MRA had attempted such a large offensive, and as such created much controversy. The response was immediate, so too were the criticisms. This World

Mission marked a turning point in MRA's history. It cut across old concepts and dealt publicly with national issues.

In the Philippines, for the first time since the war, Japanese spoke to the Philippine people. Howard wrote:

"On the green sward by the waterfront at Manila, 106,000 Filipinos were killed in the last war. Out of the grey, restless waters of Manila Bay are thrust the hulks and masts of the seventy-three Japanese vessels sunk there. Beneath those seas rest the Japanese dead, together with many of the American boys from the 150 planes lost sinking those vessels.

"The Japanese, who were among those speaking from the stage after The Vanishing Island each night, hit the headlines in Manila. Niro Hoshijima, adviser to the Japanese Cabinet, one of the six plenipotentiaries who signed the Peace Treaty for his country, apologised to the Philippine people for the wrongs Japan had committed. He said, 'We in Japan must pay reparations. But reparations are not enough. First of all we must humbly apologise for the past. That is why my Prime Minister urged me to come on this Mission. Please forgive us. Moral Re-Armament is already building a new Japan and with Moral Re-Armament all Asia can unite.'

"One could hear the angry murmurs from the Filipinos when first the Japanese language was heard across the footlights. Then, as the words were translated, the gasp of breath followed by a gale of applause.

"Afterwards many Filipinos pressed forward to shake his hand. Some wept. One of them said, 'These wrists of mine will always bear the marks of Japanese handcuffs, but tonight I have forgiven you.' "

This did not come about by chance, as Vincent Evans[1] remembers:

"Howard had brought with him from Tokyo a group of Japanese who wanted to apologise to the people of the Philippines for some of the savagery that had taken place there during the war. For an hour or so, Howard sat with these very fine Japanese people, helping them to understand the desolation that the war had brought to these gay little islands which now lay surrounded by the battered, rusting hulks of American and Japanese shipping. Gradually he won from them a warmth that transcended the cold precision of the stilted, rather fearful words that the Japanese had intended to speak before the vast audience of their former enemies."

Howard's idea of ideology was not a theory, nor simply a plan of action. It meant dealing with men:

[1] Former Fleet Street colleague, latterly Chief Foreign Sub-Editor, News Chronicle.

"Some think of ideology as kindness, what we know of brotherhood, a few corners knocked off here and there and that is it. It needs more than that. That is as selfish as the man who prefers his smokes, drinks and women to the saving of his nation.

"There can be a selfishness in being preoccupied with personal sin. It is nothing to do with ideology unless it is related to changing people. Some people recoil from the highest challenge. They will be there always, demanding human fellowship at a low level. This has dragged most great religions down to ineffectiveness, and it is moral compromise which lies at the back of it."

It was this moral compromise with which Howard dealt directly. In it he saw seeds of destruction for nations. He was outspoken in his condemnation, "I see no point in beating round the bush." He had the unusual habit of telling people to their face what he thought, and then keeping quiet about it. His conception of the work of MRA is best expressed in his own words:

"There are two schools of thought which may be called that of the 'enclavers' and that of the 'freebooters'. The enclavers are keen to create a fellowship in which the great truths of morality and God are held secure and where, in the midst of a planet that has turned its back upon such things, they can continue to live and induce some others to live in a way that seems best to them.

"The freebooters are out, night and day, with flashing swords, determined to win back from the modern world the property of God that materialists, intellectuals, Fascists and Communists have stolen, tried to destroy and hidden. They fight, sing, crawl, run, zig-zag, carving their way wherever they can. They live off the territory they move in. Establishments hate them. The hands of the powerful are against them. Millions love them. Not all understand them. They are on the rampage to create a revolution whereby God will become more authoritative to everybody than wife, husband, child, wealth, position, Mao Tse-tung, Krushchev, or even Mr. Kennedy.

"Maybe we need both enclavers and freebooters. The certain thing is that freebooters now need to shed every non-essential action from their lives, to cleave to each other with a far less glutinous and more absolute honesty, to safeguard health, strength, time and passion, to see that every weapon put to use is of a professionalism and polish that enables them to have a better chance of advance before the gaze of an earth that is beginning to pay very serious attention to their activities."

Howard was a freebooter. He added to that quality a realism and shrewdness. He was not influenced either by public response or the

reverse. MRA began to be recognised by certain governments as an impor
tant asset. There was often an effort to exploit this. Howard always refused

"If I were to allow MRA to become the tool of British or any other
foreign policy, it would immediately lose its effectiveness. MRA help
all people who love God to love their country more, not less. But it also
provides nations with a world aim beyond mere nationalistic recognition
and supremacy, without which nations today are bound to become isolated
and to risk the defection of their nationals. Personally, I remain convinced
that our one great hope is the acceptance of an idea far larger than mere
national self-interest.

"My own work, as well as the emphasis of it, would be altered and
curtailed if I were under orders from any government."

In this he was right. He knew the strength of MRA lies in the fact that
it has no politics, though many politicians are committed to it; that it
supports no government, though many governments welcome it. In this
way it can be free of man's control.

To Buchman and Howard it was the height of folly to arrive in a
situation and carry on with your programme if there was some urgent
local problem to be solved. They would abolish every programme in
order to deal with the issue on hand. Newspapers had trained Howard in
the reality of hitting deadlines and finding news. MRA trained him to
spot moral targets in a nation's life and meet them.

It was not always popular to suggest that the needs in a nation were
moral ones, as well as the obvious ones of housing, feeding and clothing
people, but Howard persisted:

"I am utterly opposed to the philosophy that God no longer works
through the transformation of the individual but only through social
operations, such as civil rights agitation in America, anti-apartheid
movements in South Africa, and the spread of Communism, which,
though godless, creates an atmosphere which will help faith forward.

"I believe that everybody on earth has some Moral Re-Armament in
them. And in that setting I believe that it is the hope of humanity.

"I am quite opposed to those Christians who say that because Christ
redeems we can go on being disinvolved with history and living much as
we are.

"A great society will never come to birth by good works that hope to
use industry and agriculture to fill belly and hand, plate and purse, but
leave self-will unbroken and hearts empty of love and faith. Political,
economic, social action alone will never touch the centre of the evil. Nor
will sluggish and surly self-satisfaction at our personal and national
perfections.

"We are in the midst of a struggle without scruple for the soul and character of the world. The question to be decided this century is whether it is to be God's earth or man's hell."

Howard believed that one test of ideology was the passion with which it was lived:

"Not long ago at an embassy party I met a leading Russian diplomat. He mistook me for a British diplomat. He asked if I knew any of the delegates at the Geneva disarmament conference. I said, 'Yes.' Then the Russian told me with force, 'We in the Soviets have one great advantage over you in the Western world. We have a strong ideology out to change the world. You have a very weak ideology.' I said to the Russian, 'Do we have an ideology at all?' He roared with laughter. He said, 'No. You have none. You do not know where you want the world to go.'

"Then I had a bit of bad luck. The Ethiopian Ambassador, who knew me, came up and asked after Frank Buchman. As soon as he left, the Russian turned on me and said, 'Moral Re-Armament? You are against us.' I said I would not put it that way at all. He asked what our attitude was.

"I told him that we knew the world had got to have a revolution if it was to be saved from war. I respected the sincerity of millions of Communists. But I thought their ideas were old-fashioned.

"He became very angry. He asked me why. I said that the theory of the class struggle, carried to its logical conclusion, must result in atomic war between vast power groups. I told him that Communism had never grown up philosophically to match the new situation created by the advance of nuclear power. It is a Stone Age outlook in the era of the atom.

"The Russian said to me, 'What is your answer?' I told him that Moral Re-Armament was a world revolution greater than Communism because it did not exclude any class, any colour, any race, but enlisted all for the great goal that all humanity can accept – the remaking of the world and the reconstruction of the whole of human society.

"The Russian asked how it worked. I told him many stories. The Russian said to me, 'If you can change men, my Marxism is out of date. We have had forty years of socialism in the Soviets – but we have not been able to cure selfishness and give men a new motive.'

"At that moment a girl came to us offering smokes of every kind. She offered me some and I said, 'No, thank you very much.' The Russian jeered at me and asked, 'Is there a rule against smoking in MRA?' I said, 'No, but every penny I have goes to my revolution. I would not waste one penny on tobacco.' He was staggered. He said, 'Does it mean as much to you as that?' I said, 'Why the devil do you Communists think you are the only people who will sacrifice for your revolution?'

"We went into the garden and around the garden there was a table loaded with drinks. Everything was there. The Russian said to me, 'Go on.

They won't charge you for it.' I said, 'Thank you very much,' and took a Coca-Cola. He said, 'Is there a rule against drinking in MRA?' I said, 'No, but when I'm with a man like you, I prefer to keep my head clear.' He laughed. I liked him.

"He asked me how my revolution began. I told him of absolute standards of honesty, purity, unselfishness and love. The Russian said to me, 'I'll tell you two things.' He looked around. 'I smoke nearly a hundred cigarettes a day and I can't stop. Can you help me?' Then he said, 'We in the Soviets know that apart from Communism, Moral Re-Armament is the only force working ideologically all over the world.' "

The passion with which Howard pursued his theme made some accuse him of thinking that MRA was the only answer at work. He replied:

"I do not believe that Moral Re-Armament has the monopoly for rebuilding the world. I am neither so conceited nor so blind. I do believe that the spirit of God in the hearts of men is the one force that will shift humanity forward."

Howard realised that this spirit was all too rare, even among those who professed to have it:

"Just as congregations in the West often influence their priests and ministers and reduce them to their worship of wealth, popularity, impurity and passionlessness, so some good people have taken on the garment of the world and become obsessed with sex and success. It helps me to ponder what God must think of us. I imagine when He weeps, He sees the colossal chasm which lies between my perception of what I should do and be and His conception of what I am meant to be. This helps me in my dealings with men."

Buchman had refused to let Howard be dependent on human approval. Buchman himself had once been offered large sums of money in America to turn his work into a popular organisation. An offer he rejected immediately. With MRA's increasing advance, Howard understood how easily this idea could attract and influence people. He knew the danger of it. After Buchman's death he wrote:

"Moral Re-Armament stands like a rock and will, I am convinced, prove the cornerstone for a new world. Buchman said, 'The one thing to do in a time of crisis is to change men.' It is a source of deep concern to me that we understand and accept this truth, which was the engine of Buchman's life.

"We seem to be reaching the masses in many countries, but we need to be very watchful that we do not drift into a movement so much in love with mass response that we are only out for the applause of the multitudes and that when that applause is not forthcoming, we develop an anti-Communism and self-justification and self-defence which is not of God, but which is indeed anti-God. I think that as God entrusts us with the masses, we need to let Him penetrate more deeply and purify our lives more absolutely, instead of allowing success to make us turn more and more to a reliance on applause.

"One man writes to me: 'The issue of fighting for God's rule in men, rather than using men to achieve a purpose born out of ambition, is a very fundamental one. Otherwise we so like the applause of the crowd that we work to get crowds to applaud, rather than to change men.' "

Howard continued:

"I believe that this impurity, which drives us to seek appreciation from everybody, can, if it is uncured and unfaced, result in disastrous national strategy. Nobody was more alert than Buchman for new ways of reaching millions. Nobody rejoiced more than he did at the marvels. But he was always questing the unexpected ways. He was resolute in his refusal to move one step unless he felt the stamp and ring of God in taking it. And he never, never, never, never yielded his passion to change every man he met, and for changed men to be the result of everything he did. I still remember his definition of the greatest words in the English language, 'Make and keep me pure within'. This means curing not just personal impurity, but also the rugged resistance to the Cross, which builds relationships with those who will flatter and praise, and builds division with those who challenge us to the highest.

"Passion is good, but passion also needs firm friends at its side to see it is passion guided by God. If we live that I believe — 'Am I therefore become your enemy because I tell you the truth?' — could become the normal salt of our life."

Buchman also trained Howard to be scrupulous over money. In many ways, Howard had already become so. He had little money himself, just what his farm in Suffolk provided for him. With what he had he was generous, sometimes impulsively. But with money that was given to MRA from sacrifice, he was extremely careful. He neither smoked nor drank. He would not spend other people's money in that way. He continued to cut down and streamline the administration of MRA to avoid any possible waste. He disliked stupid expenditure.

Howard's life was open to everyone. There was nothing private about it. He treated his secretary, his farm workers, or a hostile journalist with the same concern and directness. He believed in including everyone in his life.

In Miami at a conference for MRA, a delegate from Costa Rica met Peter Howard for the first time. He wrote at the time of Howard's death:

"I was an old man of sixty-eight then, new in MRA circles, who had come for the first time to an international convention. I was perfectly unknown to the leaders and was not supposed to deserve much attention from anybody. However, Peter Howard came to me and invited me to attend the meeting of those who were doing the programming for the day.

"Although I had spent fifty years investigating how to help humanity, this was my first direct contact with MRA. Indeed, I was delighted to see how I could get guidance from God to serve humanity, and for them to find their own spark in their hearts, to change the world.

"I was up next morning before 4 a.m. to be on the spot as early as possible. I was standing in the aisle, waiting for Peter Howard to come. One of the prominent members of the conference looked at me with surprise. My presence was not expected or desirable, I felt. He turned round and said, 'But what are you doing here?' I understood what he meant. This is not your business, how dare you come here and intrude? I answered him, 'Indeed, I am as surprised as you, sir, to be here myself, and I don't know why I am here. Please ask Peter Howard and let me know. It was he who invited me here.' I realised that I should not have answered in that way, but at that moment Peter Howard came in, pointed to a seat in the front row, and the comedy ended."

There the comedy ended for many people. For Howard believed that if you had something to say, which did not include everyone, then it was hardly worth saying it. Yet, there was nothing sentimental about him, as his secretary remembers:

"I once mixed up two letters and put them in the wrong envelopes with rather embarrassing results, and was trying to apologise for it. He said, 'If I could I would like to have a secretary who is both efficient and a Christian, but if I had to choose I would rather have a Christian.' I found that Christianity to him was very far from the purely going-to-Church-on-Sunday type, which I had rejected in my youth. He expected faith to mean for me what it did for him.

"Punctuality he insisted upon. He once left me behind in a completely unknown German town because I was two minutes late in getting to the place where he said I would be picked up. Fortunately, a passing car had someone in it who recognised me and took me on. When he saw me he said he could not be late for his appointment on my account, and that I would learn something from it. And I did."

.   .   .

As Howard's responsibilities increased, his faith deepened and his life expanded. It was perhaps for this reason that Buchman asked more and more of him. It cost Howard his time, his energy and his pride. Above all, it cost him the many occasions he would have liked to spend with his family. When his mother died in 1953, he was abroad. He went home to comfort his father, who had been blind for nearly six years.

P.D.H. to Doë   Sussex
                                                    August 17, 1953
Dad did not sleep well last night and we were off at 8 a.m. to Cheering, about forty miles away, where mother was buried. I must say it is a beautiful place, a garden. Buchman's wreath was on the coffin. I put on a sheaf of red roses from ourselves and the children. Only two of mother's own friends were there, as the notice only appeared in The Times this morning. Dad was wonderful. Two tears fell from his poor old blind eyes half-way through. Otherwise, though he trembled greatly he was fine and gave his heart in a wonderful way. When we got back here he asked if he had behaved all right and said that my support had meant everything to him.

In 1960, while Howard was in Los Angeles he heard news of his father's death. He was unable to return home.

P.D.H. to A.   Los Angeles
                                                    February 6, 1960
During my time here word came that my loved father had suddenly left us. He had been blind the last eleven years of his life, and I had never heard one whimper or whisper of complaint from him. Buchman heard the news, and later that day a beautiful vase of stately white flowers appeared in my room. Underneath was a card:

> "To a brave father —
> Who sees again in the Life Eternal
> and for the wife who gave him tenderest care
>   Devotedly,
>   Frank"

On my way back to Washington I flew to Tucson,[1] arriving at eleven o'clock in the morning. Campbell met me. And then we went and gave our news to Buchman and settled in drafting letters until late at night.

Over supper, which was served in his room to Campbell and myself, Buchman got me to talk about my father. He said, "I would like to spend half-an-hour remembering your father with you." So, for half-an-hour

[1] Tucson, Arizona, USA.

we had a foretaste of Heaven in that room, where my father and also our Heavenly Father were very close indeed. Buchman remembered how, when his mother passed away, he was in India. He was travelling in a railway carriage, and all night long the carriage was filled with light. He said, "Why, not everybody understands these things, but you could read a newspaper in that light." He said, "God will be with Peter in mighty power today and through the night." Then Buchman with great conviction, very slowly gave the whole of the 23rd Psalm. And finally, "With all the happy memories we have of the father: the games, the tears, the love he had for Peter and for his brother. Be with Anne, Ant, and Philip. Make them great men and women in Christ Jesus." When this was finished Buchman said, "Now we will do some more work."

Although Howard's parents had reconciled themselves to their son's work with MRA, they never really understood it. So he was left nothing by them. The family treasures went to others. Although this hurt him, he was not a man to harbour bitterness. After his mother's death he had offered E.C.H. a home at Hill Farm, but this had been refused. From that time, almost every week, Howard saw that food parcels were sent to his father from Suffolk. The care of the old was something close to Howard's heart. He gave both his beloved "Nanny George" and Doë's "Nursie" a home at his farm for the last years of their lives. But there was no home for Howard. For him it was to be the open road for the rest of his life.

Chapter 15

"I do miss Frank Buchman, but in a curious way. I miss him because he was always a man who would tell the truth without fear or favour and as God gave him to see it. He was a good comrade of mine through the years and paid me the compliment for a long time before he died of holding me responsible for anything that went wrong anywhere in the world concerning our work, regardless of whether I knew anything about it or not. He believed that a man like myself, as a Christian, should take full responsibility for the whole of the work. In this sense I felt myself 'in charge', insofar as a man ever is in charge, for a long time before Buchman died."

P.D.H. June 1963

On August 7, 1961, Frank Buchman died in Freudenstadt in the Black Forest in Germany. Throughout the summer he had used his energy for the thousands who attended the summer conference at Caux. When he left for Germany, Howard remained in Switzerland.

P.D.H. to Doë   Caux
                                                August 6, 1961
Campbell telephoned me last evening to say that Buchman was seized yesterday about two in the afternoon with a severe pain in the chest. It lasted for an hour-and-a-half. Campbell thinks it is serious. It is almost certain to be a coronary which in a man of that age is surely grave. They were planning to take Buchman to hospital today. There was no room there yesterday. He was comfortable last evening. We have had no word since and I await another call. The one thing seems to be to continue the fight.

P.D.H. to Doë   Caux
                                                August 9, 1961
I am off to Freudenstadt early. There are many things to be settled, as you can guess. It was such a lift to speak to you on the telephone last night.

We had a battling day here with the press prowling round unceasingly and many people to look after.

Campbell telephoned me near two o'clock on Monday. I left at once and got to Freudenstadt by ten-thirty. Let me tell you one or two things about it all. Buchman went away from here very, very tired. He was in gallant spirits, but the truth is that the struggle to get some people into the real fight has sapped his strength. He bade us the cheeriest of farewells.

When he got to Freudenstadt he loved it all so much – the cooking, the forests and the whole atmosphere of the people and the place. He said, "I would like to be buried here." He said it twice. In truth he has made arrangements to be taken home to Allentown,[1] but the question of the end of this world's journey was much in his mind. He said, "I don't think we will go back to Caux."

Just over a week ago he sent for his morning coat, saying he would need it. Now it is the suit in which he will be buried. He said to Campbell a few days back, "I am not sure I should go back to Caux. I have become a handicap to the work." It is so typical of the staggering humility of the man. While Campbell thought he was joking, he soon saw Buchman really meant it. He was worried about the necessary things which had to be done for him – the night work, the physical attention and so on.

When I spoke to him on the telephone the day he was hit by the attack he was in fighting and glowing mood, asking after all his friends. Full of plans for the future in Africa and all over the world. After lunch he was hit by severe pain. It lasted nearly two hours. Next day they took an electro-cardiogram. It showed massive deterioration of the heart. Through the day his blood pressure steadily fell. He was conscious all the time, but often barely so. Prince Richard[2] came during the afternoon. He read Buchman his favourite Psalms – the 23rd, 103rd and 121st. He said to Buchman, "Frank, I am here and I am going to stay." Buchman understood and was so pleased.

He struggled for forty minutes to get out his last words, "I want Britain to be governed by men governed by God. Why not the whole world governed by men governed by God? Why not let God run the whole world?" His blood pressure fell and fell, and finally he just stopped breathing.

One of the last things he said to me on the telephone the day before was, "Are my Americans helping you to carry the weekend?" (which indeed they were not). The thing Buchman could not bear was any lack of all-outness. He sent word to me that he thought I should take a week or two's holiday in September. Bless his heart.

He always took the time to get the space of what we are trying to do. This I mean to do myself more and more.

[1] Allentown, Pennsylvania, Dr. Buchman's family home.
[2] Prince Richard of Hesse.

I motored back here all through the night and worked like a beaver yesterday. Now I am off again to Freudenstadt and shall return here probably on Friday night, or first thing Saturday.

P.D.H. to Doë

En route to Allentown
Pan American Airlines
August 15, 1961

What awaits me in Allentown is hard to say. After lunch a black wave of depression rolled over me, probably too much to eat. But I felt I had done so many things badly in life, nothing really well – a poor sort of husband really, a failure as a father, a third-rate writer and a parody of what a true Christian should be. The overwhelming responsibilities of our work, set against the danger of our times, was too much for me. It is strange because my spirits are usually buoyant, but it was almost a physical impact. Faith lit my heart again and it passed quickly. All I felt of myself is only too true, but God will amazingly use me. The greatest years are ahead and at hand.

P.D.H. to Doë

Allentown
August 16, 1961

Buchman rests peacefully in his own home with flowers all round him and branches from the Black Forest pine from Freudenstadt at his feet. There is small understanding of the work he did, and most of his old friends in the place are gone. The service on Friday will do much for America. We will all do our utmost. The service is at two in the afternoon and afterwards we go to the cemetery. I shall try and come back via England but it may not be possible. These things weary me more than of yore.

P.D.H. to A.

Allentown
August 19, 1961

Yesterday was Buchman weather. Sunshine unfailingly. It grew as hot as Asia by the afternoon. Some were scared that the congregation would visit upon them some of the controversy which Buchman by his battle carried with him as part of his essential baggage in death as in life.

At nine o'clock suddenly the press burst in on us with cameras and women with warpaint hunting for some of the celebrities. Then we came back to this home and the men who were to carry Buchman on his last journey rehearsed. The undertaker men came, ruthless and businesslike. When you stood up to them and said, "No," they would do what you wanted. But everything they tried to do was the wrong thing.

Some wondered if the church would be full. It overflowed half-an-hour before the service began. The crowds were so vast that we had to

219

wait nearly one hour outside the church before the procession was ready to move to Fairlawn Cemetery. It stretched nearly two miles.

At the graveside, our people sang "He lives", and after the ceremony "The Hallelujah Chorus". They did not sink the coffin into the grave, but left it suspended just at the surface. That is America. They will not face reality at all. They gloss death over and pretend things like it do not happen. So they keep the coffin above ground until all the people have gone. Do not do this to me. And at my burial I'd like hot drinks for all if the weather is cold, cold drinks for all if the weather is hot (we needed them badly yesterday), and hot and cold drinks if the weather is so-so. Buchman said he wanted no sense of mourning but of triumph and victory, and yesterday did fulfil that.

After Frank Buchman's death, Peter Howard found much of the burden of responsibility for Moral Re-Armament fell upon his shoulders. There was much hostility towards this work, particularly in the British press. It was a hostility which Howard in his last four years of life did much to overcome. At the beginning of August he had written to Lord Beaverbrook explaining the unfair treatment which had been given in the *Daily Express*.

Beaverbrook to P.D.H.   La Capponcina
                                               Cap d'Ail, France
                                               August 4, 1961
My dear Peter,
    I am so sorry that you feel you have cause to complain of the newspaper.
    As you know, it has been our constant intention over the years to give a fair presentation of the MRA movement in our handling of the news.
    Perfection is denied to man, so that sometimes, in reporting the news, we may fall short of our aims.

P.D.H. to Beaverbrook   August 14, 1961
    Thank you.
    I know enough of you to understand that the tone of *The Express* and the *Evening Standard* after Frank Buchman's death owed much to your personal intervention. Derek Marks and John Redfern were not only fair, but sensitive and honourable in the way they handled things. I have written to tell them so.
    It was a joy to me that *The Express*, my old home, was the best of the British press in its handling of the event. Especially so because much of the crop of misunderstanding that he and we have reaped and still reap in Britain comes from the seeds sown in your columns by Driberg in the old days. But we survive and flourish.

In truth, Frank Buchman was one of the very few men I have met in life of whom you can say they were not only good but also effective. I remember your old verse:

"For alas it is seldom if ever
That people behave as they should.
For the good are so harsh with the clever,
And the clever so rude to the good."

It may or may not surprise you to know that you would have liked him. He had a sense of humour in some ways not unlike your own. He was always interested in the fact that I owe much of my capacity to work, such as it is, to the training and friendship you gave me.

He would have made a front-rank newspaper man. He never missed the real point of the story sitting in front of him. It has been interesting, and still is, to know so often the true facts the press miss behind the stories that they print.

One thing which would particularly have appealed to you was his lack of any snobbery. He had the genius of treating everyone as a royal soul. A miner or a cabinet minister, a cabinet maker or a king were to him people with the same needs that had to be met. And he met them.

Beaverbrook to P.D.H.   La Capponcina,
                                         Cap d'Ail, France
                                         August 16, 1961

I am deeply sorry for you.

Your trouble recalls to my mind the troubles of my life in 1923 when Bonar Law died.

I had given my whole allegiance to him. His political affairs occupied all my thoughts.

When Bonar Law died Churchill said to me, "You sat on a stool with three legs — one was yours, another was the *Daily Express*, and the third leg was Bonar Law. You have lost your Bonar Law. You cannot sit on your stool again until you have fashioned a third leg." It seems to me you are in the same position.

P.D.H. to Beaverbrook   Caux
                                         August 23, 1961

You are a loyal friend. Yours was a thoughtful and stalwart letter which awaited me when I came back late last night from Allentown.

I understand so well what Churchill said to you about the three-legged stool. But the truth is, I have no *Daily Express*, I am, alas, no Max Aitken, and Frank Buchman was no Bonar Law. He taught men like myself to rely on God before we put our weight on any living man. Through the years he helped men like me to make God our reference point beyond any human allegiance or tie and to confront all men without favour or fear. I do not say this in any pious fashion because, as you know, I am not a pious man. But it is the truth that there are many of us around the world, who, though it would be idle to pretend we shall not sadly miss Frank Buchman, have learned with him to fight for the right as God gives us to see the right, without jealousies and in unity. Our work will go forward tomorrow as it did yesterday.

People are pouring into this place from the ends of the earth. This week Kishi comes with eighteen politicians, newspapermen and others from Japan. A planeload of 126 is coming from Brazil and Peru. The Prime Minister of Burma will be here in a few days' time. A special plane from the United States comes in tomorrow. So you can see we have our work cut out and we will do it as best we can.

P.D.H. to Doë   Caux
                                        September 9, 1961

U Nu came from Belgrade weary. He had only one hour's sleep the night before they left, and says the neutral powers fought each other like tigers. One thing is certain, if Krushchev wants to blackmail modern man into another lurch towards the Communist world, he must keep on the heat as long and fiercely as he can. He dare not let up for a moment.

We welcomed U Nu in the hall at nine-forty with the Burmese National Anthem. Then we gave him Ovaltine in his room which he specially asked for. He was amazed last night at the size and strength of what he met. He said, "Is it always like this?"

His aide asked me to provide ten bananas, nine cups of coffee, plenty of fruit and two glasses at four o'clock this morning. So I went along at that time. There was some difficulty about the right size of glass but all was well. The valet and bodyguard set up some sort of Temple with twelve candles and the fruit was cut into suitable sizes. Then I withdrew to write my manifold letters.

P.D.H. to Doë   Caux
                                        September 11, 1961

U Nu's visit was excellent. The Ambassador, brother of Tin Tut, told us a good story about their visit to the Pope. U Nu went in first, then the others were sent for. Tin Tut's brother was a little shy. The Pope came forward and said, "Are you afraid of me? Don't be frightened. I am just like you are, short and fat."

U Nu tackled the Chinese general squarely at lunch on the last day and said, "If you had cleaned up years ago, you would have had no Communism." Then with earnestness, "I have told Burma for ten years that unless we clean up we shall be like the Mainland of China."

222

.D.H. to Doë   Caux
                                          September 1961
My own strong desire is to be still and cease from the striving. To
void the pressure of men who want me to do perhaps more than I
hould. The strong family ties that make me yearn to spend every minute
ft me on this earth with you and with those I love the best. All I can
o then is to do my best and go ahead stumblingly, haltingly, conscious
ften that I may be mistaken in my course but trusting God. For some
eason we have what seems to me the most responsible job on earth.
o help me do it.

Many questioned Howard's leadership of MRA. They found it im-
ossible to understand how he had acquired it, or why he had accepted
.

.D.H. to M.H.
You ask about my leadership of Moral Re-Armament. If you were
sked the question by the press about this, I would tell them very simply
hat at the time of Frank Buchman's funeral those who had worked
ogether for years decided that Howard was the most suitable figurehead
n the present situation.
Howard very much wishes that Buchman's death had altered the
ommitment of a host of people who cannot comprehend why a man
ike Howard is described as "in charge of the work of Moral Re-Arma-
nent", but refuse themselves to stride forward and take charge. It is for
he reason that so few people have been willing to do this that someone
ike myself has to become, for the sake of the work and the sake of the
nderstanding of mortal men, a figurehead on the good ship MRA. But,
f course, the figurehead is not the motor, nor the steam that drives the
hip.
If you want to know where the steam and motor come from I will tell
ou when I get back home.

A month before his death, in January 1965, Peter Howard was to
vrite:

"I feel not one whit more 'in charge' than anyone else who will bear
he brunt. It is simply that, for good or ill, in the modern world some-
ody has to wear the label of final responsibility, for otherwise men
hink there is no responsibility and, indeed, an irresponsibility that they
an ignore or destroy.
"There is a world of difference between being in the middle of every-
hing and being in charge of everything, because if you are in charge you
now that God has to be in the middle."

In December 1964 Howard wrote:

"I wish we could forget phrases like 'in charge'. So many seem to think it is a kind of grab for power. For me it means doing the simple things, like giving the best of myself to all people all the time regardless of how I am feeling or how they are behaving. It means staying honest as the day is long. It means that I shun every negative note. It means the knowledge that we must somehow get the discipline of Christ's Cross back into our affairs if we are going to go forward."

Howard did march forward. He had four years to live. It seemed probable that a man of his energy and resolve would live far longer. But he would say often and again, "We must hurry. There is so little time." His life was a race with time. A race in which he would not abate; a race which he must finish at full-speed. It was impossible to think of him as an old man. When he wrote his last play at the age of fifty-six, it was the story of the battle between the generations. He asked Doë what she thought it was like to grow old. After her reply he said, "It is funny. I am fifty-six. I don't feel any of those things. I feel just the same as I did when I was thirty."

At thirty, Peter Howard had been a man of vitality and drive, but now he possessed something more. He still enjoyed the smell of battle; he still possessed the strength to fight and win; but he had a depth of thought and faith which far outmatched both. He owed this to Frank Buchman:

"I understand the magic of that small-town American, whose personality displeased many, who was accused of snobbery, ambition and deceit, and who in an age of Satanisation got people in all corners of the world marching God-wards. This is the work of the Holy Spirit and cannot be explained by human 'whys' and 'hows'.

"Buchman was used in his generation to give millions a glimpse of God they would otherwise have lacked; to give thousands a faith; to give tens of thousands a moral challenge, greater or less, conscious or unconscious, that plays an increasing part in history. These are facts, so far as men can judge them; they will stand fire.

"Many hated Buchman's pace, his unreasonableness, his blazing resolve to hack through and crack on. They not only hated it, but thought it wrong. And it was – and is – the hope of our work. He was a man with faults. But his strength was his Christ-centredness, rather than his America-centredness.

"People will never understand the secret of Frank Buchman unless they judge him as a revolutionary. That is what he was. He did not look at life or people through the same eyes as those of other men. He did not think of people as black, white, brown or yellow, but as sons of God with the same needs which the same answer could meet.

"He did not think of people as of different classes. He did not think that a man was a better or worse man because of his wealth — or lack of it. He sympathised with poor men and did his best to help them materially and in every way — but he was far from that patronage of poverty which refuses to face the need of the poor for the same honesty and purity that the world rightly demands from the rich.

"Buchman for half-a-century strode fearlessly forward, proclaiming old truths in new ways, facing decadent generations with a decision to let God clean up themselves and their nations from top to bottom. He challenged the statesman and the ordinary man with standards which, if accepted, mean revolution in all they think and do. In the landslide of morality and the shifting sands of an age of licence, he gave the solid rock of eternal values and truth.

"Of course he was persecuted. Men with such a message have been persecuted all through the ages."

It was under the fire of persecution that Peter Howard set forth to take up this battle.

Chapter 16

BIRTHRIGHT

Britain, a thousand of your men
Have praised you with their voice and pen,
And millions more their blood have shed.
Your life, you owe it to your dead.
But who will now arouse and save
Your birthright from a common grave?

Island of grey and green and gold
When autumn mists your fields enfold.
Island of sap and blossoming
When earth first sprays her lap in spring.
Island of coal and cliff and sea,
Of commonplace and mystery.

The smooth green of the southern downs,
The gaunt grey shapes of northern towns,
The mediaeval bells that chime
And wood fires in the winter time —
O Britain, we of you are part,
Your bloodbeat fills and warms our heart.

The humble, nameless, godly folk
For centuries they drew the yoke,
Their stubborn arms and hearts upbore
A nation out of peace and war.
They laboured loyally as they died
And left an empire to our pride.

Yet not by might and not by power
Can Britain answer at this hour;
Nor can we from the past inherit
A living victory of the spirit
To seize the moment that remains
Ere Britain crumbles into chains.

Yes, we could bear in war to die,
Slain by the blows of tyranny;
Up held our banners while our breath
Remained — courageous unto death.
Better to fall beneath our shield,
The Cross, than to a dragon yield.

But bitter when an isle, once free,
Rots from within, and liberty
Unearned is lost; the land which braved
The centuries becomes enslaved;
The blight and blindness of small men
To turn the ages dark again.

So not by power and not by might
Can Britain resurrect the right.
By renaissance alone can bring
Freedom to commoner and king.
God redirect us and forgive.
Lord, teach a nation how to live.

Britain, a thousand of your men
Have praised you with their voice and pen,
And millions more their blood have shed.
Your life, you owe it to your dead.
But who will now arouse and save
Your birthright from a common grave?

Peter Howard fought a forthright battle for Britain. He fought on national issues; on public platforms, in full-page announcements in the press; in speeches; in plays. He fought for the young, for the old, for the women, for management and workers. He fought also for his children. He was willing to sacrifice everything, even the family relationships he held most dear, to see his country brought under the control of God.

As a result some people regarded him as hard and ruthless. In truth, he was sensitive, with almost Victorian good manners. He would go nowhere uninvited. He would receive no hospitality without thanking by letter within an hour or two of leaving. He disliked rudeness or brashness in the young. He equally disliked superiority and indifference in the old. To his home he would invite generously. He hated leaving people out, especially those in trouble or need. However difficult he found them he would ask them. But he would offer them no cushions of comfort, only the challenge of a Cross. It made some demand from him that he become more "human":

"I am more vulnerable to wounds, having less time for adjustment than most people. But I do not want to become the 'human' who in the name of tolerance lets others down and out. I have seen the gleam in man and seen it flicker and begin to fade. I do not know what is the right life for others. I am always in question about what people should do, never in doubt about what they should be. Absolute honesty is right for everybody. I feel the same about the other standards of Christ.

"*The Spectator* says I am Dr. Goebbels. Brebner, formerly Brendan Bracken's side-kick, says I am a comrade of brother Krushchev. In truth, I am just an old newspaperman, inky but unbowed."

Howard was not one who thought that Britain was finished or that it would be better to be born in another age or another country. He told an audience of businessmen in Leeds in April 1964:

"I would not choose to be living at any other time, nor would I choose at this time to be anything but an Englishman. For I believe this unknown age will be captured by courage in experiment, craftsmanship in industry, care from man to man. In our country, these qualities of brain, hand and heart still abound. Sometimes observers, who do not know us well, under-estimate us. Only this week I heard some foreigner say that our country is finished. This is a form of folly that has afflicted tyrants and dictators through centuries. The best of Britain does not make the biggest noise or the big mess.

"The world looks on us as a nation of blockheads, not eggheads. But in truth, with the majesty of our mongrel ancestry, we are a nation of prophets, warriors, poets.

"A Briton saw an apple fall from a tree, and this theory launched an historic leap ahead in science and experimental mathematics.

"A Briton saw a kettle boiling, and created an age of steam that revolutionised society.

"A Briton saw mould in a jar, and led man to penicillin. Our people first split the atom, invented jet engines, pioneered trade unionism from Tolpuddle, ended slavery, ended the degradation of child labour, educated, emancipated and finally liberated millions of our fellow men in Asia, Africa and elsewhere.

"This age of adventure was built for men like us. But we refuse to make it our own.

"Englishmen who once felt a stain on their honour more deeply than a wound upon their flesh, do so no more. Family life is not so sound as once it was. Vice is not everywhere regarded as gross. Faith lacks moulding

228

force upon our generation. 'British made' does not always mean best made. Estimates are often exceeded in industrial contracts, and jobs are not always done when they have been promised. The word of those who negotiate at breakfast tables, board rooms or conference tables is not always their bond.

"The gap in leadership whether from Right or Left is the gap of purpose. All parties concentrate on things, on materialism, and neglect a theme, a motive for our nation."

He thought that political leaders evaded this vital point. In a full-page announcement in the *Daily Express* on December 22, 1964, he wrote:

The Prime Minister said at Brighton, "Only by a massive sense of dedication by every individual can we get the national sense of purpose we need." But this is harvest before seedtime. It is upside-down thinking. The truth is that only by proclaiming a national purpose which every individual can understand and love will a "massive sense of dedication" be created. Until the British people are told where the nation is heading they will not dedicate themselves to head there.

What is our national purpose? What is the theme, the goal, that will capture the mind, inflame the heart and put the will of the people into gear?

He was not pessimistic, but he held with Thomas Hardy that "if way to the better there be, it exacts a full look at the worst".

"Britain will have to decide whether to help mould a new type of human society, with a new type of man to live in it, or to stand aside, filling her pockets, shrinking to insignificance and hoping for the best. No country in history has been greater than our own. The image of no great country has been dragged so low so swiftly by such petty men.

"Today our country is regarded as a humbug and fraud by millions of people in other countries. Surely we have enough men free from the problems of adultery, homosexuality, viciousness and drunkenness left in our society to govern us and to govern us well?

"The terror of our times is not that they are evil, but that they call in question the very existence of right and wrong, of absolute standards. There has always been wickedness in Britain. But it is the first time in history that outsiders who hate us are cultivating our decadence in order to destroy us, and when sincere men in our midst say good and evil no longer have relevance or meaning.

"British hearts are still hungry for God's truth. The ordinary man and woman in their homes or at their work, uneasy, inarticulate, almost lost in the modern maelstrom, will respond in millions to a clear lead given by convinced people, whether they come from pub or palace, from Left or Right, from Conservative or Labour. The nation is waiting for some modern Churchill to do for our morals in peacetime what he did for our guts in time of war."

Howard went on the attack. He felt that if nobody else would raise their voice in Britain, MRA had to do so:

"There is a yearly Festival at Edinburgh, a city which once stood for faith and decency. The Festival has produced good shows and entertainment. It has also produced a posse of poets and playwrights who use their talents to thrust godlessness and dirt down the national gullet, to proclaim that God is dead, and that right and wrong no longer exist. It has produced a troupe of African ladies, naked to the waist, who display themselves in their dances to the slobbering eyes of art-lovers. It is typical British hypocrisy that while we rightly complain of colour prejudice in other parts of the world, we pay black women to dance in public in ways we would not allow British girls, in the name of decency, to perform.

"The Edinburgh Festival has produced an image that we are no longer a Christian nation and that our god is flesh, with sex our aim and object."

The Lord Provost of Edinburgh, Duncan Weatherstone, described Howard's remarks as "impertinence". He added, "I hope he will have the courage to apologise."

Lord Harewood, at that time the Festival's artistic director, said, "Mr. Howard seems to have a very restricted view. If he thinks this then it is entirely up to him. It is all in the mind you know."

Howard said a few days later:

"I am in the dilemma of giving offence either to the Lord Provost of Edinburgh or to the Lord God Almighty. So, reluctantly, I must risk the displeasure of the elected ruler of the earth.

"I love my country. I do not intend to be bullied into silence if I choose to point out trends in Edinburgh or elsewhere that in my view may destroy the tradition and liberty which millions of our brothers, sons, husbands and fathers died in war to preserve."

In London on July 28, 1963, Howard said:

"There is a conspiracy against our traditions and our power. Monarchy, Church and Parliament, the solid institutions of our forefathers are under attack.

"The Royal Family hold a special place in the affection and allegiance of our people. Their example could do more than a million exhortations. They should refuse to consort with any whose habits are known to be debased. If their advisers are unable to tell them the true nature of some who try to use friendship at Court as a cover for moral compromise, they should get new advisers able and willing to do so.

"Government should make it plain they will not elevate public men with vulnerable private habits.

"Parliament should deal with the corrupting influence of the BBC. From some programmes of the BBC a spiritual sewer flows out into the homes of Britain. It infects the community. They broadcast dirt with the air of intellectual authority. It is a legend that all young people like immorality. The truth often is that the older generation has decided to live in dirt and excuses itself with the lie that modern youth demands dirt of them, and like lice, feels more at home with filth."

The BBC retorted that they gave equal time to God and anti-God. But Howard was not satisfied:

"The times may be the same, but some of the people offered the freedom of the air to put the case for God are often defeated men, dullards or dupes who have no idea how to hit as hard and as entertainingly as these smutty satirists. They make Christ more boring than anti-Christ. And He is not."

Elements in the Church of England opposed Howard strongly:

P.D.H. to H.H.   December 28, 1964
I never thought in my lifetime I would see bishops and prelates in our country electing themselves as pall-bearers at God's funeral and inviting us to join them. But on the fundamental of faith in God and in His standards of morality, we will never yield nor abate. It still grieves me when I think of all our country could yet do and be in the world. But people say to me, 'Britain is leading us into the new morality.' By this they mean a rationalisation of faith so that men no longer believe in miracles or in the divinity of Christ. They mean an interpretation of liberty which says that it is wrong to feel guilty about anything, and that whatever people like to do is all right for them to do. I think this is a misinterpretation of the heart of most of the British people. But God help us. It is the image that our Establishment and some of our more vocal public figures are giving to the modern world.

The Bishop of Southwark attacked Howard and MRA on a television programme. Howard wrote and asked him for an explanation:

Dear Bishop,   July 15, 1963

I am writing to ask sincerely and seriously why you go out of your way to make such an offensive reference to myself and my friends. . . .

If we cannot work together as Christians are meant to work, surely at least it would be reasonable and fair to refrain from hurling into millions of homes insults which it seems impossible to have any chance of answering? . . .

Like many others, I found Christian faith and returned to the Church as a result of meeting Moral Re-Armament. So long as men like myself are in charge, the work will be rooted in Christ.

Disagreement with methods is one thing. We want to learn how to do better. The broadcasting of smear is another matter. And I would truly appreciate it if you could explain to me why hindrances by a man with the influence you possess should be set in our path.

                                        Bishop's House
                                        38, Tooting Bec Gardens
                                        Streatham, S.W.16
                                        July 19, 1963

Dear Mr. Howard,

Thank you for your letter which I much appreciate.

There is no need for me to give you a detailed explanation of my attitude to MRA. I do not question the sincerity of MRA, but I doubt its wisdom, its balance and its orthodoxy. In the television interview I felt it necessary to draw attention to these doubts.

My position can be stated simply. I am interested in the conversion of Mr. Rachman[1] because I hold the Catholic faith with regard to his eternal salvation. But I am not so naïve as to think that the housing situation in England can be "changed" by "changing" Mr. Rachman and his like. What is needed is a ruthless onslaught on a damnable system of property rights which is corrupt as it is immoral. Is MRA with its campaigning for absolute standards prepared to take part in the onslaught? If so, I shall be glad to reverse my attitude with regard to its integrity and I shall have more respect for its supporters who hold positions in my diocese.

                        Yours, etc.
                        Mervyn Stockwood

P.D.H. to the Bishop of Southwark

Moral Re-Armament is not a political party, nor a Church. You would not wish us to be either. Having said this, of course my answer to your question about Mr. Rachman is that I would fight to win him to conversion, but I would also fight like hell to end the shameful conditions in

[1] Property racketeer, from whom the word "Rachmanism" was derived.

housing which make it possible for men like him to prosper. I yield to nobody in my determination through the law of the land and through social and economic revolution to change the material situation in the modern world. If Moral Re-Armament was a reactionary force, simply designed to keep people quiet and conditions as they are, please believe me I should not stay a day with it. How well we do our job is a matter of opinion. Personally, I feel we could do it better. Certainly we need and welcome help to heighten our aims and deepen our penetration.

I believe that there is a universal need for Christ and that we should hold the challenge of His Cross to the anti-Christ of totalitarianism, whether it comes from Right or Left.

In an interview with Dr. W. J. Bolt in the *Church of England Newspaper*, June 19, 1964, Peter Howard was asked:

W.J.B.: "What has MRA to say to the more pressing needs of today?

P.D.H.: "If you are thinking of the widespread demoralisation caused by sexual vice, drink and gambling, we affirm that God, Who gave man his body, mind and will, can guide and assist man to control them. We Christians must be eager and alert to demonstrate to others who lack our experience and our enlightenment that we can live full and happy lives without indulgences which, to others, seem indispensable necessities.

W.J.B.: "Do you consider that MRA has made any substantial impression on the Christian Churches, or on the outside world?

P.D.H.: "I cannot measure the success of a spiritual plan by statistics, or by the amount of outside publicity it attracts. As long as we are bringing Christ's life and His standards into deeper observance in the life of the world, we do not care whether or not our organisation is a numerical or financial success."

P.D.H. to F.C.   June 5, 1963

The Christian life is a fighting life. So many people have such a phoney idea that if you are guided by God, you lose all feelings and become a kind of hulk in a rosy glow. This is not my experience. I feel the wounds. I feel the lures of the devil. I feel the discouragement of sinful men and adversities more than I ever did in my life before. But I have firmly determined, in the power of Christ, not to be guided by anything except God.

By some within Moral Re-Armament Howard's outspoken assault upon immorality was regarded with suspicion, especially when it incurred the displeasure of leading Churchmen:

M. to P.D.H.   May 27, 1964

Today in MRA we are much more down-to-earth and are concentrating on realisable ends. "The secret of success is to concentrate on finite ends" says Cosimo de Medici. Would it not be possible to change the image of MRA from starry-eyed enthusiasts content to murmur, "The solution is a God-controlled nation," and create a new image of realists who correctly diagnosed the evil, and who were longing to co-operate with other well-intentioned groups anxious to arrest decadence?

If you can create a new and, for ordinary folk, far more sympathetic image of MRA, it will perform an invaluable service.

Howard replied: June 3, 1964

Your outlook would be the death of MRA because your road is Cross-less. You want to rob Moral Re-Armament of its genius as God's answer architected for this century. Once we accept that position we not only make respectability our aim, but we yield responsibility in return for a possible response from those who don't do much anyway. We can deal with a whole lot of minor issues, and at the same time miss the needs of men.

I believe one of our great needs is to make Moral Re-Armament work. You see, our books, our theatre, our publications, our life in our homes is not so dynamic, so profitable, so real, that it jolts the nation to a halt. I think we ought to co-operate with everybody who is willing to co-operate with us, but it must be co-operation in the task of changing men rather than starry-eyed enthusiasm which thinks that evils will be arrested while everyone stays the same.

Howard believed that the measuring rod of a healthy Christian or a healthy Church was whether in fact people were changed. Addressing a conference of clergy and ministers at Church House, Westminster, he said:

"Frank Buchman used to say, 'If you're not winning, you're sinning.' He meant that if you call yourself a Christian and people around you are not changing, there is something wrong with the way you live your faith. I do not talk about it as a point of doctrine. I talk about it as a point of experience. In my own life, if I am living straight and the maximum God shows me, people change. If people do not change, there is some sin, definite, concrete, which is preventing that happening around me.

"It is true of a Church. It is true of a so-called Christian nation. It is true of Christendom. If we are not winning, we are sinning. If people in their millions are not being changed and won to the truth of Christ, there is something wrong with the way Christians are living their Christianity.

"Every non-Christian in the world should be saying, 'What are the Christian nations thinking about now? What is their next move? What are they saying? What are they doing?' We ought to be the focus of attention at this time of crisis instead of being a pattern of disunity and ineffectiveness.

"What does God mean to modern man? A God passionate to win the world? A God with a master-plan for every human being in the world? An unexpected God? An adventurous God? Somebody who is more interesting, more loving, more dynamic than any human person you know? Not on your life.

"Moral Re-Armament is the true and traditional property of the Church. It takes a man like myself with no faith; it gets me straight; it gives me a friendship with Jesus Christ which is the most precious possession in my life. It teaches me, such as I am, to be available to God for His plan. Isn't that the work of the Church?"

In his diary, Howard was to record a conversation with Lord Beaverbrook. It took place in September 1963:

"Beaverbrook asked me, 'Why do you think religion has lost its impact on the nation?' I replied, 'Because history has passed them by. Because they are living in the past.'

"Beaverbrook said, 'That's true, but it is more than that. They have become comfortable. In the old days, they were on the attack, they were fighters. Don't ever let your crowd become too comfortable, Peter."

It was a piece of advice Howard did not forget.

.   .   .

In January 1962, Howard's only daughter, Anne, became engaged to the young Member of Parliament for East Aberdeenshire, Patrick Wolrige Gordon. In the months that followed, an attempt was made to remove Wolrige Gordon from his seat because of his association with MRA and, in particular, because of his engagement to Howard's daughter. This attempt was supported by senior members of the Conservative Party. It failed because the ordinary men and women of East Aberdeenshire refused to submit to pressure. At a special meeting of the constituency party, they gave the young Member a three to one majority.

Throughout these months, Peter Howard was abroad. He never went to East Aberdeenshire until the political battle was over, and then only to see his daughter and the house she and her husband were buying. Afterwards, one of Wolrige Gordon's opponents said at an Executive meeting, "We do not want Howard up here indoctrinating us and pushing his nose into our affairs." Howard never returned again.

P.D.H. to Doë   January 25, 1962

Thank you for your tender care. Perhaps if I were a saint I would not feel the need of it. But I do. I do. It is a mighty reinforcement in life. We have lived good years, but we have great years ahead. I realise more than ever before the magnitude of the heritage that is MRA. It is a trust from God. I believe you and I are entering the best years of our lives. I feel utterly inadequate to match the needs of the challenge. There is a gap in my ways and thoughts when you are not there. It is odd but we do seem to have been propelled to a place in the centre of this world struggle. We must learn to live in that knowledge and with a child's faith in Him. It is our only way and it will win. Sometimes I wonder why we are placed in the position where so much seems to depend on us, but there it is and we will forge forward. I must shed everything from me that does not help change folk.

It was noble of you to come and see me off. My heart was wrung to see you through the window of the grim airport. We seem to spend much of life saying farewell, but never mind.

P.D.H. to Doë   April 1, 1962

Anne and Patrick make me happy. They love each other and that is much of what is needed. Patrick has a love of God too. How the battle in Aberdeen will go is hard to foretell.

P.D.H. to Doë   Los Angeles
                                                    April 4, 1962

My heart is torn by the struggle in which Patrick and Anne are engaged. I long to do much but can do little.

An odd thing happened to me when I spoke at the theatre. The Biltmore Bowl lay-out was fine and all went well, but as the final speaker of the evening after the play, I suddenly found my knees wilting and my feet buckling. I nearly fell over. It was just tiredness I think.

P.D.H. to Doë   Los Angeles
                                                    April 5, 1962

Odd. It has been a night of vigil. I could not sleep for thinking of Anne and Patrick. And there came as a flood the sureness of God's love and mercy. It is not our job to protect them, but only to share the battle with them.

As I write this, they are preparing for what is sure to be an ordeal in Aberdeen. I live through it with them. Persecution is the fire that forges prophets. You do not begin to measure the love of God until you experience the hate of enemies. There is nothing new in all this.

Some are shocked by the venom of their enemies. They live in a dream world much of the time because they refuse to grapple with iniquity.

On June 2, 1962, Peter and Doë Howard received over seventeen hundred guests at Hill Farm for their daughter's wedding. Howard insisted that friend and foe alike should be bidden. The numbers grew out of all proportion, but Howard was undaunted. On the eve of the wedding he saw that every guest received a hot meal and the warmest of hospitality — even though some did not arrive until midnight.

Among the journalists who came to cover the wedding was one from Scotland, Pat Strachan, Editor of The Buchan Observer. He wrote:

"The blackbirds were trying out the first notes of the dawn chorus over Hill Farm, Brent Eleigh, one glorious morning in May 1962, when Peter Howard introduced himself in all his stature. Most carefully he opened the guest room door, silently crossed the few feet of floor to the bedside and laid down with barely a clink of china — a cup of tea. Silently the door closed behind him, certainly without his knowing whether his overnight guest was asleep or awake. It is an old English custom (so they say) and a delightful one.

"As the guest sipped his very early morning refreshment, two Post Office vans arrived and stopped below his bedroom window with the household mail — his own, no doubt, as one might expect in a man with his world-wide interests, and that of his only daughter whose wedding was to take place a few days later.

"Here was a man, up with the lark, attending to his guest, and ready to scale a mountain of mail even before some of the birds had opened their eyes, let alone tuned up! His guest, the writer, leisurely sipped his tea, drank in the glorious morning, and surveyed the astonishing scene below as two postmen shuttled mailbag upon bulging mailbag from their vans into the repository of Hill Farm. Indeed, the guest was dressed and ready for the morning air outdoors before the vans moved off.

"That morning, before breakfast, I saw the impact of Peter Howard's vitality on Hill Farm — from the fish pool beside the farmstead, to the broad acres around — themselves a tribute to his thorough grasp of the fundamentals of life. Those around him in his employ had caught his vision of what a modern farm could be with just that extra concern for man and beast. 'A good master,' as one in fact readily conceded.

"In the briefest of interludes, Peter Howard gave the impression of preferring the role of the 'working farmer' to that of the farming laird or Lord of the manor, apparent in the fact that he was dressed to work the farm not simply to supervise. At the same time, the farmer had his eyes on other horizons, east and west, and far beyond the range of fatstock and marketing, in conversation seeking always complete understanding and, as I saw him, relating what he had seen and heard to what he was seeing and hearing."

Howard was to describe the wedding day as "the happiest of my life". With infinite care he had prepared every detail — the food, entertainments for the children, where guests should sit, at what time each car should leave for the church, how the special trains from London should be met, and above all how each person should be cared for individually.

He had insisted that his daughter write and thank for every present within twenty-four hours of receiving it. Sometimes this meant writing over thirty letters a day by hand. "To you it may mean a little hard work," he said, "but to the other person it means everything. Never take generosity for granted." After the wedding was over, every person who had helped on that day received a letter of thanks within a week. For him it was rudeness to wait longer.

.   .   .

The events in East Aberdeenshire had convinced Howard that all was not well within the Conservative Party. When the Profumo and Vassall affairs followed hot foot the following summer, he was not surprised. He wrote:

"Events seem to hint that it is not always wise to regard a public man's private life wholly as his own affair. The answer is not McCarthyism, a police state, or the banning from high places of men who have made mistakes. Nor is the answer the protection of those in power from the penalties of private folly. The answer is honesty. Men with secrets to hide are not always able to keep, when under pressure, secrets of state. Blackmail plays an increasing part in national and international affairs. Modern governments are prone to have much the same standards of honesty and behaviour as the people, neither better nor worse. It seems a shock to both when this comes to light.

"Some believe it is dangerous to insist on high character in high places. They say it may lead to moral dictatorship, the enforcement of a code of conduct on men unwilling to accept it. If right and wrong do not exist, this argument counts. If right and wrong should exist, the argument vanishes. And it is yet more dangerous to accept a dictatorship of immorality, the enforcement of a code of moral laxity that destroys ancient virtues and makes the 'done thing' out of what men know should not be done."

Conservatives and Socialists wrote to him asking him to stop his public attacks.

P.D.H. to an M.P.   June 14, 1963
My own difficulty is that many among your colleagues, in ways that some would call 'persecution' and that others would call 'arrogant con-

tempt', have for a long time helped to smear, misrepresent, belittle, or swamp with studied silence the work we are trying to do. They have treated us with contempt and, in some cases, with venom. I do not say this in terms of personal complaint. I say it in terms of spiritual diagnosis, which the present administration certainly needs and seems in a large measure to lack.

My own belief is that our own nation will in the end stand or fall by whether it accepts or rejects God. A witch hunt is wrong. Give me Macmillan before McCarthy any day of the week. But a national moral aim, proclaimed and lived by our leadership, is right and has, so far as public image goes, and indeed in my view so far as reality goes, been wholly lacking.

For his statements Howard was accused of meddling in politics. He replied:

"We use political issues to advance Christ's Kingdom, and we do not try to use Christ in the furtherance of political issues. There is an important difference."

From many countries in the Commonwealth he received letters. One came from India:

G. to P.D.H.   August 4, 1963
The Profumo affair is a main topic and it is sad to see how this has grievously blighted such a lot of Indian regard for Britain. We expected this sort of thing from some European countries. But to have a British Minister behaving so – cheaply! There seem to be no moral standards in Britain any more.

P.D.H. to G.   August 8, 1963
Thank you for your interesting letter. I hold no brief for Britain, but the most significant part about the Profumo affair was the very strong outrage from every section of British life when it came to light. There is a lot of hypocrisy in Britain, but other countries also have their share of this tranquilliser and energiser.

I personally thank God that Profumo has at least given a jab to the conscience of the nation and that there still is such a vigorous life revealed.

Howard disliked bandwagons. And the post-Profumo months provided plenty of them.

P.D.H. to S.   July 30, 1963

There is no particular virtue in attacking immorality and saying, "What brave men we are." The point is to live out in the light of the nation so normally and steadfastly that at any point all men know what is the right battle to fight, and the right stronghold to assail.

I want Moral Re-Armament to be a keg of God's ants in the nation's pants, not a secret chrysalis behind the closet door.

Howard felt that it was no good attacking what was wrong unless you also created new life. His plays, produced in London at the Westminster Theatre, was one way he did this.

P.D.H. to W.W.   August 14, 1963

What is in my mind is to create in the world of theatre a group of actors and actresses who will fearlessly, constantly and with all their professional genius and flair carry a new spirit into the heart of the stage and screen world. I am not looking for actors and actresses who will do the sort of play that is running at the Westminster Theatre and explain it to others. I am asking for people who will actually understand the need of a regeneration of art in modern England and be willing to play their part in creating the plays, producing the plays, acting the plays and winning the nation.

P.D.H. to A.B.   September 23, 1963

Art is meant to illustrate the highest aims of humanity, the part each can play in achieving those aims and to show everyone how playing such a part is not only possible but normal. An artist should be a mixture between a surgeon, a physician, a prophet, a poet and a priest.

For many artists it was a new and strange conception, particularly in an age of "kitchen sink" theatre and pornographic books. They felt Howard's approach meant that he despised D. H. Lawrence and Wesker. This was not true as Howard explained:

P.D.H. to P.B.   August 14, 1963

I think Lawrence is a very great writer and his greatness lies in the fact that he was a pioneering pen. He broke through many of the encasements and moulds that had crippled conformists for nearly a century.

But I do not believe that men with great talents should use them to debase humanity. My conviction is that man is not a beast. And if I find people with great literary and artistic gifts bestialising their fellow men with them, it is to me rather like seeing a surgeon of genius using his skill to cut up rotten carrion for the sake of making a smell and creating sensation.

Literature is literature and there are no frontiers in the pen. There are certain barriers of language but sensitive translators leap beyond them.

You are right that my own writing has undergone a radical reappraisal. I will tell you about it when we meet. Perhaps the best advice given to a writer was by Arnold Bennett who, when asked how to do it replied, "Apply a pen to paper, a seat to a chair and remain there until results are obtained."

Howard understood the difficulty of creating good plays and books. He was never satisfied with his own, and he received much criticism for them. In this he sympathised with other writers.

P.D.H. to J.G.   October 29, 1962

Your finest, freest, fullest, most creative years are ahead for you if you follow God's star. It gleams fitfully from time to time in life. That I know. I also know that, though not an artist like yourself, I have passed through valleys of dry bones where you are tempted to feel that life and colour and warmth and vitality will never again be given to your genius. But they are. They are. These dry times, I think, are meant to hold us to the realisation that God is the source for us all of everything we put forth. And He likes us once or twice in a lifetime to understand it more fully.

Although Howard was keen that the productions at the Westminster Theatre should be perfect in every way, he had severe conditions:

"I want to be sure that every play we do involves the will and imagination of modern man. Everyone will say, 'How lovely.' Everyone will say, 'What wonderful people you are.' But will anybody say, 'My God, I never felt so uncomfortable in my life in a theatre.' If we are to shift Britain some of the audiences must feel like this."

Howard's plays did, in fact, shift thousands of British people – and many British situations. A thousand shipyard workers and their families from the Clyde travelled down to see his play *Through the Garden Wall* and shop stewards there reported that the new climate among them had made possible the discarding of cherished restrictive practices. Similar parties came, weekend after weekend from industries in the North East, the Midlands, Lancashire and South Wales, with similar results. The Chairman of the Building Trades Workers in Coventry stated publicly that, on some of the sites for which he was responsible, production had risen by as much as 30 per cent because of the new approach he had found at the Westminster.

The Westminster Theatre paid. It did so without subsidies, and in the face of much competition and opposition. This spoke louder than words to Howard.

P.D.H. to K.B.   October 27, 1964

The theatre has done more to bring the truths of God home to modern Britain and other countries than any other single activity in which we have all been engaged.

Howard's principal work was still and always his personal work with people. After the plays or the speeches, he would often be talking with them until a late hour:

"After my speech a young woman said, 'Will you sit with me on the sofa?' Well, it might have been misunderstood, but I took a look at that girl and I knew it wasn't that. So I sat down with her. Other people went out into the garden. She said to me, 'I find it awfully hard to say some things to my mother and father.' I said, 'Why on earth?' She said, 'Well, they don't understand me. Tell me this, is it all right for me to sleep with men before I am married? I just want to know.' Now that was not a cheap question – it was not a daring question. It was the question of a hungry human heart of a child who did not know the answer. Her parents said to me later, 'Of course, the one answer is a faith, not just a personal faith, but a faith strong enough to change the trend in our nation.' And the mother said, 'I haven't got any faith. What am I to do?' Now there you have got the dilemma of our times."

It was from talks like this that his plays emerged. Perhaps it was this talk which led him to create the teenage girl in his last play, *Happy Death-day*, bewildered in her relationships with her parents and with her father's scientific assistant, a part so powerful that it left the audience silent and often speechless.

Howard spent a lot of time with children – and few of the thousands he met will forget him. One of them, Mary Lean, daughter of Garth Lean, whom Howard had first met in Fleet Street, wrote:

"I was twelve years old when he died, so all my memories of him are as a child. He always seemed to have time for me. When he was leading his daughter up the aisle at Lavenham Church, he noticed me standing at the end of a pew fascinated by my first wedding, and gave me a dig in the ribs as he moved past up to the altar.

"He always teased me a great deal. Once, when he came to our home he spent a long time trying to convince me that my chilblainy finger would fall off, although I assured him it wouldn't. Another time I met him in one

242

of the long passages at Caux. He immediately leapt into the air, clicking his heels together in what he called a 'Christmas jump'.

"Once I had earned some money which I sent him to help pay for one of his full-pages in the *Daily Express*. I said I thought it would make a lot of people feel very uncomfortable. He replied:

Dear Mary,

You are a humdingerdinkle, which is a mixture of Joan of Arc, St. George and the dragon, and the best of both your parents. I have passed the money on.

I am sorry you think my page would make people feel uncomfortable. I used to try and make people as comfortable as possible. Then I met your father!

"Once he had a party for children. Before you were let into the room you had to answer an impossible question. Mine was, 'How many fishes are there in the sea?' It took us some time to see that we were meant to answer, 'I don't know.'

"Somehow, in spite of all the bustle and business of his life, he always managed to have time for me. I have been told he once decided to treat every child as though he were his own. He certainly treated me like that whenever I met him."

Vincent Evans, one of Howard's friends from Fleet Street, writes:

"I once lay in a hospital bed in London. My sight was gone. Not much of it would ever return. My career as a Fleet Street journalist was certainly ended and a period of deep reappraisal of the lives of my young family lay ahead. The evening on which the surgeon had told me that there was little more that he could do for me was not the gayest of my life.

"I had no reason to believe that Peter Howard was in London. In fact I knew that a couple of days before he had been in South America. The door opened and I heard that odd limping gait coming across the room and the moment of something like despair became light and vivid.

"As he left a couple of hours later, Peter said a very simple but infinitely loving thing: 'I wanted to share this thing with you.' And I knew that, for the rest of his life, he would carry in his mind and on his heart the cares of people like myself.

"It was Peter's immense gift that, in a life in which the days often began and ended in the early hours of the morning, his thoughts were populated by a cavalcade of friends.

"The day after he came to see me in hospital, Peter was gone again to some other part of this world which he had made his own – but, at odd moments of stress, a letter or a 'phone call or a cable would tumble out of the blue and add some new quality to the days that followed.

"Peter lived through his own moments of tremendous personal sadness — often caused by what he felt had been his own mistakes and sometimes when he saw his own work shattered by someone else's folly. He would sink to the very bottom of his faith, stay there for a while and then begin to claw his way back again to his pinnacle of certainty. 'Nothing in my hand I bring,' he would say. And he would begin to rebuild with that as a foundation.

"Peter was a tall, gaunt, striding, but very gentle man, who would bring to the smallest duty the devotion and concentration and energy that most of us reserve for the great moments of life. You would notice that, as he grew tired, his limp would grow more pronounced, but his deep, penetrating eyes would swing round his companions, seeking a little more knowledge of them, measuring their strengths and weaknesses and asking from them a little more than their minds and bodies were prepared to give. At his moments of greatest weariness, he was still probing with tender care for the things that would nourish our faith.

"There are things which stay alert in the memory about Peter Howard — this probing for the best depths of one's character, his fastidious attention to the details of friendship, his sense of impious fun and the unrestrained laughter which accompanied it, a love for every member of his family which often tore at his heart, and the gradual expansion of that love until it wrapped its hands around the world.

"I remember the day when he was introducing some of us to an Asian potentate in his gilded palace. The man's marriage was on the verge of breaking up on the rocks of a political struggle within his own country and among his own followers. Peter suggested that, as a mark of respect, we should give him the Eastern salute as we were introduced — with bowed heads and hands pressed together as if in prayer.

"We all did so — with the exception of a high-ranking British army officer — who explained with more than a little irascibility that he was British, that he was a Christian, and that this Eastern gesture was totally foreign to him. Peter gazed at the officer in his serene way, sucked in his breath, as he sometimes did in moments of irritation, and said, 'My dear general, if I felt that, by standing on my head, I could add one inch to that man's faith, then I would stand on my head.'

"I must add that later that evening, I saw a humble and contrite British officer practising the Eastern salute in the solitude of the palace car park.

"One of Peter's greatest qualities was that he could see through men and yet love them. And this was because he had dealt faithfully with the problems in his own life that destroy relationships with people. He had rooted out the jealousies, the ambitions, the self-seeking, the search for

244

wealth, the impurities and selfishness that bring anger and division into friendships.

"I recall one night in London, after a long day's work, a colleague of Peter's sought him out and wanted to sit down and discuss his personal problems. He was a man who revelled in his own discontents. Peter was very firm with him. 'We've done this over and over again,' he told him. 'You have the answer in your own hands.' But on another day, when another man was bedevilled by something in his life that he couldn't conquer, Peter gave of his time and love with a generosity that was born out of the man's need. Peter would unfold his own life before the man, tell how he had met his own deep problems, and then show the man new vision out of the rock bottom of despair and defeat.

"I have no doubt that many others are finding the same thing about Peter — that when their instinctive pettiness and self-seeking threaten to take over, the gay memory of Peter Howard steps in almost demanding that they keep their faith. It is in fact not a demand — it is a yearning that he always felt that other people should find the truths that he found."

Howard thought that much of the trouble with the nation went back to parents:

"Parents have forgotten that it takes more creative energy to bring children up right than to bring them into the world. Instead homelife in its traditional form has almost vanished from the land. Women go to work. Their homes are deserted by day and sometimes by night. Children have to fend for themselves and seek their own amusement.

"The cure for teenage thuggery is adult unselfishness. We cannot expect youth to accept standards of morality which we older people disregard or deny.

"God is no gentleman. It is not on record which public school, if any, He attended. Nobody can tell where He cast His vote at the election. The colour of His skin, the nature of His accent, the length of His hair and the cut of His clothing are all mysteries. What is still certain and a matter of experience is that He can, will and does talk to anyone at any time who is willing to listen. For those who have no faith in God, there is the honest experiment of the absolute standards of morality that we so urgently desire those we criticise to accept. Absolute moral standards are a guide in life. They are like the North Star. For centuries mariners have steered by the North Star. It is a fixed point in the sky. It is yet to be recorded that any ship has reached the North Star, but it is true that on every ocean mariners discern from that star where their position is and where they need to head. And absolute moral standards for those who lack faith may be a good starting point if they wish to play their part with all of us in a revolution that will change this country and the world.

"God is not dead. God is the great progressive. He is far more radical than any Russian. Far more modern than any Mod or Rocker. And far more interesting than the dirty books, filthy pictures or even the matchless pop music that is such a delight to so many nowadays in this Beatle Britain.

"I feel myself a man of many frailties and much weakness. I hope that before I die I shall have changed out of all recognition and be wholly different tomorrow from what I am today. Just as indeed I am different today from what I was yesterday. But I tell you without soap or sentiment that as I begin each day by listening to God, it is a time of enthralment and fascination that I would not miss. It is like a great shoal of silver fish flashing through your heart and mind — new ideas for people, fresh approaches to problems, deeper insight into the mood of the times, costly, daily, personal decision that is the price of shifting our force and our nation ahead. I am not much of a fisherman but I try and snatch one or two of those silvery fish as they fly from the Mind of God into the mind of men and women and children like ourselves."

Chapter 17

"Asia hoped to teach the world the art of unity. For years India practised the policy of 'neutrality', which was praised to high heaven by the Red Chinese giant. Now that giant has crossed the nation's frontier and swallowed 30,000 square miles of Indian soil.

"The Communists say that the free world is divided within itself. That is true. But the Communist world has failed to answer the hate and bitterness in their own ranks.

"Hating Russia or hating America or hating another class, colour, race or country multiples the problem and cures nothing. The free world as well as the Communist world needs help not hate."

P.D.H. December 3, 1962

Peter Howard journeyed several times to Asia.

In October 1961, he went with his son, Anthony, and Lawson Wood (Dr. Buchman's secretary from 1936–39). Rajmohan Gandhi, the son of Devadas Gandhi,[1] and the grandson of the Mahatma, met them there. His father had sent Rajmohan to learn journalism in Edinburgh where he lived with a doctor long identified with MRA:

"Forty years after Frank Buchman first met his grandfather, Rajmohan Gandhi was working as a newspaper man in Britain. He was so impressed by what he saw in Frank Buchman's work that he resigned his job and decided to make Moral Re-Armament his calling. One of the leaders of India urged him that his duty lay in the newspapers. Rajmohan replied, 'When my grandfather came back to this country from South Africa as a lawyer, his family urged him to continue his legal practice. Instead, he put aside his private plans in order to free our country. Now there is a bigger job than freeing one country. The job is to save the whole world from dictatorship, corruption and war. I am going to put Moral Re-Armament in first place.'

"More than a year later this same Indian leader was going out of a building with Rajmohan Gandhi. They called a taxi. Rajmohan stood

[1] Editor of the *Hindustan Times*.

aside to let the older man in first. But the older man insisted on Rajmohan going before him, saying, 'I want you to go first to show you that you were right and I was wrong.' "

The Howards, Gandhi and Wood first visited Burma at the invitation of U Nu who had been at Caux earlier that year. It was at Caux he had found himself sitting next to a docker from Brazil:

"The docker told U Nu how he had begun to change, losing his love of violence and taking up the struggle to remake the world. 'I was a drunkard,' he said, 'and this nearly destroyed our home.'

" 'I used to drink far too much also,' said the Prime Minister. 'I began at the age of ten. Then I gave it up. But being a weak man, I took to the bottle again. At the age of twenty-six I stopped, and I can say that today I would sooner die than drink too much.'

"The docker talked about his hate. 'Have you lost that too?' asked U Nu. 'Do you feel sure you are permanently free from bitterness? Not one drop left?'

"With care and sensitivity he dug to the root of the docker's life, helped him to bring to the surface the causes of his bitterness and to find a cure.

"U Nu said at Caux, 'If we want to stop Communism taking hold of the world we must deal with corruption, bribery, drink and womanising.' He has seen the effects of Moral Re-Armament in his own country. In 1961, the Conference of the Presiding Abbots' Association, representing 75,000 Buddhist monks, spent much of its annual session on MRA and, as a result, five senior abbots joined Buchman at Caux for his eighty-third birthday."

P.D.H. to Doë

Prime Minister's
Residence, Rangoon.
October 26, 1961

U Nu is keen we help him solve the problems of the country. The situation is complicated by the fact that the American and British Embassies and the Burmese Army were against U Nu in the recent election which his party won. U Nu is so unpopular in some parts of the country now that he dare not go there. The military men respect U Nu but nobody else in government.

No welcome could have been warmer than ours. We went in the car put at our disposal and saw the Shwedagon Pagoda at night when the Festival of Lights was just ending. Every shrine was lit. Patterns of little oil lamps spelling out prayers and hopes stood around the Buddhas. Many were praying. Many out on a Bank Holiday spree letting off crackers, playing with the children and chewing the nut. We also paid respects at the Aung San Memorial and visited the Peace Pavilion. The night was full of saffron smells, the whistles, and the bonks and signs of the Asian night that I love so well.

P.D.H. to Doë   En route to Taunggyi
                                                       October 31, 1961

We are flying over the jungle land where the fighting was during the war.

U Ba Than, who escorted us, is amazed at the progress we made yesterday. We saw the elders of the tribes, the Catholics, who pressed whisky upon us, the Baptist parson at the head of the anti-Government agitation, who sang hymns to us in a loin cloth.

In the place where we stayed last night they have had four sets of rulers in twenty years — British, Japanese, Free Chinese and Burmese. They say the Free Chinese were far the worst, next come the Burmese. Japan and Britain they feel treated them better than the others.

P.D.H. to Doë   Rangoon
                                                       November 3, 1961

We have just returned from a magic land. It is a place called Taunggyi — 4,790 feet above sea level and a thousand miles from the Chinese border in the Shan State. The Shan Princes, who were friends of the British, have been driven from the kingdom by the Burmese Government. They roam the mountains and pounce on the unwary. They cultivate the poppy lands which produce opium, which is a valuable part of this country's trade. They cross to and fro between China and Burma. The MacMahon Line has recently been extended by a series of concrete posts marking the frontier but nobody heeds them. There is danger in these mountains and we have been guarded by up to twenty armed police in jeeps every inch and hour of our way since we came here.

Krushchev, Bulganin, Mao Tse-tung have all been here. Princess Alexandra will be the next guest to come. Until twenty years ago the only road to Taunggyi was by bullock and mule. The newest building is a 200-bed hospital, a gift of the Russians, staffed and manned by Soviet doctors and nurses with every modern resource and the talk of the state.

We went early this morning to Lake Esile, where the Inthas live. Out in the very centre of the lake is a town on stilts — shops, temples, everything. Bare-footed we paid our respects and homage to the Buddha there. Around him today were literally hundreds of gifts of rice, fruit, candles, money all arranged in beauty.

We spent more than an hour yesterday at the feet of U Narada,[1] the

[1] Secretary of the Presiding Abbots' Association who led the delegation to Caux.

oldest of the Sayadaws. It was a full-scale meeting with the elders of the place squatting around with us. He said that Caux had been the peak of his life and all begged us to come soon to Taunggyi.

Earlier we had a wonderful time with the Chieftain and leaders who came, twenty-four of them, to talk with us. One of them was drunk. It turned out that he is a Member of Parliament who was sent down from New College, Oxford. He recognised my Oxford tie I happened to be wearing. All took away literature. All begged us to return with a force.

The Russians as I say are here. The Chinese come and go. The Czechs were here with dancers and singers in May. If we do not do something soon this section of Burma in my view will drop into the Communist lap. We need masses of literature, many films, money and men for this job.

P.D.H. to Doë   Rangoon
                                                      November 5, 1961

U Narada came to see me late in the day. Two Cabinet Ministers had asked 180 of the leading monks to come and see them yesterday. One monk came. This is deadly serious. It is the first time in the history of the land that such a thing has happened. The reason is that henchmen from both Russia and China have been spending money freely and much of it goes into the begging bowls. The thing was organised by certain men in the Secretariat. The senior Abbots did not know what had happened until after the event. U Narada says that unless it is sorted out, it would mean the fall of U Nu. The hatred between the Moslems and the Buddhists is the mainspring of the division that is being used. U Nu has remained steadily out of town. Many of the monks are here seeking for him. He says he wants to see me today or tomorrow, but the plain fact is that we are in the middle of a gathering crisis here which might easily mean the reconstruction of affairs at the top.

P.D.H. to Doë   Rangoon
                                                      November 6, 1961

This will be my last letter from Burma on this visit. We go to the Foreign Office this morning. U Narada sees us for an hour or so. Then the British Embassy for tea. Then back to the guest house to say good-bye to the families of the staff who are coming to see us. Then the State dinner. Then Burmese dancing laid on for us by the Government. Then back here to write reports for the Prime Minister and letters. Then we leave at 3.30 a.m. on the same plane as the Prime Minister for Calcutta.

Tell the farm men that if they ever think they work too hard, they ought to come on this venture.

P.D.H. to Doë   Calcutta

November 8, 1961

We had an important morning. Some of our people have not truly thought through what our work is. One man was quite pathetic. He said, "Once I had passion but it went." I suggested that honesty might help to recapture it.

We went to dine last night with Kanti Ghosh,[1] the Indian journalist. It was a perfect first day in India. It was Divali, the Festival of Lights, which celebrates the return of the good Prince Rama to India after fourteen years of exile in Ceylon. The whole city was flickering and blazing with lights. All the temples were going full blast.

We were given a two-hour firework display by our host before we ate. Some of the best fireworks and without exception the biggest bangs I have ever heard at close range. They are homemade by the villagers who let them off in their hand, and showed a courage at which I marvelled. Not so the son of our host, aged five, who every time there was a bang left his father's side and scampered howling indoors. This greatly pleased the father who proudly told me, "You see, he is a real coward." (Just as some British Pa might say of his son, "How brave he is.") I think Ghosh felt his son gave signs of early wisdom in life.

They flew on to Japan.

P.D.H. to Doë   Tokyo

November 10, 1961

Switzerland, England, Switzerland, France, Switzerland, England, America, Brazil, America, England, Germany, Switzerland, Italy, Switzerland, Italy, Switzerland, England, Switzerland, Germany, Switzerland, Germany, Switzerland, England, America, England, Switzerland, Scotland, Switzerland, Scotland, Norway, Germany, Switzerland, Burma, India, Japan. These are my travels so far this year taken from my diary. I was weary this morning so looked through the year to see why. It is the diary Philip gave me for Christmas, bless him.

P.D.H. to Doë   Tokyo

November 11, 1961

We saw Yoshida[2] yesterday. He has one of the loveliest Japanese homes I ever have seen. He is a great personality. He said, "I do not know much about MRA." I said, "Forget that. Everything you have said here and all you have expressed is MRA. That is exactly what we are fighting for."

[1] Editor of *Amrita Bazar Patrika*, and former President, Indian Journalists' Association.

[2] Mr. Shigeru Yoshida, Japanese elder statesman. Successively Prime Minister and Foreign Minister of Japan.

The glory of the work we are in struck me afresh this morning. MRA is the element of this century that God remembers and some of the leaders of the world forget. It is the vein of metal in the nation. It will shift the compass of humanity.

In Japan, Howard and his friends were the guests of Masahide Shibusawa and of his father, Keizo Shibusawa, the former Finance Minister and Governor of the Bank of Japan. Another of his hosts was Saburo Chiba, the Chairman of the Security Committee of the Diet whom Howard had first met with Buchman in America two years earlier:

"Chiba arrived with his wife. He was an agnostic. He was friendly, but cautious. He sat down to breakfast at a quarter-past-eight in the morning. The breakfast lasted until twenty minutes to twelve. After breakfast the men walked together in the garden and talked. Lunch was a Japanese meal, perfectly cooked. Chiba was so impressed he insisted on going into the kitchen to meet the cooks.

"At the end of that afternoon, as Chiba and his wife were preparing to leave, Buchman said to him, 'I had one thought early this morning for you.'

"Chiba said, 'What was it?'

"Buchman said, 'The whole world will walk into your heart. You will let the whole world walk into your heart.'

"As Chiba, the agnostic statesman, said goodbye at the airport that evening, he turned to his friends with these words, 'Today, for the first time in my life, I have found God. I shall never be the same again.'

P.D.H. to Doë   Tokyo
                                         November 14, 1961

We whirl forward here at a pace that is sometimes that of God and sometimes not. The Japanese think that unless you have a programme then you have nothing to do.

Today we breakfast, lunch and dine with Chiba, who has political figures to meet us at two of these events, and the press at the third.

Yesterday we had a battle at lunch with six of the top pressmen of the country. They shouted and roared and we shouted back. One said, "The thing which interests me is your passion." Frankly, they seem to have lost hope of an answer and the idea that we could win was like a dynamo in their anatomy. They want now to plan and carry through a mass demonstration for MRA in the largest hall in Tokyo.

Keizo Shibusawa had some of the industrialists to meet us for two hours in the Industrial Club. One of the men summed up by saying, "Until this afternoon we all thought MRA was a hobby. Most of the industrialists of Japan think the same." This may be broadly true. Until people are clear on the impurity which puts them on the get in every relationship, they are bound to draw men into a little group centred on themselves instead of reaching the nation.

We are finding it is essential to deal with real issues in real terms; in Burma the answer to the division between races, the corruption in all races and the money Communism was spending to use that division and corruption.

Here they are interested in how Japan, helping her neighbours to re-arm morally, would not only wrest ideological initiative from China but would create a climate in which a final settlement of reparations could be reached.

Yesterday the cable came saying they want a script of a film from me at once. Well, I will get to work. It is not easy in days that from their nature are full to overflowing, and I am not as strong nor as young as I would like. I also have on my plate 13,000 words[1] for Gollancz by December 31.

P.D.H. to Doë   Tokyo
                                                       November 16, 1961

We spent last night at the Kabuki Theatre. It was a strange medieval pageantry — heads cut off, wailing women, men acting the parts but brilliant in their portrayal. The theme was the importance of duty over feelings and emotions. The story of the play last night was of a Samurai warrior who cuts off his own son's head in battle by mistake, but then with his wife he has to pretend it is the son of his enemy. By orders of the Shogun the warrior ends as a Buddhist monk.

An Ambassador's wife came in the afternoon when we were out and apparently left saying, "Peter Howard can go to hell," though I have had no word or communication with her or her husband since I came here. My only comment is that if her wish comes true, we shall certainly meet again.

P.D.H. to Doë   Grand Hotel
                                                          Taipeh, Taiwan

We had a good journey in a CAT plane — a Mandarin flight with all the glories of old China in decor and service. At the airport we found pressmen with scores of flashing bulbs, generals, professors, Madame Ho[2] and all the company. After a rapid dinner we were rushed off to the university where we all spoke to about 2,500 people.

Today we have a breakfast date, a mass meeting at ten o'clock, a lunch

[1] For Three Views of Christianity.

[2] Wife of General Ho Ying-chin, former Prime Minister of China and Commander-in-Chief of the Army.

253

date, two tea dates – one with the President – a dinner date and an evening meeting.

P.D.H. to Doë
Taipeh
November 20, 1961

We had an hour with the Chiang Kai-sheks yesterday. Suddenly she suggested flying to Quemoy. So at a very early hour this morning we are off in a government plane and will spend the morning there and broadcast to the Mainland. I like the President. He is a man of courage. Few could have come through all he has endured without becoming sad and sour, but he is neither.

P.D.H. to Doë
Hong Kong
November 21, 1961

Yesterday we flew into Kinmen, which is high Mandarin for the Island of Quemoy and the name which they prefer, with lifebelts strapped around us and skimming the waves. This is for security as the Chinese Communists have built forty airfields along the coast opposite Taiwan in the last two years.

Kinmen is a fort – 46,000 islanders live there and 70,000 troops. They keep the troops happy, as they proudly explain, by having recreation centres where Taiwan whores keep them going. (The girls are inspected once a week for venereal disease.) The children are happy but covered with scabs and sores through lack of proper care.

Howard went to Viet Nam as the guest of President Diem.

P.D.H. to Doë
Saigon
November 26, 1961

We are in the hands of God and Father de Jaegher. He is a Belgian, who has been thirty years in Asia. We see Diem tomorrow. Meanwhile, Father de Jaegher has been wonderful to us, meeting us at the airport, taking us to see the Minister of Education, the head of the Psychological Warfare branch of the army and everyone else under the sun.

Today we go with him about one hundred miles into the country. The Viet Cong are active all round here. They skinned a colonel two weeks ago about fifteen kilometres away. They tossed a grenade into the car of the American Ambassador in the main road of Saigon the other day, but de Jaegher says we can only die once. It is no use being afraid. They offered me an escort today but I refused. Safer without. They are liable to shoot at escorted vehicles. The President's aides expressed their fears at taking the guests of the President on such a journey. The President himself likes people to see the country, and I told them we were not frightened.

In truth, there is the air here of a big push to come. The American advisers are everywhere and much disliked. The rich French rubber planters have stayed in the country and are far more popular than the Americans. There is in some quarters, not many, nostalgia for the good old days.

P.D.H. to Doë   Saigon
                                                 November 27, 1961
Ant has just posted a letter to you which I am sure has the details of yesterday's adventure.

There was, in truth, little danger. I saw for myself the ruthless and indiscriminate nature of the Communist attacks. Their main motive seems to be to get food for themselves from the villages. They are prone to behead those who will not supply it. They are also determined to stop the supplies of rice going from the country to the towns, so they now and again kill a few innocent folk on the road. We saw the remains of a whole village burned.

The other day a big hole was dug by night in a main road. The soldiers got the local villagers to fill it in. The officer said, "Do you know who dug this hole?" To his surprise the men said, "Yes, we did. The Viet Cong come by night and make us at gun point dig these holes. You come by day and make us fill them in. What are we to do?"

Howard saw President Diem, a shy man who spoke French, and was stiff at first but unbent later:

"Diem said to me, 'Help me to save my country.' I said, 'What can I do?' He said, 'Can you do anything with the Americans?' I said, 'What do you mean?' He said, 'We owe everything to America in South Viet Nam. They have made the country economically viable. They have sent their sons to fight, they have built us roads, they have poured out their dollars, but they will not listen to anything I try to tell them about Viet Nam. They think they know better than me about my own country.' "

President Diem said he thought the only lasting answer for Viet Nam would be for MRA to do a "saturation penetration" of North and South, bringing a new climate of opinion. He invited Howard to bring a large force to attempt this, but the initiative was stopped by the Americans.

P.D.H. to Doë   Aboard BOAC flight
                                                 November 29, 1961
Here we are above the waterways of the rice lands on the road from Bangkok to Delhi. A marvel from the air to see the hundreds of homes hidden in trees standing on stilts with only the rivers and rice fields to

reach them. Love, birth, death, sweat, tears, laughter — all as real to them as to us on these islands. Millions whom we shall never meet who are just like us and whom we shall have to help.

In January 1962, Howard returned to Asia, and again in the autumn of the same year.

P.D.H. to Doë   Trivandrum, India
                                                       January 12, 1962
Lo and behold, I am back in our old room in the Residency. The same men look after us and clustered around last night asking, "How is Memsahib? Where is she?"

It was an exhausting flight — Bombay, Madras, Kottayam and finally here. As soon as we landed we were rushed off to the stadium — football in progress and a crowd estimated by PTI (Press Trust of India) at around 5,000 — where Chiba, Gandhi, myself and others spoke.

A drunken Indian Cabinet Minister stayed here last night. He made much noise and bullied the staff. When he saw me he became subdued and servile. It is an illumination of what really goes on here. The Chief Justice dined with us last night. He is a nice man. He says all the business-men give equal sums to the Congress Party and the Communists as a form of insurance against the future.

P.D.H. to Doë   Tokyo
                                                       October 17, 1962
I am baptising my new machine with a letter to you. Ant is in here with me. He is a good comrade.

We had a typical Japanese breakfast yesterday with Members of Parliament, bankers and industrialists. Chiba presided.

It seems to me that responsibility in this work means having nobody but God back of you — any number of those who will carry the adventure at your side, but nobody but God behind you when the decisions have to be made that risk so much and need either man's approval or naked faith. I am plumping on faith.

P.D.H. to Doë   Tokyo
                                                       October 26, 1962
Yoshida at lunch yesterday gave the heart of the reason why Japan loses her way in Asia. He said, "A few years ago I travelled in South East Asia. I did not think much of the people. I lost interest in that part of the world." I said, "I think we had better get Krushchev and Mao Tse-tung to visit South East Asia in that case." He is a shrewd old boy. He peeped at me over his tiny glasses, then grinned but said nothing.

Yesterday, British and American pressmen came out to tell the Japanese that they could not grasp why the Japanese were so keen on MRA, as in the West it was laughed at. The Japanese were unshaken by this and indeed dealt forthrightly with the villains. The UPI have asked me to do 450 words on Cuba. But the damage these monkeys do with their venom and ignorance is beyond belief. I will give my days to take us past it.

P.D.H. to Doë   Tokyo
                                        November 5, 1962
One man spoke today saying that we had to have the voice of labour because some people think we are a rich man's dream or something. I said forthrightly something I have itched to say for a long time, namely, that I am not giving my life to a class movement and that I am not for a man because he is a worker, or because he is not a worker, but I am for him if he fights.

The Japanese do not always make it easy to get to the point. They are more interested in campaigns than people, and in plans than God.

Honda, who is the Beaverbrook of the country and has the largest newspaper and three TV stations, was with me for an hour. He said, "You must stay here right through December. You must soak Japan in this. I thought you were some sort of Rotarian Society but this is the one thing that will save my nation." I told him that Buchman had had a high opinion of him. He said, "He rated me too high." I replied, "He said if you changed you could be the lighthouse keeper of the lighthouse of Asia." He thought for some time and then said, "I would like to be the lighthouse keeper." He told me he had retired from the chairmanship of the paper. I said we then would offer him a new job. He said, "I do not have to be chairman to control them."

P.D.H. to Doë   Tokyo
                                        November 6, 1962
We had a tempura lunch today with Idemitsu, who is the head of a shipping company that has just built a 130,000 ton tanker on government order. An American gentleman was there, fat and foolish. I said we ought to get the Americans to put up a statue to Abraham Lincoln and himself. The translator did as I hoped he would, and said, "Abraham Lincoln and George Washington." I corrected him. Idemitsu laughed heartily, but the American quite seriously said, "It is very good of you to suggest it, but I probably would not deserve it." These Americans are as much at home with a man like Idemitsu as a Brent Eleigh villager would be with the Lama of Tibet. It is simply another world.

We need men and women who are incorruptible by Satan. Not lured by desire, driven by demand, forced by fear nor sunk by defeat. Men in authority and mad mobs have persecuted and sometimes destroyed

God's soldiers for centuries, but God and His truth are unconquerable and indestructible.

P.D.H. to Doë

Hokkaido
November 13, 1962

We flew up here yesterday. It is so like England at this time of year, much colder than Tokyo, with skeleton trees, the dark brown earth with collars of frost round the paddy fields. It is far to the Left, the coalmines are having to sack 70,000 miners from the pits because Russian oil is cheaper to fuel industry, and they are importing it in big quantities. They risk a general strike next week.

Salmon still swarm in the rivers and it is a country which has only just begun to be exploited industrially and bears all the stamp of a pioneer town of the last century in America.

The hunger of people here is shaking. The youth are bitter and savage. Ant and I were up to a late hour last night talking with some of the students. One of them said, "Is there any answer at all to dirt, hate, ambition to get on, even if it means breaking your word or hurting friends? Nobody at the university thinks there is. We often talk about it."

I met the President of the university yesterday. He said, "I have done my best for the youth but we have no teachers who believe in anything except economic revolution. I wish we could have had MRA in the university ten years ago."

P.D.H. to Doë

Hokkaido
November 16, 1962

Yesterday was dramatic. The police came to us having heard we were going to the university and asked if we wanted protection. We said, "No, thank you."

Three-quarters of an hour before we began, when, on account of the savage hostility of hell-hounds, we had only sold twenty-two tickets, the President and Secretary of the Zengakuren[1] were brought into the hall by a rugger man and made straight for me. It was plain they were trying to break the thing up. I girded up my own limbs and went at them with all the force I could command. There was such a row that we were all asked to leave the hall. We did so and were followed by a mob of the Zengakuren and a number of our folk. We had them laughing, then silence, and then back into the hall with their friends having called off the demonstration. You felt God shifting young people who had never been given anything but stones all life long. They all stayed talking long afterwards. Their line is that men like Stalin and Krushchev have betrayed the Lenin revolution and become bourgeois. They think better of Mao Tse-tung, but not all that better. They fired many questions, such as, "What sort of

[1] National student organisation of Japan.

world do you see if you win?" Ant stuck with me and was marvellous and so was Gandhi.

P.D.H. to Doë   Tokyo
                                                  November 21, 1962
When we came here there was an excellent luncheon with the press, but a Japanese spoke likening us to Rotary and the Lions. I interrupted him to say, "We are no more like them than a cabbage is like an elephant." He was angry.

The Indian news looks dangerous here. The Chinese press on and have no limit to their aim that I can see. Sooner or later Nehru will have to face reality and declare war. Then there will be a bang. All governments will have to re-assess their attitudes towards Communism. It is a mad world.

P.D.H. to Doë   Tokyo
                                                  November 22, 1962
I went to see Matsushita.[1] He lives in a vast industrial palace with Gobelin tapestries on the walls amid the electronic devices. He is quite clear about his industrial might. I said to him, "Some people dare to say you are ahead of the Americans in electronics." He replied, "In consumer electronics we are way ahead of them." They are making computers that count your hair while you drink a cup of coffee and all sorts of funny things. He is what used to be called a gentleman.

P.D.H. to Doë   Tokyo
                                                  November 25, 1962
We journeyed to Kobe to see the head of a shipyard. We saw the yards. They are perfect. They build an 80,000 tonner in six months, delivery date guaranteed and a 38,000 tonner in four months.

I had a long interview on TV. The odd thing was that when the interviewer asked me, "What is MRA?" a local enthusiast answered in my stead, "Unselfishness and walking in heaven." I roared, "Bunk," with such vigour as I could.

P.D.H. to Doë   Tokyo
                                                  November 26
We came flying to Tokyo on one of Sogo's trains — 500 miles in six-and-a-half hours. It was glorious and we saw the fishermen and farmers, the temples and the castles, the seas and the snow mountains as we came. The thing I love about Japan is that it is so alive, afraid, jumpy, jerky, godless, cruel, sad, lonely and hungry — in more ways than one — but alive. It is like America when first I went there. God help us if we allow Japan to relapse into fat, as the USA seems to have done.

[1] Head of National Electric and Electronic Industries of Japan.

Meanwhile, we speak today to 2,000 women. Japanese women have successfully risen above their servility to the male. They run things quietly but decisively in many homes.

P.D.H. to Doë   Tokyo
                                                 November 27, 1962

Yesterday in the midst of my speech to the women, every light in the place went out. The mike went off and there we were. The translator was scared and I must say it was eerie, but when I roared, "Don't worry. I am not afraid of the dark," they all hooted with laughter.

P.D.H. to Doë   Tokyo
                                                 November 29, 1962

Today Yoshida has asked us to his home. I like him. He is a unique and cunning old fox, in the mould of Churchill, Lloyd George and Beaverbrook.

P.D.H. to P.W.G.   November 30, 1962

Yoshida received us in one of the most beautiful Japanese rooms I have ever seen looking out across a flower garden, with ornamental Japanese lakes, to the pounding ocean, while through the other window you could see Mount Fuji with the sun going down behind her and a sickle moon gleaming among the stars.

He said, "You can take it from me that in the next few months Japan is going to reach an agreement with South Korea. We have to help South Korea economically. It is our job to do so because nothing will impact the Communist world more than a unity between Japan and South Korea and a South Korea more prosperous than North Korea. North Korea has the industry so we must make South Korea prosperous."

Yoshida went on to express his view that prosperous Western Germany and prosperous Japan were the greatest pains in the neck to the Communist world and a constant challenge to Russia and China. He quite naïvely said that if his nation and West Germany continue prosperous, sooner or later the Communist world would want to be like us. But he added that this would take some time.

He spoke of Nehru and told the story that when Nehru came to Japan three years ago, he presented Yoshida with a baby elephant called after his daughter, Indira. Yoshida said he would give Nehru a Japanese bear named after his daughter, but Yoshida said, "My daughter refused to allow the bear to have her name, so Nehru never got it." When I remarked that Nehru seemed to have a bear of a different kind coming in at the North right now, he laughed and said, "But Japanese bears are very harmless creatures."

He spoke with affection of Churchill and, puffing at a cigar, vigorously said, "Churchill taught me to smoke cigars. He likes painting and always

260

wanted to come to Japan to paint. He told me his mother once came to Japan and described Mount Fuji to him. So I sent him a painting of Mount Fuji."

He then went into a long discourse saying that the secret of prosperity was to get rid of colonies. He said, "Japan used to have colonies and we got rid of them and now we are prosperous. In Belgium last year I saw a prosperous country because they got rid of the Congo. France has got out of Algeria and is becoming prosperous. Britain has lost her Commonwealth and has begun to prosper. My theory of prosperity is not to spend too much money on armaments and not to waste money on colonies." I ventured to say that there were certain nations spending a great deal on armaments nowadays and perhaps he would agree that it was excellent for the more powerful rivals of Japan to spend their money in this way. He thoroughly agreed that the more money America and Russia spent on armaments, the better it suited Japan, although he added that he hoped they would not use the armaments they were making.

He pressed us very hard to smoke, so after a bit I said, "You, Mr. Yoshida, have told me of your theory of national economy. I have never been a prime minister, but in personal economy I decided to give up cigars as you decided Japan should give up colonies." For some reason this amused him.

He said, "Japan is a small and ingrown nation. I am grateful for your vision for her and also grateful that you feel we can play a key part in South East Asia. I agree with this. When I saw Mr. Macmillan last year, I urged him to invite our Prime Minister, Ikeda, to come and see him. I was so glad when I got home to hear that Macmillan had sent the invitation." Yoshida also said that following his visit to Australia three years ago he was very happy that the Australians took a far more kindly view of the Japanese.

I send you this rather long account of this interview because I think it represents the reality of Japan's outlook and policy at this point. One of Yoshida's last comments to me was, "I wish you would see Krushchev. Have you seen him?" I replied, "No," and said I had not been invited yet. Yoshida added, "But there is such a thing as an uninvited guest." I answered that the British had often been to places without being invited and that I, personally, preferred to await an invitation. He said, "I would like to go and see Krushchev." I said, "I think he is a human with a spirit that can be won." Yoshida nodded very seriously and said, "I agree with that. I think it is true. We cannot be in a hurry with the Communist world, but we have got to win them."

Yoshida also said, "Britain is the only country that America will heed now. You must speak to America." An interesting challenge if it is true.

The American Embassy here say we equate American democracy with

Communism. They mean that we say Krushchev and Kennedy both need to change, which they do. Gandhi wrote the Military Attaché saying if we declare that a hairy gorilla and a man who has not shaved for two days both need shaving, it does not mean we think a man is a gorilla.

In the Spring of 1963, Howard was in Japan again. On April 25, he addressed the students of Waseda University, Tokyo, in Ono Hall, where Adenauer, Nehru and President Sukarno of Indonesia had spoken before him. And more recently Yuri Gagarin[1] and Robert Kennedy, who was subjected to a particularly rough ride. Waseda is one of the most politically aware of Japanese universities, and is traditionally far to the Left. Howard's theme was "Beyond Communism to Revolution". The hall was packed and Professor Nakatani, the Professor of Modern Japanese Literature, described the speech as "one of the greatest this University has ever heard":

"I am talking this afternoon to those who in twenty years or less, if they so decide, will be leading Japan and the whole of Asia in a new direction. It means putting revolution before career, private plans, and personal fears or hates. It means the acceptance of a goal for your nation and a theme of history bigger than Communism, militarism or intellectualism. It is the hope of a remade world.

"Since the end of the war, both Japan and Germany have been told by the West to keep small, keep quiet, keep out of the game. It was not just defeat in battle that we inflicted upon Japan. We came to Japan as occupation armies and deliberately destroyed your traditions. I do not say all those traditions were good. But certainly they were not all bad. We taught you to sneer at patriotism and told you love of Emperor and of country were out-of-date. We brought our metallic Western materialism and thrust it down your throats. We said you had made so many mistakes in the past that you could and should play no part in the leadership of the future.

"Japan is not meant to be like America or like Russia. Japan is Japan. She can, she must and she will leave the past behind and, with the rest of us, have the privilege and burden of building a new and sane civilisation from the ruins of the old.

"The Soviet magazine *Kommunist* two weeks ago in an analysis of Moral Re-Armament said, 'MRA is the most prominent association in the world aiming to save civilisation from Communism.'

"But our aim is far larger than that. I would not be in Japan if that was what Moral Re-Armament was about. We aim to save Western society from moral decadence, and Communism from the contradictions inherent in its own dialectic. We want a revolution that works. We offer Com-

[1] First Soviet cosmonaut, killed in a plane crash in Russia in 1968.

munist and non-Communist the challenge to play their part in the greatest revolution of all time."

In December 1963, Howard again visited Asia:

P.D.H. to C.B.   Delhi
                                          December 4, 1963
We just returned to Delhi after an important and adventurous journey up the foothills of the Himalayas to see the Dalai Lama. We were told beforehand that we would have half-an-hour with him and that he would tell us when to leave. In fact, he kept us for almost an hour-and-a-half sitting on the floor at the foot of his own saffron throne, serving us tea, laughing, meditating, questioning.

He says that the whole world needs a fresh concept of morality, and that unless and until this happens there will be neither peace nor justice. He feels the first step is a real accord between East and West, and until this happens there can and will be no significant disarmament.

One thing clear to me is that fellowship without the salt of absolute moral standards is the downslide of every great movement of the Spirit of God. Putting plans of action before people is no more virtuous than putting profits before people.

Rajmohan Gandhi has a towering vision for his country. I believe he is going to lead a new salt march for a nation. No nation needs absolute moral standards more than India. Almost everything is done in a sloppy, second-rate way. Poverty and "backwardness" are used as an excuse. In fact, not everyone in India is poor, and so far from being "backward", the people are as clear and able as any people I know. But if you refuse to go along with their own slovenly, second-rate style of talking, of punctuality, of human relationships, you are accused of being snobbish, proud and un-Indian. It occurs to me that there are a lot of people who treat MRA just like this. They squander our spiritual heritage with their second-rate aims and fourth-rate discipline, and then growl at anyone who tries to maintain the pace and depth of God.

During this visit, Howard took part in Gandhi's march from Cape Comorin to Delhi. In writing of it later, Howard said:

"Last year 63 per cent of India's taxes were unpaid. The head of the railways says over 6,000,000 dollars of cheated fares were discovered. Corruption and bribery have become nationwide. Divisions of caste and hate of race abound.

"Gandhi led a 4,000 mile march through India. Everywhere he has gone he has held mass meetings. He has asked for Indians to come forward and be trained in Moral Re-Armament.

"A few days ago, speaking to 75,000 people on Chowpatty Sands, a traditional meeting place of his grandfather on the shores of the Arabian Ocean at Bombay, he said:

" 'We are determined to raise up a force of able, intelligent young men and women who will live straight, who will not be corrupted by money or power, who can lead this nation. This can be done sooner than people think. Every weak link in the chain inside India must now be strengthened. Corruption, jealousy and division are an open invitation to aggression.'

"Mr. Nehru told me in Delhi in November that Gandhi had achieved a contact with the youth of India which Indian leaders and Cabinet Ministers had, for the last five years, lost."

Howard was pressed by some Socialists to deal only with India's poverty. He wrote:

P.D.H. to W.   Delhi
                                           December 6, 1963
I wish we could help sentimental Socialists to feel as concerned about hatred as they feel about hunger. They get all upwrought about material misery and completely ignore the spiritual starvation of the man next door to them. In the mind of God a dead conscience is, I believe, more damaging than a half-empty belly. Naturally, we have to fill the stomachs. But these sentimentalists spend their lives fussing about things which are not the essential thing in the modern world.

Very few people have any idea what leadership is. They think a leader tells everyone else what to do, and does no work himself. That is the reverse of leadership.

In Asia, Howard was often questioned about how a Christian like himself had a common platform with other faiths.

P.D.H. to G.C.   July 5, 1964
Moral Re-Armament is for everyone, everywhere. It is not, has not been, and never will be "another religion". Nor will it ever be segregational.

It is true that a Christian believes that absolute standards of honesty, purity, unselfishness and love are Christ's standards and that the guidance of God is the way Christ calls His followers to live. It is also true that Moral Re-Armament holds all Christians to living the standards of Christ, which he professes, and that most non-Christians rejoice when they see an effort made to help Christians live what they talk about.

Absolute moral standards represent a common battleground and a common step for the whole of humanity. Many agnostics and many atheists, in my experience, have begun to take their stand in the moral re-armament of the nation when they make an experiment here.

Change is for everyone. It begins when these standards are applied drastically. Men with this experience have something real which they can pass on to others.

A colonel from Korea asked me once, "Are you a Christian?" I said, "Yes." He said, "I want you to know what many Christians are like in South Korea. I have a nation on my hands. We are in desperate straits morally and industrially. I need help so much, but these Christians are not a bit interested in the problems on my cabinet table. They are only interested in getting Christians from one Church into another. They are the most self-righteous, exclusive, divided and divisive group we have in South Korea."

I said, "We are sorry." Then I began to tell him what I thought real Christians could do in a country like Korea if they were revolutionaries. He said, "Of course, if they were like that, the whole country would be with you."

It was not on public platforms that Howard spent himself most. It was with individual people. Often his talks with them were of a depth not normal in Asia, where reticence is strong. But Howard was a man who was instantly sensitive to the needs of others. He could rejoice with those who rejoiced, and mourn with those who mourned. Above all, he could be honest with those who longed to be honest themselves.

When he put foot on Asian soil he did not arrive with a British point or view. He had the gift of putting himself at once into the framework of the person next to him. It was hard for some to realise that this outspoken and thunderous personality had an unseen, but ever present, side to him which was silent and questing:

"The way to change people on a massive and colossal scale is to change some individuals deeply and permanently. It takes time, it takes trouble, it takes prayer, it takes imagination. But there is no short cut to it."

Youth responded to him, but he was not dedicated entirely to youth. He wrote:

P.D.H. to U.C.   Sao Paulo
                                                 January 29, 1965

It is fine to have a conference of a thousand picked youth, but we must not make ourselves into a youth movement. We must move all the time with the leadership of our countries. The point of moving with youth is that it is an instrument to affect the thinking, living and planning of the leadership, but we must not avoid the hard crunch of materialism in mature, cynical minds by merely sliding along with the *joie de vivre* of the young.

Politicians wanted to support him, but he did not want their support unless it involved changed men. He wrote to one politician who wanted to co-operate with MRA.

P.D.H. to C.   Buenos Aires
                                                           February 12, 1965
There are many organisations of Members of Parliament for many purposes and reasons in many lands. In some parts of the world these organisations have often failed because they do not change the people who are organised, but simply let them continue as before, attempting to put the world right but determined to remain themselves in the grip of the old ambitions, prejudices, greeds and corruption. Unless men change nothing really changes.

We have to outbid Communist China in the hearts and minds of men. But mere anti-Communism by itself will never do the job. If that were enough, America and her allies, with their wealth, power and ceaseless propaganda, would long ago have succeeded in pushing back the frontiers of the Red Empire in Asia, Africa and Latin America.

If your organisation intends to make Moral Re-Armament and the changing of men its theme and aim, I believe you will render a supreme service to history and humanity.

If, however, any of your friends from these other countries intend, as some of them have done in the past, to pay lip-service to "MRA methods" while suppressing the reality and name of Moral Re-Armament, and quietly continuing to do things the same old selfish way, they will frustrate your best efforts and in the end rob Asia of liberty, unity and prosperity, which she so richly deserves after centuries of wrongful exploitation.

The above was Peter Howard's last letter to Asia.

Chapter 18

"Freedom is good and is coming like a flood to Africa. But where yesterday black men hated white, now black fears black. And tomorrow may see black or red imperialism where white imperialism reigned yesterday."

P.D.H. December 3, 1963

Howard only once went to Africa. But he had many friends throughout the continent, and at Caux and at other centres he had taken part in events which had played a part in helping a number of countries to gain independence without bloodshed.

One such occasion was when a French journalist brought two North African exiles, Si Bekkai[1] of Morocco and Mohammed Masmoudi of Tunisia to Caux. Howard, in 1957, described the effect on Masmoudi:

"Masmoudi was an exile. The French had arrested his brother. He himself had once been in the death cell, his head shaved ready for execution. In Paris he was the spokesman of Neo Destour, the party fighting for Tunisian independence and regarded by the French as a dangerous and revolutionary body. At Caux, Masmoudi found the answer to bitterness. Changed Frenchmen melted the hate in his heart without melting the iron of his resolve to win freedom for his people.

"While he was at Caux, his eighty-year-old mother sent him a letter which ended, 'God bless you, my son. God curse the French.'

"Masmoudi replied, 'God bless me, mother – yes. I need it. But don't curse the French. I have found French with whom we can work without distrust for justice in our problems and aspirations.'

"Masmoudi is a Moslem and so was expected by his faith to pray five times a day. And he accepted the normal discipline of listening to God each day for His direction. He wrote down the thoughts. He formed a plan.

"He returned to Paris free from bitterness, filled with hope.

"Peace and war were in balance. The French had imprisoned Bourguiba, the much-loved leader of the Tunisian people, on a Mediterranean island. Land was being harvested under the protection of French tanks. The

[1] First Prime Minister of independant Morocco.

267

fellaghas descended from the hills to attack and kill the French settlers, and fighter planes patrolled the hills where the fellaghas made their plans.

"Masmoudi went to see the new French Prime Minister, Mendes-France. He told him of Moral Re-Armament. Mendes-France flew to Tunis and promised autonomy. In the long negotiations which followed, Masmoudi brought an answer each time there was the threat of deadlock. He said later, 'I fought all through according to the principles of Moral Re-Armament.'

"Today Bourguiba is Prime Minister of Tunisia. Masmoudi was Minister of State in the Central Government and is now Ambassador to France.

"Masmoudi travelled with me to the United States, Japan, the Philippines, Thailand, India and Pakistan with the World Mission.[1] In Washington in June 1955, he said, 'Never forget. Were it not for MRA, we Tunisians would today be engaged against the French in a war without mercy. Moral Re-Armament is bridging the gap between France and Tunisia, between Africa and Europe. Africa is awakening. She is determined to play her part in world affairs within the framework of MRA. Without MRA Tunisia would have been another Indo-China.' "

Howard played his part in these events. He held a vision for Africa and the Africans until he died.

P.D.H. – speaking to Nigerians in London, September 27, 1963

"I believe that Africa can, if she will, play a concrete part in creating the right revolution for the modern world.

"It is perfectly clear to me that old Europe has failed to do it. It is perfectly clear to me that modern America is failing to do it. With the massive lack of unity now being displayed by China and Russia, I do not exactly see that they are going to unite the earth. But who is going to undertake the task?

"God is colour-blind but character conscious. Man is character blind but colour conscious. Now we have got to reverse that and we can reverse that if it is true in our own hearts. You will never get unity unless you have a real faith. It is a very easy thing to say, but has there ever been a time in history where men are more foolishly and needlessly divided?"

Howard appreciated more than most men the service many British people had rendered in Africa:

"No other empire has triumphed over all her enemies and, after that triumph, has handed back freedom to nation after nation, because she thought it was the right thing to do. But it is one thing to give nations

[1] See chapter 14, page 208.

their freedom. It is another thing to establish in them the quality of character and ideology that preserves and guarantees that freedom."

In this respect, he felt Britain had failed:

"The answer to colour conflict is to build a society free from prejudice and hate of every kind. Theoretical agreement with civil rights and colour equality, coupled with practical hate of another class, race, nation or individual, will never work. Any man who hates another man is part of the problem of colour and class conflict that burdens humanity. For those who hate cannot cure hate. And those who cannot cure hate today help it to multiply. Idealists who despise everyone in disagreement with them are like doctors who warn us all of the dangers of smoking but never think of stopping it themselves."

Howard's own visit to Africa was made when he led the World Mission, with his play *The Vanishing Island*, into Kenya. He arrived in the middle of the Mau Mau emergency. During this visit. Howard and some of his friends went to the Athi River detention camp where, behind barbed wire fences and watch-towers, twelve hundred Mau Mau detainees were confined. They were the hardcore of Mau Mau — the original thinkers and political leaders. They wore yellow shorts and their heads were shaved. They sat in tight rows under a blazing sun. It was Peter Howard who spoke to them first:

"They covered their faces as I drew near. They would not look at a white man. My first words were, 'I was born white. I could not help it, could I?' They began to look at me. It began to slide upon their understanding that it was as immature and ignorant to hate a man because he was born white, as to hate him because he was born black, brilliant, foolish, ugly, beautiful, big, small, Jew or Arab. When I had finished speaking, their leaders came to me and said, 'We were educated in Christian schools. We lost our faith and became cynical of everything except violence to achieve liberty, because of the way we saw white Christians live. We want you to know that if we had dreamed white men could speak and think as we heard you speak today, there would have been no Mau Mau in Kenya.

"I felt in my heart the shame and agony of the words these Kenyans spoke to me. I wept. Some of these former Mau Mau leaders have become my friends. They saw white men change. They learned that black men, too, could change. They changed. They understood that violence, sometimes regarded as a good servant, can swiftly become a bad master, and that history never long remains on the side of hate. Hate knows no colour bar. Neither does love.

"Out of their wages of one shilling a day, the camp prisoners collected £26 in pennies as their contribution to the expenses of the Mission."

Later Howard spent long hours talking with the Mau Mau men. They told him they had sent their African women to sleep with the white soldiers and receive ammunition in payment. This ammunition was used to kill white settlers. Howard dealt with the Mau Mau men, like everyone else, on the basis of absolute moral standards. One of them was to say later, "If we had known the answer to lust, there would have been no killing."

Howard's conception of the new Africa was a continent with her eyes on the world, rather than on her own internal problems.

P.D.H. to I.A.   February 12, 1963
The African problem will never be solved in Africa alone. It is a world-wide problem. It is an organised revolt on a world scale against the sovereign rule of God. It takes place in every heart and every Cabinet. Africa still remains a pawn in the eyes of some men of power.

Many felt that it was possible to jog along with the humour and friendship of Africa, and in that way create a better atmosphere. Howard did not share their views.

P.D.H. to G.   March 15, 1963
I am not devoting my life to seeing that black and white Africans find some means of living together without cutting each other's throat. I am not a bit concerned with whether white people stay too long, or black people behave badly, or all the things that seem to preoccupy so many. This one thing I do — to live and breathe and fight and, if necessary, die to see God rules in the affairs of men, including the African continent.
Cannot we raise a few men in Africa who actually will take on the commitment of Frank Buchman? He did not appear to me to be a man concerned all the time with how white people or black people would treat him. Had this been his main concern, personally he would have bored me to death, and I get extremely bored with the white people of life who can only think of whether the black people will leave them alone, as well as with the black people of life who appear only to think of when the white man will leave their country. To me, both points are divisive and futile.
God came not to bring an inter-racial cuddle, but what He described as a sword cleaving through families, classes, colours and continents. Oh God, oh God, oh God, give us that sword.

Howard felt that the intense nationalisms in Africa were bound to destroy a continent which could otherwise become a voice of sanity:

"I need apart from God's grace, courage and humour, a definite, final and decisive 'yes' to God's claim upon me. Africa needs this experience. So many of her people are only prepared to go forward as long as others behave the way they think they should, or treat them well. Alternatively, they build up a province for themselves in their country or their continent, and that becomes their realm. It is quite possible to have a wrong relationship with a nation, as it is with a man or a woman, a colour or a class."

African nationalists found this hard to comprehend. They asked Howard if he did not love his own country. He replied:

P.D.H. to I.A.   May 15, 1962

I do not think that you regard me as a de-nationalised person. If you do you must tell me so. I am British to my cuticles, with all the follies and other things that such a background denotes. My attitude to my country is what Doë said to me when I was honest with her, "I love you as you are, but will fight to make you what you are meant to be."

At the same time, that is my attitude to your country, and to Russia, and to America, and to every country under the sun. And I will tell you why. God once said clearly to me, "I want you to love everybody in the world as you love your own children." I knew that was humanly impossible, but on my knees I asked God for the grace to give my heart and mind in His way to everybody. Of course, I have not fully succeeded, but it has made a profound difference to my life.

Not many years ago I used to get desperately home-hungry and heartsick when, for weeks, months and sometimes a year or two, I was separated from my loved-ones and from my land. Naturally, I thought of fifty good reasons why I should get back home, but what I really meant was that I liked my home and wanted to be in it. The issue was whether, if God wanted me never to see my home again, I was willing for that to be so. On my knees I said, "Yes." The result was an amazing liberation. I have loved my country far more since then.

This happens to be the first springtime for sixteen years I have spent in my own home. But I have also felt absolutely heart-free to fight all-out with no strings attached and no limits on my sojourn wherever I go in the world.

Howard never visited South Africa, though he had many friends from that country. He also had enemies. But he was not a person who compromised with people, and he refused to do so with governments.

I am not so foolish or conceited as to attempt to tell any government what should or should not be done. Nor equally am I going to be told by any human government what my attitude should be towards my fellow men whatever the colour of their skin. I maintain the liberty of the human conscience is a sacred charge of every individual and no coterie is going to bully me into attitudes with which I disagree. If I and my friends had had the chance, we could have been the truest and most understanding comrades in the crisis that is now developing with such terrible speed from north to south of the African continent.

We white people need not justice but mercy. Indeed, humanity needs mercy. We are facing now the breakdown not just of East and West, of black or white, of rich or poor, of young or old, but of mankind. We simply have failed to measure the challenge of the century.

I only pray that in time the white Africans may learn the lesson of history, which is that goodwill is no answer to hatred, and that patronage is no answer to the bitterness that springs from social injustice and inequality.

For my part, my life is given — and I mean given — to shifting the whole world, Communist and non-Communist alike, to the Cross.

I feel so sad at the plain cowardice of some of the men of Africa who have caught a glint of God's vision, returned home and turned their backs upon it. History in the last years could be different if men on that great continent would understand the truth, "No Cross, no crown."

Howard's challenge was not a comfortable one. Nor was it exclusive:

London
July 30, 1963

"Last night we entertained the South African netball team. They were all Afrikaners — Dutch-speaking, white South Africans. They represent their country. I, personally, am strongly opposed to the policy of apartheid. I think it is utterly wrong. I think it has got to be stopped. But how do you do it?

"Those girls were in England. They behaved absolutely beautifully. They took infinite care. They were very much on their guard. Soon I found out why. We English, in order to demonstrate our disapproval, have put them in unpleasant lodgings, where they live four in a room with one bathroom between them all. Men can look through the bathroom door as they try and get clean. That is to show them what we think of their country.

"The effect it has had upon these women is for them to say, 'We never want to see your country again. As far as we are concerned we like home best.' Now that is one way of doing it. But it is not mine.

"Some people think you are going to create the right revolution in South Africa, and many other countries, with a bloody revolution. I, personally, do not believe that everyone with a black skin is perfect and everybody with a white skin is a swine. Nor do I, oddly enough, believe that everybody white is superior and everybody black is inferior. I think we are all sons of God.

"I want to see in Moral Re-Armament not a destination, but a road — a road all can travel. Not the ultimate truth, but a way in which everybody can be pointed towards truth; a common battlefield for everybody in life."

To his home in Suffolk, Howard welcomed the men and women of Africa. Jomo Kenyatta had been there before his imprisonment in Kenya. And at the time of Howard's death, nine of the Kenya Cabinet were to cable Doë: "The philosophy and practice of Moral Re-Armament have contributed decisively to our stability and progress."

It was from meeting and knowing such people that Howard caught a glimpse of what Africa could be:

"The world is waiting with an eager heart and hungry mind to listen to the voice of the new Africa. It must be a voice so revolutionary that China, Russia, America, Europe, black men, brown men, yellow men, white men say with one accord, 'That is the way God's earth is meant to live.' "

Chapter 19

The old, staunch house safeguards its mystery —
The part it played and plays in forging history.

Through centuries its back and bone
Weathered the storms and stood like stone.
The cannons and the curse of war
Closed not its open heart and door.
Paint may have changed, and so may size
But still the place with steadfast eyes
Gazes across the corn and cotton.
Its spirit big with unforgotten
Memories of the man who came
Out of its acres into fame.

Washington, plodding through the mud,
Was here before, with brain and blood,
He forged a nation out of men
And handed it to God again.
His heart with love of freedom burned
But oftentimes it homeward turned
To the quiet fields and wild geese flying
Into their rest at daylight dying.

McClellan's Army camping there
With some afraid and some at prayer —
Between the red earth and the stars —
Watched morning climb through night's black bars,
The battlefield to illuminate
That welded union out of hate.
And many an unknown hero crossed
This doorway who, in history lost,
In heaven has his name secure,
Who died that freedom shall endure.

Christ, too, came walking through this land
Into the home and laid His hand
Upon the heart of a loved son, a true, a tried, a valiant one.

Unhesitant and unafraid,
He gladly, gloriously obeyed.
Like Washington, like Lincoln, he
Went out to meet with Destiny.

This old house whispers in my ear
That though one day it disappear,
Though Time on Time may melt its stone
Back to the earth which made its bone,
Yet never more shall pass away
The record of his choice that day.
It shall outlive, outlove, outlast
The whole long pageant of the past.
For we shall see from man to man
The pattern of God's master plan
Fashioned by men like your loved son
Who from this home his race doth run.

P.D.H.
(Written for an American family.)

Peter Howard spent most of the last months of his life in the United States of America. His love for that country and her people had grown with the years. He possessed none of that stuffiness or superiority which make many Americans regard Britain with sympathy or indifference. He was almost un-British, not in his language or his affection for his country, but in his commitment and enthusiasm which were like a gust of fresh air. He spoke to Americans with hope:

"The hard truth is that our fate, like the fate of the rest of humanity, rests in your hands. Without American blood and treasure there would be no liberty left on earth today.

"If America fails, the world fails, but America will not fail. America morally re-armed will capture the allegiance of the entire world, Communist and non-Communist alike, and will lead man into an age of justice, sanity, freedom and lasting peace. This will be not by the gold in your purse, which will increase; nor by the gun in your hand, which must be maintained; but by the guts of your youth, the genius of your multi-racial society, and the guidance of Almighty God in Whom, according to the words on the dollar, we already place our trust."

Howard also spoke to America with honesty. That was true friendship as he understood it. He did not flatter and he did not condemn. He said what he felt and bore no ill-will for it afterwards.

Howard's programme in America during 1964 was heavier than any other he had undertaken. In one ten-week visit he made forty-six speeches in twenty-five cities. This was followed by longer visits and more intensive speaking.

P.D.H. to Doë   November 14, 1964

There is a crushing programme arranged for me, but I will do it gladly. Our hour has come in this country and the world, and we must claim the faith and strength to meet it.

In May 1964, the Archbishop of Boston, Cardinal Cushing, wrote the foreword to Howard's speeches in a book entitled *Design for Dedication*:

"Peter Howard is a friend of mine. To his talent and training as a newspaperman he has added the moral insight drawn from experience with men in many lands.

"He has made some of the finest addresses I have read in modern times. To Americans, carrying a larger load of world responsibility than ever before in history, they point a leadership that could preserve faith and freedom for millions.

"His words are a challenge for all. They bring an extraordinary clarity about America and the world."

P.D.H. to A.T.   New York
                                                                    March 5, 1964

In America the tide of the answer runs deep, strong and powerfully. But it is a different America from the country of even two or three years ago. It is cynical, rude, divided and dying.

Peter Howard devoted his mind and strength to preventing this cynicism and death creeping through America. On February 4, 1964, he spoke in the Town Hall, Los Angeles:

"One man stands at my side as I speak. He is my young and only brother, John. He fought through the last war in Africa, in frozen islands of the Arctic Seas, on blood-soaked mountain slopes of Italy, amid the heat, flies and fury of North Africa, finally dropping with the Paratroops at Arnhem, where death met him. Like millions of others he gave his life so that we could inherit freedom. This freedom, dearly bought, is dear to me.

"America is a giant Father Christmas staggering through Asia, Africa, Latin America with a pack of goods, handing out gifts to the children, behaving with a generosity never before shown in the history of man. The children grab the gifts, scream for more, pick the pocket of Santa

Claus as he passes by, try to trip him up, knock him down, abuse him and destroy him. It is a puzzle and a paradox. In the short time at my disposal, I mean to tell you why it has come to pass.

"America needs an aim for humanity. She needs an idea in her head and an answer in her heart, as well as a pack of gifts on her back, a roll of dollars in one hand and a holocaust of bombs in the other. I thank God on my knees each day for the strength of America. But without a revolutionary plan in which all men can share, without a faith which all can understand and love, without a self-discipline to match that plan and faith, America may become a dead knight in armour."

On February 28, 1964, at a time when the Viet Nam war was not yet at its height, Howard spoke to the Commonwealth Club in San Francisco. President Diem had been assassinated a few months before:

"Soon President Johnson may be forced to grave and agonising decisions.

"If the present Saigon regime is threatened with disintegration, America will have to decide whether to withdraw, to fight an all-out war, or to institute reprisals against the North Viet Namese intervention. Such reprisals might involve the bombing of selected targets in North Viet Nam. And if the Chinese intervene, which would mean they were ready to risk war with the USA, it would, according to one Washington policy-maker, offer 'a heaven-sent opportunity to hit certain targets in China'. Those targets are, of course, the Chinese atomic plants.

"In these circumstances, the death of Diem may have been a costly miscalculation. On my recent journey through Asia, in different countries, in different cities and in different languages, people asked, 'Do you believe violence is a legitimate means of obtaining political ends?' They meant, could they use force to destroy capitalism – should they kill rich men? When I replied that this seemed to me a bad plan, with one accord these Asians asked, 'What about Viet Nam? America showed us there that she now is ready to encourage violence in order to achieve her political purposes in another country.' I do not say this is just. I do not say it is true. I do say it is a view running like a prairie fire through millions of hearts in Asia, Africa, Latin America today.

"I do not express views for or against Diem's policies in Viet Nam. He had his follies and his weaknesses. He had his difficult relatives. Most of us do. I can say from knowledge of the man that the stories that he was some kind of Fascist beast are lies.

"Since Diem fell, seven other Buddhists have tragically immolated themselves in and around Saigon. Nothing, or very little of this, has reached the Western press, though before Diem's fall the punjis who poured gasoline over themselves and burned themselves to death were heralded everywhere as a symbol of the rebellion of tortured people against a cruel oppressor.

"At this moment, in paddy fields and swamps, jungle darkness, slime, stench and mud of fetid rivers, Americans, Viet Namese villagers and soldiers are putting to the test with their blood and suffering whether freedom shall or shall not endure in Viet Nam. Without expressing views about the policies or character of Diem or the Nhus, one thing is certain. The United States, for the first time in its history, encouraged the overthrow in time of war of a duly elected government fighting loyally against the common Communist invader.

"The full bill for the destruction of Diem has yet to be presented, and the fuller truth has yet to come out. But be assured that bill will be presented.

"Diem was the head of a friendly state engaged in a common struggle. He was put to death with the connivance of certain American authorities. All Asia knows that. And Asia has not forgotten.

"People sometimes think of Diem as a little jumped-up Hitler or dictator who bullied and tortured people, and was ineffective. It is very far from the truth. It is a fact that he closed Saigon's bars and brothels. He told me why. He said there were serious security leaks which threatened the safety of his troops. He said his information was that these soldiers — and soldiers are soldiers everywhere — got tight at night and talked when they shouldn't in these bars and brothels. He felt for the sake of his army they should be closed. I am not asking whether you would have done it or not. I am telling you why he did it."

On November 15, 1963, Howard had written from New Delhi:

"I knew Diem. I feel the failure of American diplomacy to establish a relationship with him which I think could have saved much tragedy. I can only say that in my conversations with the man, I found him extremely open to suggestions if they were made from the Cross and not from the throne."

Howard's speeches, which dealt openly with topics that Americans regarded as their own private concern, did not win universal approval. But, with hindsight, they often seem prophetic. The majority of Americans responded, even though he was often extremely blunt in what he said.

P.D.H. to M.H.   February 6, 1964

There is an American idea of at all costs avoiding blame, and consequently achieving credit. It makes you prone to take colour from the nation instead of giving the nation the colour of God.

I am amazed at the way in which America over the Olympic Games, or sending a space camera to the moon, boosts itself to the sky beforehand, beats its breast and says, "My, we are terrific," and then when something not quite right happens, says, "Well, after all we did our best. We tried hard and it is much better than people think." We must stop this. Let us learn to fight and not to heed the wounds.

P.D.H. to R.P.   February 13, 1964
    It seems to me in America that so many people will only do what they are fully convinced is bound to be a colossal and recognised success. It, therefore, renders them insecure and frustrated half the time, and foolishly arrogant and cocky the other half.
    This mentality represents a determination to make the rest of the world like America, and a belief that anybody who says America needs change is anti-God. It is folly. I do not at all mean by this that we must ruffle American feathers and make people sour and deliberately provoke them. But we must deal with the colossal perversion that this attitude of protectiveness towards America represents.
    I know full well that in the mind of God, America is still meant to tilt the world towards Him. But I feel frankly the demoralisation of a decadent giant in some of the actions and utterances from this country, and I must say so. We must avoid the temptation to become apologetic to the point where we water the truth down to suit the compromises of the comfortable.

On February 16, 1964, Howard spoke in Phoenix, Arizona:

    "I do not think that America as a gigantic do-gooder, or as a gigantic one-worlder, is very effective. You have given the whole world the impression that you want everybody on earth not only to like America but to be like America. You may not stand for one world, but the world thinks you do. And it is an image that needs very rapidly and intelligently to be dissolved if you are to out-revolutionise in Asia, in Africa, in Latin America and in Europe the titanic bid of Communism to capture the heart of humanity.
    "Unless your country and mine choose to be governed by God, we may condemn millions of others in Africa and Asia and elsewhere to be ruled by tyrants. And choosing to be governed by God does not just mean a formal Church attendance, important as that is. It does not just mean saying I am a good fellow and I wish everybody were like me. It means accepting a passion, a philosophy, a plan, a discipline to establish what is right in family life, in industrial life, in American life and in the life of the modern world."

Earlier in January 1964 Howard had said:

"You may have read a book called *The Ugly American*. I happen to love this country as I love my own. I did not like the story of the ugly American. But the ugly American may have added to the modern problem. The lovely American certainly will not cure it. What the world is looking for is a new American, a changed American with a fresh aim, a fresh character, a fresh philosophy, a new passion to shift Communist and non-Communist alike into a fresh dimension of living. A man and a nation whose strength is as the strength of ten because his personal and family life is pure. Supposing that became America. The whole world would follow you."

It was in search of this new American that Howard spent himself totally. He had no sense of his own ability in the task before him.

It was this sense of need, plus his passionate, all-out fight, which enabled Howard to win young people. It was not his charm which drew them, not just his intellect. He neither spoke down to them, nor sucked up to them. He spoke of a need which he felt they could answer, and he called them to a revolution which they saw portrayed in his own life and bearing. "He was moving faster than we were." "He lived more vibrantly than anyone I'd ever met." "He expected us to be the finest Americans in history." "He was challenging – and compassionate." Such were the reactions of young people he met.

Typical of them was a girl called Linda who saw his play, *Through the Garden Wall*, at the Westminster Theatre in 1963, and wrote to him to ask for an interview. In the end he went to a meal with her and her mother. She had red hair and he christened the girl she could be "Ginger".

In America, on March 2, 1964, he wrote to her:

Dear Ginger,

Returning home at two o'clock this morning after a television panel that lasted for two hours and left me exhausted, I suddenly thought of Ginger.

I had the clear conviction that Ginger is meant to be a Joan of Arc for modern America. A Joan of Arc for her generation, which means I suppose that you put the right sort of ginger into everybody's guts. You have the get-up-and-go to do it.

Please thank your mother again for her courteous hospitality and I wanted to thank you, too, for all the fun you gave this old gentleman, and for the hope you gave me of the young women and young men of tomorrow. With people like you guided by God this country will be a country such as the world has never yet known.

I hope to see you soon.

Always your sincere friend,
Peter Howard

March 6, 1964

Dear Mr. Howard,

Needless to say, I was very surprised to receive your letter, and want to thank you for your kind comments and hopeful convictions.

But I can't help thinking you also noticed quite clearly a different side of Ginger — a girl named Linda, who is not ginger, nor hopeful, nor possesses any strong convictions concerning a better and more hopeful America, but rather a girl who feels rather rootless, uncertain and full of fear. This girl named Linda knows this side far better and is aware she knows it by choice, not chance. Yet Linda can't see faith and hope nearly as clearly as she can see confusion and fear. But Linda also realizes that Ginger is a possible reality for certain people, and doesn't mean to insinuate they are off their noodle. It's just that Linda has really never met Ginger.

But Linda also appreciates Mr. Peter Howard and considers him one of the most impressive and genuine humans she's ever met. And she thanks him sincerely for taking the time to send her such a thoughtful and warm letter.

Your little lost friend,
Linda

March 10, 1964

Dear Ginger,

Your old and tottering friend, Mr. Peter Howard, knows Linda as well as Ginger — and loves 'em both.

Linda needs to decide to meet Ginger soon. She'll be enchanted by her.

I'm just off to Europe. But I hope to see you at Mackinac? There is an answer to Linda's fears.

Ever hopefully and merrily,
Peter Howard

Mackinac Island
June 30, 1964

Dear Ginger,

We have over a thousand heads of youth here — blond, black, brunette, copper-coloured, every kind. But I searched vainly amongst them for Ginger.

Truly, I was sad you could not come. I think it is the kind of assembly that would have rejoiced your heart. I also have ever remembered our talks together and believe you are meant to find a root in life and a course to take that will satisfy and fulfil that wonderful, wide and adventurous heart of yours.

We are running all kinds of exciting things here, including hootenannies in a huge tent, workshops on theatre, art, photography and so on. Indeed, it is the most extraordinary event I have ever attended.

Give my greetings to your family.
Always your true friend,
Peter Howard

November 17, 1964

Dear Peter Howard,

I thank you for your letter dated June 30. As punctuality is not one of my most shining virtues, my reply has become long overdue.

I just found out that you will be in Portland the first of December to speak at Marylhurst. If you are able I would like to invite you to an informal dinner Tuesday evening (December 1) in our home, which is just a half mile from Marylhurst College. I would like you to meet my father and also my brother's father-in-law who has been active in politics in Washington State. He heard you speak at Lewis and Clark and was much impressed. And I, of course, would like to talk with you again too.

I'm sorry you didn't find Ginger at the summer conference. She's somewhat rebellious actually, but we're both glad that it proved effective (the conference that is). Actually Ginger is enjoying life more than she was the time you met her. She seems to be finding her own personal goal too.

I thank you again for remembering me and I hope to see you when you come to Portland. In case I don't see you on your arrival I shall send you my greeting in advance.

WELCOME TO PORTLAND, PETER HOWARD!

Most sincerely,
Ginger

November 22, 1964

Dear Linda,

I was sad you didn't come to Mackinac. But I am coming out in your direction again. I do hope we shall meet.

You still stick in my mind as a torch bearer for the adventure of truth in America.

Greet your parents.

Your ancient but extremely active
and affectionate friend,
Peter Howard

P.S.

I just arrived in Boston and found Ginger's letter waiting. Believe it or not, I had dictated this letter before I knew you had written to me and am now adding the postscript. You have been strongly in my thoughts all through the day.

I would love to meet your family and if the programme permits, would love to dine with them. Let's see when we get there. This old gentleman sends not only his firm affection but a strong conviction that you can be a source of light and fire to a generation.

Ginger did not get to Mackinac in 1964, but two thousand four hundred other young Americans did. Many of them had heard Howard speak on university campuses or elsewhere. They came to a conference for Tomorrow's America under the chairmanship of Mr. J. Blanton Belk, Jr.

One of them was a girl called Kathy from California. She wrote:

"I can say that in my twenty-three years no person has ever had more effect on me than Peter Howard. He was the one person who had the ability to capture my imagination. I had become so accustomed to people telling me 'no' and 'don't do this', or 'that', or 'why can't you be like so and so?' that I became numb to what anybody had to say.

"Peter's genius with me and my generation was that he went beyond criticism to the 'action' one could do. I was causing a disturbance by my behaviour. I was rebelling. I expected my elders to say how awful I was, and why couldn't I do something worthwhile, etc. Peter came to me and said, 'I need your advice.' Well, I just about dropped. What on earth does *he* want my advice for? He wanted me to tell him what was on the hearts and minds of the youth. He wanted to write a play that would capture our minds. This, after the general shock, brought me out for the first time, made me think, made me feel, made me talk and communicate. And that is where it began.

"Then he realised my interests in life were involved in the entertainment world. He sparked me into singing, writing, etc. It didn't stop with just creating – he instilled the fact that in order to do the job completely you must learn to deal with people – especially the ones you work with. And in order to do that you have got to be able to deal with your own nature. He taught me the key to this art – honesty with myself. He also said, 'Never speak beyond your own experience. Experience is a fact. Long-winded ideas are theories and can be knocked down.'

"He was a man of pace and grace, and because of the way he lived, people caught it. What he gave to me and others lasted because he made it become reality in my own life. He led me by the hand till I was strong enough to stand on my own. Then one day he said, 'You have to have your own faith. You have to be able to stand alone, secure in your own beliefs.' He was right because when I was finally put on my own, I found I was like a tape recorder, repeating what others had said. It wasn't until I had my own experience that I began to feel and live all that I had heard.

"Peter was marvellous with children. They flocked to him like bees to honey. It was because he kept no skeletons in the closet; he had nothing to hide; he didn't push; he had fantastic humour; and he had the ability to be as free as a child and as open as the sky. He felt everything around him – and he was honest. Children trusted him – grown-ups sometimes shied from him because they knew they couldn't fool him. But if you were willing to change, you loved being around him and respected him because

283

he never judged or ridiculed. He always looked for the new and unexpected way.

"Peter Howard was just a man but he made the best of it. And a shallow kid like myself grew to love him, and began to grow in depth and to give to others what he gave to me."

Howard warned those who lived in the MRA conference centre on Mackinac Island that there would be a flood of young people, but they hardly believed him. Some were horrified when the mass of youngsters, with their jazz bands, guitars and wild clothes began to arrive on the island.

Many of the young people came from difficult backgrounds. "We discovered that 90 per cent of the Californian delegation came from broken homes," wrote one of the older people present. "Some of the girls had no idea how to set a table. They were used to getting their meals out of the icebox and eating it before the television set. One girl said her family had not sat together at a table for seven years. A boy had seven divorces between his two parents."

The fight was not for self-improvement nor to create a youth movement, but for a new America and a new world. The aims of the conference, as set out in the invitation, were:

To build homes in which families learn to live together.

To build industries in which labour and management learn to work together.

To demand schools and colleges which build faith and character as well as brains and skills.

To produce films, plays and books which give a new purpose to America and mankind.

To challenge promiscuous parents, cynical teachers, watered down religion and polluted politics.

To make absolute honesty, purity, unselfishness and love the standards of America.

To raise a force of young Americans more disciplined and revolutionary, and more dedicated to building a world that works than any Communist, Fascist or other materialist.

Howard was clear that it would take change and thought to achieve these aims. On the morning after one of the hootenannies in the big tent, he spoke to the conference:

"Last night we rejoiced in the talent, fun and magic of youth. It was an evening to remember. But with all the force at my command I tell you, it will take more than music and laughter to carry us through the crisis that confronts America. You have to save a corrupt society from self-destruction, and to bring sanity back to a civilisation that is becoming a moral and spiritual nut house. And time is running out.

"Somebody called me the janitor. I am proud to accept that title. In a sense it is promotion. What is a janitor? Look it up in your dictionaries. It is an old Latin word and it means the man who keeps the gate, who opens the door. Today, American youth is confronted by a choice – which gate is it to be? Wide is the gate and broad is the path that leadeth to destruction. Narrow is the gate and straight the road that leads to life and liberty for all men everywhere. If it falls to my lot as janitor to help even a few choose the right gate, and come away from the wrong gate, I shall rest content. If together you decide to help America turn aside from the wide gate and the broad, downhill track she risks treading today, your name will be carved in history.

"What image of America are we going to give mankind?

"Is it the Hollywood image – sex and violence?

"Is it the Pentagon image – reliance on hardware and bombs alone?

"Is it to be the Madison Avenue image – you can tell a slick American anywhere but you cannot tell him much?

"The CIA image – pulling secret strings in other countries and sometimes the wrong strings?

"The Wall Street image – trust in the mighty dollar?

"The Mississippi image – violence, intolerance and hate?

"I am telling you the images the world sees today.

"Or shall it be the image of Abraham Lincoln? A figure of justice, charity and honour lived out personally and nationally against a global background.

"America needs a passion for what is right, rooted in absolute purity. Otherwise, she may succumb to the passions of those who are wrong, rooted in impurity. Do not fool yourselves. No man or woman run by sex can answer the needs of somebody run by hate.

"We need and can have an uprising of youth that will reshape history. But we need to face the truth that it is not the old or the young, the black or the white, the Communist, Fascist or phoney idealist that is to blame. We are all to blame for the state of our society. That is why all of us have a part in putting it right."

During these summer conferences, Howard worked hard. But he did not forget his friends elsewhere. In August 1964, the father of his school friend, Tony Carter, died. Howard immediately sent a cable, followed by a letter of August 18:

"Don't trouble to answer this, my old friend. I just wanted you to know that I was thinking of you and your family as I often do, and praying for you all. Pray for me, too, if you can ever make the effort. I find myself responsible for a world work of immense size and feel grossly inadequate for it.

"It is funny how sometimes my heart yearns to do something as ordinary and simple as go and watch a cricket match. I have not seen a ball bowled all through the season."

Tony Carter replied:

"Having read *Design for Dedication* I have some little idea of how much spare time you have on your visits to America, and it warmed my heart at a time when it needed warming that you should have heard of my father's death and cabled a message."

Howard's intense application to his work made some wonder whether he really enjoyed anything else at all. Those who knew him well realised how much of his own desires and wishes he was sacrificing.

P.D.H. to G.T.   Mackinac Island
                                                  July 12, 1964

You ask me whether I really enjoy an assembly like this. Humanly, it is the last thing I enjoy. Humanly, my longing and my heart is for quietness and the countryside and a chance to walk the fields and smell the air, and do the writing that I have always longed to do. But I can, indeed, say that when I commit myself to what I believe is God's calling for my life and for this time of it, my heart is satisfied. Of course, I get tired. Of course, the constant drainage of being available for people and giving them of your best and often feeling that you have failed to give them all you should have given them, is painful.

But the honest answer to your question is that I do find in pursuing the path of God so far as He makes me aware of it, a satisfaction and a depth of joy that cannot be described but is true.

Each week, Howard dealt with the report from his farm in Suffolk, and kept a close watch on all sides of the farm policy. Even when several thousand miles away, he had a knack for issuing relevant orders and asking probing questions.

He wrote his farm manager:

                                                  Mackinac Island
                                                  August 18, 1964

I cannot tell you how strongly I am alarmed at your news at the serious drop in pig margins. If we have gone down from £5 a pig to £2 a pig profit in the last four months, it is one of the most serious pieces of news I ever had from Hill Farm. It must be something to do with the conversion rate. Are we using different food? Is it simply the new building that is the trouble? What do you think is the reason for this very grave statement, which must affect the whole future of our enterprise if we cannot bring the cure?

In fact, the cure was brought. But this was Howard's idea of responsibility. He could not understand people who, while making new openings in life, were constantly forgetting their old ones:

"The basis of all responsibility is to be responsible every day for yourself and for one other person. It means also that every day we consciously bring at least one other person to their next step of change and advance. Of course, it ought to be and can be far more than one other person. But the word 'responsibility' seems to have lost all meaning in the minds of many people."

At the end of the summer of 1964, Howard spoke to the young delegates before they left.

Mackinac Island
August 1964

"There was a man called Paul Revere and he rode, and certain people rode with him. The great majority did not. Some of them never left their wives, their beds, their comforts and their corn. Some turned back. But the people who built the nation and who are remembered by history were the men who rode.

"Do not be a bit disconcerted if not everybody rides with you. They will not. Do not be a bit disconcerted if some people get the collywobbles when the bullets fly. They will. But the people who ride and keep on riding are going to make a permanent mark on the history of this country and on the story of liberty."

The impact upon America of those young men and women was to be great. But Howard was quite aware that it would take far more than one summer to do it:

"We must understand that if these young people are going to give new leadership that America needs, they have to live the life, as well as to be natural. There has been so much talk about being natural. So I put to the young people that they write down what is the difference between being natural and being guided by God. We cannot afford a spearhead that is vulnerable.

"The real link, the chains, between emotionalism and experience, are concrete, costly, daily decisions."

The response from the youth of America was overwhelming. Many wrote to Howard and remarked on the great advance that was being made. Howard replied:

"People talk about a colossal shift. I pray that this year will mark a colossal shift in me.

"It seems to me it is a sort of scatterbox time. People are taking up old impurities, rationalising things they know are wrong and generally trying to muck around with absolute moral standards. All of us, young and old, need a wisdom, strength, dare, restraint and faith beyond our own. We need the Holy Spirit."

Howard addressed himself to the needs of America. One of them was the colour issue. He spoke at the Wheat Street Baptist Church in Atlanta, Georgia, to the Negro people of that city. The title of his talk was "What Colour is God's Skin?":

"The different races in America are her strength and glory.

"God made men in different colours. A white man's world, in the sense that a white man, because of the colour of his skin, is closer to God than is his neighbour, affronts the will of the Almighty and the understanding and conscience of humanity. So does a black man's world. So does a world of yellow or red domination. We need a world where all men walk the earth with the dignity of brotherhood that should be normal to all who accept the fatherhood of God.

"Today, the long-awaited tide of history flows towards the non-white races. Those tides will lift burdens of the centuries and wipe out blood-stains in the sands of time. Be sure that tide elevates all humanity. You cannot expect every Negro, any more than you can expect every white man, to be a genius of ability, a paragon of virtue, a miracle of grace. But I hope, pray and expect that the Negro people of the United States will have the wisdom, understanding and human greatness to avoid mistakes that men like myself have made before them.

"The black man's chance is surely coming. What will he do with it? I do not say, 'Be patient.' I say, 'Be passionate for something far bigger than colour. Be passionate for an answer big enough to include everybody, powerful enough to change everybody, fundamental enough to satisfy the longings for bread, work and the hope of a new world that lie in the heart of the teeming millions of the earth.' "

In Albuquerque, New Mexico, Howard spoke to a conference of American Indians. He said:

"You won't get promises of material advancement from me. You will get an offer to play an equal part in shaping history. The Indian can be a prophet voice in a prophet nation.

"We cannot allow white men from the privilege of state position to tell Indians what they should or should not do in matters of conviction and commitment. I want the Indians to speak up now with a voice of authority because for a century they have been some of the greatest men in America and they have remained silent.

"It doesn't need great wealth or high education or a white skin to meet the needs of modern man. What it really takes are clean hands and a pure heart. It takes lips that are free from lies and mouths that are free from the domination of the bottle. It takes hands that do not pick and steal. It takes pure hearts, because the problem for many people in the modern world is not colour; it is chastity, and the passionate commitment, 'Thy will be done on earth as it is in Heaven', so that we live, speak, breathe, work, sweat and fight to help God's will be done in the affairs of men."

Howard spoke to American Labour:

"I rejoice at the prosperity of the American unions. I thank God for the conditions you have achieved. I know the struggle you have had. But I beg you all, by the mercy of God, do not forget the people who do not have unions. Do not forget the people who are still oppressed. Do not forget the people who this day as we sit here are going to bed hungry, and waking up tomorrow without hope. If we in the free world forget those people for one instant, the world we create is going to be destroyed."

On this and on his subsequent tours of America that year, Howard spoke on many university campuses. But his audiences were, as the editors of his American speeches pointed out, "remarkable for their variety". "They ranged from university professors to high school students, union officials to Wall Street bankers, liberal intellectuals to the conservatives of Palm Springs and Westchester." He wrote to Doë:

"The theme of my talks here is that we must enlarge the aim of democracy. A democracy that lives to keep things as they are for the sake of its own wealth and comfort, has no hope of victory in a world where vast societies are committed to revolution. We must launch a greater revolution. The history of freedom is like a great circle. Men struggle upward through sacrifice to achieve it. They grow selfish in the enjoyment of it, so they are thrust down to slavery again."

.   .   .

In November 1964, Howard returned to America, on what was to be his last visit.

P.D.H. to Doë   In flight

This is a comfortable plane but no writing paper, so I make the best of it. It is always a wrench to leave you and may be when we meet again we can stay longer together. They have been golden months for which I am grateful. You are a marvellous mother to our children, for which I owe you one more debt.

My own life must be different. I am clear I must not shrink from the decisions that Buchman so often made and which now go by default. I see the shining size of it all and I sometimes feel dismayed at the smallness of the negatives that so easily burden the human heart.

We are lucky. I suppose in life that no two people know each other perfectly. There are bound to be secret reactions, attitudes and feelings, unknown even to oneself, let alone to one's partner, that only the mind of God grasps. And as one gets older, perhaps fear or misunderstanding or a technique of life and association to cover up coldness and boredom, seem to assail many. We have been spared this.

I do not doubt your love for me and it still amazes me. There isn't any doubt of my deepened love for you. It grew so much through the years, especially, I think, in some strange way through the difficulties and battles of the last twenty years. Nobody could have been humanly less equipped for the adventure of MRA than myself. All my instincts and desires are so contrary, but your sense of right about it was a lasting buttress to my own. You helped my faith so much and so far as I have grown in God's grace, it has been much due to your loyalty and belief in me.

Now I look with intense curiosity towards the future. We are lucky in all our children, and we are going to see staggering events of fulfilment.

P.D.H. to Doë   American Airlines
                                                          November 13, 1964

Last night I spoke at Dartmouth. There has been much opposition from the faculty. They had spread many lies, including one that Buchman was never for MRA, but that it was the development of wicked men around him. Our student hosts were very nervous. They spent all of dinner telling me the things I must not do.

The great hall was packed — about 1,100. Everything went with swinging power, though I was dead weary. Then they took me to a fraternity house for private conversation. I was met at the door by three men saying, "You can't come in. No more room. The place is full." After explanations they let me in. Over 150 were jammed in with question, question, question, question until at last we had to go, near on midnight.

Six o'clock this morning they came again banging on the door — question, question, question through breakfast. A radio interview of thirty-five minutes and then I dashed away to catch this plane.

In my view, the death of the West or the death of Communism are false alternatives. We need to plan for the rebirth of humanity. As people we cannot help nations satisfied with their own condition if we are smug and static about ourselves.

P.D.H. to Doë   Nashville, Tennessee
                                                November 19, 1964

Last night I spoke at the Tennessee State University. It is Negro. They had questions by the carload. Today I speak at Vanderbilt University, which is white. Their paper has attacked us in an editorial called "Morality Gone Mad". It is violent. So I have been up from an early hour preparing. I have a TV interview immediately afterwards. Then another major speech. Tomorrow is Washington. The Brazilian Ambassador gives a reception for us.

There is a strong response to our work. My insistent thought is that only in the future will the fulness of harvest be seen, but it will be seen. There is very deep in the human spirit a conviction that it knows what is best for everybody. The confusing element is that it is so often right, but not always — certainly not on occasions when it is necessary for people to find their own way to the right, and not just to be told what is right.

P.D.H. to Doë   Toronto
                                                November 25, 1964

I always miss you but today more than usual, for I have to speak to Montreal University and then answer questions in French.

The coast to coast TV went well. The four questioners were all hostile, but we fought a merry battle. When they said, "No British politician supports MRA," I said, "What about my son-in-law?" They said he had had a lot of difficulties. I replied, "He had one of the best results of any Tory in Scotland." The audience applauded loudly.

I must off to catch another plane. Have done 10,000 miles in the last ten days, but am still breathing.

The interviewers on CBC[1] television were hostile to Howard, but he gave them a good run for their money. He wrote to one of them after the programme:

"Next time we have a programme I would like you to attack me on the sounder and, incidentally, more challenging line that we should be doing our work far better, going much faster and reaching more people — why are we so reticent, so lazy and so slow? And why don't we do more Moral Re-Armament?

[1] Canadian Broadcasting Corporation (Radio Canada).

291

"I should feel much more vulnerable and, I believe, you would have more fun. I can guarantee you the victory on this more positive assault."

P.D.H. to Doë

Fredericton,
New Brunswick
November 27, 1964

It was an interesting day. The country is lovely. The Chief Justice, a former Prime Minister, who was one of Mike Wardell's dinner guests last night, told me that his young daughter caught a 37 lb. salmon last June.

At the university where I was going to speak pickets were out and around with slogans — "Absolutes don't feed hungry men", "Down with MRA" and so on. The young man who had invited us did nothing for us. The meeting was excellent.

The student revue that was put on at night was the product of a sick society, bogus beyond belief. No Oxford college would have endured its badness for five minutes. It had no merit, only a rather silly sort of dirt.

Canada seems to me in real peril. I mean to say so in Toronto tonight. The French in Quebec feel they are 80 per cent of the population with but 20 per cent of the wealth in French hands. The English are blind and bland.

The theatre Beaverbrook built and the gallery of art are perfect. I spent an hour looking at the pictures and wished you were with me — Constable's "Flatford Mill" is there. Also a Dali of Lady Beaverbrook on horseback. I sent postcards to Philip and Anthony of portraits from the gallery, and one to Anne of Janet Kidd as a child, as I remember her. I will be so glad to see you all again. I am counting the days.

P.D.H. to Doë

Tucson
November 29, 1964

I came yesterday from Canada. Tomorrow I heave forward to Oregon.

It was a golden evening. Arizona at its best, blues, greens, pastel reds, the quail among the cactus and a letter of yours dated November 20 waiting for me.

I have to speak to Michigan University on the day of Pearl Harbour. It will give me a chance. There is still the fire and fury of sane patriotism in America if only it can be sparked. But evil seems to have dug deep into the body of the land. There is so much wrong thinking wrapped up in the wool of wet and sentimental impurity.

I want to write. I want to write. I want to write. The peril of humanity sometimes bangs into my guts like a boot. Things are galloping on so fast and the leaders of the free world, with all their power and opportunity, seem to me to have decided on suicide for the West, but the values of the West hold some of the best treasures of heaven. We have the answer to the splintering and chaos that presses on, and I want to reach as many as I can, as swiftly as I can, and while there is still time to do it. But there are so many things to do and so few folk with the bite and muscle of the heart and will that compel relentlessness.

P.D.H. to Doë   United Airlines
                                                        December 3, 1964

We are *en route* to Wyoming. There the university paper has declared, "These people are charlatans who exploit man's desire to believe. We have asked them here to create controversy." So it looks as though we shall have fun and I am limbered up for it.

Last night at Tacoma was one of the best presentations of the tour. The questions were fast and funny. My best shot was when a professor. trembling with rage, challenged me to name any two well-known literary works that supported my views. I said, "The Old and the New Testaments," which made him hop higher and sparkier than ever.

I am weary but not woeful. I look forward very much to seeing you. The Christmas trees are all out in the streets gleaming and twinkling. Let's try and have one meal or evening with the family.

P.D.H. to Doë   American Airlines
                                                        December 6, 1964

I am just on my way to Kalamazoo via Chicago. I speak tonight at Michigan State University. Then tomorrow to Minneapolis where I speak to the college in the morning. Then five hours to Iowa. I speak to the faculty there in the morning and the students of the university in the evening. Then by night to Chicago. Fly to New York 6 a.m. Leave New York 10 a.m. Reach home around 9.30 p.m. (your time).

I long to see you again. You rest me and I need rest.

Howard went home briefly, but returned to spend Christmas in America. On January 8, 1965, he left the United States and returned to London, where he was installed as the Renter Warden of the Wheelwrights Company. It was the City Company of which he had been a member for over thirty years. His appointment in it meant a very great deal to him. He was to spend barely four days in London. During which time he saw all his children, his two grandchildren, and visited his farm. It was the last time in his life he was to see any of them. His wife, Doë, was on her way to Latin America where Howard was to join her within a week.

P.D.H. to Doë   January 8, 1965

This is my first letter of the New Year to you, and if we stick together perhaps it will be my last. I enjoy living life with you and look ahead with joy. I love our children. They are one of the blessings of life.

Forgive me for being less than I should be. I love you so much and with boundless thankfulness.

P.D.H. to Doë   January 11, 1965

Last night Philip and Myrtle, Anthony and Elisabeth dined with me. I took them to the Trocadero, which is closing on February 13. They talked away and seemed happy. The evening before, I took the big dog and the pecking hens round to Ladbroke Grove and gave them to Julie and Jocky[1] from you and me. Enormous excitement and pleasure.

Peter Howard spent his last evening in London with his daughter and son-in-law. It was a quiet supper party. He talked. The talk was mostly of his forthcoming visit to Latin America. He said, "The Latin America venture is in some ways the biggest yet." The burden of it fell heavily upon him, yet he was optimistic about it. Although he was leaving for Rio de Janeiro the following morning himself, he went to Kings Cross late at night to see his family off to Scotland. It was a cheerful goodbye. Within twelve hours he had bidden farewell to Britain and America for the last time.

[1] Peter Howard's eldest grandchildren.

Chapter 20

PETER HOWARD flew the Atlantic for the last time in a VC10. Rajmohan Gandhi, who accompanied him, remembers his intense pride in the performance of this British aircraft, and Howard himself took the time in his tumultuous Brazilian tour to thank the company:

P.D.H. to British United Airways   January 21, 1965

I spend far too much of my life travelling in aeroplanes. But I say without hesitation that that journey in the VC10 was one of the most pleasant I ever enjoyed.

I also liked the quickness of the meal service. So often on night flights you have to wait for two hours, or even three, before you have finished with dinner. On your flight the stewardesses served the meal swiftly as soon as height was gained, and those who wished to sleep could sleep. I enjoyed every minute of the journey.

Howard and Gandhi arrived at Rio de Janeiro in the early morning of January 15. They were met, as they came down the steps, by the representatives of President Castello Branco and Dr. Chateaubriand, the newspaper proprietor and former Ambassador to Great Britain, who had first suggested the visit. With them were members of the Cabinet, Generals and the Secretary-General of the 4,200,000 strong Industrial Workers' Federation. Behind them was a vast crowd, including the leaders of ten of the *favelas* or shanty towns of Rio, holding aloft banners reading "Favelados march with Howard for a revolution of character." "In my thirty years here," an airport official told the press, "I have never seen anybody from abroad received by the people of Brazil as Howard was received today."

Brazil had, ten months earlier, undergone a revolution which had ousted the Goulart Government and prevented a Communist take-over. One of Howard's first speeches was to officers at the Naval Club:

"It would be easy to praise you or to pour the soft oil of flattery down your back. But I want to tell you the truth.

"The March revolution was a marking event in history. But today, that revolution is incomplete. If it is completed so that divisions are healed, social and economic injustice ended, homes and industries united in a way that unites the nation, Brazil will become the pace-maker of the century. If we stop short of that, the revolution might fail. Its failure could condemn a continent to godlessness and a tyranny that might put out the lamps of liberty and faith itself for a hundred years.

"There are two sorts of revolution. In one, men use revolution to save their property, their place and power, their skins. In another, men hazard their lives, their place and power, their property to save and serve a nation. The future of your revolution depends on whether enough Brazilian patriots can be found to sacrifice their selfishness for the nation. Or whether they sacrifice the nation and the revolution for their selfishness.

"The test of the revolution will be whether the government is more keen to crush Communism or to cure the causes of Communism."

Dr. Assis Chateaubriand, the head of the largest newspaper-radio-television empire in the Western hemisphere, in inviting Howard to Brazil, had asked him to "launch a civic offensive for Moral Re-Armament from Amazonas State to Rio Grande do Sul", and to "help answer the economic inequalities and social injustices of the continent".

"My belief," Howard had written to him, "is that there resides in the heart of Latin America the spirit to demonstrate to America and the whole world a new path and a new discipline to pursue it." At a banquet given by Dr. Chateaubriand's picture magazine, O Cruzeiro, Howard outlined the uncompromising discipline required:

"The kind of discipline the future depends on is absolute honesty, absolute purity, absolute unselfishness and absolute love. There is nothing mysterious about them. Honesty means not just telling no lies, but it means no corruption. It means that employers who criticise the workers for dishonesty start to pay taxes honestly. Unselfishness means that we either sacrifice our selfishness for our nation or our nation for our selfishness. It means stop shouting about liberty in public life and live like dictators in our homes. Purity means simply the end of a double standard. We husbands always want our wives to live purity, then so should we. It is quite simple – difficult but simple."

The following evening, Howard was received in the poorest part of Rio de Janeiro by the Favelados. After his death they were to erect a memorial to him on the mountain side above their little hillside shacks. Howard spoke to them:

"Poverty is hell. But sometimes it creates a spirit of community and solidarity which is part of heaven on earth. The true spirit of community in some of these favelas is something the world needs. And our revolution is not going to stop until every hungry stomach on earth has enough to eat, and every man, woman and child on earth has a decent place to live in. It is perfectly possible. But there is nobody more mystical and idealistic than those who talk about remaking the world and do not tackle human nature. They sit around the conference tables, they sit around the cabinet tables, they sit around the tables of the press giving idealism to humanity. I know, because for a long time I was one of those men. Idealistic – and absolutely ineffective."

The Favelados entertained Howard and the party of fifty people travelling with him to drinks and iced-cake which they could ill afford. Exactly two years after this event, the President of four of the Rio Favelado associations, Euclides da Silva, travelled to London to report that he had, through the inspiration of Howard and MRA, been able to help rehouse 500,000 shanty dwellers up to that time.

Three days later, the dockers of the Port of Rio decided to entertain Howard and his party to tea. The docks had been going through a hard time, and the dockers were hard-pressed financially. But so great was the enthusiasm that the tea was transformed into a dinner attended by a hundred people. The dockers of Rio had been the pioneers of MRA in Latin America. Howard wrote of this in 1957:

"Towards the close of 1956, a group of portworkers from Brazil travelled to Argentina to tell the President of the new life flooding through the waterfronts, purifying homes, bringing unity at an industrial and national level and winning men back to the Church.

"The President was so impressed by the news that he kept the Economic Council of his country waiting for thirty minutes while he continued his discussions with the Brazilian portworkers.

"The story which moved the President most deeply was that of Damasio Cardoso, a leader of the Portworkers of Brazil, who in 1952 was responsible for one of the longest strikes in the history of the Rio waterfront.

"Cardoso came to a Moral Re-Armament assembly in 1953. At that time he was Vice-President of one of the two trade unions competing for the loyalty of the Brazilian dockers. With him was Nelson Marcellino de Carvalho, a leader of the rival union.

"These two men honestly faced the ambition and rivalry that divided them. They saw that division in labour was the greatest weakness of labour. They went back united to Brazil.

"Cardoso was at once under pressure from Communism. He was labelled 'traitor'. When a strike, which he thought unjustified, was proposed and he spoke against it, he was hit on the head with a bottle and gravely injured.

"In the end, he was forced out of the union by its President, but the best men saw that the President was using the union wrongly and they left it with him.

"Today it is men trained in Moral Re-Armament who run the *Uniao dos Portuários do Brasil* (the Portworkers' Union of Brazil), which is virtually in control of the waterfront situation. During the last three years the membership of that union has multiplied itself by thirteen.

"Cardoso related all these events to the Argentine President. He also said that he had had the conviction to be married for the first time in the Church to Nair, with whom he has lived for twenty years and who has borne him seven children.

"In the Port of Rio de Janeiro, in April 1957, elections for trade union leadership were held. A week before the election the Chief of Police in charge of security sent for Marcellino and Cardoso, and their friends, Henrique and Carlos Pinto, Secretary of the Union. He told them the Communists were determined to win the forthcoming election. They were offering free lunches in the port, and pensions after twenty-five years of service as part of their election programme.

"Marcellino and his friends replied, 'We will promise nothing we cannot perform. How we fight the election is as important to us as winning it.'

"In the previous 'election' a few men, without calling a meeting, chose the new President and officers, and then secured sixty signatures on an attendance list to make the election 'legal'. This time, out of the union members who were not absent on holiday or ill, 83 per cent voted.

"The votes were counted in the U.P.B. Hall, on the wall of which hangs a Crucifix. The MRA vote was almost three times as great as the vote for the Communist-supported candidate — 1,672 votes to 587.

"Henrique was the winner. Joel, who was at Caux for training in MRA in 1954, ran second. When the result was announced, Joel said, 'Victory for Henrique is victory for me and my friends. We are united in a common programme of absolute honesty, absolute unselfishness, absolute love and absolute purity.'

"The main daily paper of Rio, *Correio da Manha*, reported, 'For the first time in Brazil, an association of public servants has held an election within the framework of electoral justice.' Other papers commented, 'A step forward for trade unionism in Brazil.' 'Simple, honest, clean victory.' 'The workers benefit. Trade unionism benefits.' "

One of the most important speeches of Howard's first days in Brazil was to diplomats and Foreign Office officials at the Itamarati Palace, when the Foreign Minister, Dr. Vasco Leitao da Cunha, presided. Howard drew lessons from the history of post-war Europe:

"In Western Europe at the end of World War II, the Communist

Parties were strong. They had been a mainspring of resistance to Hitler. They were led, for the most part, by highly sincere and intelligent people. But in Western Europe, Communism has, if anything, retreated. The reason is simple. In Europe some of the great post-war leaders understood the need for ideology to answer ideology. They believed that an ideology of freedom was necessary if free men were to show the Communists that their philosophy was wrong and that there was more in a man than liquids, muscles, fats and bones that would all turn to dust in due season.

"The Americans poured money into Europe. They poured arms into Europe. By their policies they built NATO as a political and military shield. But no great idea came from America to Europe that could include everybody – Communist and non-Communist alike – in the supreme purpose of putting right what was wrong throughout the continent.

"Three men – Adenauer, Schuman and de Gasperi – from three different nations – Germany, France and Italy – decided to stand together to build Europe. Those men were united in their political philosophy by being pupils of Don Sturzo. They were helped to this effective action by their conviction about Moral Re-Armament. Schuman would have retreated into private life in 1949 but for a conversation with Dr. Buchman. Instead he took up the task he most feared – that of reconciliation with Germany – and for which he faced bitter criticism from his own people. Adenauer knew the part played by Moral Re-Armament in the creation of the economic unity of Europe. When the Schuman Plan agreement was signed he said, 'MRA played an unseen but effective part in bridging differences of opinion between the negotiating parties in recent important international agreements.' De Gasperi echoed this in his conviction that MRA went to the 'root of the world's evils and will bring about the understanding between men and nations for which all people long'.

"Robert Schuman wrote, 'If Moral Re-Armament were just another theory, I should not be interested. But it is a philosophy of life applied in action, which I have seen reaching the millions. It is a world-wide transformation of human society which has already begun.'

"Don Sturzo, who had trained these three great Europeans, described Moral Re-Armament as 'fire from Heaven' before he died. And two years ago, Adenauer told the press, 'Unless Moral Re-Armament is extended, peace cannot be preserved.' "

Howard knew and respected Adenauer and Schuman, but his admiration was not blind. He had written to Doë some years before:

P.D.H. to Doë   December 15, 1960
It was an interesting time with Adenauer. You would like him. He is

299

shrewd, polite, seemingly docile, with an eye like a razor, and not missing one trick.

Adenauer thinks that Krushchev would prefer him to Willy Brandt as Chancellor, for he thinks, "I am unyielding but Krushchev trusts me." It is amazing how these top executives suffer from *folie de grandeur*. It was the same mistake Chamberlain made with Hitler. There is a curious form of personality worship that comes into men in possession of supreme power. They suffer from the illusion that all the world is left to them.

P.D.H. to H.K.   Buenos Aires
                                                      February 11, 1965

I have an enormous respect for General de Gaulle. I do not, however, think his concept is big enough in the long run to unite Europe and secure freedom. For good or ill, Britain has to play a part in the rebuilding of Europe, and Britain has to be helped to become a true European. Britain will not be helped to take those decisions by treating her now as she has wrongly treated so many other nations in the past, with a stiff arm and a stand-offish atmosphere.

In the midst of his tour, Howard kept in daily touch with people all over the world. It was from Brazil that he despatched the last of the twenty-two full page announcements which he had written for the *Daily Express*. It was written just after the funeral of Sir Winston Churchill and was entitled, "National Aim 1965":

"Soon buds will blaze in Bladon Churchyard. The casual, the curious, as well as a host of others who care for Britain's glory, will flock to Churchill's grave.

"It is one thing to mourn that mighty Englishman. It is another to live so the country he loved offers new greatness to the world. All should remember the warning theme of his last war volume, *Triumph and Tragedy*: 'How the great democracies triumphed and so were able to resume the follies which had so nearly cost them their life.'

"Moral Re-Armament points a finger at nobody. It points a finger at absolute standards of honesty, purity, unselfishness and love as Christ's standards, as standards of common sense for those who lack faith, as standards of society which alone can preserve the peace and build the new world.

"The world must be rebuilt. If this task seems difficult it is well to remember that when Britain faced her finest hour, some said and more believed victory was impossible. Churchill's word was, 'Never give up. Never give up in things great or small. Never, never, never give up.' If we do not fight in the life of our island now for the Moral Re-Armament of Britain, we may have to risk the life of the island in war later."

This was Howard's last word to Britain. He was wearied by all that was demanded of him, yet determined not to abate his efforts and seeking for new ways for the future. From Brazil he wrote to a friend:

"Frankly the burdens that fall on my shoulders are too heavy to bear. I have enough correspondence for three ordinary men, and I am bombarded with requests for speeches, plays, journeys and visitations. But I do my best and shall so continue.

"I feel an awful dud. I'm aware that my brain and spirit are utterly inadequate. My body, though older, remains strong which is a blessing, but body is the least of things in our sort of warfare.

"When Buchman died, God must have wanted more of us to carry the central load, and to carry it together. Instead, so many people seem to have used his going as an excuse to do more of what they wanted all along.

"The past has been wonderful. But nothing past is adequate for what lies ahead. We are in the midst of the mightiest convulsion human society has ever known. It has only just begun. Those who want to drive God into His grave are moving relentlessly and far more rapidly than us. We have got to change. I know I must. I want to be more like Christ, to streamline my life, to deepen my penetration."

At a reception given by Marshal Guedes Muniz[1] on January 12, he added:

"I will tell you the truth about myself. I am a very ordinary man. I have many fears, many hopes, many longings. But I do not belong to myself. Many years ago when I met this work it struck me as the best hope of a revolutionised world. I then gave the rest of my life to God under His direction to help this revolution. Frankly, I don't think I do it too well. I make a lot of mistakes. But I do not belong to myself. And until I die I shall continue to fight as God shows me to fight, to bring my country, your country and the world, under the control of the Living God."

Later speaking to the military chiefs he said:

"Moral Re-Armament is not an army. It is a war. It is not a regiment you can join. Nobody can join Moral Re-Armament. I am not a member of Moral Re-Armament. Moral Re-Armament is a battle all should fight."

His last speech in Brazil was made to the women of São Paulo, the women who had, in large measure, organised the March revolution:

"What Brazil needs is not a tranquilliser to keep discontented men quiet. It needs a galvaniser and transformer to make decent people effective."

[1] Distinguished Brazilian military and industrial figure.

Before he left Brazil, the Brazilian Government awarded him the Cruzeiro do Sol for his services to the nation. The British Foreign Office refused, on various pretexts, to grant permission for the decoration, and it was never presented. It did not greatly matter to Howard himself, but he minded that official Britain was unable, or unwilling, to grasp the truths for which he strove.

After Howard's death, the Brazilian Government asked the British Government for permission to present the decoration posthumously to his widow. This request was also refused.

The response in Brazil had been great. But Howard was not influenced by that. He had written three years before to Latin America at a time when MRA was drawing great crowds:

"It is better to have one man 100 per cent committed to God than 99,000 men 99 per cent committed."

It was still his belief.

Leaving most of his party to follow up the openings in Brazil, Howard, with Doë, Gandhi, Dame Flora MacLeod of MacLeod and a few others, flew on to the Argentine, Uruguay and Chile, meeting the Presidents of each country and conferring with their other leaders. On February 21, he landed at Lima, Peru. Gandhi recalled that he himself had been there three years earlier, when Frank Buchman died, and had been present when 75,000 people stood silent in his memory in the main football stadium.

Howard was weary, but in high spirits. He gave a press conference on arrival, and attended a party at a friend's house. He had written that morning in a letter to one of his children:

"I do not forget the force and rancour of the enemy, but millions are hungry for what we believe. I am resolved to put on a new Spring coat of Christ and never take it off again. Many of our people work for recognition and not from obedience, so there is a demand in them from everyone they meet. They are swayed backwards with every cold wind and are carried into a false enthusiasm by any compliment.

"I am a shabby fellow. My handwriting is hard to read. My books and plays are second-rate. I do my work in MRA in a way that is so far from what would satisfy me. My failure is apparent. But God loves me, and He even uses me, and though I should not be, I am happy. My eyes are sore and my heart aches from many hours of toil . . ."

Late that night, after returning from the party, Howard was shaken by a severe fever. "I have not felt my body shake so strongly since I played rugger," he said. At first it was thought to be a chill or a tropical infection which would pass, but the temperature mounted and, on February 23, he was taken into hospital with virus pneumonia. He was fearfully weak. In the ambulance on the way to the hospital, he dictated the outline for the final act of the play which he had been writing in the early mornings during his trip. It was a story of three conflicting generations which had been in his mind for many months, a play which he had long ago named, *Happy Deathday*. In the telegram he sent to London with this outline, he added a message to his daughter: "Tell her not to worry. I shall be out of hospital in a week." It was hard for a man who had overcome so many obstacles in life to conceive that he had met one he would not overcome in this world.

Doë was able to be with him in the hospital, and he was well cared for; but the virus was not checked and at 1 p.m. on February 25, 1965, he died. Doë cabled his friends:

"He belongs to the world. He had done for twenty-five years. He is of the long line of those who have fought for good against evil and spent himself wholly in the doing of it. He has passed from death into life.

"He had the thought from God to love every child he met as if it were his own. His revolution goes on. And we women must carry it on if our children and their children are to live free."

Dame Flora MacLeod of MacLeod, then eighty-six, the grandmother of Howard's son-in-law, was with Doë in Lima. She wrote later:

"On these great journeys I saw little of Peter. But we triumphed in his achievements. The load he carried was tremendous. Besides his external work which was never-ending and of first importance, he had to train and teach his own staff from different countries. He carried the burden and the worry, and the disappointments — I am sure there must have been some, although we never heard of them.

"There were so few years with Peter, but they were my crowning experience, and have made me young enough to believe there is still something I can do.

"Times with Peter were tremendously inspiring and revealed a new vision to me. I learned of the immanent presence of God in all our life. But the sacrifice of the Cross was always there.

"How often I have heard him say, 'When I survey the wondrous Cross, on which the Prince of Glory died,' a Cross which he himself bore in failing strength till his life ebbed away and there was nothing left. I do not believe he ever ceased to say, 'Work harder, work harder.' He could be very stern but he was never unkind. Sometimes I thought he was unfair, sometimes I have been eaten up with remorse . . . *mea maxima culpa*.

"When he drove to hospital in an ambulance on February 23, two days before he died, he sent me pink roses. He must have divided the flowers in his hotel bedroom between his friends. What wonderful thought and care he had for all of us."

The President of Peru arranged for Howard's body to lie in state in the City Hall of Lima.

.　　　.　　　.

March 5, 1965, the day that Peter Howard was brought home to Suffolk, was a cold winter's day. The great church at Lavenham was once more full with a thousand people from many lands, as it had been on that June day three years earlier when he had led his daughter up the aisle to her wedding. Now he was carried on his last journey by the men of his farm.

Men of renown from all over the world were present. He would have been glad to see them, but it would have been the homecoming to his own country folk which would have meant most to him. His coffin was placed on a farm cart and drawn by two great horses, Suffolk punches, past the gates of Hill Farm, through the lanes to Brent Eleigh churchyard. There, as a flurry of snow settled on the surrounding fields, he was laid to rest, looking out over the rolling East Anglian fields which the Howards had farmed for generations.

In March 1964 he had written, "If you ever have the burying of me, make it merry, militant and many-voiced. Let my enemies have their whack also. That is the time for them to get rid of it." And so it was to be. The only voice chosen to remember him on the BBC was that of Tom Driberg, who had opposed him and what he stood for without respite since *Daily Express* days. When friends protested, Sir Hugh Greene maintained that Driberg was an impartial expert – and the talk was repeated on another channel.

Howard's friends in Scotland sent a granite stone to stand over the grave. Supported by the Rev. C. Dobree, the Rector of Brent Eleigh, the Parochial Church Council refused to grant permission for it to be raised. His grave lies unmarked save by the flowers and heathers which are put there by friend and stranger month after month. In death, as in life, he fought a battle which was as he would have wished it.

"The great issue in the modern world is Almighty Man or Almighty God. At a time when all negative forces are chipping and filing away at the Rock of Ages, we must perceive the danger and the challenge, and fearlessly in the midst of misunderstanding and misrepresentation, and opposition, even from within the compromised camp of Christianity, build Almighty God once more as a modern and revolutionary factor into the lives of millions of our fellow men."

Years before, at Hill Farm, he had written at the end of *Ideas Have Legs*:

"So we come to the end of our journey, you and I together, and together we begin the new. We have never met before, and shall never part again. We can be numbered among the powerful of history. From this day we can march in the ranks of the swelling army of ordinary men and women whose destiny it is to make all nations greater.

"There are so many things in our countries which touch the human heart. Both you and I, know parts of our lands, her sounds, her sights, her smells, which penetrate and stir the deepest corners of our nature.

"Perhaps it is memories of the waters, the slick shadows of trout in tumbling streams, the slow and thoughtful glide of deeper rivers among the pasture land, and the sea, multitudinous, savage, restless, cold and grey and green.

"Perhaps it is the sound of laughter around a fireside, of country voices floating homeward across the field in summer dusk, when the last load of corn has been drawn into the stackyard and a mist is rising from the meadows; or the cough and whistle of wind in trees and around snug dwellings on a cold winter night.

"Maybe we remember and love the springtime valleys of white blossom furrowing the red earth, the wind across the mountains, the rustle and gossip of the corn, the silences and songs of trees in the deep forests, the granite of the hillsides and the warm hearts of the people.

"Maybe the thing which most catches our breath and heart is the subtle, simple smell of wood-smoke on an autumn evening, that same smell which our ancestors knew from generation to generation.

"All these things we inherit, you and I. And we inherit the green fields and thorn hedges and wild flowers, the treasures of the ages in literature and art, and above all the accumulated character and experience of great people.

"All these things are ours by right of legacy and life, no matter what circumstances surround us now, no matter if we spend our days at home or abroad, amid the stir of cities, in buses, planes and trains, in the sweat and danger of coalmines or the strain and clamour of factory or office or dock.

"These things we have inherited. History will record what we make of our inheritance.

"Many plan the future. But you and I live the future. We are the future.

"For you and I, ordinary men and women, our frames dust and dirt and water, stirred with the same desires, wooed by the same temptations, borne forward by the same power if we choose, have this distinctive contribution to make.

"We know the most precious secret of this and every generation, the secret which can remake the world. We possess the idea big enough to outmatch all other ideas, to mobilise the minds, hearts and wills of millions to unity and action.

"Time is not on our side — unless we grasp it.

"Tradition is not on our side — unless we live and create it.

"God is not on our side — unless we listen and obey.

"History will be written about the choice you and I make today. It will be the most momentous choice in human history.

"For one thing is certain. We do stand on the threshold of a new age. A new age of some kind is about to be ushered in, with all the sweat and blood and agony of new creation.

"It can be God's idea of a new age. If not, it will be a new age of another kind. And we, we alone, the citizens of destiny, decide.

> "Once to every man and nation
> Comes the moment to decide.
> Then it is the brave man chooses
> While the coward stands aside,
> Till the multitude makes virtue
> Of the faith they had denied."

Address by the Rt. Hon. Quintin Hogg, Q.C., M.P. at a Memorial Service for Mr. Peter Howard in the Royal Parish Church of St. Martin-in-the-Fields, London, April 12, 1965.

We are here in gratitude and love for the life of a man by most standards remarkable, by any standards lovable and by all human standards good.

Many in this great congregation, probably most, and conceivably all, were more closely associated than I with Peter Howard's public work and therefore better qualified than I to assess it. But from about 1926 onwards I knew him as a friend, generous, gay, loyal and understanding. Presumably it is as a friend that I have been asked to pay this tribute to his memory, and I do so willingly. I was proud of his friendship, but I do so sadly because by any earthly criterion, he died too soon.

I think first of his courage. Physical courage, by which I mean the will-power necessary to give mind the mastery over matter, was, I am inclined to think, the foundation of his whole character. From his childhood he was compelled to face an almost crippling physical incapacity which many of us would have found overwhelming. His courage treated it as a challenge rather than as an affliction. And even before his character was fully formed or fully seen, brought him the captaincy of England on the rugby field.

This courage never deserted him, though the power which it gave him to work his body unmercifully may have betrayed him in the end. No one who saw the extent to which he drove himself in the last few years could fail to wonder how he could possibly maintain the pace and no one now, reflecting upon his early death, can fail to speculate how far his resistance to infection may have been undermined by the tremendous impetus he maintained year after year. But it would have been unlike Peter to spare himself. The astonishing thing is that he never permitted the immense strain under which he compelled himself to live and work to show in any loss of patience or understanding towards the host of those whose need he sought to serve.

I have already mentioned Peter's gaiety, his sense of fun. No one enjoyed life more than Peter. The things that he enjoyed were the good things of life — sunshine and fresh air, friendship and family, farm and country, the company and the laughter of children, the unending fascination of human idiosyncrasy. Joy, we are assured, is one of the chief fruits of the Spirit. Peter's simple gaiety was undoubtedly a mark of holiness.

I think next of his unaffected goodness. Goodness is not an easy thing to define, for it is not a quality. It is an orientation of the whole being. Despite limitations and defects of character, each of us in his own individual, uniquely different way can be good. Very few of us are. Even ordinarily good men are not so common that their passing can go unremarked.

But Peter's simple goodness was not ordinary. His was *anima naturaliter Christiana*, a soul naturally Christian, as perhaps at bottom all human souls are. But in him it was the combination of this natural goodness with the acquired determination following his religious experience which gave him the moral earnestness and power of his later years. He was determined that goodness should not perish from the earth, that light should conquer darkness, that sinners should repent and be redeemed and that perfectability should in the end become perfection.

He was untroubled by doubts about the nature of goodness and in this surely he was wise. It does not need a philosopher to tell right from wrong, courage from cowardice, integrity from deviousness, kindness from cruelty, purity from its opposite. If it did, it would be a poor look-out for most of us.

But most of us are inhibited by modesty or shame from becoming open advocates of goodness. Perhaps we are afraid of unction or hypocrisy or too conscious of our own shortcomings.

Peter was not, and in this too he was right. His was the vision of Isaiah in the year when King Uzziah died. He heard the word of God in the smoke-filled temple asking, "Whom shall we send for us?" And like the Prophet, Peter, reassured by the live coal from the altar, protesting his unworthiness and without the least hint of self-righteousness, replied in the end, "Here am I. Send me." And in truth if someone did not answer so, there would be no one left to send. For we are all men of unclean lips and we live in the midst of a generation of unclean men of unclean lips.

So Peter answered the voice he heard and because Peter was good, the world not merely heard but listened. He saw in clear terms the essential drama of the individual's life, the pity of it and the terror of it, the ceaseless longing of it for redemption. He saw clearly that life is never the tragi-comedy so often portrayed. Strip off the mask, remove the wrappings of self-protection and it is sheer melodrama — poignant as tragedy, heroic as epic, demanding compassion, capable of triumph, threatened with disaster, but never trivial, never to be written down as absurd, never more perilous than when dull, never more tragic than when played flippantly. He knew that there is more joy in heaven over one sinner that repenteth than over ninety-nine just persons. This is what added the earnestness and force to a character full of natural virtue.

I approach the central experience of his life with reverence but reticence. It is not for me to explore the intimate secrets of the human soul, nor to seek to evaluate and unravel its relationship with the Divine. But no one who knew Peter as I knew him can doubt the reality of the experience of conversion or, as he called it, change, which he underwent in the early days of the war.

It was this experience which dominated the rest of his life. It gave to his life from that moment onwards a wholly new direction and sense of purpose and it brought him in his later years, though he did not see it, a national — even an international renown. Like the mighty and venerable figure whose first name he bears, Peter became from that time onwards a fisher of men.

This is not the time or place to describe his work nor to speculate what, had he been longer spared, he would have accomplished. But we can remember with gladness as well as sorrow the friend we knew. Here there were no sins unrepented and therefore none unforgiven. Here there were no opportunities missed, no qualities unrealised to the full. If ever a man went to his Maker with his baptismal robe restored to its original freshness, surely it was Peter Howard.

Christians, I feel, are conventionally taught to make too light of death. This, I am sure, never quite comes off. We may comfort ourselves with the thought of the vision of the Divine, the beatific vision which makes us forever happy, with the sight face to face of what we now see through a glass darkly. We may talk, as we do, to one another about the communion of saints, the resurrection of the body and the life everlasting, but somehow nothing really blunts the pain of parting.

I do not think we need be ashamed of this. When Jesus was told of the death of Lazarus, He did not lift up His eyes to heaven and say, "Thank God, Lazarus is in heaven." Jesus wept, and because He had the power, He summoned His friend back from the tomb. Perhaps for the human reason that He loved him and He wanted him back.

The pain of bereavement is the price we pay for love. It is a high price but those who have paid it never regret their bargain, however often it may be repeated in their lives. All the same, when a Christian dies, though there is always pain, there is also consolation. We can thank God for a life well spent; in Peter's case, very well spent and in his case, too, very greatly enjoyed.

We are allowed to tell one another that somewhere in the universe Peter still exists at peace, we may be sure, but not perhaps wholly at rest, for inaction would be strangely unlike our friend. In the mysterious interplay of the seen and the unseen which we call the communion of saints, somehow, somewhere it is permitted us to believe he still shares

309

with us and with our Master the unending task of the redemption of the world. It is the work of God and the true function of the Church. Lux perpetua luceat ei. May light perpetual shine upon him, and I am sure it does. Blessed are the pure in heart, for they shall see God. Blessed are they that mourn for they shall be comforted.

.   .   .

The following were among the messages and letters received by Peter Howard's family after his death:

"Since the days when Lafayette and von Steuben gave our infant republic a decisive help in the revolutionary struggle for survival, few if any citizens of other lands have rendered the American people services comparable to those of Mr. Peter Howard."
Speaker McCormack,
U.S. House of Representatives

"I had for him a great esteem: he was so devoted to the good of others. His death is a great loss."
Cardinal Tisserant,
Dean of the Sacred College of Cardinals

"Leaders of nations in all continents will miss his guidance."
Keith Holyoake,
Prime Minister of New Zealand

"Peter Howard had the wavelength of our generation in America. We were some of the lucky ones who had him on our campuses. He was a true statesman for this age who gave us a great aim for our lives and a hope for the America we want to see. We are eternally grateful. Now it is for us to match his commitment."
Signed by 12 university student body Presidents

"Peter was great. Because Peter's heart could contain all the nations and people of the world, just as it could Britain and the Britishers. It could contain me — an ordinary and physically-handicapped man of Kerala, the southern-most part of India.

"Our friendship began on January 13, 1962, when we met in my village for the first time. That day he attended a meeting in my place. It was the Foundation-laying ceremony of our Children's Centre. Our State Governor and ministers were present.

"Mr. K. M. Cherian, Chief Editor of *Malayala Manorama*, a leading daily newspaper of Kerala, brought two honoured guests of MRA to the meeting. I was sitting on the rostrum in the back row. Peter took the seat beside my wheel chair. Thousands were gathered in front of us. People were listening to speeches with eager ears. Peter turned and looked at me, an invalid sitting in a wheel chair, leaned towards me and said, 'George, I too am an invalid. I have conquered it. So, be cheerful and face it courageously.' That was the beginning of our friendship. I was honoured with that friendship. It meant much to my life. It shaped my life. It gave a greater aim to my life.

"His last letter came to me on December 15, 1964 from London.

"Then came the sad news. I was shocked. I have rededicated myself for the great revolution — God's revolution, for which Peter worked, died and entrusted us. He was my best friend."

George Mathew,
Kerala, South India

"I was very sorry to hear that Peter Howard who wrote the pantomime, *Give a Dog a Bone*, had died. I wished I could have met him because I heard he had many good ideas under his belt for plays and pantomimes. He was a good man and very determined. I sent him a wreath, as I want to say thank you to him."

An eight-year-old schoolboy

"Peter Howard saved my life. So I'm giving the rest of it to Moral Re-Armament, to be part of the fruits of his life."

Found on a wreath in the churchyard

"My mind goes back twenty years to the time when Philip was a small boy in College and I first made Peter Howard's acquaintance. From then onwards, all through the time when Anthony was in the house, he was the most kindly and considerate of 'parents' to a housemaster. Indeed, if there was one thing I regretted, it was that he was so self-effacing; one enjoyed his company so much that one would have liked to see a great deal more of him."

F. J. A. Cruso,
Eton College

"Peter Howard was the true friend of the miners. He came to us at a very dark time when over a thousand men had lost their jobs as a result of the disaster in the Barony Colliery, Auchinleck.

"We felt we had been forgotten, but Howard brought us hope and showed us that people really cared.

"We believe if what he brought to us in Ayrshire is applied nationally by leaders and led it would solve not only the problems in our industries but in every other sphere as well."

Signed by Miners of the Ayrshire Coalfields

311

"Some of the highlights of my life have been listening to Peter Howard's speeches. His plays have given me purpose, discipline and faith. His books have given, and will go on giving, me challenge and adventure.

"The way he lived has meant that millions like me have felt the full blast of God on earth and we will never be the same again."

Signed "A humble soldier", B.A.O.R.

"Not long after World War II, and back with the London *Sunday Express* after serving overseas, I met Peter Howard by accident in a Glasgow hotel. I couldn't believe he was the man I used to know. The change shone in his face. You could see it in those dark eyes under the beetling eyebrows. It was the second face of Peter Howard. The face of a man who had come to the end of an old journey and was embarked on the new. He said he had discovered an idea bigger than all the rest. Alas, like jesting Pilate, I did not wait for the answer to that one. Sometimes, when I recall that second face of Peter Howard, I wish that I had."

Paul Irwin,
Sunday Times Magazine, Johannesburg

"I did not think of Peter Howard, primarily, as the leader of an international movement, but rather as a stalwart ally, as, in his own phrase, a 'comrade in arms'. I learned upon meeting him what had made him such a formidable Crossbencher. The nimble brain, the ready wit, the shrewd tactical appreciation, the sharply-ground phrase — all were there, together with a youthful zest for smiting the enemy where it would hurt most and a gleeful viewing of the results. And yet, he was sorry for them, too, and reluctant to apply the coup de grace. Mercy stopped him short of being ruthless, and humour tempered even his most biting attacks. He taught me a lot about this kind of journalism . . . A well-written article was sure to bring a note from him, however busy he might be. His encouragement was unstinted, and all the more valuable for coming from a master of the craft he liked to call the Black Art. When a titbit of political information came his way — and he had many sources — he was generous in passing it on, knowing its value to me . . . This is my impression of him. A powerhouse of brilliant energy, with a central core of warm, human compassion. In the Christian ethic, death has no terrors. It is the fulfilment of life. In his own terminology, it is the final triumphant change. Few men have left their families such a magnificent legacy of love and pride as Peter Howard. His memory is a treasure for them to cherish all the days of their lives and an inspiration to all who knew him."

Charles Graham,
Scottish Daily Express

Books and Plays by Peter Howard
from many of which quotations are made in the text

Books

Guilty Men (with Michael Foot and Frank Owen), Gollancz, 1939
Innocent Men, Heinemann, 1941
Fighters Ever, Heinemann, 1942
Ideas Have Legs, Frederick Muller, 1945
Men on Trial, Blandford Press, 1945
That Man Frank Buchman, Blandford Press, 1946
The World Rebuilt, Blandford Press, 1951
Remaking Men (with Paul Campbell), Blandford Press, 1954
An Idea to Win the World, Blandford Press, 1955
Effective Statesmanship (with Paul Campbell), Blandford Press, 1955
America Needs an Ideology (with Paul Campbell), Muller, 1957
Frank Buchman's Secret, Heinemann, 1961
Three Views of Christianity (with L. J. Collins and T. S. Gregory), Gollancz, 1962
Britain and the Beast, Heinemann, 1963
Design for Dedication, Regnery, 1964
Beaverbrook, A Study of Max the Unknown, Hutchinson, 1964

Plays

The Real News, Blandford Press, 1954
The Dictator's Slippers, Blandford Press, 1954
The Boss, Blandford Press, 1954
We are Tomorrow, Blandford Press, 1954
The Vanishing Island, 1955
Pickle Hill, Blandford Press, 1960
The Hurricane (with Alan Thornhill), Blandford Press, 1961
The Ladder, Blandford Press, 1961
Music at Midnight (with Alan Thornhill), Blandford Press, 1962
Through the Garden Wall, Blandford Press, 1963

The Diplomats, Blandford Press, 1964
Mr. Brown Comes Down the Hill, Blandford Press, 1964
Give a Dog a Bone, 1964
Happy Deathday, Westminster Productions, 1965

Any discrepancies between the dates given here and those given in *Who's Who* are because *Who's Who* gives the dates when the plays were written, and this list gives the dates they were published.